CW00471210

Easily Led
and
Hard on His Shoes

by
Geoff Mullin

Grosvenor House
Publishing Limited

This book is published by
Grosvenor House Publishing Ltd
Link House
140 The Broadway, Tolworth, Surrey, KT6 7HT.
www.grosvenorhousepublishing.co.uk

A CIP record for this book
is available from the British Library

ISBN 978-1-80381-284-7
eBook ISBN 978-1-80381-358-5

All proceeds from the sale of this book will go to Prostate Cancer UK
Prostate Cancer UK is a registered charity in England and Wales (1005541)
and in Scotland (SC039332).

For Lesley

from Terry Wogan

Sunday 20ᵗʰ Jan.

Dear Geoff,

A brief, and therefore inadequate note of thanks and appreciation for all the help, good times and good friendship that you have given me so unstintingly over the past four years. Those years have been the happiest and most successful of my professional career, and its no coincidence that they've been spent with you as my producer and friend.

May you go on to the success and promotion that you deserve, and will undoubtedly achieve.

Here's to the next time — Yours,

Terry.

Preface

Sir Terry Wogan couldn't have written a better introduction had he been alive today. I think it might have been penned with a tear in his eye and a crystal ball on the table, the one he used on a regular basis to tell my future, as you'll soon discover. What he couldn't know is that I would write and publish this book, for which I must credit my daughter Krystle and her persistent insistence that I put it all down for posterity. Most of my friends say they will buy a copy so that should boost the bank balance by about a tenner, if I'm lucky, which I have been during most of my life, and that theme, plus a deep love of music, permeates this tome throughout. I wouldn't say it's a rags to riches story but I can still hardly believe that a little lad from the back streets of Manchester could have had the fun journey I have enjoyed. I hope you'll travel with me through childhood and teens to the Swinging Sixties in London and Manchester, where I briefly found employment as a schoolteacher and civil servant, through my time as a singer/songwriter/record producer and pop star in Norway (Oh yes I was!). From the seventies onward the BBC was my main focus as a producer with thirty years before the mast on the Good Ship Radio Two working with some of the all-time great broadcasters like Jack Jackson, Simon Bates, Sir Terry Wogan, Jimmy Young, David Hamilton, Kenny Everett, Wally Whyton, Anne Robinson, Michael Aspel and Ken Bruce. The cream on the top during those years was meeting my heroes Gene Vincent, Jerry Lee Lewis, Johnny Cash, John D Loudermilk, Neil Sedaka and Roy Rogers. Did I mention The Beatles?

Acknowledgements

My deep gratitude to my old mucker Paul Phillips, whose invaluable assistance and indefatigable dedication to the cause practically guaranteed I would receive more rejections than Quasimodo (only joking, Paul, you've been brilliant). To my wife Lesley, my soulmate, my proofreader, censor and conscience, without whose restraining ropes litigation was sure to follow. To Paul Gambaccini for his initial advice and guidance to get me started. To the BBC for the chances and to the British Music Industry for the weight gain. To my regular support crew who have boosted my energy levels with their good humour and sneery cynicism (untrue), so thanks Ron Stratton, Dave Lee Travis, John Rostron, Martin Kearney, Martin Bishop, Michael Gouby, Tony Walmsley and all their delightful and tolerant wives. Thanks to my family and Lesley's family, especially our regular fridge cleaners Jamie and Kerry Davies, two highly efficient food processing machines, a loving, caring pair and great games players, not forgetting Billy, the incorrigible canine, and lastly to Denise and Roger Grant for their introduction to Becky Banning at Grosvenor House Publishing, without whose inestimable help you would not be reading this book.

Foreword by Lesley Mullin

Geoff Mullin – an amazing man who lived a charmed life. The only plan he had was to play rugby and teach sport but when an early knee injury put paid to any sporting career, he was able to pursue his other passion – music – and nearly all music! Classical, big bands and music from the 20s onwards: brass bands, jazz bands, rock 'n' roll, pop, country – he loved it all.

The 60s were a wonderful time for Geoff; he was singing and managing bands, he was the first DJ at the famous Twisted Wheel in Manchester and he became a pop star in Norway before finally settling in London initially with a job at Billboard magazine. "Being in the right place at the right time" could have been written with Geoff in mind as he then landed a dream job at BBC Radio 2! Throughout his lifetime, Geoff met and worked with so many of his heroes and the stories and anecdotes from the fun times he has had have always entertained and amused his friends and family. His daughter Krystle endlessly encouraged him to write it all down and so here it is – his autobiography .

Geoff's life wasn't all about working in music; he was equally passionate about sport -nearly all sport – and he refused to buy Sky Sports TV because he said he would never do anything else! His favourite sport was rugby – union and league - but he was always sorry he hadn't been able to live in America when he was younger so that he could play American Football. I remember once, when we were touring in South Africa in 2003, we were in a pub in the middle of nowhere watching England playing South Africa and we were obviously the only England supporters! Such a fun afternoon! Baseball was another game we always watched while travelling in America and we finally got to spring training in Arizona to watch a live game – thank goodness for the very helpful man in the next seat who explained it all! I've always said that if there is a ball is involved he'll watch it but actually that wasn't completely accurate - he always enjoyed athletics, winter sports, rodeo – particularly bull riding - and was recently enjoying horse racing.

Geoff had a very happy family life; he enjoyed good food and good wine, going to the theatre watching films both at home and at the cinema and playing games. At one stage we had a pool table and everybody's aim was to beat Geoff; and he always took it in good part if anyone did manage to beat him. Nobody ever wanted to play him at Trivial Pursuit though; his knowledge of music and entertainment always put him streets ahead. Christmas was always a family occasion with long-standing traditions: a mince pie and sherry out for Santa, a carrot for Rudolph and no prodding presents! Even Billy the dog has to abide by the rules! The Christmas board game is another tradition Jamie always has to be talked into but me, Geoff and Kerry are always raring to go. We enjoyed playing 221B Baker Street over the Christmas of 2019 and it stood us in good stead during the 2020 lockdown, when we were able to continue our games over Zoom, helping to keep everyone's spirits up.

Party animal Geoff only needed a hint of an excuse and off we would go… themed parties such as "When I'm 64", where everybody had to wear something to do with the Beatles and we really had some very imaginative and creative friends. Murder Mystery dinner parties… nobody really cared whodunit by the end of evening! New Year's Eve parties were always great, hot cross buns and bucks' fizz on Good Friday was always a favourite… I'm sure you get the picture.

Geoff was 80 in September 2022 and we had a last-minute party in the garden where Kerry introduced him to Aperol Spritz which was definitely a hit! Sadly, it was to be his last hurrah as his particularly aggressive form of prostate cancer took him from us on 30th September. A great memory from just a few days before he died was sitting in the bedroom with him and Jamie, Kerry and I all had champagne but his last toast was with Aperol Spritz – keep on rockin'!

Contents

CHAPTER ONE

The Mancunian Kid

The great northern city of Manchester was an education, an inspiration, an introduction to my two great passions, music and sport, and a springboard to explore the wider world, which I did on many occasions from a very young age, being regularly parcelled off to stay with relatives in Yorkshire, and once to friends on the Isle of Man. All this before the age of twelve when I took matters into my own hands and began a love affair with Vienna and Austria by taking part in a student exchange programme every year until I was eighteen. Maybe my parents were relieved to be rid of me for a period of time and I certainly enjoyed my holiday visits away from home. It was always a great adventure, which is how most of my life has been ever since.

It's January 2020 and I've already accomplished my New Year's resolution, which was to start writing this book, after much cajoling from my daughter Krystle who's heard me telling stories over the years and insisted I put them all down for posterity. I've been compiling and collating dates to bring the memories into focus and I'm attempting a chronological presentation but obviously there'll be lots of going off on a tangent as things inter-connect all over the place.

It all started with a bass guitar. A Fender Precision Bass, to be exact, about which I knew nothing at the time I bought it, but which put me on a trajectory to a life-long involvement with popular music and the rarefied atmosphere of stars and celebrity, about which, more later. I could have called this book "All About That Bass" but Meghan Trainor beat me to it.

So it became "Easily Led And Hard On His Shoes" which were a couple of the many things my mother called me, the first for being a little naïve and credulous and the second for my inability to resist kicking anything in the street, be it a stone, a stick or a tin can. That seems like a good starting point for some family background and historical context. I was born in Nell Lane Hospital, Withington in Manchester on September the 11th 1942, the same day and month, but not year I hasten to add, as D H Lawrence, I was later to find out with a fair degree of pleasure. I arrived on a Friday and so, according to the rhyme, I am "loving and giving" – quite true, of course. I only recently found out that I was born into "The Silent Generation" (1928-1945) which immediately preceded the Baby Boomers. We are regarded as Traditionalists because we were brought up with the old-fashioned notion that children should be seen and not heard. We were also called "The Lucky Few" due to the low birth rates during the Great Depression of the 1930's and the Second World War and, although there were not that many of us, we did make the biggest generational leaps in education, affluence and life expectancy in history. Many will live to be a hundred. I hope I'm one of them.

By family tradition I should have been named Stanley Gibson, the names given to the first-born male of each Mullin generation. My mother was having none of it and defied my grandfather by naming me Geoffrey Kenneth, for which I'm quite relieved as I can't see myself as a Stan.

Both my parents were Butchers – my mother, Lily, by name, and my father, Ken, by trade. Lily was born on August 4 1911 to John Warner and Emily Butcher (nee Horner) 0f 146 Harcourt Street, Ardwick, Manchester. Ken was born on August 19 1912 to Stanley Gibson and Kate Mary Mullin (nee Shaw) of 49 School Lane, Didsbury, Manchester. They were married on July 30 1937 at St Christopher's Church, West Didsbury, attended by my mother's sisters Edith, with husband Eric, Doris with husband George and the adorable Elsie, who never married. My father's brothers Stanley and Ronald were with their wives Phyllis and Edna.

My Dad joined the Territorial Army when he was 17 because he liked all the physical stuff and made a bit of a name for himself as a boxer which is how he got his broken nose. He was also a fully qualified butcher and slaughterhouseman and that was to stand him in good stead in the jungles of Burma during the war. At the start of WW2, as far as I can ascertain, my parents were running a fish and chip shop business in Bangor, North Wales and because of his work in a reserved occupation Dad was not conscripted but he decided to enlist in the regular army on 24 June 1940 joining the Royal Welch Fusiliers No S/46251 where his occupation was listed as "bacon curer". His army records show that on 26 September 1941 he forfeited 8 days pay for "driving a WD vehicle at a speed in excess of that laid down for its type" – an early example of speed-freakery in the family. My mother thought he was cracked for volunteering when he needn't have, especially when she fell pregnant in early 1942 leaving her to cope alone when he was shipped out to India on the 12 April 1942 to join the 14th Army under General Slim. He didn't talk a great deal about his experiences in Burma but he did relate how he was involved with food supplies and how there was so little food he caught monkeys and snakes to provide some protein for the troops. They were in awe of the Americans who got regular drops of all the food they needed, including chewing gum – lucky bastards he said they were. On the bloody side of the conflict he told me how he had dispatched about a dozen enemy troops in hand-to-hand fighting and the terrible shock when comrades were falling and on one occasion his best friend's head went whizzing past him. He suffered from malaria and dysentery while in Burma and was shipped home via Rangoon and Bombay on 29 October 1945. As a leaving present he was given a ceremonial Kukri knife by a Gurkha friend he served with. He arrived home on 15 November 1945 and was finally demobbed on 12 March 1946. On leaving it is remarked that "Lance Corporal Mullin K has, during his army service, been a very hard worker, cheerful, loyal and trustworthy. He has done his job well and is well qualified for the accolade of Exemplary" – pretty good, I think.

I don't know much about my mother's occupation other than she worked as a seamstress, sometimes in retail and served as a nurse during the war.

I spent the first three years of my life with my mother in a two up two down terraced house at 146 Brailsford Road in Fallowfield with no bathroom or hot running water, an outside toilet and air-raid shelter in the back yard behind which was an access entry for the dustbin men and coal deliveries, beyond which were small allocated allotments backing on to a main railway line. Next door at 144 was a lovely spinster lady called Edith Meakin who I called Auntie Edith. I enjoyed going into her house and particularly playing with her very modern push-button radio set. There was electricity in her house but the lights were still lit by gas, which I found quite fascinating as they were brought to life. She was the manageress of the best milk bar in town and whenever we went into the city-centre we could be sure of one or two free milkshakes and ice-cream sodas.

When I reached three I was eligible to attend Mosely Road Infants school, about a hundred yards away at the end of Brailsford Road. I don't think I took too kindly to being separated from my mother and my house and I particularly disliked the routine of having to lie down on a little trestle bed for an hour in the morning and an hour in the afternoon. That was seriously boring and I've never been interested in taking an afternoon nap my whole life. Maybe that'll happen when I get old. Other than the daytime naps I can't remember a thing about that period at the school.

Not too long after my third birthday I was awoken one night by the sounds of laughter coming up from the kitchen into my bedroom. I got up and walked down the stairs and put my head through the kitchen door to see what was happening. My mother saw me and picked me up and showed me to this man in uniform. I said "Oh look mummy, it's the man in the photograph", at which the whole room burst into laughter. That was the first time my Dad and I had seen each other and from that day on my life changed considerably. There was always a lot of activity going on at the house with regular visits from the rent man, the insurance man, dustbin men, the catalogue man, the coal deliveries, daily milk deliveries, the pedalling knife and scissor sharpener and the rag and bone man with his horse and cart but my favourite delivery was the lorry with a new supply of stone flagons full of ginger beer, sarsaparilla and delicious dandelion and burdock. I'm still partial to a fizzy drink even today but it's now mostly tonic with five parts gin – I call it gin and t. I remember visits from our local GP, Doctor Beattie, and on visits to his surgery with my Mum there would always be a payment due, usually about one shilling or a little bit more. Those payments all stopped with the introduction of the National Health Service in 1948. It was an interesting time and looking back on it I think I may have been left alone some of the time as on one occasion I answered the front door and a man asked if my mum and dad were home and I said "No, they've gone to get married". He was taken aback but, obviously, they'd gone to a wedding. There was another time I decided to help clear things up, being the good boy I was, and put the newspapers away in the oven. It was fortunate they were found before they caught fire because the oven was connected to the fire in the grate which was burning away at the time. On another occasion I tidied up and shut the oven door not knowing our cat Susie was in there keeping warm. Again, fortunately, Susie was rescued before she expired.

My best pals were Stanley Oakes and Jackie Battersby and I have two abiding memories of the pair of them from around the time I was five or six. The first was going into Stan's house to play some games, probably bagatelle or marbles, when we had a disagreement which ended with him chasing me out of the house with a carving knife and running after me all the way back to my house where I managed to shut the back gate on him. That was my first ever near-death experience. We soon became pals again and spent a lot of time together, as did our parents, and I still have a photo of us all together at Blackpool Pleasure Beach around 1947/8. Stan and I would go to The Church Of The Holy Innocents on Wilbraham Road where we were in the choir together. Other pals from the choir were Rodney Bracewell and Frank Nelson, who always insisted he was related to Horatio. Having no reason to query this assertion, I believed him, it was a great claim to fame. One day in1956 after choir practice we were walking home when Stan started singing this rock and roll song he'd heard. There may be quite a few "if only I'd known" and "I never really knew" events in this book as you'll find out when the coincidences start to stack up and this is one of them. The song was by Bill Haley called "Razzle Dazzle" and it absolutely knocked me for six, so much so that I asked Stan to sing it at least another three times on the way home. Stan had a great voice and was really into this new music but

I didn't know he was learning piano and would turn out to be a star performer. Not only did he have tremendous talent but he also had an undeniable look of Elvis about him and he wore all the right clothes. Ten years down the line when I was looking to recruit a piano player into our group, I went to see Stan playing in a local pub and asked him if he'd like to join up with us. He didn't take long telling me that he was earning much more as a solo artist than we could pay him to be in the group. When I told him the fringe benefits of female fans he just laughed and I last saw him that night walking down the road with a cutie on each arm. Boy, did he have it made – yes. Sometime after that I heard that Stan had moved to South Africa and become quite a star. I often wonder how he got on.

One of the funniest things I ever saw happened to another pal from church, Timothy Broughton, when we went with our nets and jam jars fishing for sticklebacks and tiddlers in Platt Fields Lake. I was behind Tim and as we walked along the edge dragging our bamboo cane nets one of the flagstones gave way under him and, as if in slow motion, I watched the stone and Tim slide into the water. Both went completely under the surface and Tim came up and out in one movement with a shocked look on his face and almost in tears. Needless to say, he was thoroughly soaked and shivering so the only thing we could do was make our way back to his house. As we trudged along I was trying really hard to suppress my laughter as every step Tim took there was a loud squelch from the water trapped in his shoes and socks. You never forget moments like that. We had a good friendship for a while and I was even invited to go with him and his brother, Michael I think, to stay with his grandparents at their lovely house in Grantham, Lincolnshire. Tim's brother had a Vincent motorcycle and took me for rides on it where he scraped both exhausts pipes along the ground causing sparks to fly. Terrifying would be putting it mildly.

My other pal, Jackie Battersby, was a real bundle of fun and got up to all sorts of larks. He had a shock of ginger hair and was a lively lad – we were like two Just Williams. Back in those days we had very little in the way of toys to play with, not even a ball, although I did have Meccano and Bayko sets to play with, these were solitary pastimes and so we spent as much time as possible playing outdoors.

Just remember this, most people in our road had no cars, no telephones, no fridges, no central heating, no televisions and many of the houses were lit internally by gas lights. I well remember the lamplighter coming every night to light the street lamps. At least most people had a radio, some had a gramophone and some, like us, had an upright piano. My mum could read music and was pretty good at knocking out a tune. My dad could also play but not as well and rarely touched the keys. Anyway, one game Jackie and I invented was played on what we called the croft, basically a bombsite where a house once stood. The challenge was to pick up half a brick off the ground, which was just rubble, and see how far we could chuck it up the exposed wall of the house and make a mark. We were supposed to watch each other throw but one day Jackie threw one up while I wasn't looking and it came down and hit me just above the eye leaving a bit of a gash which was stitched and patched by my mum. The house wall we were throwing at belonged to Mr Williams and one day Stan was with us and said "Whatever you do, don't go into Mr Williams back yard". We asked him why and he said "Because Mr Williams breeds rats in his shed". We were horrified and asked what on earth he was breeding rats for and Stan said "Oh, they're to feed his snakes". Not surprisingly that was the end of our brick throwing Olympics.

One of the highlights of the week for me was the Sunday afternoon arrival of Wilkie the ice-cream man with his donkey and cart. Done out like a circus carnival float, Wilkie, who had a look of Mr Pastry about him, would announce himself with a very loud handbell around 3pm and provide a cornet or wafer for threepence or sixpence and ask if you wanted raspberry sauce on it, which most of us did. I always had a wafer. The other major event happened weekly with Saturday morning pictures at the Kingsway cinema, only a five-minute walk away. I was taken there by a pair of sisters who sometimes were my babysitters. I loved those girls to pieces and they looked after me through films of Tarzan, Laurel and Hardy, Three Stooges, Buck Rogers, Bowery Boys, Hopalong Cassidy, The Lone Ranger, Flash Gordon, the wonderful Mighty

Mouse cartoons and my great favourite Roy Rogers, "King of the Cowboys". Little did I know, again, that one day I would meet my hero in Nashville, Tennessee.

Many things changed in the last couple of years in Brailsford Road. My Dad couldn't get a job as a butcher so he got work as a tram driver with Manchester Corporation. I always thought it was great fun if we got on a tram he was driving and I could stand up front with him. At that time he was my hero but the effects of the war and continuing bouts of malaria which laid him low for weeks at a time gave him dark moods and angry episodes. My Dad's brother Ron said he was always prone to be reckless, telling me of the time he threw a knife at him which missed his head only by inches. He was a naughty boy, too, as he brought home from the army a service Royal Enfield Rifle but he handed it in some years later during an armistice. Around this time, to make ends meet, my parents took in lodgers. The first two were shopfitters from Bristol who were working in one of the department stores in the city centre. One was called Desmond and he rode a motorbike, which impressed me greatly. They took over my bedroom and I got relegated to a cot under the stairs. That really upset me, as you may imagine. It was highly unsuitable and caused me so much misery that my parents decided a move to a bigger house was the only answer – correct.

Events took place in my early childhood that I have been unable to reconcile, namely this. On 12 October 1944 my paternal grandfather, Stanley Gibson Mullin, died in the Royal Infirmary from a perforated duodenal ulcer, diabetes and coronary thrombosis. I have no recollection of him at all but he obviously loved me a great deal as the following account will confirm. I was two years old when he died but he had made contact with an elderly couple who lived at 133 Brailsford Road, almost directly opposite to 146. They had been looking after me in a babysitting sort of way and he knew they were good people. For some reason he didn't think my parents would be able to look after my welfare as well as he thought they should and so he entrusted them with £50 and charged them with being his substitute as my grandparents. This they willingly accepted and became my adoptive Granny and Grampa. Obviously, I didn't find out until many years later that we were not related but I could not have loved them more for the kindness, generosity and protection they so freely and lovingly gave me. Additionally, not only did I not know my paternal grandfather, I also didn't know his wife, my grandmother Kate, nor my maternal grandfather Stephen John Warner Butcher, who died on 23 October 1934, 8 years before I was born, only his wife, Grandma Emily, whom I loved very much.

This lovely couple who vowed to love and protect me were not married and although they lived together there was no hint of romance with Mrs Hindle acting as cook and housekeeper to James Bailey. And what a cook she was with amazing stews and puddings the like of which I haven't tasted since. The best suet and rice puddings and wonderful baked egg custard which I put down to the fact that she used sterilised milk, not particularly nice to drink but oh, those puddings. She also helped to provide a celebratory feast for a Brailsford Road street-party at the end of the war with various jellies, cakes and my favourite pink blancmange. Mrs Hindle followed the regular hard graft routine of many women in those days with Mondays as laundry day and several days a week cleaning the front door steps and windowsills with what they called a donkey stone, which came in white, cream, yellow and brown and was given out along with dusters and bars of soap by the regular rag and bone men in exchange for old clothes and general junk – a sort of mobile dump. I think she had been married but he not and they had separate bedrooms, he at the front, she at the rear and they both had commodes by their beds, which somehow amused me but then they also had an outside toilet to cope with. She came from Stalybridge and he had served in the Merchant Navy during the first World War. They lived a simple and frugal life but they looked after me as if I were their own, always giving me pocket money and a few pence for an ice cream, taking me on trips by charabanc (coach) to places like the wonderful Trentham Gardens and the seaside at Southport. Grampa was also a dab hand at what became known as DIY and for many years he did all our shoe repairs. Their house was also my refuge and where I would run to when my Dad had one of his rages and frightened me nearly witless. I had nightmares for years as I associated him with a giant coming for me shouting "Fee-fi-fo-fum, I smell the blood of an Englishman" and I dreamed I sought refuge by hiding under Granny's sewing machine. That image is still vivid in my mind today – it terrified me so much.

Another thing that drove a wedge between me and my Dad came at mealtimes when he added various spices to our food, a habit and taste he acquired while in Burma but which made me feel sick to the point of the occasional vomit. It was curry powder, ginger, caraway seeds, cardamon and worst of all he sprinkled brittle cinnamon bark onto rice pudding and said things like "Get that down you, it'll do you good" – which it didn't and neither did his refusal to let me have a drink with my meal because he said you only drink after a meal, not with it. Hardly any wonder that it took me years to even try any kind of spicy food. Obviously, I'm over it now as I love Mexican, Indian, Chinese and most European cuisines. Those were distressing times for me with all his nonsensical rules and regulations and with the added restriction about not getting any pudding if you didn't finish your main course there was many-a-night I was sent early to bed very upset, very miserable and very hungry. In hindsight it's not hard to see why I never had a great rapport with my father or that we never bonded as I would have wished. That lack of closeness and interest in me continued through to my later school days when, unlike my team mate's dads, he never came to see me play a game of rugby – not once. Ha, I say, ha.

My parents

Mum

Blackpool trip With Stanley Oakes riding pillion on the motorbike

Aged 11 - the Holy Innocent

CHAPTER TWO
The Growing Years Where Nothing Much Happened

My musical influences and education began when I was about three years old and well aware of the popular wartime songs I heard on the radio and which my Mum played on the piano. My all-time favourite was Glenn Miller's 1939 hit "Moonlight Serenade" which I like to think I first heard while still in the womb. Songs in those days remained popular for many years after their initial release like my Dad's favourites "Whispering Grass" and "Java Jive" by The Ink Spots, novelty items like "Mairzy Doats and Dozy Doats" and songs by two artists I would meet 30 years later as a producer at the BBC. They were Bing Crosby "You Are My Sunshine" and Anne Shelton "Lili Marlene" – another one of those "who would have known" moments. Two of my parent's favourites are the now largely forgotten singer Issy Bonn and bandleader Nat Gonella, whom they claimed to know as a friend although I never met him as far as I know.

The first songs I learned to sing were both Frank Sinatra hits from 1947 namely "Five Minutes More" – my pleading song to be allowed to stay up a little past my bedtime and "The Coffee Song" which often got a laugh as I mis-pronounced the word politician as alopecia - a condition which causes bald spots on the scalp. Lots of other songs captured the imagination in the mid-40's such as "Hey Ba-Ba-Re-Bop" and "Open The Door Richard", then later on came "So Tired", "The Woody Woodpecker Song" and "On A Slow Boat To China" to which I knew all the words. That wasn't much use to me in 1949 when two of the biggest hits were instrumentals – "Bewitched" by Bill Snyder and "The Harry Lime Theme" from the film "The Third Man" which was set in Vienna, and though I never saw the film at the time it would only be five years before I was in that beautiful city. We had a summer holiday in Llandudno in 1951 and I well remember going to a matinee performance of the big hit film of the time "Annie Get Your Gun", where I fell in love with June Hutton.

One other thing that amused the family when I was very little was my insistence on wearing my brand-new blue wellington boots to bed. I was so pleased with them that I really never wanted to take them off but, strangely enough, they always came off during the night and were beside my bed next morning. I wonder how that happened?

Two major changes occurred when I was about six with a house move to 62 Osborne Road in Levenshulme, about half a mile from Brailsford Road. It was a much larger house with a kitchen, dining room, living room , six bedrooms and a bathroom with an indoor loo. This was to be my home throughout my teenage years and, apart from a brief escape in 1962, until I left for London in 1966. The other was starting at Birchfields Junior School in Lytham Road, just a ten-minute walk away – or a five-minute sprint if I was late. Life then pretty much revolved around school and school friends from a wide range of families and fortunes. Birchfields was a good school and my classmates included the Lord Mayor's son Richard Harper who lived on Slade Lane and who invited me to go to his house to play with his train set. Well, talk about another world, this was spectacular and totally exotic to me. It was a large detached house in a grand style and as we walked through the hallway to the rear there opened up in front of us an enormous glass room, obviously a Victorian conservatory, filled with potted plants and all kinds of collected memorabilia and there in the middle was Richard's train set laid out on top of a full-sized billiard table. My mouth must have been wide open but I still let out a shriek at the sight of a massive stuffed bear standing right beside me. It's always the unexpected that gets you that way, isn't it?

My first year at junior school was one of wide-eyed innocence and a degree of bewilderment as new information was implanted in my brain. As I recall this was the first time my mother said I was easily led when she found me following a friend who had persuaded me to go with him looking for the pot of gold at the end of a rainbow. She called me a daft ha'porth and marched me back home. Well, I was only six years old.

Another pal I visited was Oliver James, whose father was the High Master at Manchester Grammar School, and whose house sat directly opposite the main entrance gates of that august institution. Another lovely home and a great place to play our various games. There's not much in my memory banks regarding the years 1947-1950 except that at some time I joined both the Wolf Cubs and the choir at Holy Innocents church in Fallowfield and settled into a routine of Cubs one night a week, choir practise on another and three visits to church on Sunday - morning service, Sunday school and evensong. At least I earned a few bob for singing in the choir, especially if there was a wedding. I had a great affection and respect for our vicar the Reverend T E Kennaugh who was married with kids and always had a friendly disposition. He ran a youth club on Sunday evenings after church and you could only get in if you'd been to church but it was worth it. I got kicked out of the Cubs for boisterous behaviour so I never joined the scout troop either. I think I was about fourteen when I gave up the choir and the church, apart from the youth club.

For the next few years there was that church-related routine together with regular visits to see my mother's mother Grandma Butcher and Auntie Elsie in Tunstead Avenue, Didsbury. I got to love my Grandma greatly once I realised she was not as fierce as at first I thought she was with her instructions to sit up straight in the armchair and not rest my head back in case I got grease on the antimacassar cover. Macassar, a hair grooming product for men, had been a very oily stainer of fabrics in earlier times but was superseded first by brilliantine and later by Brylcreem, thanks to Denis Compton's adverts. More about meeting him later. Christmas Day was almost always celebrated at Grandma's house and I have such fond memories of lying on the floor avidly reading my Rupert Bear Annual from cover to cover. Auntie Elsie was a most lovely person and she devoted much of her life to looking after Grandma. She was the top designer of ladies corsets at J S Blair, one of the top foundation garment firms in Manchester, where she originated both the classic Slim Jim and Chainmail lines, were these the spanx of the time? She passed away far too young due to a weak heart. I adored her and she was the one who took me on my first visit to a theatrical performance, which I think was at The Manchester Opera House, to see the magical Peter Pan starring, if memory serves, Dorothy Tutin in the lead role. It made such an impression on me that I can remember it clearly to this day.

The rest of the family at those Christmas gatherings included my mother's other sisters Doris, a lovely lady with a beautiful voice who sang with The Halle Choir and her husband George, a fine sewing machine and clock and watch repairer who always teased me and challenged me with play-fights telling me he was a professional wrestler. In my childhood innocence I believed him, but I should have known he was just kidding because he was only five foot nothing and thin as a rake. Doris and George (Hill) never had children of their own and doted on me and my cousin Susan, the daughter of Edith and Eric Taylor. It was their house in Earby in Yorkshire that I went to for holidays from time to time. I don't know how or why those trips were arranged but I can tell you I really enjoyed it every time I travelled there. It was a world away from the big city, surrounded by wonderful countryside and even though I was quite young at the time I was free to wander every day as I pleased. My favourite place was the park, a short walk away down the main road. It had two bowling greens but what I enjoyed most were the swings and roundabouts and especially the slides, which on one occasion I hammered so hard that when I got home Auntie Edith took one look at my backside and said "Oh Geoffrey, you've worn a great big hole in your pants and you can't wear them again until they are repaired". "Oh", I said, "can you mend them for me, please?". "Yes", said Auntie Edith, "but I only have red material and your pants are green, what are we to do?". She then offered me the choice of a red patch or the only other option of painting my bottom green. Guess which option I chose? That's right, I decided to have my bottom painted green. My one regret from those halcyon days was my failure to protect my very young cousin Susan, who was about four at the time, and I would be about nine. In the park one day she inadvertently walked past a swing on its rearward trajectory and caught a huge blow to her forehead. As you can imagine, I was mortified and rushed her home for attention to the bump which was now as big as an egg. Auntie Edith did the necessary and Susan recovered quite quickly and I hope by now she has forgiven me. As well as the freedom and fresh air in Earby, Auntie Edith dispensed various medicaments such as cod liver oil, California syrup of figs (to keep you regular) and my absolute favourite, which came as a reward for taking the others, the thick, dark, sweet and treacly extract of malt, given as a mineral and vitamin supplement. Another daily routine was the mostly unwanted 6 o'clock in the morning alarm clock delivered by the loud percussive sound of the women in their clogs making their way to the factory along the cobblestones behind the house and directly outside my bedroom.

You can tell from the above that I spent a great deal of my childhood with my mother's family and hardly any that I remember with the Mullin side. My dad had two older brothers, Stan and Ron, and Stan's kids were my cousins Judith, Brian and Geraldine but we saw very little of each other in those early years due, I suspect, to stories I heard about a family rift following a death in the family.

Life at number 62 began quietly but soon picked up speed as my mother started her Bed and Breakfast business for any passer-by in need of accommodation. This included some quite extraordinary characters, most of whom moved on very quickly and others who stayed much longer, like Ron Crank, a gentle man, a painter and decorator who spent most of his working life painting the Manchester Corporation's fleet of red buses. Now that was a job for life if ever there was one. Ron really became one of the family and moved with my parents to Blackpool and stayed with my Dad until he, my Dad, passed away. Ron helped me make a few quid at the weekends assisting him painting the outsides of various houses. I learned to use a blowlamp and became a bit of a dab hand with a paintbrush. One guest who was with us for a while was the amazing Mr Frank Wilson, an intelligent and eccentric scientific man who wore plus-four trousers, a cape and strange hats. He had white hair, was probably about 70 years old or more but was as fit as a fiddle due to his daily walk, with his trusty cane, from our house to his "laboratory" (whatever that was) in the centre of Manchester. Another who stayed during one summer was an Armenian Jewish gentleman whose business was selling shirts and ties from a suitcase on street corners. He was only a small man and his suitcase was so huge that he often had trouble lifting it. There was Geoff Shotter with the biggest motorbike I had ever seen who took me on a death-defying ride to Alderley Edge, telling me to lean with him as he went round corners like a lunatic. I only ever went with him once. Our most exotic visitor, in my opinion, was Trevor Davies, a sun-tanned god of a man who was better looking than most film matinee idols. He stayed with us for quite a while and we got to know him well enough to be invited to his wedding, which if memory serves, was held in London.

After some time doing B & B there was an approach from Manchester University asking if we could take students during term time. This type of accommodation was known as "digs" and meant full occupation but involved also cooking an evening meal for the students. Very soon we had a house full with up to 8, mostly lads, at any one time plus the 3 of us and Ron Crank making 12 in all. The main downside to this arrangement for me was that to earn my weekly pocket money I had to do the washing up after every evening meal. I can't tell you how I came to loathe that job but I did become a bloody good dishwasher. My other main jobs were to chop firewood, fill the coal scuttle, bring it up from the cellar, fold old newspapers into twists and light the front room fire, which always seemed difficult to start until we got a fitted gas poker, oh joy, no more paper, no more wood just pop it under the coal and let it go. As a special treat on very rare occasions I accompanied my mother into town on a shopping trip and was rewarded with afternoon tea at the Midland Hotel which was certainly worth being dragged around all those department stores for a day. There were some great times and a continual change of faces over the years, although most stayed with us for the full duration of their courses. There was never an excuse needed to have a party what with birthdays, Bonfire Night and Christmas, when everybody joined in to decorate the house in all sorts of ways from pirate themes to ghostly spider's webs it created a great atmosphere which was so much fun but as I was only a youngster I couldn't stay up too late, unfortunately.

I remember some of the students more clearly than others, although they were all happy to help me with my homework when I was sitting both my 11-plus and my GCE exams – it was like having 8 brothers. Many of them were quite sporty, like footballers Colin Eastwood, Charlie Woodward and Bob Price. It was Bob Price's lovely mother who I stayed with in Bootle when I was 15 years old. The time is very clear in my mind for one specific reason because in her house she had rediffusion radio, which meant you had a speaker on the wall with three options, Light Programme, Home Service and, joy upon joy, Radio Luxembourg coming over clear as a bell. I was listening to 208 when on came a new record that absolutely knocked me out. It had a super fresh sound, great rhythm and the most amazing vocals and the announcer said "That's the Everly Brothers with their new single Bye-Bye Love". Well, that did it for me – I was an Everly fan. Now, Buddy Holly and the Crickets were also just about to arrive on the scene and they often get cited as a great inspiration to the Beatles and the Hollies but the Everly's deserve equal credit in my opinion. My days in Bootle were carefree and I could wander along the docks and watch the ferries and ships getting on with their business. Mrs Price looked after me really well and I look back to that time with great affection.

My time with Mrs Price wasn't the only student-related holiday I went on without my parents. Around 1951/52 we had our first female student, Hilda Corlett from the Isle Of Man. Hilda had two brothers and her family had a farm outside Ramsey to which I was invited for a short stay. I loved it there, having the freedom of the farm and local fields where you could see the rabbits eating early every morning. I was very taken with the calves in a pen and when I went over to them they came across and seemed so affectionate I made the mistake of getting into the pen with them. I didn't stay in there long after one of them butted me in the stomach, not too badly but enough to teach me a lesson and about just how strong they were. The farm was also the location for my second "near-death" experience as, having the run of the place, I climbed up onto a tractor and pretended to drive even though I had no idea what I was doing. This became very obvious very quickly as the tractor began to move slowly forward and I had no idea how to stop it as it picked up speed down an incline heading for a dry-stone wall. As the ensuing collision became inevitable, I clung on to the steering wheel like grim death and awaited the impact – ouch. I escaped unscathed but frightened and I think the tractor survived although not sure about the wall. The brothers gave me a bit of a bollocking but forgave me and said to leave things alone in future. They were a lovely family and took me on various trips around the island and I especially enjoyed the famous Great Laxey Wheel and the Snaefell mountain railway. Once again, little did I know I would return to the island for a Radio Two Outside Broadcast with Terry Wogan some 30 years later.

There was another student I got on with very well and with whom I maintained a friendship into the 1970's. His name was Beverley Leatherbarrow and he was a great cricket fan who very generously took me to Old Trafford to see England beat Australia in July 1956 in a match that has gone down in history, as Jim Laker took 19 wickets for 90 runs, a feat that has never been equalled. The resulting sunburn I got was worth it just to have been there for such a momentous event. Bev was a photography student who went on to great success as Beverley Le Barrow, snapping glamourous ladies for a series of James Bond novels. He moved to London and I believe one of his early associations was with the famous photographer Sterling Henry Nahum, known professionally as Baron, the Court Photographer to the British Royal Family. That's not a bad place to start your professional life, is it? Bev also took some excellent family portraits while he was with us and did a session of publicity shots for me in 1967 when I made my Jason James records, of which more later. I never got a set of those shots and I'd love to see them now with me decked out in my fashionable Carnaby Street gear – ah well.

I often got homework help from the boys but they never ever told me the answers and made me work things out for myself, which was always the best policy and it got me through my important exams. It didn't stop me getting into trouble at Birchfields

Junior School, though, and I was hauled up in front of the Headmistress Mrs Pine a few times for a good telling off. One of the naughtiest things I did, and I probably shouldn't be owning up to this, but it was while the class was waiting for the bus to take us for our weekly swimming lesson at the High Street baths in Longsight and I was standing behind a girl called Beryl who had a long plait down her back. You know what's coming, don't you? Yes, I took out my penknife and cut off about 3 inches of her hair. Naturally, she screamed, the teacher came along, and I knew I was in big trouble. That episode lasted long in the memory for me, but especially for Beryl, who never forgave me. However, I did learn to swim at those baths thanks to the hardest instructor you ever saw, with his bald head and brown lab coat he would shout at you very loudly until you got it right. In fact, he frightened me into learning to swim. I didn't realise the correct name for those baths until they came up as a contender in the BBC's Restoration programme in 2003 when viewers were invited to vote for what they deemed to be the most-worthy cause. Knowing those baths so well, it was also where we went swimming from Burnage Grammar School later on, I was very happy to join in, basically voting multiple times for what I then knew to be Victoria Baths, the eventual winner. I did my bit.

Looking back, it seems I was either daydreaming or totally boisterous most of the time, for instance, during an arithmetic lesson I was brought swiftly to my senses by a sharp punch in the back by Mrs Maxwell, who said "Stop looking out of the window, Geoffrey, and get on with your work". She was fierce but I had great respect and admiration for her, often speaking to her over the years away from school as she lived in the area. I was regularly getting into fights with other kids and although I don't recall having a nasty streak to start a fight, I always came out winning. In my last year there I got into a fight with Pete Dunkerley over a girl called Gillian Kelsall, whom I thought rather ravishing. I had no idea Pete felt the same way about her until he challenged me to fight for the right to this maiden's hand. I accepted, all the while knowing there was nothing going on between me and Gillian and that she probably had no idea what it was all about, either. Still, the time for the bout was arranged for lunchtime behind the canteen and Pete and

I squared off against each other as some of the class watched on. I stood there waiting and Pete rushed forward. He met a straight jab from my left hand, staggered backwards with a bloody nose and declared that that was enough. Only the one punch was landed and we shook hands and became quite good pals for a while. It was no surprise in my last school report that our teacher Mr Flockton wrote "Geoffrey must learn to control his robust energy". How right he was and that energy was channelled very effectively just months later when I got to senior school and started playing rugby. One last word on my misdemeanours in Mr Flockton's class was the heavy price I paid with the writing out of "lines" for bad behaviour. This was almost always 50 or 100 lines of "I MUST NOT TALK IN CLASS" in my best handwriting. Will I never learn? Apparently not, because the last time I got hauled up for a dressing down (oops) was during the summer term when a group of us lads were sitting on the grass discussing our futures and which schools we may be going to next when my best pal Michael Rowe brought up the subject of babies. He said he thought they were made by some remarkable process when a man and a woman were in bed together. The other lads, Leslie Grindle, the class comedian who made me laugh every day, and Colin Wood, first choice on the team sheet for football games, both denied any knowledge of the subject. Well, here comes the big reveal – just a couple of days earlier my pal Victor had told me all about the process of getting harder and longer and entering the unknown lady territory. I was keen to divulge this secret knowledge and did so very convincingly as my pals sat there open-mouthed at this outrageous and extraordinary information. Unfortunately, ahem, one of the girls had been eavesdropping behind us and went immediately to report this disgusting conversation to the headmistress. Needless to say, I was well and truly carpeted and told under no circumstances to discuss the subject of baby production ever again. She didn't say whether it was true or not but it did give me a bit of notorious celebrity and status for a while – hey, the man who knew too much.

Two major events occurred towards the end of my time there. The first was the Queen's Coronation on June 2nd 1953 which was a Tuesday and we all got a day off school – hooray. Lots of neighbours gathered around to watch the ceremony on the only television set in the road, not ours, followed by a great street party which was unfortunately marred by rain but we still thoroughly enjoyed it. The last was a year later on the 30th June 1954 when all the kids at school were able to witness the most amazing solar eclipse of the sun. We were under strict instructions not to look at the sun, always keep our backs towards it and use the pinhole projectors we had all recently made in class. It was a most unusual event but I wasn't to witness another until 1999 when I became a bit of a "shadow chaser".

CHAPTER THREE
Life, As We Know It, Starts

My best pals during my last year at Birchfields were Clive and Victor Sayer who lived in the next street, Windsor Road. You may have drawn the connection already between the street names as they all referenced Queen Victoria with both Albert and Victoria roads. The area was in Levenshulme and known as West Point, probably due to its being a bus terminus and going back to a time when it may have been the furthest outlying district from the city centre. Clive was the youngest of 3 brothers. Don, the oldest, worked in the television industry and their father was a famous circus clown who appeared with the legendary performer Charlie Cairoli at Blackpool's Tower Circus. Clive and Victor had already started senior school when I took my 11-plus exam and I desperately wanted to pass with good enough marks to join them at Burnage Grammar school. The day the results were announced I couldn't have been happier – my wish to join them and go to an all-boys rugby-playing school had been granted. My parents had promised to buy me a bike if I passed and, even though I hadn't learned to ride, a few days later the big unveiling arrived. Hidden in the garage and wheeled out by my Dad it was a new but somewhat old-fashioned sit-up-and-beg bike, disappointingly unlike the drop-handlebar racer I was hoping for. Nevertheless Clive, Victor and I stood there admiring this new means of transport which I could use to cycle to my new school. As we were checking out the tires, brakes, pedals etc, Victor said he could ride and would I let him have a go. He mounted with great confidence and set off down the passage running straight out into the road, where cars were a rarity, and yes, that's right, he got run over by a car. Bloody hell, upset was probably a mild description of my reaction to this appalling event as we all rushed into the road to see what had happened to both Victor and the bike. Needless to say, Victor was fine, having taken a tumble over the bonnet of this car but the bike was wrecked with both wheels and the handlebars bent well out of shape. Just recently Victor wanted to know if he still owes me money for the repairs. Rather magnanimously I let him off. It was a very long time ago. The bike was fixed and returned a couple of weeks later, after which I quickly learned to ride and gained the freedom of the open road. Clive and I became the best of friends and spent a lot of time playing together right through our teenage years and into our twenties before he decided to emigrate to Canada. That didn't work out for him and he returned to the UK, by which time I had moved to London and we never saw each other again, sadly.

Perhaps the greatest fun day of the year for all us teenagers was Bonfire Night or Guy Fawkes Night when we made a model Guy and paraded him round the streets in a cart asking passers-by for "A penny for the Guy", which usually resulted in enough pennies to buy a few fireworks. One of the funniest sights I ever saw was when Clive and Victor purloined a couple of huge thunderflash type bangers from their dad's circus storeroom. They were seriously loud with an epic bang and one night as all the kids were standing round the bonfire, they were invited to come to stand by the drain in the street to watch this banger go off. Well, I didn't know what to expect and it seemed very exciting but Victor whispered to me to stand well back as the banger was lit and dropped into the drain. Nothing happened at first but then came a whooshing sound as all the kids looked down into the darkness of the drain and then, with something approaching the velocity of a tornado, up shot a plume of water about twenty feet into the air and, yes, you guessed right again, those poor kids got absolutely drenched. Oh boy, did we laugh, even the soaked kids, and all was dried out in front of the fire with large helpings of my Mum's delicious treacle toffee and ginger parkin cake.

At about this time Victor's entrepreneurial ambitions began to surface and he decided to mount a puppet show depicting "When World's Collide". To facilitate this, he commandeered our back garden gate as the venue where he could put a curtain across and use as a stage. The puppets obviously came from his father's stock and they were very realistic in a Punch and Judy sort of way. All the local kids were invited and admittance to this great spectacle would be sixpence each. I thought that a fair price, especially as I was expecting to share the ackers with Victor, but no, not only wasn't I getting a share of the proceeds, he actually had the gall to try to charge me to watch. I said I wasn't about to pay and if I didn't get a share-out he could mount his production elsewhere – or words to that effect. Result was – he paid up.

Soon after we moved into Osborne Road we went to the Kingsway cinema to see the 1949 film "The Blue Lagoon" which I found both enchanting and scary and had nightmares for weeks afterwards about one particular scene which I recall vividly to this day. The cinema that night was totally packed out and our party couldn't all sit together so I was seated with family friends about 4 rows back from my parents. The story is about two children, a boy and a girl, shipwrecked alone on a desert island where they learn to live and play as they grow to be teenagers. As they mature, I become totally confused by the plot and shout to my mother in front for an explanation, with "Mum, where did that baby come from?". Well, you can imagine the reaction – the entire audience collapsed with laughter for several minutes – my second unintentional funny. The image that stayed with me from that film which caused me to not look forward to going to bed was this. The children find an old sea-dog who lives in a cave, and this is the terrifying part, they are with him the moment he expires, which is depicted in the film by the image of a skeleton rising from his body in a swirl of smoke and mist. No wonder I was scared, don't you think? At the moment you are not able to watch this film as it has been withdrawn from public viewing, apparently because of the nakedness of the children. If needed I wish they could edit those scenes out and let us watch the rest of it if only to see that damned skeleton again.

From our new home I had access to five cinemas within easy walking distance – Kingsway, Regal, Palace, Grand and Arcadia – the local fleapit. The Regal was the ABC Minors Saturday morning club where we watched all the classics and was well worth the sixpence entrance fee. The Regal later became a Ten Pin bowling alley where young Ron Stratton and I honed our chucking skills.

There was also the Levenshulme swimming baths and a roller-skating rink where I first heard and enjoyed The Skater's Waltz by Waldteufel, which means wood devil in German, which is all very Teutonic, except that Waldteufel wasn't his real name and he was French. Other films that caught my attention in the early fifties were Cinderella and two great favourites Peter Pan and Treasure Island with Robert Newton, after which we practised limping, closing one eye, inclining our head to one side and shouting "Ah harrr Jim Lad", bringing about ructions from the grown-ups, which only encouraged us do it more. On the musical side it was becoming a rite of passage for me that whenever we went to a family friend or relative's house I would, whenever possible, closet myself in an adjoining room with a gramophone and listen to every single disc in their collection. Some equipment was still wind-up but most were electric and virtually all were 78rpm. Disc sizes ranged from 3 inch to 5 inch to 7 inch to the standard 10 inch and some with orchestral works were much larger still. That was the start of my obsession with recorded music which I still haven't fully exhausted.

I don't know about other 8-year-old kids in 1950 but when I heard Teresa Brewer sing "Music Music Music" my ears became attuned in an entirely new way. We still had some of the old sounds that year such as Guy Lombardo's "Enjoy Yourself (it's later than you think)" – still popular today thanks to Jools Holland and The Specials but there was movement a-plenty on the popular music front. The Mambo arrived and new stars appeared in the early fifties with more modern songs and sounds, destined to be with us for the long term like Guy Mitchell, Frankie Laine, Kay Starr and the latest to be crowned "heart-throb", Johnnie Ray, who, because of his massive hit song "Cry" became known as the "Nabob of Sob" and the "Prince of Wails" – where do they get this stuff from. Another form of entertainment was a Saturday night outing to cheer on and support the Belle Vue Aces speedway team. It was an exciting night out and we boys would don our protective goggles and stand right up to the barrier as our heroes hurtled by throwing up grit which got lodged in our hair, on our clothes and in our mouths if we weren't careful. I was lucky enough to see many world track champions there – Ove Fundin, Ivan Mauger, Barry Briggs,

Split Waterman and our local stars Jack Parker and Peter Craven. It was at the track one night in the summer of 1954 that something struck me as so far out, beyond anything I'd ever heard before, when over the Tannoy loud and clear came Johnnie Ray singing "Such A Night". Well, that was it for me, as close to an original rock and roll song as you got at that time and one you probably wouldn't hear on the BBC because of its overt sexuality.I loved it. This was before either Bill Haley or Elvis hit the charts. Elvis himself did a great version of that song too and it's come back again recently with Michael Buble's version. After the racing was over we would go to the fun fair with rides on the terrifying "Bobs" rollercoaster and play some games on the various stalls. All in all it was a very exciting night out.

My new surroundings were an adventure playground compared to Brailsford Road because there was so much more to see and do. West Point had a sort of village feel about it with a small park, a grocer, greengrocer, butcher, baker, newsagent, off-license, sweet shop and a fish and chip shop all within 100 yards of our house. Next door at number 60 were the Bowers with two children Michael and his younger sister Joan. Michael and I started playing games over the back garden fence, deciding by the toss of a coin which super hero we would choose to be. If Michael won he would choose my favourite and be Superman. I then chose to be Tarzan and off we'd go into our fantasy world chasing the evil baddies out of our realm until we were exhausted and went inside for tea. After one of these adventures my mother said I shouldn't play with Michael anymore and when I asked why she said it was because he was a Catholic. I asked what that was and she said they believed different things to us and that we shouldn't mix. I was totally perplexed by this and soon after I dragged Michael away from the environs of our house and asked him what a Catholic was and why we were different. He said we didn't share the same religion and at his church their services were held in a foreign language but they felt superior because they had the advantage of Holy Water. "Blimey", says I, "what is Holy Water?". "Would you like to see it?", said Michael. Would I, are you kidding? Off we went immediately to his church, creeping in very quietly and a soon as we entered Michael pointed out the Holy Water. I said it looked perfectly ordinary to me but he said no, you have to dip you fingers in and you'd be cleansed and protected. I didn't ask where the soap was but dipped my fingers in anyway, Michael did the same and then we scarpered in case we got caught. This Holy Water made no impression on me at all, so naturally I couldn't possibly be a Catholic.

Michael and I stayed friends for a long time and he joined in with Clive and Victor in all our various street games such as marbles, cricket down the alley and, most popular of all, stone throwing battles. Yes, can you believe it, we would run up and down the road, hiding in gardens and picking up stones to throw at one another whenever another boy became visible. It's amazing that no one got seriously injured during those "games", which we all got into trouble for playing, especially on one occasion when we had the nerve to disturb the peace and tranquillity of the local "Witch Lady", as we called her. Nellie Wolstenholme was a spinster with a shock of red hair and a bizarre dress sense who frightened us all into submission whenever we came across her. It wasn't long before we got to know and like her when she generously employed us for the Cubs annual "Bob A Job Week" initiative. That's when we raised money by going door-to-door offering to do any jobs for the donation of a bob (one shilling). Some of the work was easy and the bob was handed over with a knowing smile but on others we were taken advantage of by unscrupulous adults who expected our blood for their money.

Speaking about the sordid topic of coin (love that phrase, don't you?), my parents never owned our house, they always rented, hoping that one day they would be able to afford a home of their own. They filled in their football pools coupons religiously every week but the dream of landing the £75,000 jackpot was forever out of reach. The only other form of gambling they indulged in was a flutter on the big horse races like The Derby and The Grand National, which was a real pain for me as I had to walk a considerable distance to place the bets with the backstreet bookies, which were illegal before 1960. The only other place you might get a bet on was in the pub but I was too young to go in there. Honestly, the things little kids had to do in those days.

CHAPTER FOUR

The Student Years – Me And Them

In September 1954 I began my incarceration at Burnage Grammar school and with my birthday being the 11th of September I was always the oldest in the class, which were now known as forms. My form was 1B, one of four first year classes. One thing that happened there early on gave me a nickname which was to stick with me for most of my time there and this is how it happened. Every day we had to hand in our books for marking by the teacher and when he called out our names for us to receive our books back he got to mine and called out "MUFFIN", because some wag had altered my name easily enough by turning the letter "L" into an "F". Well, that was it, ever after I bore the name of a famous television puppet "Muffin The Mule". I didn't like it at first but soon got used to it in the shortened form of "Muff" carrying it as a badge of celebrity and woe betide anyone who laughed at me.

My first year was plagued by illness and time away from school with all sorts of ailments, the most serious of which was a bout of shingles, followed by a couple of weeks convalescing at a children's home in Morecambe, which was good fun with lots of other kids from all over England and it certainly aided my recovery. One of the friends I made there came from Devon and he had a wonderful accent which fascinated me and the other kids. We loved to hear him speak and always asked him to say "how now brown cow", which had us all in hysterics. He knew what he was doing this lad and laid on the old Devonian with some relish. Due to these absences, I was way behind in some subjects, particularly German and algebra, which, if you don't get the basics, is very hard to catch up on. My favourite subject was always English, especially lessons with Mr Hughes, who once wrote on the blackboard this indecipherable gibberish, "o ony o yer ony o it on yer" and challenged us to translate it. Unsurprisingly, no one had a clue, until he explained it was the way Yorkshire miners would speak when they wanted some tobacco from a mate. He then translated it as "Have any of you any of it on you?", a request for some baccy. Hughes was also keen on handing out "lines" for bad behaviour but these were not easy scribbles, for instance "A Psychopathic Tendency Is Symptomatic Of Insanity" was one of his favourites. The algebra was rescued just before I sat my maths GCE with intense study of the text book but the German was to take a dramatic turn for the better almost immediately. At the end of that first year's exams I did OK in science and English but I was last in German and this is how the improvement came about, which, in many ways, changed my life for the better. During assembly one morning the Headmaster Mr Spencer announced that there was an opportunity for a student exchange with some Austrian schoolboys whereby we would have them to stay with us in England and they would have us return to Austria for a visit to their homes. This really got me interested and right after assembly I went to see the head in his office to tell him that I would like to be considered for one of the exchange students. He said I was a bit quick off the mark and I would have to ask my parent's permission. I said could I please be first in line and I would be back after lunch with permission from my mother. I think he was impressed by my enthusiasm and initiative and said to come to him after lunch with my mother's agreement. When I got home I had little difficulty persuading my Mum that this was a good idea as it could improve my German, and she agreed. So it was that that very summer, via the good offices of The Anglo-Austrian Society, we were host to a boy from Vienna called Horst Hofer, with whom I became very good friends for many years until he got married and sort of disappeared from my life.

That was the start of a sequence of yearly exchange visits with various Austrian boys and more or less the end of summer holidays taken with my parents at English and Welsh seaside resorts like Blackpool, Southport and Morecambe in Lancashire, Bridlington, Mablethorpe and Skegness on the east coast. The places we seemed to visit most in Wales were Colwyn Bay and Llandudno where

I won a prize in the open-air Happy Valley competition for singing "Unchained Melody", a Number One hit for Jimmy Young. How could I know that many years later I would be his radio producer, very weird.

The following year I went to stay with Horst and his parents Karl and Elfriede at their apartment in the northern Viennese district of Floridsdorf, which had suffered badly at the hands of the Russian occupying forces after the war when the Allies divided the city into four zones. Karl had lost a leg during the war and told me of the cruelty inflicted by Russian soldiers, which lasted until all foreign troops withdrew in 1955, just a year before I arrived. Their apartment was just a short walk away from the Old Danube and Donau Kanal where we spent carefree days swimming and sunbathing with Horst and his friends Heinz, Seppl and a very pretty girl, Renate Albrecht, with whom I fell hopelessly in love but, sadly, all to no avail. Well, I was only thirteen. However, Renate and I became pen pals and due to my writing to her and Horst my German improved to such an extent that I always came top of the class from then on. Result.

My next house guest was Hans Hirschl, with whom I am still in touch and whose family made me feel so welcome in their home in Vienna. His older sister Christa was wonderful company, too, and we all went on cycling trips together, where I first rode a bike that you could brake by pedalling backwards – very strange. Relief on very hot days was to be found at a huge public swimming pool where I first experienced a wave machine. The weather that summer was perfect as we spent time in the garden eating apricots straight off the tree, it was idyllic and strangely exotic, being a world away from Manchester. I was given the grand tour of Vienna and went to the Prater amusement park and rode the Riesenrad wheel, famous from the Orson Welles film "The Third Man". It was also the place I had my first real French fries otherwise known to us Brits as thin chips. The other foods that really took my taste buds to another world were Wiener schnitzel, goulash with brat kartoffeln (small fried potatoes), Sacher torte and Christa's delicious pflaumenknoedel (plum dumplings). You know, I could easily survive on the food over there. Their house in Stefan Fadinger Platz was lovely with green shuttered windows and where I first enjoyed sleeping under a duvet, which were thrown over the windowsill every morning to air. I came back from that visit with a pair of lederhosen, short leather trousers, which caused some amusement back home for their eccentricity but I loved them and wore them quite often. Hans, proper name Georg, was a terrific basketball player and later did the usual thing - he grew up and married a lovely girl called Bobby, the daughter of a diplomat. They came over for my 50th birthday party and we went over to Vienna for his. Long lasting friendships are a thing to be treasured very highly.

The next exchange wasn't. Yes, we had another boy to stay but he didn't seem very interested in joining in and spent a lot of time playing patience with his cards. His name was Klaus and he came from Graz where his family business was a brick manufacturing facility. I think he just got homesick, nothing we did seemed to please him and I never got to visit him.

Erich Zojer was my next exchange, a clever boy and an outstanding athlete from a small village in the south of Austria very close to the Italian border. Erich enjoyed his time with us and in the summer of 1958 I enjoyed my visit back to his home in Kotschach-Mauthen. I was 16, Erich a little older, and his brother Herbert was a little older still. Their house in this tiny hamlet was very much in the alpine style and I spent many afternoons helping with chopping wooden logs out in the back yard. Herbert worked in the main industry of the area which was logging timber. Both Erich and Herbert were fully qualified skiers and mountain guides, always ready for a call-out to help on a rescue mission. They took me on a trip over the mountains into Italy where we posted a route by painting the rocks red and white as we passed on our way up to the peak. We had an overnight stay in a mountain hut about half way up and the next day on the way down we were mostly sliding at some pace over the scree. We finally arrived at the base of the mountain and made our way to the nearest town which was Cortina d'Ampezzo where I had my first lesson in how to eat spaghetti – delicious. The Zojer family looked after me really well and took me on several trips including one to Austria's highest mountain, the amazing Grossglockner (big bell) and back into Italy to Udine to see the famous castle there and drink a refreshing glass of the local lager Birra Moretti. This was where I bought some clothes that were to get me into a fight on my return to England – stay tuned. As I said, Erich was an ace athlete and had been entered into the state athletics meeting to select runners for the Austrian team and yes, he was that good. These elimination rounds were held in Klagenfurt, the capital of Karnten, which we call Carinthia. In the days before the meeting Erich had been training hard for his 400 and 800 metre races and I had joined him in his runs through the local woods every evening. I thought I was fit playing so much sport but he left me for dead every time, his stamina was extraordinary. Come the day of the competition I went along to support Erich and as we entered the stadium the coach came over to us and had a few words with Erich, who then turned to me and said that, if I wanted to, I could take part as a guest competitor. Well, what was I to say? The coach asked me what my best events were and I knew I couldn't match up to Erich on the track and I also knew there wouldn't be a cricket ball throwing event so I said I wasn't bad with a javelin. I was entered into the Junior section as a competitor, Erich managed to find me a pair of spiked running shoes and you've probably guessed by now that I wouldn't be telling you this had it been a disaster. Well, it wasn't, and to my utter amazement I came first and somewhere in the archives from 1958 I am down as the winner of the Carinthian games Junior Javelin Competition – a most unexpected champion. Having spent much of those summer weeks in the local swimming pool I arrived home with a healthy tan and the aforementioned clothes which I wore the very next day when my pal Bob Morrell came to call. He mightily approved of my new Italian gear which was a pair of tailored trousers in a silvery shot-gaberdine type fabric, a pair of lightweight latticed slip-on leather shoes along with a short-sleeved polo shirt – the very image of a mod which hadn't yet arrived in England. We decided to go for a game of bowls at the little park in Fallowfield and as we walked along I told Bob about Austria and, as I hadn't heard any pop music while I was away, I asked him what was number one in the charts. That started a hilarious round of question and answer that carried on for some time and it went like this – me to Bob, "So, what's number one this week?", Bob, "When", me, "This week", Bob, "When", me, "Now, today, what is the top song you idiot?" At this point Bob fell about laughing knowing he had played a blinder on me, finally explaining that The Kalin Twins were at the top of the charts with a song called "When". I saw the funny side of it and said "You bastard". This was July 1958 and the teddy boy fashion trend was still very much in vogue and as we arrived in the park there were a couple of teds we knew from the youth club sitting on a bench being all grown up and smoking, something I didn't do at that time. One of them, Joe Elson, decided to take the piss out of me and called me a queer and accused me of wearing girl's shoes. I replied it was better than being dressed like an old rag and bone man. He took more offence at this than I had and stood up ready to grapple. This we did for a couple of minutes and I gave him a bloody nose before we were separated by a couple of older lads. Joe realised I wasn't what he had called me so we shook hands and made up, his umbrage entirely dissipated. The end of that summer came and as we went back to school one of the first opportunities for sport was the gym class where I got well and truly lambasted by all the lads as I got undressed to reveal a rather magnificent golden tan. They couldn't believe it as the best they could show were a few pink and painful sunburned backs. Jealous or what?

The last exchangee to arrive was Adolf Mattersdorfer from Bad Voslau, a village about 30 miles south of Vienna famed for its Thermalbad spa waters and situated in the heart of Austria's red wine growing territory. Addi was a couple of years older than me and therefore my mother let him come and go as he pleased, unlike the vice-like grip she had on my freedom of movement, which was another bone of contention. One of the differences between the Austrians coming to me and my going to them was quite stark because they always came at the end of our school term and were required to come to school with me for a couple of weeks, whereas when I went to them it was always in the school holidays – lucky me. My return visit was another idyllic summer in the usual hot Austrian sun but this time I had access to the most wonderful water playground. Bad Voslau is a renowned spa town and it just so transpired that Addi's sister Edith ran the local bath and swimming pool complex which also included a restaurant, a bar and a nightclub – heaven. Lazy days were spent around one of the two large pools, food was always available and in the evening we had fun playing the jukebox and dancing with the local ladies. Shangri-la. That was the last of my school exchange visits though I did go back just a few years later with Ron Stratton to visit both the Hirschl and Mattersdorfer families, who welcomed us with open arms and treated us right royally. The last time I spoke to Addi he told me that he was now The Burgermeister and I congratulated him on this well-deserved accolade.

One final note on these wonderful travels must be many thanks to the Anglo-Austrian Society who organised all the transport and excursions on our way to Austria such as a visit en-route to see the sights of London and particularly the 1958 visit to the World's Fair at the Brussels Expo where we saw the amazing, never to be forgotten depiction of an atom known, naturally, as the Atomium.

CHAPTER FIVE

Burnage Grammar School

At the start of every new school year we would have a new form teacher and as we left Mr Bateman and Form 1B behind we were split up into our supposed varying ability groupings where the streams reflected either mostly a scientific or a language leaning. I went into Form 2 Beta together with friends Paul Grundy, Jeff Ward, Chris Kershaw, Geoff Mann and Rob Crompton. With Geoff and Rob I enjoy an ongoing friendship to this day. Rob was part of a group of lads who practised guitar down in the cloakroom during breaks and that group included my good friend Pete Bocking who emerged as the premier guitarist in Manchester just a few years later playing in The Fourtones with Allan Clarke and Graham Nash who would later become The Hollies. If we'd known at the time we could have formed a great little band with Pete on lead guitar, Rob on rhythm, Chris on drums, Ian "Big Wal" Waller on bass and my other good friend Pete Howarth on piano. There'll be more to come regarding their musical futures later on although the first of our contemporaries that I know of who made a mark in the music industry was an older boy who formed a group called Paul Beattie and The Beats, one of the first Manchester groups. Paul grew up in Fallowfield, like me, sang, played guitar and signed a recording contract with Parlophone Records who released his first single "I'm Comin' Home" in 1957, regarded as George Martin's first rock and roll record. He made a few more records but was never able to get into the charts, unfortunately.

I began taking piano lessons locally with Miss Morris but, much like my reluctance to do homework, my piano playing took second place to my love of sport, particularly rugby. In the first year I played full-back at football for the house team and the rugby coach Mr Starkey was watching when I booted an extremely wet and heavy ball down into the other half of the field. He spoke to me afterwards and said he'd like to see if I could kick a rugby ball like that. Well, we discovered that I could and he drafted me into the school Under 13 team where I thrived and became devoted to the game. As I was quite tall for my age I played in the scrum where my height was an advantage at the line-out but it was my kicking that really marked me out. I would practise spot kicks for ages, long after the regular training sessions finished until I could send the ball a very long way with great accuracy. I wasn't too bad in open play either and in the Under 14 team I managed to score half the team's points with tries and kicks. As we reached the Under 15 stage we were entered into the Manchester Schools Sevens tournament. It was pretty tough but we had a good team and triumphed in the final by only five points to three. I scored the try and converted it from the touchline as it hit the crossbar and bounced over – a bloody miracle The other six on the team were Paul Grundy, Stuart Ashworth, John Hobson, Ray Wills, Billy Wright and Arthur Rule, otherwise known as Six-inch, for obvious reasons. We were awarded our medals by the headmaster a few days later in morning assembly and the whole school gave us a great cheer as we mounted the steps onto the stage to receive them. Doesn't get any better than that.

There was a marked difference in disciplinary measures between Birchfields and Burnage, which usually left its impression on our backsides. Yes, we still had to do lines for naughtiness and sometimes detention but some staff had a slightly more sadistic solution, which might be the slipper, a plimsoll, across your tender parts or a ruler smack on the palms of your hands. Even the Headmaster gave you the cane in his study but the most feared of all was the chemistry teacher, Mr Brackenbury, who would stand in his classroom doorway and ambush any boy silly enough to run along the corridor outside his lab. It wasn't the getting caught so much as the method of retribution Mr B would administer, delivering justice with the weapon of his choice, an enormous squeegee, combining great energy with enthusiastic relish. Most boys only ever ran along that corridor once. There was another master with a fearsome reputation and that was the metalwork teacher Mr Todd, who was equally ambitious in his aim of turning us into cowering wrecks, but he did it once too often to Pete Bocking who, on his very last day of school exacted his revenge by giving Todd a massive punch in the face which produced the biggest "shiner" you ever saw.

During the first years at Burnage you were not allowed to leave the compound at lunchtime, which meant school dinners, which were OK but we envied the older boys who could go to the shops and buy what they liked to eat. When we earned that freedom by dint of our age my daily fare would start with the bakers to buy a bap, a flat round bun, from which the bread inside would be scooped out to make way for the chips with lashings of salt and vinegar, all washed down with a bottle of fizzy pineapple juice from the greengrocers. Pudding was the great treat of a large cream doughnut. I survived on that diet for months.

It wasn't too painful though and there were some funny incidents along the way such as the day Pete Howarth turned up for school in a pair of jeans, strictly against the dress code, and was told to go home and not return until he was properly attired. We didn't see him for two weeks – hilarious. He was a rebel with a cause. There were odd disturbances of the peace by the boys which could have had serious consequences, especially those in the chemistry class who learned to make a bomb using fertiliser in a lead pipe and sending a dustbin lid about fifty feet into the air. Not me, m'lud. We heard a funny story about two schoolmates after they were marched off to a local police station for questioning. They had been caught smoking in a shop doorway by a copper and he wanted their names and addresses, so the first lad, who had a very obvious silver incisor, front tooth, told him his name was David Tooth, which was true. The copper gave him a funny look and asked the other lad his name and got the reply Sedmiradsky. Well, that did it, he didn't believe them and they had to accompany him to the nick for their identification to be verified and their parents contacted. They really didn't get into any trouble but we all thought it a very amusing confrontation with the law.

The teachers were mostly older gentlemen and generally quite restrained and sober types but we did get many a giggle in our maths lessons with Mr Mathias who had a string of phrases that he trotted out on a regular basis. Here's a couple of them "Keep your eye on the board while I run through it" and the classic "Every time I open my mouth some damn fool speaks". His favourite form of admonishment was the standard "You're a donkey, laddie" which I got a few times until he came to watch a rugby game against St Bede's college. We had scored a try right in the corner and I took the conversion kick from well behind the 25-yard line in order to widen the angle. That ball sailed through those posts as straight as an arrow and at a great height too, causing him to shout "Bloody marvellous, Mullin, bloody marvellous" in his Welsh brogue – good old Taffy, who was very helpful with my maths lessons after that display. One of the things that helped my kicking was the square-toed boots I favoured which were unusual in those days when kicks were almost always toe-ended except by ex-footballers who favoured the instep kick now used almost universally in the game.

The other rugby coach at school was the admirable Mr Starkey the woodwork teacher and the man who led us to victory in the Sevens tournament. He was the polar opposite to Todd and really helped us all with our work, especially when we had to make a piece of furniture for our final exams. I chose to assemble a drinks trolley which didn't look too shabby after I stained and varnished it and as we were allowed to take them home upon completion, I took mine and gave it to Granny and Grampa as a present, which they really appreciated.

I told you earlier of my night frights from seeing The Blue Lagoon but there were other things that my young mind fretted over and one was a local man who appeared, in the true sense of the word, as grotesque. He was a large man around thirty years old who wandered around with an enormous growth coming out of his neck and head that rested on his left shoulder. It was white and bulbous with the veins clearly visible and it sent shivers down your spine, so much so that if I saw him I would quickly cross to the other side of the street. It was obviously very sad for him but to us kids all we could think of was that he was some kind of monster. The other reason for my apprehension was any visit to the shoe repair shop on the parade. A bell rang as you entered but the desk was never manned as the cobbler was always hard at it in the rear workshop. He looked like the original Doctor Who, William

Hartnell, and he had a fierce manner about him when he came out and only said "Yes?" You then popped your shoes on the counter and he would say "Soled and heeled or just soled?" very bluntly. You'd say both please and he would bark again "Leather sole or rubber, leather heel or rubber?" You'd tell him what you wanted and he'd just say "Ready on Tuesday" or whatever day of the week it would be. He was another man who wore a brown lab coat to work in and he was never one to smile or chat with you, until one day I met him at the bus stop and he was well-dressed and carrying a violin case. I tentatively asked him about the case and he opened up immediately and told me with some pride that he was going into town to play with The Halle Orchestra. Well, that was some revelation for sure and ever after that I came to rather enjoy my visits to his shop as his attitude towards me changed very much for the better.

There were two major community events every year in Manchester city centre which drew huge crowds to watch them. The famous Whit Walks saw many churches and Sunday School children in their all-white outfits parade around the town with their banners, often accompanied by a brass band, in a procession which eventually ended up in Albert Square. I took part in several of these marches and can't honestly say that I enjoyed them.

The other event I really did enjoy were the University Rag Weeks where the students would man various exotically designed floats which toured the main streets collecting money for charity. It was always hilariously riotous with some crazy, maybe insane, antics being performed by the students, all in a good cause. As I got older I was able to join in more and give a little help where needed.

There were a couple of frustrating things I wasn't able to join in with during the early 1950's because I was too young. The first was not being allowed to stay up to listen to the Goon Show on the radio, which followed Journey Into Space, which was allowed. Once again, I had no idea then that one day I would produce one of the cast members, David Jacobs, who played Captain Jet Morgan and a host of other characters. The second was the student's trips to the pictures when they would come back and talk enthusiastically of the films they had seen and been influenced by. Two I remember clearly, "Monsieur Hulot's Holiday" in 1953 when they all came back doing Jaques Tati impersonations, which lasted for weeks afterwards. The other was "I Am A Camera" from 1955 which seemed to make quite an impression on them, especially literature student Colin Eastwood who started using long words like vituperation, misogynist and recidivistic. It's a good job we had a dictionary in the house. Colin had a great sense of humour and delivered his verdict on nearly everything as "splendid, splendid" in a slightly posh voice. He was also the one who gave William the soubriquet of "Curly Bill" – because, unusually for such a young man, he was bald as a coot. Sunday morning would always make us smile when one of the boys, David Iny, an Iraqi student, would get up and wander over to the newsagent for a paper and cigarettes wearing just his pyjamas, dressing gown and slippers. Nobody seemed too concerned at this somewhat eccentric behaviour, least of all David. His letters from home provided me with a steady stream of postage stamps for my collection, which I finally sold in 1969 when Stanley Gibbons in The Strand made me an offer I couldn't refuse. Well, it wasn't cheap living in London those days.

There was one rivalry I had with the boys and that was to see who could get up first on Tuesday morning. The reason? That was the day The Beano was delivered so whoever came down first got the comic and it was nearly always me, probably because I hadn't been out drinking the night before. Casting forward, here's another one of those "who'd have thought" memories as I would meet a man in the 1970's called Rod Buckle who had been an editor on both The Beano and The Dandy but more of that later. Some of the lads drinking sessions were legendary, usually starting and finishing at The Kingsway pub from where they would lurch back home with young David Staniforth shinning up a lamppost and on one occasion having great difficulty getting down, much to the amusement of the others but to the consternation of the local bobby. I tried to emulate the great Staniforth and ended up falling off and getting a greenstick fracture in my left hand. Two months later I got another one in my right hand when I fell off my bike in the park. Disaster-prone me? Yes. These breaks occurred at about the same time as I had my third "near-death" experience when I fell backwards down the cellar steps while playing hide and seek in the dark. I didn't notice the cellar door was open as I pressed myself back against it to hide my profile. That was a shock to the system, I can tell you, but strangely no damage was done. David Staniforth was also the one who stood up on the bus all the way home because he couldn't sit down after an evening out at Cheetham Hill ice rink where he spent most of the time with his arse on the ice. All the boys decided he was nesh. There were a few times when some of the boys failed to return home after a night out and my mother called them "dirty stop-outs" and laughed when they told her they'd been at an all-night tiddledywinks competition or a high stakes Ludo game, or as one wag put it "lewd-o" – like as if.

I'd been wondering how I could supplement my pocket money and the day finally arrived when I turned fourteen. That was the age you had to be before you could be a delivery boy for the butcher or the grocer. So, when I wasn't playing rugby or cricket for the school on a Saturday, I would be cycling around Levenshulme knocking on customer's doors with their orders which more often than not ended up with a small tip. All good for the pocket. I did that for a couple of years until I was sixteen when you were allowed to work in a shop. I managed to get holiday work with some of the large stores in the city such as Paulden's, Affleck & Brown, Woolworths and mostly Lewis's. That's the store where a common phrase originated to indicate somebody not doing very much, and this was it "Don't just stand there like one of Lewis's". There were some funny times at that store and some stories of unscrupulous, nay, criminal behaviour. Apparently, because the tills did not give out receipts, cashiers would ring up lesser amounts than the goods cost and pocket the difference. Very naughty, and the other thing that happened was when an assistant wrapped up an item, let's say a tennis racquet, and put a name on it with a sold label. A friend of theirs would come by and collect it, which was cheating and theft. Some people were surely caught doing that kind of thing and one of my pals there made a big joke of it. His name was Paddy, from Galway Bay in Ireland, who limped in late one morning and when the floor manager confronted him he said he was very sorry but he'd dropped a till on his foot when leaving the night before. I fell about laughing but the manager was not amused. Paddy and I got along famously and at the end of one shift we went to get our wages from the office on the fifth floor. Well, this absolute stunner came out with our envelopes and I just had to speak to her. Her name was Elaine and right there and then she invited us to a party that same night. Naturally, we went and for a short while afterwards Elaine was my girlfriend. It was great to have this beauty by my side but she was a little older than me and the affair fizzled out and our paths parted. The lovely Elaine was not my first girlfriend. My first ever date was a trip to the Kingsway cinema to see "Rock Around The Clock" in 1956 with Valerie who was the same age as me. Going to see that film could be a worrying experience if the teddy boys decided to jump, jive and riot by ripping up the seats which is why we paid extra to sit up in the balcony well away from any trouble. Nothing happened that night to frighten us but I was aware as we sat there holding hands that my palms were getting sweaty – I wonder why? Nothing else happened, either, no snogging or necking as we called it then and Valerie and I went our separate ways until I met up with Kathleen Day – more later.

The other quite exciting thing I did to earn a few extra quid was when the funfair came to nearby Cringle Fields once or twice a year and I would go and ask if they needed any extra hands. Luckily, I was assigned to the dodgem cars and thoroughly enjoyed myself riding round on the back of them collecting the ride money and listening to all the latest hits over the thumping sound system, one of which seemed to come up with monotonous regularity in 1959 was "The Happy Organ" by Dave Baby Cortez, an absolute classic.

I was now at that stage of having, seemingly overnight, changed from boy into man and was ready to leave behind my boyhood passions. No more dreaming of joining "Fudge The Elf" from the cartoon strip in the Manchester Evening News, goodbye Rupert, Just William, Beano and Eagle comics and even my great favourite The Wizard with its tales of Wilson the Wonder Athlete. Now it was to be the triple attractions of girls, music and sport – a most tremendous improvement, I think.

Let's start with the girls and in particular the ladies from Fallowfield Girls School where some of us boys would cycle to at lunchtime to meet up with several young ladies there. I don't really recall how it started or how we came to pair off but three of us embarked on our first serious relationships. I started going out with Kathleen Day, Paul Grundy took up with the head girl and Ray Wills partnered Ann Higson, a gorgeous girl who many years later I helped move to London to start a job with United Artists Records where she met and married a member of the Australian group The Easybeats. These relationships lasted quite a while and one summer we even accepted a challenge from the girls to take them on at netball. They were no shrinking violets those girls but we were the rugby boys and never shirked a challenge. Naturally, they hammered us, our strength and speed was no match for their movement, discipline and cunning, a most humbling defeat. I was crestfallen when Kathleen told me she and her family were moving to London on a permanent basis and that we had to say goodbye to each other. I tried to keep in touch with letters but time and distance put paid to our romance. In fact, all romances were off later that year when my friend Paul Grundy was caught in the most compromising situation with his girlfriend and had to go to see their Headmistress and apologise. Henceforth we were banned from all and any contact with the Fallowfield girls. Still, that left us the option of Levenshulme Girl's School where Paul and I vied for the luscious lips of Wendy Bland – a contest I prevailed in and spent many happy hours with Wendy – playing tennis, obviously. Paul and I had another contest over a local girl that we both fancied a great deal, and she didn't play tennis. That was Sandra Turner, a great looking girl and an amazing kisser who spent many happy days with me one long hot summer. Our favourite spot was The Galleon outdoor swimming pool in Didsbury, long gone now, but a magnetic attraction to all of us, even to the extent of skipping school on sunny afternoons just to be together. In our last year we got to be a bit more devil-may-care with the odd afternoon of truanting when we went into town for a jive session at the Plaza ballroom, from where we couldn't possibly get back to school for more lessons. We took off our ties and turned our jackets inside out so we didn't look like schoolboys. Golden days for sure.

There was one Fallowfield girl with whom I stayed friends long after we left school and that was Christine Mulligan, my sometime tennis opponent but never lover, who was wont to throw a party any time her parents went away for the week-end, which was quite often. It was open-house there with booze and dancing and a chance to let rip. Ron, Pete McNulty and Paul Grundy would be there and some of Christine's girl friends would make an appearance so it was the perfect social mix. One of her friends drove over from Buxton with her caravan in tow and I asked her if she was a gypsy. She said to come to the caravan and she would tell my fortune. I can't remember what she foretold but even though that caravan was stationary it rocked and rolled that night.

Leonie Rosenbloom was not allowed to attend those early parties because she was too young and her parents banned her from mixing with such unsuitable types as us. They did have a point because sometimes there would be an eruption of violence when two studs would fight over a girl such as the night when Paul Grundy and Mike Ward got it on over one of the Fallowfield girls. I helped to break it up before too much damage was done but it was hard to restrain Paul Grundy in those days. He was fearless both on and off the rugby field but he did get his comeuppance when he was standing at a bus stop near school and eyeing up a teddy boy's girlfriend. The ted said what all teds said "What you looking at?" in a menacing way and Paul thought he'd try his luck with this guy. Big mistake. The ted gave him a "Glasgow Kiss" which knocked him to the ground and then put the boot in a couple of times so that he couldn't get up. The ted then straightened his jacket and got on the next bus along. Next day at school Paul arrived with face all swollen and a black eye and told me what had happened. That was one lesson he didn't learn at school and he certainly seemed to calm down a bit after that.

Those Mulligan parties went on over the years and Christine got into group management when she took on the representation of Manchester singer Johnny Peters, whom she absolutely adored. It also seemed highly coincidental to me that Christine lived on Parrs Wood Road where so many other friends of mine lived. From school there was Geoff Mann, Chris Kershaw and Billy Wright and later on Leonie Rosenbloom (later Mrs Leckenby), Pete "Nobby" McNulty and Tony Walmsley with Trevor and Barry Whitwam also nearby That's a lot of friends in such a small area, maybe there was something in the water.

Next of the three disciplines was music, which led to my longest lasting continual friendship of all, the aforementioned Ron Stratton. This is how it happened. All us rock and roll fanatics shared our passion and our records with each other listening to new arrivals. Russell Alt lent me his Buddy Holly records, Ray Wills blew my mind when he played me "Whole Lotta Shakin" by Jerry Lee Lewis. I spent many happy lunch hours during term time with my pal Pete Howarth who had a great record collection and was the first to have a copy of "Sweet Little Sixteen", which led me to wrongly believe that Chuck Berry played piano, purely because of the instrumental solo break. Pete was great on the old Joanna and learnt to play all the latest hits by ear and he was also very generous by dint of lending me his record player which I took home on a regular basis because my folks only had a large gramophone and I wanted to listen to my records in my bedroom. And so it was that one Sunday afternoon I had possession of Pete's player when there was a knock at the front door and there stood a young lad with a shock of red hair who boldly told me that he was there to collect Pete's record player. Well, I wasn't having that and told him two things, one was that I hadn't finished with it and two, I wasn't going to hand over the player without Pete's say-so. That was my first meeting with young Ronnie Stratton and though he looked a little crestfallen, accepted my decision not to part with said machine and asked politely if he could come back and collect after I had Pete's OK. That was where we left it until a few days later when he came back and I duly handed it over. We struck up a conversation about various artists we liked and decided to visit each other to listen to music. That was the start of a friendship that continues to this day.

Ron and I became great friends and spent most of our free time together going to the cinema, youth clubs, bowling alley, snooker hall and anywhere we could enjoy a friendly competition with each other, eventually followed by our other great passion – the pursuit of the ladies. Our favourite weekly visit was to the local Methodist church youth club where I danced and got friendly with a tall blonde beauty by the name of Helen Lake and Ron chatted up her friend Joan Hackett, who proved to be a fantastic source of new music as her father had a record shop on Slade Lane where Ron was able to get all the latest releases to listen to. That was such a boon as we couldn't possibly have afforded to buy all those discs. Coincidentally, the premises next door to Mr Hackett's was a sweet shop owned by Paul Grundy's father, so that particular dot on the map became a regular haunt.

Ron was a little younger than me and left school at fourteen to start as a trainee at a small butcher's shop near his home. I was still at school and would cycle over to see him at work and when there was not much going on we would have a game of darts in the back room with his boss Sam Garner. Ron quickly figured out that this was not the future he had envisaged for himself and, even though he got great steaks for his dinner every night, he decided he had to make a change. I don't know where he got the inspiration from but he decided he would try for a job at Culvers Car Mart, a mere 100 yards from his house on Moseley Road. To make the best impression he had a haircut at our local barbers Joe Riley in Brailsford Road. (Years before we had always wondered why Joe asked all the men leaving if they wanted "Something for the weekend, sir?" Now we were of an age to understand that question perfectly well). Ron put on his best bib and tucker and went down the road one morning to speak to the boss Alan Culver. The interview didn't last very long as Ron offered to help him sell all his stock on the forecourt in double quick time. He assured Alan that he was the man to do it and Alan Culver simply said "Start on Monday". And what a start that was as Ron proved his worth beyond all measure, eventually starting his own business with dealerships for all the major manufacturers, becoming hugely successful and undoubtedly the best car salesman in the North of England, if not the country.

We certainly didn't have any idea where that initial foray into selling cars would lead but it did mean that we always had wheels to go out and about on our various trips, one of which took us to the Levenshulme Conservative Club one evening when we were at a loose end. Neither of us were members, nor were we politically motivated but there was a snooker table, a table tennis table and some very genteel young ladies. Well, we played snooker and table tennis but the ladies proved to be extremely elusive and the only scores that night were marked up on the snooker board. There was an introduction made that night that was to influence my life for the next few years as I shook hands with the man running the club, Alan Johnson. He asked us a few questions to get to know us and one of my answers was that I attended Burnage Grammar which prompted Alan to say that he had also been a pupil there. I told him I was in the first fifteen rugby team which seemed to interest him even more as he told me he was a member of Burnage Old Boys Rugby Club and asked if I fancied coming down to have a look and maybe join with the possibility of playing for the Colts Under 19 team. There was a caveat, however, in that the head of rugby at school, Mr "Taffy" Mathias, had fallen out with the club and barred boys from membership directing them instead to Heaton Moor rugby club. I thought that wasn't good and surely ex-pupils should go to the Old Boys club. Alan agreed and said they hadn't had any boys join the club for quite some time but that he would be happy to introduce me there. In my usual rebellious mode I said I would be happy to break the cycle and come along and join. Alan asked if there were any other lads I would recommend and I said the best player on the team was my pal Paul Grundy, an elusive runner and fearless tackler, and I would be happy to bring him along with me. So Paul and I went along, were accepted into the club to play for the colts and our joining was even mentioned in the Manchester Evening News green paper for sport – we were famous.

That was the start of the third discipline, rugby, and for the next few years I played rugby every Saturday morning for the school and afternoons for the club. The school team was moderately successful but the club team, in my last season there, never lost a match. The only game we drew was when fielding a slightly weakened team away to Fylde on the Lancashire coast. They were a well-established top club, a bit toffee-nosed we thought, who couldn't understand how they didn't beat us. They found out in the return fixture when we totally thrashed them in Burnage. Ah, the sweet taste of victory. Probably my most exhilarating and also humiliating day at the club was a home match against a very weak team who turned up a man short. In those days there were no substitutes so a 15-man team was announced plus a reserve in case a player was sick or didn't turn up. I had never been a substitute until this very day when the opposition asked if I could make up their numbers. Our captain Dave Gray was a bit dubious because we didn't know the strength of this team but reluctantly he agreed. I played at full back and after the first half the Burnage boys were about 30 points ahead with no chance of a challenge in the second half. Until, that is, by some miracle the ball came out of a scrum and along the three-quarter line which I joined on the left wing. The ball came to me and I sprinted all the way to the try line for their first points of the match. I then converted the place kick and added the extra points. To add insult to injury I crash tackled our captain Dave and put him down just yards from the try line causing him to yell out "You bastard, Mullin". Well, I just smirked at him and said "It's all in the game". The smile was wiped off my face in very short order after we had our showers and the opposition captain was talking to me and asked if I'd be interested in joining their team. I turned the offer down and went back to the dressing area only to find my clothes had all disappeared. Oh yeah, I thought, where are they? I looked around and by this time the place was empty and the team bus had gone back to the main clubhouse about a mile away from the pitch. The realisation dawned on me what had happened, they'd swiped my clothes and buggered off leaving me with only my muddy shorts, shirt, socks and boots to walk all the way back to the clubhouse. This was my punishment for being such a smart arse and the whole club had a good laugh at my expense but I have to tell you I was never on the team sheet ever again as a reserve. Being an ex-rugby player, my mates have often asked me why I don't drink beer and I'll tell you now. All the colts games were played on the same day as the first team matches and after every away game on the coach home there would be much drinking and singing of filthy rugby songs, which was very enjoyable but the home games were a different kettle of fish altogether. There would regularly be a hotpot supper served in the clubhouse and all the senior players would put ten bob (shillings) into the kitty and us young 'uns would have to put in a couple of bob or what we could afford as we weren't working. Well, and this is the problem, most of the older guys were serious drinkers knocking back 8 to 10 pints with no trouble. I, on the other hand, was a complete novice and after two or three pints of mild would be quite woozy and after five I would be in the loo throwing up my Lancashire Hot Pot. It was really unpleasant being in such a state so often and it cured me of ever wanting to drink beer again. Not only that but I had to explain my state of being to my mother when I got home. She was always hard on me about that and about smoking and coming in late. Many's the time I've got back home to find the lights out and the front door locked and bolted, meaning I had to ring the bell to get her to let me in and then the Spanish Inquisition would start "Where have you been, who have you been with, what time do you call this to be coming in?" This routine carried on long after I had started work which prompted me to consider leaving home and even sending away for papers to enlist in the army. I would have gone, too, but my parents refused to sign the papers. It also wouldn't have bothered me too much had I been called up for National Service but lots of my mates were terrified at the idea, though fortunately we all missed it by the skin of our teeth as conscription ended officially at the end of December 1960. I did do a runner when I was about 16 for a couple of days but I did it for real a few years later after my mother's domineering ways drove me to it. I was twenty by then. Two final words on my rugby playing highlights, both came in 1959, firstly, in April, I played for Cheshire Schoolboys against Yorkshire Schoolboys and shortly afterwards I trialled for England schoolboys playing for the possibles against the probables. I didn't make it and that was probably right.

Winners – Manchester Schools Under 15's
Sevens Tournament 1957/58
Back Row L-R – Mullin, Wills, Grundy, Hobson
Front Row L-R – Wright, Rule, Ashwoth

CHAPTER SIX

The World Of Work Beckons

I suppose I must have been a trial to my mother in some ways that I don't really understand, for instance on one occasion I was cleaning my shoes in the kitchen on an old newspaper when she told me not to make a mess and go and clean them outside. I must have made some surly remark as she picked up a kitchen knife and came at me with a murderous look in her eyes. Naturally I bolted out the back door like O J Simpson and didn't come back for a couple of hours. She also came at me once with a pudding bowl and aimed it at my head. Fortunately, I ducked just in time and she smashed the bowl against the wall. It was all quite frightening, particularly when she would wait until my dad came home and say to him "Ken, he's been very naughty, give him a good hiding" and my father would just do as he was told and I got a good thumping. She was just as hard on my dad though and on one occasion it delivered one of the funniest things I ever saw. Dad came in one sunny day with a joint for dinner which he handed over to my mother who took one look at it and said "What the hell is this? I said beef and you've brought lamb. Take it back". My dad was adamant that he'd brought what she asked for and then a major argument ensued, escalating to fever pitch until mother finally lost her rag and threw the joint at my dad, who ducked, and the joint went straight through the glass in the kitchen window and out into the garden, whereupon our dog Trixie leapt up and raced outside to get her teeth into it. I thought that was simply hilarious and it took my parents quite some time to simmer down. I think we had baked beans on toast for dinner. As well as the dog we had Jet, a black cat, and chickens in a pen in the back garden. Their demise was not to my liking as my dad either wrung their necks or chopped their heads off and let them run around till they expired. Most distressing of all, though, was the fate of the cat's kittens, as those that couldn't be found a home were put in a sack and drowned outside in a bucket of water. When I found out what had happened to them it broke my heart and added a further strike to my dislike of my father who had absolutely no conscience about that sort of thing at all. As for the beatings he gave me, they stopped abruptly at the age of eighteen when he came at me with violent intent and I grabbed him by the throat, held him up against the kitchen wall. and said "If you ever raise your hand to me again, I will lay you out". He never bothered me after that. Domestic bliss was a rare thing in our house.

The last couple of years at school passed quite quickly I seem to remember, with lots of interesting things going on with girls, music and rugby, although there were a couple of pretty low episodes, the first in 1958 when, on February 6 the Manchester United team were devastated by the Munich air disaster. It was particularly poignant at school because Roger Byrne, the captain, had been a pupil just a few years earlier and there was a deep sense of sorrow for weeks after. My earliest allegiance had been to Manchester City because I could get to the Maine Road ground much more easily than Old Trafford but that event divided my loyalty so much that I now support both teams but with a slight, almost imperceptible leaning towards United.

The second awful thing happened almost exactly a year later on February 3 1959 when the great Buddy Holly died, also in an air crash. It's been well documented what a great influence he was on groups and guitarists who were to follow but it would never have occurred to me then that some 40 years later I would sit down to dinner with his backing group The Crickets at the house of my great friend John Rostron in Southport.

On a very personal note, there was a tragedy much closer to home with the death of a good friend from school, the first death of a friend I'd had to contend with, and it hit me pretty hard. I had been spending time with Trevor Whitwam, a sporty lad and music lover much like myself, and we went to local youth clubs and movies together. One day I went to call for Trevor at his house in Lynnwood Road where he introduced me to a little chap in his school uniform with short trousers and a cap called Barry, his younger brother, who would later be the drummer in our group The Wailers and later found fame with Herman's Hermits. More about that later but the heart-breaking news came some days later when I arrived at school one morning and heard one of the lads whisper, "Don't tell him, don't tell him". "Don't tell him what?" I asked and he very sheepishly told me the awful news that Trevor had died the night before while taking a bath and reaching out to his Dansette record player had electrocuted himself. Such a tragedy that affected me quite badly and a terrible loss of such a young life so full of promise.

It's now 1960 and I have decisions to make before the summer regarding my future employment options. I want to go to teacher training college and qualify to teach PE (Physical Education) and games My idea is to teach during the week and possibly play rugby league at the weekend, thereby earning an extra few quid. The careers advice officer listens to my plans and tells me that it is possible to reduce your time at college by doing a year or possibly two as what they called a "student teacher". This sounds like a good idea to me, reducing my college time by a year and learning and earning in the meantime. I tell him I'm very interested and he says he will make enquiries regarding any available posts. Not long afterwards I'm invited to an interview at the offices of the Bury Education Committee where they offer me a position teaching at St Paul's Bell secondary modern school, which I accept and agree to start at the beginning of term in September. As the minimum age for this work was 18 and my birthday was on the 11th I became the youngest teacher in the Lancashire Education system, strangely following in the footsteps of Aunt Edith who had been the youngest Headmistress in her day. I had no idea how I would control mixed classes of eleven-to-sixteen-year-olds, many from socially deprived backgrounds, as I was only two years older than they were but ignorance is bliss, as they say, and somehow I was confident I could cope.

The end of the school year culminated in the annual Speech Day at The Free Trade Hall which I attended with a terrific rugby playing pal Brent Ashton – great name. eh? Brent was a year below me but wise to the world beyond his years and he knew the city centre dives pretty well. After the boredom of the evening he suggested we go for a coffee at a place he knew in Lloyd Street off Albert Square called the 2 J's club. Well, that was like a religious conversion for me as I went down those steps into my first cellar club and I knew right there that I had had a revelation and that I would belong in these magical and mystical surroundings for many years to come. Thanks Brent, wherever you are. I believe he went to America to play gridiron.

It was Brent who introduced me to the dubious joys of smoking, easily led again, you see. My mother disapproved of me taking up this habit even though both she and my dad were smokers and, as was usual with young beginners, the starting brand was Woodbines because they were the cheapest, after which you aspired to Senior Service and Players. It seemed in those days that everybody smoked and I only half-jokingly say that was why nobody ever needed to worry too much about personal hygiene or deodorant because the only thing you could smell was nicotine everywhere you went. Ron and I went through a phase of trying every brand available at a dedicated tobacconists in Longsight where the brands on offer included State Express 555, Pall Mall, Balkan Sobranie, Passing Cloud, Peter Stuyvesant and many more, even the killer tubes Capstan Full Strength. None of these stuck and for several years we enjoyed the heady pleasures of Consulate menthol cigarettes, which are now totally banned, I believe. There were times at our house during card sessions when everybody lit up that an industrial-size ashtray, probably nicked from a pub, would be overflowing with dimps (fag ends, if you don't know the local lingo, a.k.a. cigarette stubs).

As was usual for me I got a summer job, this time working as a gofer and general dogsbody in the offices of the Daily Mirror and Sunday Pictorial in the city centre. It was here that I struck up a friendly conversation with the sports writer Arthur Brookes and told him of my inclination towards playing rugby league. He thought that was a good idea and very kindly organised for me to meet two of the greats of the game, Gus Risman and his son Bev Risman, who at the time were running Oldham rugby league club. I went for a trial there and in discussions afterwards I told them of my teaching plans and college which they encouraged me to pursue and to come and see them at a later date when I was more settled in my studies, which I was happy to do. Working in those offices was quite interesting for me and I tried to learn a little about the business until one day an old pal of mine from junior school, Pete Donovan, turned up to start work there – problems. We were a bit of a bad influence on each other and at every available opportunity we would sneak off to the staff snooker room for a game. It wasn't long before we were discovered and given a stiff warning, which lasted about a week until we did it again and both got fired. One good thing that came from meeting Pete again happened not long afterwards when I invited him to a bit of a daytime music session at my house. The students were away and I took my new record player to a large room at the top of the house, cleared the floor for jiving and waited for a few pals to turn up. Ron Stratton, Clive Sayer and another couple of lads and lasses arrived including Pete with a girl called Denise Jenkins, who turned out to be a great jiver and full of fun. The records we played that day give a clue to the timeline as the top tunes then were "It's Now Or Never" by Elvis and Cliff's "I Love You" although I preferred the "B" side "D In Love", both from the end of 1960. After we'd had enough jigging about somebody suggested we go to the movies and we all agreed it was a good idea. All, that is, except Pete who said he wasn't going even though Denise was very keen to go. Pete said no and I said "Well, if Pete won't take you, I will". That was brave as Pete was a hulk about six inches taller than me but he just shrugged his shoulders and said "OK then". This gentle giant then took off on his enormous Triumph Bonneville motorbike leaving me, Denise and the others to go to the pictures at the nearby Palace Farmside. You've probably guessed by now that Denise and I embarked on a deeply romantic episode that lasted nearly two years. It was bliss, my first real long-term relationship and the first "love of my life". My parents thought the world of her and, even though I wasn't aware of them, I'm sure they could hear the sound of wedding bells. However, it wasn't to be, fortunately, because we were really both too young for that kind of commitment.

Shortly before I was due to start my teaching career in Bury, I went for a meeting with the headmaster, the intriguingly named

Johnnie Walker, and his second in command Mr Crick. These two were tough old campaigners well able to put the fear of God into their charges, including me. They needed to be both feared and respected by the kids because some of them came from the less privileged local community and required a very firm hand to keep them in line. Personally, I had very little cause to worry about bad behaviour and there were only limited times I had to discipline any of them. Possibly one reason was that, although I was required to do a fair amount of classroom teaching such as maths and english, I was the games master and could match the boys at football, cricket and cross-country running. The "cock of the school" was a tough lad named Billy Booth, a very good swimmer, and the best footballer was Alec Lindsay, who went on to play professionally, firstly with his home team Bury and then for Liverpool when Bill Shankly signed him to play left back. He made his mark there and was also selected to play for England. Obviously, it was my training and encouragement which led to his great success.

Because so many of the older pupils were interested in music, I started an after-school session where I would bring some records, they would bring their favourites and we would all sit around and enjoy the music together. I thought that was quite a good bonding exercise and it did work very well.

There were a few, shall we say, interesting episodes while I was at St Paul's, the first of which was when one of the older boys turned up late for class with the excuse that his house had caught fire that morning and he wasn't able to get to his clothes. Later, during the lunch break, I mentioned this to Johnnie Walker and he said "Yes, I know", telling me that he (the pupil) had started the fire and it wasn't the first time he'd done it, either, a regular pyromaniac. One of the other boys was pretty popular and often shared his sweets around which prompted me to ask, knowing that he came from a very poor home, where he got the money from to buy so many sweets, "Well", he told me "My uncles usually give me half a crown when they come to visit". "Oh, how many uncles have you got?" I ask and he says quite a few, although he doesn't remember all their names. Again, in my innocence, I mention this to the other teachers in the staff room and they all laugh and tell me that the "uncles" give him money to get him out of the house because his mother is on the game. By now I'm realising that this is a bit of a naughty area and a school with a poor reputation, quite different from the ones I'd been accustomed to in my short life. No wonder they needed the stiff authoritarianism of Walker and Crick, a point brought forcefully home to me when I tried to encourage a rather shy and quiet younger lad and help him along in class because one of the stranger things I had to contend with was that whenever I wanted what was called "scrap paper" for a drawing project I had to send someone to get it from Mr Walker's office. Goodness knows why it was so closely guarded – maybe to stop it being used to start a fire – you never know. By doing the right thing, as I thought, I would give this lad some responsibility and send him off to fetch the paper. He came back a few minutes later in floods of tears and without any paper. He was inconsolable and wouldn't say what had happened so I reassured him as much as I could and he sat there for the rest of the lesson with his head in his arms on the desk. In the break that followed I spoke to Johnnie Walker and asked him what had happened and his explanation pretty well floored me as he said "He's always in trouble that one so as soon as he arrived I just gave him the usual six of the best". I told him I'd only sent him for some scrap paper and he said "Well, he probably deserves it for something else". That was how JW ruled with a rod of iron, he took no prisoners. My time at St Paul's was completed at the end of the summer term when the senior class went on a week's holiday to Pontins Holiday Camp in Lowestoft in Suffolk, the most easterly point on the English coastline. It was a good break for the pupils, who were mostly very well behaved, and we organised competitions, music evenings and lots of swimming and sunbathing. I was in charge of the boys and Miss Pat Fogg was looking after the girls. She and I got on famously and by the strangest coincidence my next place of employment also had a Miss Pat Fogg. Unusual to say the least, but then my whole life has been full of such coincidences.

During that year in Bury I kept myself really fit with the games at the school and rugby at the weekends. My daily routine was to get up at six o'clock, put my track suit on and get my breakfast which consisted of two raw eggs whisked together in a glass of milk with a spoonful of sugar stirred in – delicious, eh? My usual running route would take me past the university sports ground, the Reg Harris cycling track and around Platt Fields lake, a distance of about five miles. This kept me in fine fettle and ready for my college interviews which had been arranged at St John's in York, St Luke's in Exeter and the ever so prestigious Loughborough Teacher Training College. These took place in the winter of 1960/61 and I travelled to them by hitchhiking all the way, sometimes quite arduous in the pouring rain and freezing cold. I'm not that tough now, I can tell you. My offers of transport from both private motorists and truckers may have had something to do with my attire of a Royal Air Force greatcoat and a khaki backpack, which probably made them think I was in the Armed Forces. Whatever it was it worked really well for me. I think the interviews went well enough for me to be considering my choices for the next September intake but all my grand plans were about to be thrown into total disarray in just a few months' time.

And so it was, at the very end of the rugby season in May I got crocked good and proper. A knock on the knee did for me and my sporting career and at the end of the summer term I went into Manchester Royal Infirmary to have a cartilage removed from my left knee. The operation was performed by the well-respected orthopaedic surgeon Sir John Barnes who gave me the devastating news that I wouldn't be able to take part in any athletic activities for six months and therefore all my plans came crashing down around me in that one short conversation. For the next six weeks I had a metal splint from my arse to my ankle and attended regular physiotherapy sessions at the hospital. At this point I had to seriously consider my future employment options in the knowledge that I couldn't carry on teaching, play any kind of sport nor go to college. As Peter Green once sang "Big Change Is Gonna Come".

CHAPTER SEVEN

Tune In Turn On And Drop Out – Life In The Sixties

And so it came to pass, hmm, that, with no little trepidation, I sat the Civil Service entrance exam in central Manchester. I naturally assumed that if I passed I would be working in my home town. It never occurred to me that because of my almost fluent German and knowledge of Vienna that I might possibly end up in the Foreign Office in London, a prospect I certainly wouldn't have relished at that time. As luck would have it I was relieved to find that there was a job for me as a Tax Officer at the Inland Revenue, Manchester First District, situated just south of Deansgate in Albert Bridge House. And that was where the fun really began, against a counterpoint of utter boredom in the workplace.

Working in the city centre afforded me the opportunity to familiarise myself with some of the many clubs and coffee bars which young Stratton and myself would frequent over the next few years. Weekends would include a late Sunday morning visit to Amigo's for a frothy coffee and a session with the jukebox which always seemed to be playing the same two tunes, Jim Reeves "He'll Have To Go" and, in total contrast, "Tintarella De Luna" by Bob Azzam. Our other haunts included the Cona in Tibb Street, Kardomah on Market Street, the Three Coins and the Mogambo, run by Jack Jackson (not the famous DJ) who would one day be my landlord when I was living with Pauline, more of that later. Jack also owned and ran the 2 J's jazz club for about a year before selling it to Rick Dixon who turned it into the much more pop-oriented venue The Oasis, calling it "Manchester's Most Fab Club For Young People". It was and the place where many of us spent a great deal of time enjoying all the best groups in the country playing there during the sixties.

Nearer to home Ron and I would visit Frankie's 700 coffee bar on Stockport Road in Levenshulme. It was a great meeting place and the motorbike boys would often turn up and dominate the jukebox, which saved us putting money in it. There was a one-armed bandit machine which once delivered the jackpot for Ron. That was where we first came into contact with the singer Wayne Fontana who, as plain Glynn Ellis, was the washer-upper for the owners Graham and Pauline Clegg who would go on to manage Wayne and run the Oasis Club. Some step-up from serving frothy coffee in a glass cup and saucer. One evening there we were visited by the police who asked us to volunteer in an identity parade they were organising to put some criminal in the dock. Somewhat foolishly, I suppose, we agreed and off we went to the local nick. Some of the local Teddy Boys declined to take part and that may have been because some of them were not exactly sainted. They may have been part of the much-feared "Bushmen" gang, led by Smokey and Louie, who frequented the 700 as well as Sivori's ice cream parlour down the road. They reportedly threw a policeman through a plate-glass florist's window and regularly organised fights with rival gangs from as far afield as Sheffield and Liverpool. To be avoided at all costs although as far as I knew they never caused any trouble at Frankie's.

Away from the daily grind life carried on in quite a busy way with me and Denise and Ron and his girlfriend Maureen going to the cinemas and youth clubs, although we were just getting to be a little too old for them by 1960/61. There was one dance we went to in Withington where they had a jiving competition and just as I was about to take Denise onto the floor Stratton jumped in, whisked her off and next thing I know they've won, thanks Ron. Denise was a great dancer. Another place we went was at St John's Church in Longsight where I got involved, Ron didn't, with a hiking group which would set off early on a Sunday morning for walks in the Peak District, leaving Piccadilly station for Whaley Bridge. We would trek to Castleton, Hope and Edale, where my Dad told me in his youth they used to kick around large lumps of Blue John stone. He should have kept some as it's now quite rare and valued for its beauty. The views from the top of Kinder Scout were also beautiful with striking views in good weather back towards Manchester and even as far as Snowdonia in Wales. Conditions up there could be treacherous, and mis-placed bravado and stupidity led us to do some crazy things like swimming across a freezing cold tarn in the middle of winter. I only ever did it once.

Clothes became a big issue between me and my mother as I wanted to appear more modish and she continued to insist I wore cavalry twill trousers and a Harris tweed jacket, total anathema for a young buck in those days. I resolved this conflict one day when Ron and I were out looking at shoes and I spied a pair of green crocodile leather winklepickers that looked amazing and I wanted them. At this point Ron showed true friendship and said I could leave them at his house and come over to change before we went out. What a great solution, which led to my having a whole outfit of clothes stored at Ron's including denim jeans, drainpipe trousers and one of those shaggy mohair jumpers, in purple if you please.

My other great pal during that time was the aforementioned Clive Sayer, who came to our house on a regular basis as he only lived around the corner. Clive was prone to the odd pang of hunger and would regularly raid the cupboards for something to eat but on one occasion he made a huge mistake by opening a catering jar of Horlicks malted milk powder. What he didn't know, and neither did I, was that my mother had taken the empty jar of Horlicks and filled it up with white pepper without putting a label on it. Clive took a heaped tablespoonful of this powder, which looked identical to the Horlicks, tilted his head back and took it all in one go. Well, within a second he went bright red and stumbled over to the sink and lay back with his mouth under the tap and let the cold water run for at least ten minutes. It was a major shock to his system and to me as I didn't know what he'd done until I examined the contents of the jar and checked to find that a switch had been made. He never foraged for food in our house ever again.

The kitchen in our house was always the focal point but one day it disappeared. A bunch of us had been visiting a local girl called Barbara Pilkington, a friend of Denise, and as we were walking back towards my house a fire engine went by with all bells and sirens going. My friend John Wilson mused "I wonder where that's going?"and I jauntily replied "Oh, probably to our house if my mum's set the chip pan on fire", which, I hasten to add, had never happened before. It proved to be quite prescient as when we turned the corner into Osborne Road there was the fire crew and a large crowd of neighbours gathered round watching proceedings. The fire chief stopped me as I walked up the path and I explained that I lived here and he let me in to find my mother in tears in the front room being consoled by my father and the fire crew in the kitchen ripping out the windows and throwing all that remained of the kitchen cupboards out into the back garden. Therein lies the danger of getting too involved in a TV show in the front-room and forgetting the chip pan back in the kitchen. That was one joke that backfired spectacularly and literally.

In the course of our perambulations around the clubs one of my earliest memories of seeing a live band was at the Birch Park skating rink in Rusholme where my pal Pete Bocking was playing with a group called The Fourtones, who have since gone down in history as the forerunners of The Hollies because of the vocalists Allan Clarke and Graham Nash. The guitarist Derek Quinn also played that night and he was later to join Freddie and the Dreamers so it was no surprise to me that they sounded so damn good. Groups were the coming thing in the clubs as the appeal of Trad Jazz began to fade and my pal Pete Howarth told me he was joining an outfit called The Phantoms and would I like to come along and see them play. Would I? No question about it, the answer was a resounding YES. That started a long association with the group and I helped lug equipment into dancehalls and clubs all over the Manchester area and beyond. They were a crack combo consisting of Trevor Jones on guitar and vocals, Keith Shepherd on bass, Graham Smith on drums and Pete on piano and an electronic keyboard instrument called a clavioline, as used on the Tornados massive hit "Telstar" and Del Shannon's first number one "Runaway". After spending some time with them they began discussing the prospect of bringing in a lead guitar player and wondering who they might approach. My immediate suggestion was Pete Bocking and they all shook their heads saying "He'll never join us, he's far too good". I told them Pete was currently without a band and what did they have to lose. I knew where Pete lived and the next day we tipped up at his house, went in for a chat and sealed the deal there and then. From then on they became the "go to" backing outfit for many solo artists appearing in Manchester. They played brilliantly for Susan "Bobby's Girl" Maughan at the Three Coins and backed Danny "Moon River" Williams at the Oasis. I was at both those gigs and after the Oasis one I was talking to Danny who said he hadn't booked any accommodation for the night and did I know where he might get a hotel room. Bearing in mind this was late in the evening I said he could sleep on the couch in our front room if he wanted to. He accepted very readily and when we got back to our place everybody was in bed so I gave Danny a pillow, a sheet and a blanket and left him to it. The next morning I was greatly amused when my mother came into my bedroom with a shocked look on her face and blurted out "There's a pair of black feet sticking out of the end of the sofa". I explained what had happened and told her who it was and she said "What, Danny Williams the singer?" I said yes and she asked straight away if he'd like a cup of tea. We all had breakfast together and Danny left around midday and I never heard from him again. Funny times, eh?

All this time spent with the Phantoms gave me a real taste for that lifestyle even though I was content to only be a bystander because it was so fascinating and exciting watching and learning how things worked in this corner of the music business. The group would rehearse regularly every Saturday afternoon at the Scout hut on Burnage Lane and I would often drop in for a listen. One time Trevor didn't turn up and the lads played a few instrumentals to pass the time until they turned to me and said that I should get on the microphone and sing a song or two. I just laughed and said I had no idea what to do and Pete Bocking in his usual short manner said "You look the part and anyway anybody can sing this stuff". I said I'd give it a go and suggested doing the latest Bobby Vee hit "More Than I Can Say", so this must have been around early summer 1961. Well, that was one failed audition as I realised later I had picked the wrong song and when I met the writer Sonny Curtis some thirty years later and recounted the story he smiled and said to never do a ballad for an audition with a rock band, always do a rocker. If only I'd known that at the time.

Many memories like that are linked to the popular songs of the day, never more appropriately conveyed than when Cliff and The Shadows later sang "Time Drags By Real Slow", a perfect description of my time in the tax office. The section I was in was commanded, and I do mean commanded, by Mr Alec Dick who ran his empire like a headmaster out of a Victorian novel. Desks were spaced far enough apart to discourage talking, the telephone rarely rang and silence reigned in tandem with Mr Dick. Each of us had an allocation of P.A.Y.E. returns and questions to deal with and these were supposedly distributed on an equal basis but it took the newer intake far longer to process their workload than some of the older more experienced staff. For instance, immediately behind me sat one Sidney Smith who regularly got through all his paperwork long before it was time to go home. Occasionally he would do some of my work but mostly he'd sit behind me having imaginary conversations with his budgerigar in a sibilant hissing voice through his teeth, whistling things like "See here Sidney, see here, who's a pretty boy", getting as many sibilant "s" sounds in as possible. It nearly drove me mad and I'd often turn round to him and tell him to shut up. Didn't make any difference as he started again after a few minutes. This was to go on a lot longer than I thought I would be able to stand but salvation in female form was just around the corner as you will shortly find out. I almost didn't live long enough to enjoy my reprieve as I had an argument with a lorry going the wrong way down a one-way street just outside the office. Fortunately, in one way, was the fact that I was sprinting back to work in the same direction as the vehicle so the impact was much less than it might have been. Nevertheless, I was thrown up into the air and landed on the pavement. The lorry stopped and the driver came to help me and apologised as a small crowd gathered round to check what was going on. The driver gave me his details and reported the incident to his insurance company who came to see me a few days later to settle the claim which amounted to £50 for a new pair of trousers, shoes and jacket all ripped to pieces, and a goodwill gesture for a gash on my leg. That claim would probably amount to tens of thousands of pounds these days. That, I considered, was a lucky escape from my fourth near-death event.

My love affair with Denise lasted all the way through 1961 and Christmas that year was very special as we spent all of our time together still deeply in love but a family tragedy was waiting in the wings. Grandma Butcher was staying with us and had jigged away merrily on New Year's Eve, she especially liked Bill Haley's "Rock Around The Clock" and I was amazed at her energy and enthusiasm. Early in January she took ill and was confined to bed in a downstairs room so that we could look after her more easily than her being upstairs. On the morning of the 26th of January I took in her usual cup of tea and was shocked and scared to discover that she had passed away in her sleep. My mother took over from that moment and I wandered around the house in a daze for the next few hours. No way I was going to work that day.

The mood lifted after Grandma's funeral and Denise and I carried on as before with trips to the cinema to see Cliff in "The Young Ones" and Elvis in "Blue Hawaii" plus nights out jiving and generally enjoying ourselves. However, the intensity of our relationship wasn't meant to last and the flame began to splutter somewhat, possibly due to the amount of time I was spending with The Phantoms or perhaps she was hoping for a more permanent arrangement between us, I don't know, but whatever it was we began to drift apart.

That was when my relief from boredom at work presented itself with a naughty little minx called Veronica. She and her friend Joan were clerical officers and they used to tease me in various ways to see how I would react. One day Veronica put out the ultimate challenge when, after a bit of cheeky banter, she said "Oh, you're all talk, you are". Well, what red-blooded youth wouldn't rise to that? And rise I did by telling her I'd show her the error of her ways next time she was going down into the basement to look for files – a euphemism if ever there was one. A little later she said the file search was on and proceeded to leave the office. A few minutes later I was going down in the lift with my heart pumping away in anticipation. There we met, in Row H, where I proved conclusively to Veronica that I wasn't all talk.

That was the end of my affair with Denise and the start of a most enjoyable time with Veronica. We'd usually go out for a jive and a twist at lunchtime to the Plaza ballroom or the Oasis and sometimes Joan would make up a foursome with her boyfriend Dave. Joan was a fun-loving girl and Dave was a window dresser at the top department store Kendall Milne on Deansgate. For the next six months the Oasis became our favourite haunt both at lunchtime and in the evening when we would watch all the top Manchester groups like Johnny Peters and The Crestas and, in my opinion, the best of them all at that time Pete MacLaine and the Dakotas. I'm still in regular touch with Pete, who I think was well and truly shafted when Brian Epstein lured The Dakotas away as a backing group for Billy J Kramer, who never was as good a vocalist as Pete. That must have been a crushing blow for Pete as he had to start all over again with a new band and I have every sympathy for him as something similar happened to me when Peter Noone stole my band to form Herman's Hermits, more on that later.

This was the time when Joan's boyfriend Dave decided that his future did not lie in the design department of Kendall Milne and embarked upon a career as a Disc Jockey. To facilitate this move he decided on the stage name of Dave Lee Travis and began his rise to fame spinning discs at the Oasis. To say he was successful at this new career would be the ultimate understatement as he went on to become one of the most famous voices and faces in the British media. His stellar rise began in those early days and I'm proud to call him great friend to this day. He was best man at my marriage to Caroline in 1970 and I would be his best man when he married Marianne six months later in 1971.

CHAPTER EIGHT
All About That Bass

This is where my total immersion into the music business really started and it's an extraordinary story of being in the right place at the right time. I don't know if you'd call it luck, coincidence or random chance but the improbable events that happened have always been a mystery to me, especially as I never engineered or pushed for any specific outcome. I don't think I was particularly ambitious or driven to achieve anything. I just went with the flow and good things mostly happened for me. I think of myself as extremely fortunate to have been involved in so many interesting situations.

In among all these varying distractions my friendship with Ron Stratton held firm and in the summer of 1962 I took him with me on his first visit abroad to stay with my friends in Vienna and Bad Voslau. Having done this journey several times I was used to the idea of sleeping on the overnight train from Ostende to Vienna but it was an eye-opener for Ron, sleeping in a compartment of eight, some of them female, wow. One of the first things Ron noticed in Vienna was that many of the shops seemed to have my name on their doors. "What does it mean,'geoffnet'?" he asked. I burst out laughing and said it was German for "open" and because of the way it was pronounced some people also said my name in the same way which phonetically sounds like "gay oaf", a most unflattering name in English. Then it was Ron's turn to laugh. We stayed with the Hirschl family in Vienna and the holiday was a great success with Ron thoroughly enjoying the experience, especially the night clubs in Vienna where we experienced the unusual music break when the band took a rest and the roof opened to let the hot air out and the air-con came on. We thought that very sophisticated. In Bad Voslau we stayed with the Mattersdorfers and Ron got his first taste of Austrian wine on an evening when he was supposed to have a date with a local girl called Dietlinda. He totally collapsed in an alcoholic stupor leaving me to explain his absence to his date. Forever after he accused me of stealing his girl and despite all my protestations to the contrary, I have never been able to convince him that my intentions were purely honourable. Although we're still the greatest of friends I do wonder if he's been holding a grudge over all these years, or is he just teasing me?.

In July we saw our hero Gene Vincent play at the Oasis and in August we watched The Fourtones play their last gig together at the Three Coins before planning their re-emergence as The Hollies.

In early September the stars conjoined to deliver a great gift to me. Yes, I am lucky. My parents took me on a weekend trip with them to see friends in Bristol, possibly to attend a wedding, and on the return journey we stopped off at a petrol station to fill up. I was sitting in the back of the car and as I looked out of the window I saw the most incongruous site. There, in this tiny cash kiosk just big enough for one person, was hanging a large guitar. I was filled with curiosity and got out of the car to have a look at this beast in the window. On it was a sticker saying "For Sale £5". Now, I had no clue as to the cost of a solid body guitar but I suspected it was worth more than a fiver. Admittedly it was minus a couple of strings and had a few scratches but I recognised it as a bass guitar of some quality. I asked my dad to lend me a fiver to buy it and he said "You can't play a guitar" and I said I could learn and anyway it was my birthday very soon and it could be my birthday present. He agreed, gave me the money and this guitar became mine. There's no doubt in my mind that the guy in the kiosk had no idea what he had and for sure it must have fallen out of the back of some group's van, which would explain the gouges on the body and the missing strings.

When we got home I wasn't sure what to do with this beast I had bought and decided I'd better show it to Keith Shepherd in The Phantoms. As luck would have it, just as I was deliberating what to do an old school chum Dave Chalmers suggested I take it to another ex-Burnage boy Ian Waller who lived in his street and who had made his own bass guitar. I took it round to Wal and his eyes popped out of his head as he said "Where did you get that? Do you know it's a Fender Precision Bass and very rare and very expensive?" I said I had no idea but thought it was worth buying on the off chance. I said I might learn to play it and Wal said it needed new strings and a possible refurbishment which he would be happy to do as it would help him to understand the design and electronics involved. He told me his dad was an engineer at Fairey Aviation who would help him with the project. I had no qualms about letting him have a crack at it and told him to go ahead, at which he seemed highly delighted.

A few weeks later Wal told me there was a problem with the paint finish on the guitar because they couldn't reproduce the famous "Sunburst" lacquer of the original and how would it be if they sprayed it white. I said no problem with that and a week later the bass came back looking absolutely stunning and as good as new. Wal was kind enough to make me an amplifier from an old valve radio so that I could practise and offered to give me lessons. With that I went home with my new equipment and started practising, all to no avail as I had little ability and even less desire to spend time practising. Wal asked me how I was getting on and I told him not very well but that I would like to settle the bill for the work he and his father had done. He said there was no charge as he had learned so much about the construction of the guitar but could I do him a little favour and let him play it the following Saturday at the church youth club dance so as to test it out. Naturally I agreed and he said that I should come along to see and hear the results of his labour. That was the start of my association with The Demons guitar group and total immersion into the music business which would provide me with a career for the rest of my life. How extraordinary is that?

Shortly after that first gig Wal gave me a ticket to a Youth Dance on Saturday 13 October 1962 at The Hall, St Ann's, Burlington Street, Ashton-Under-Lyne with "Jiving To The Demons" and the price was two shillings and sixpence, about twelve pence in today's money. My total involvement with the group happened very quickly when Wal told me they were trying out a new lead guitar player called Lek Leckenby at their next gig at

Levenshulme Palais/Sporting Club and that I should come along. They sounded pretty good and after their first set, as I was standing outside the dressing room, the Palais manager came up to me and said "Tell the boys to hurry up now it's time for their second set". Even though it had nothing to do with me I went in and told them to get a move on as they were due on stage. My demeanour must have been quite forceful because after the gig we had a conflab where they asked me to be their manager. I was quite taken aback by this request and asked them why and they said because I knew all the clubs and so could get them work and besides which I had a white suit. It wasn't white, it was very light grey but obviously it made a big impression. A deal was agreed whereby I would try to find them work and all the proceeds would be shared equally between us, which was Lek on lead guitar, Lawrence Jordan on rhythm guitar, Wal on bass, and Barry Whitwam on drums. It seemed obvious to me that we needed to move on from being an instrumental group so when Brian Smith was brought in on vocals we changed the name to Danny and the Demons. There was a proviso attached to these developments and that was that I was to be the one to tell original lead guitarist Bobby Ainsworth that he had been permanently replaced. Such is the manager's lot and very soon after that I was to have the job of telling Brian that his services as a vocalist were no longer needed when the group decided they'd had enough of copying Cliff and The Shadows and wanted to move on without Brian. Auditions were held and a lad called Malcolm Roberts got the job and joined towards the end of 1962 or early 1963, I don't have a date for that change. About the same time as Malcolm arrived we parted company with Lawrence Jordan who had got a job as a policeman and decided to quit the group. We also thought the group needed a new name, something with a bit more bite, and Lek and I both remembered the 1961 Richard Todd movie The Hellions and thought that would be a great name. Wal, Barry and Malcolm agreed and so The Hellions were born in Manchester, not to be confused with a similarly named group from the Midlands. To avoid a clash with this other group we also decided that Malcolm should have a stage name and finally settled on Dean West and The Hellions.

Getting gigs wasn't quite so easy as you might think as there was a massive growth in groups starting out and all wanting work. We did well with bookings through the Paddy McKiernan agency and a few other clubs and bookers as we started to build up quite a good reputation. This meant travelling further afield and it soon became obvious that we couldn't keep going to local gigs on buses and heaving Barry's kit around as well as increasingly large amps and speakers. A van was needed, and a driver as none of us had passed the test, so I went to see Pete, our friendly greengrocer with a van and asked him if he'd be our "roadie". He liked the idea and said he had his evenings free and would love to be involved with all this pop music stuff. And so we were ready for the road.

Things on the home front had deteriorated very badly and came to a head one day when my mother came into my bedroom, yanked the plug out of my record player, picked it up and threw it down the stairs along with a pile of my cherished discs including the first record I ever bought "Stagger Lee" by Lloyd Price. That was absolutely it and I resolved to leave home as soon as I possibly could. As luck would have it I was very soon able to rent a flat above a barber's shop in Stanley Grove, Longsight. Without telling my parents a thing about it I began surreptitiously moving clothes and other stuff out before taking the final plunge. That happened in the most clandestine way as I waited until my parents had gone to bed and slipped quietly down a strategically placed ladder outside my bedroom window. I didn't see my parents for quite a few months after that, even though they tried initially to find me by going round to all my friend's houses. Cat and mouse tactics were employed and one rehearsal Saturday they arrived at Wal's house demanding to know where I was. Wal's mother was on my side and told them I wasn't there, even though she knew I was out the back hiding in their coal shed.

Freedom at last meant I was able to traverse the streets of the city centre visiting all the various clubs and live music venues, promoting the group and looking for work. It certainly wasn't a hassle in any way as it allowed me legitimate free entrance into all those premises. Ron, Lek and I would be in town on a regular basis to check out the competition and talk to other musicians and club managers. That was how we were able to see many visiting acts as well as local groups like the newly-formed Hollies at their audition in the Oasis on a Sunday afternoon session in late September where my new pal Dave Lee Travis was the DJ. Lek and I had a smile on our faces as we looked at the stage set up to see what looked like a couple of plywood wardrobes with round holes in them and thinking that nothing good would come out of them. We couldn't have been more wrong as the group just blew the place apart and Allan Clarke and Graham Nash delivered fantastic harmonies backed by a blistering band. That certainly took the smirks away for sure. We congratulated them after the show knowing that we had witnessed something really amazing. The Hollies had arrived and sometimes I would visit them as they rehearsed in a small room above Barratt's music shop in Oxford Road. I knew that original line-up quite well with Don Rathbone on drums, Eric Haydock on bass and Vic Steele on guitar. The lead guitarist would change not long afterwards when Vic decided he didn't want to turn professional with the others and I had some input into his replacement in the shape of Tony Hicks. There was a group called Ricky Shaw and the Dolphins playing at The Oasis in late December 1962 and I checked them out as per usual, noting that Ricky Shaw had an Elvis/Cliff approach and wearing his gold lame jacket he looked like yesterday's pop idol. Not a bad singer but pretty dated in his style and delivery. During the intermission Tony Hicks came into the coffee bar at the rear of the club and sat down with me for a chat. He asked me how I thought they'd done and, being diplomatic, I said "The group is terrific but what on earth are you doing backing this guy? You'll get nowhere with him". Tony nodded, reflected on what I'd said and thoughtfully agreed with my assessment. A few days later at the Hollies practise session I mentioned this great guitarist I'd seen playing with Ricky Shaw and the Dolphins and suggested to Graham Nash that he should check him out, he was that good. History records that Tony did replace Vic and that eventually Dolphins bass player Bernie Calvert and drummer Bobby Elliott would complete the line-up. Glad to have helped, guys.

These were wonderfully memorable and halcyon days for a young twenty-year old and none more so than when this Liverpool outfit came to play The Oasis in early December 1962. Our favourite group at the time were also from Liverpool, The Big Three, a hard-rocking band and by far the most exciting we had ever seen, but this wasn't them. This group was the first, to our knowledge, to have released a record and scored a chart hit with "Love Me Do". They were, of course, The Beatles, and they put on a pretty good show that night and later on they would make another appearance at my flat. On coffee and coke duty that night were three of the regulars, Lesley Earith, who lived near me, Allan Clarke's sister Cindy and Rose Eccles, soon to become Mrs Graham Nash and the inspiration for the Hollies hit "Jennifer Eccles". Rose served me my coffee and said, with incredible prescience, you should get these boys autographs because they will be huge stars in the future. I just shrugged casually and said I didn't have any paper or a pen, thinking that was that but two minutes later Rose was back with a pen in her hand and a sheet of Oasis headed notepaper telling me to get in the dressing room and get them to sign it. "Yes, Rose", I said. You didn't argue with Rose. The tiny dressing room was all steamed-up like a hothouse conservatory and as I walked in John Lennon said "It's so bloody hot in here I can't even tune this bloody guitar", to which Paul McCartney replied "Mine seems to be OK", and I think I heard John mumble under his breath "That's because you're just a plonker", or words to that effect. Ringo Starr got in on the act and said he thought it was like the Black Hole of Calcutta but George Harrison was a little more erudite remarking "Well, I think it's more like one of those sweaty Swedish saunas they have these days". It was all good-humoured banter and they were very happy to sign and I'm sure they, and I, thought nothing more of it but it was to prove to be one of the smartest things Rose ever told me to do. More on that later. I went back into the bar area and sat with Veronica, remember her(?), and Joan and Dave, who by now was a regular DJ at the club along with resident DJ Mac Magonegall Lacy. We sat and chatted for a while when both Lesley and Rose came over and said the boys, i.e., The Beatles, were wondering if there was anywhere to go for a party after the gig and could we organise one at my flat in Longsight for later on. That was OK by me but

I said was short on booze but they said that wouldn't be a problem and they'd bring some beer and spirits.

That small one-bedroom flat, with two single beds, was about to host the biggest musical phenomenon of the twentieth century but we surely didn't know it at the time. Well, Rose Nash did. The Demons were playing a gig in Stockport and Lek and Barry turned up later, our pals Pete MacLaine (Dakotas) and Wayne Fontana (Mindbenders) were there and Veronica, Joan and Dave plus several other friends. The Beatles turned up with John in the lead coming up the stairs and he said to me "Hello La, where's the beer?" I pointed him towards the lounge, the others followed and everybody got friendly with somebody. Lesley Earith was madly keen on the boys and put "Love Me Do" on the record player at which Paul McCartney turned round and said "Who put that shit on?" Everybody laughed and we went back to playing Ray Charles, Chuck Berry and Little Richard records. About half an hour in Lennon came up to me and asked if I owned the barber's shop below and I told him I only rented the flat. I asked him why and he said "Oh, I thought it was your place so I went to get some johnnies for Johnny and the boys". He said not to worry as their roadie Neil would sort it out before they left and guess what, that bill has never been settled. That's why The Beatles still owe me for four packs of condoms. Ringo was enjoying himself jigging about to the music and George was getting friendly with a girl on the stairs until the group commandeered the bedroom for a while before shooting off into the night without so much as a thanks or goodbye – nobody cared, we were all enjoying ourselves. It was like two speedboats passing in the night – flash, splash, bash and gone. There were only a couple of people left as the party wound down in the wee small hours, Lek and a lady friend in a corner all snuggled up and we four, Joan, Dave, Veronica and me. As Dave and Joan tried to get into bed Dave realised one of the legs had been broken, most likely due to over-enthusiastic activity by you know who. He cleverly fixed it for that night at least by replacing the wooden leg with a Guinness bottle which proved to be somewhat precarious to say the least. And that's another thing I put on The Fab Four account although over the years I have been more than adequately compensated for that night of fun and frivolity as you'll find out later. There was a girl called Edna at the party who fancied Paul and I think the attraction was mutual but I never got to see her again after that night. Neither did I see the girl that Lek spent the night with but she was still there in the morning when I got up to find she was the only one who hadn't gone home. I asked her if she'd had fun with Lek and she said "No, it was very disappointing, he didn't touch me all night". I asked her why she didn't take the initiative and she said she wasn't that kind of girl, then immediately proceeded to prove to me that that was exactly the kind of girl she was. Ships that pass in the night – and the early morning.

CHAPTER NINE
Twisted Wheel Time

Bongo Van Dort, now there's a name to conjure with. His real name was Peter Lyne and he'd been a pal of mine since he was around eight years old when he came to live with his grandmother in Osborne Road. His parents had divorced and his mother moved from the south of England back to Manchester and set up home with a gentleman friend in Mauldeth Road, Burnage. Pete was then placed with Granny Van Dort and one day she brought him round to introduce us in the hope that we'd become friends, which we very much did. It was obvious that Pete was going to be a character when the first thing he said as he came into the kitchen was "Who's that man in the mirror there?" He had never seen a serving hatch before and assumed it was a mirror but couldn't work out where the image was coming from, very sweet, and observant too. He was very well looked after by his gran, a lovely lady who welcomed me into her house and always had lots of good things to eat. One afternoon, sitting in the back garden, she asked if we'd like some sandwiches for our tea. The choice was peanut butter or honey, which sounded very exotic to me as I'd never had either before and hadn't a clue what they were. She said she'd make both and I could decide which I liked. The peanut butter left me feeling quite queasy, still does, but the honey sent my taste buds into ecstasy, still does.

Pete was one of the local gang with Clive and Victor Sayer and Michael Bowers and we'd spend most of our time together outside, especially on a hot sunny day when we'd pick the softened black tar out of the kerb cobblestones and make missile balls with them. Pete turned out to be a very good quick bowler at cricket and a ferociously fast cyclist on his racing bike, which we all envied for its state-of-the-art design and a classic Claude Butler frame. In later years when

I got involved with the groups Pete was one of a bunch of friends who would come to see us play at local gigs. That's when and why I gave him the monicker "Bongo" because he always brought his bongos and would sit by the side of the stage playing along with us, even though he wasn't in the band. That nickname stuck and he became quite well known around town for a few years. Other group fans, helpers and friends included Clive Sayer, Pete "Nobby" McNulty, and a chap known to me only as "Kiwi" who would later be the group's roadie along with Dave Chalmers.

Early January 1963 saw the start of a new cellar enterprise opening in Brazenose Street just around the corner from The Oasis. It was owned and run by two ex-Burnage Grammar boys, Jack and Ivor Abadi, who were well tuned in to the new club zeitgeist for the young generation like me. They named it The Twisted Wheel, serving coffees and coke during the day and I often had my favourite lunch there – cheese on toast and a portion of chips, delicious. Lek managed to get himself a job there serving behind the counter and it became quite the place to be. Jack and Ivor were very keen to promote the club and chatted to me about their plans. I suggested they could up the ambience in the place if they played some music in the background and I offered to bring in some of my records to play, which they readily accepted. One thing led to another and I started spinning discs there in the evening becoming the first DJ at what would become one of the most famous clubs in the country, which you can read about in the book "CENtral 1179" if you can find and afford a copy. That book title was the club's phone number, by the way. The discs I played were mainly up-tempo for dancing containing a mix of current chart singles like "Let's Dance" by Chris Montez, the Four Seasons "Sherry" and the Crystals "He's A Rebel" together with some rhythm and blues tracks like the Isley Brothers "Twist And Shout" and "Money" by Barrett Strong. I got a lot of help from a great old guy who ran the Hime and Addison record shop in John Dalton Street where I would call in after work and he would let me stay and listen to all the new releases from such labels as Sue, London American and Stateside. That was a wonderful source of some great soul records but I was resistant to some of the new pop stuff coming through, especially when a girl came up to me one night and handed me the first Gerry and the Pacemakers single "How Do You Do It" and insisted that I give it a spin. Reluctantly I put it on the turntable and was a bit surprised at the positive reaction it got from the crowd that night. So, the customer is always right – and she was a very pretty girl.

I also mentioned to the Abadi boys that I was managing The Hellions and what about having some live music sessions in the evenings. They thought this was another good idea and booked The Hellions to play at the official Twisted Wheel opening night on 27 January 1963. Dean West and The Hellions played the afternoon session at The Oasis and opened The Twisted Wheel in the evening, appearing as The Hellions, which was recorded for posterity by a Norman Jopling article and photograph of the event in the pop music weekly New Record Mirror. That was another "little did I know" event as in later years I would be the Advertising Manager for that very same paper.

The group made many appearances over the coming months at The Wheel, as we now called it, and bookings were coming in on a regular basis, mostly at weekends but requiring us to travel much further afield. This led to a great conflict of interest for me, what with my job at the tax office, disc-jockeying at the Wheel and managing the group, something had to give. My boss the Tax Inspector called me into his office one day and said my late arrivals would not be tolerated any longer and in order for me to keep my job I would be allowed to start at nine o'clock each morning, half an hour later than everybody else, and stay later in the day until five o'clock. This seemed very fair to me but it was a bit lonely for that last half hour of the day when everybody else had gone home. My boss knew, and I knew, that I probably wasn't cut out for a lifetime of employment in the civil service. My time as DJ at the Wheel was also proving too much to handle with all the group commitments and I had to tell Jack and Ivor that I was leaving but I suggested my old pal Pete "Bongo" Van Dort would be a good replacement as he was enthusiastic, knowledgeable and had a very good record collection. They agreed to this arrangement and Pete got the gig, becoming famous around Manchester.

My eclectic tastes in music had started very early in life but was finally confirmed to me on April 13th 1963 when I attended my first live jazz concert at the Free Trade Hall featuring the great Ella Fitzgerald, the Oscar Peterson Trio and the Roy Eldridge Quartet. That kind of supreme talent line-up comes along so rarely and it made a great impression on me. A night to savour, remember and live long in the memory.

The scene in Manchester was taking a new direction with The Hollies, Wayne Fontana and others trying out more rhythm and blues material from the likes of Bo Diddley, Chuck Berry and The Coasters. Malcolm had been with us for several months and we had regular Saturday afternoon practise sessions checking out new songs to refresh the act until one afternoon things changed dramatically. Wal had a copy of the Beatles "From Me To You" and I brought along the Johnny Kidd hit "Shot of Rhythm and Blues", which we all liked except for Malcolm, who either didn't want to sing them or felt that he couldn't. I cajoled him and encouraged him to put a bit more "growl and gravel" into his voice which was, admittedly, very much a smooth tenor more suited to ballads and softer pop songs. He just couldn't get his tonsils around these new, more aggressive vigorous sounds we wanted him to produce and he left that afternoon in a somewhat despondent mood. After he'd gone Lek and Wal asked me if I'd have a crack at singing a couple of numbers and I said I wasn't sure about that but they said they'd heard me singing in the van and believed I could do it. Well, I had to take the microphone into the hall so they couldn't see me and I had a go at "Shot of Rhythm and Blues", which they applauded when I'd finished. Then we did a few more songs and they said they'd decided I was to be the new singer in the band – bloody hell. There was a gig coming up at a small club on Stockport Road where I would get my first introduction as the singer. We were to do two spots but after the first one I was very upset with my performance and told the lads that I'd messed up and sang the wrong lyrics to a couple of tunes and maybe I wasn't cut out for it. They just laughed and said the audience were very enthusiastic and I'd been fine and there was no need to worry. That was the start of my singing career with a beat group. Sadly, Malcolm got the boot, and we changed the name of the group once again, this time to a name Bob Marley saw fit to use later – The Wailers. We concentrated on mostly up-tempo numbers like "Lucille", "Hippy Hippy Shake" and "Money". Gone were the cover versions of Cliff and Elvis songs although we did keep some Coasters numbers like "I'm A Hog For You Baby", "Three Cool Cats" and "Little Egypt" which always seemed to go down well. Bookings were often made well in advance which is why in June we were billed at the Oasis as The Hellions with the Unknown because they didn't know who the new singer was going to be nor were they aware of the change of name to The Wailers. Our performance was well received, we went down well and I enjoyed my first appearance at this iconic venue. Shortly after I became the vocalist we thought it would be a good idea to increase the band size by adding a tenor sax to the mix and so we advertised for one in the local paper. The first person to apply was the one we picked because he was very good and just what we wanted. His name was Dave McShane and he fitted in really well but what we didn't know was that he was a deserter from the army and so just three weeks later he was obliged to do another runner and we never saw him again. We didn't replace him, either. Strange times.

In July Ron and I booked a holiday in Sweden in the hope of finding "free love". We didn't find any, but we did have a very good time on the overnight ferry to Gothenburg which had a disco for dancing to keep us entertained and exhausted enough to get some sleep before we reached port. We had a good look around the city and found the best steak and chips were to be had at the railway station and at a price we could afford. We then made our way to our accommodation in the coastal resort of Tylosand and checked out the local activity where we might find the thing we were hoping for. You know what that was. There was a dance on the second evening we were there and we were totally taken aback by the reception we received on account of being from England, land of the Beatles and popular culture. Not only were they fascinated to hear about the groups and the music scene but they were offering us quite good money for our clothes, which they couldn't get in Sweden at that time. Like many of the young dudes in our area we spent most of clothing money at the "in" place in Stockport called

The Toggery, which was the general meeting place for groups to congregate on a Saturday. They had all the "gear" there and it was run by Michael Cohen, the Hollies manager, who also employed Graham Nash to work on the shop floor. Needless to say, we didn't sell any clothes because we needed them but I did sell one pair of shoes that I could manage without. After a few days by the sea, and no luck, we decided to get on a train and head for Copenhagen in Denmark. That was our first sighting of the Little Mermaid and over a couple of days we saw the city and very much enjoyed evenings in the Tivoli Gardens. Then it was time to return to Gothenburg and the ferry back to Blighty. I bought a half bottle of scotch whisky in duty free and the first night after we got back I sat in Ron's kitchen and shared it with his dad. Ron said he was tired and went to bed leaving me and his old man to chew the cud and polish off the whisky. I knew Mr Stratton liked a drink because I often saw him going into our local "The Old House At Home" and returning home with a quart of beer in one of those white enamel jugs which he would drink sitting in front of the fire watching television. He was happy as Larry. Who was Larry, I wonder?

Girlfriends? Yes, there were one or two, and after splitting up with Veronica in early 1963 I tried hard to find love and affection wherever I could but I failed to maintain a permanent relationship for the next few years, possibly because they wanted to move on to pastures new – or was it me? As it happened, Veronica found comfort and connubial bliss in the arms of Pete McNulty, the undisputed King of the Manchester Jive and they did make a great dancing partnership. My next girlfriend presented me with a very tricky dilemma just a month or so after we started dating. Her name was Christine and we went to several clubs and cinemas, after which I would take her home, say hello to her parents and be on my way, except one night when we got back her father and mother said they were going to bed and the lounge was ours. This seemed somewhat unusual, as did the fact that I had noticed Christine seemed to have gained a little weight, especially around her middle, and when she became extremely compliant as we kissed and cuddled, alarm bells started ringing. This was all far too easy and, keen though I might have been previously, those bells were ringing very loudly and consummation was not about to happen. I made my excuses and left for the walk home with all sorts of "what if's" and "maybe's" flashing through my mind. Needless to say, that was the end of a brief affair and I never saw Christine again. The first "Great Escape" of 1963, with Steve McQueen's version to follow later in the year.

My next girlfriend also almost got me into trouble but from a completely different direction. Her name was Gel, short, I think, for Geraldine, and we met at the same dancehall where Ron and Denise won the jive competition. Gel was good dancer and seemed very happy to strike up a friendship with me and being a fun-loving girl arranged to have a party at her parent's house one Saturday evening. What I didn't know was that her ex-boyfriend had turned up and was threatening to do me some serious damage for pinching his girlfriend. This news came to me via Lek, who was also at the party and had overheard these threats in the kitchen. He came into the lounge to warn me and I said "Who is this guy?" and Lek said "His name's Butch, he's the bass player in the Pete Bocking Six and he's mad as hell". Lek was all prepared for a major confrontation and stood behind the door with an empty pint pot in his hand and said "If that bastard comes through this door with a knife in his hand I'm going to brain him". Now that's the kind of support you need in these situations. As it turned out bloodshed was avoided, Gel calmed things down and Butch left without me ever seeing him. The second "Great Escape" of 1963 and still no sign of Steve McQueen.

Things were going along quite well in most directions until one morning in the summer of '63 I received a letter from my mother asking how I was and that she was missing me and would I agree to a reconciliation meeting as she and my father wanted to clear the air. As I hadn't seen my parents for many months I knew this meeting had to happen one day so I phoned and said I'd come over to see them the next day. My mother told me in floods of tears how worried she was about me and how I was coping on my own and surely I could come home where she assured me things would be different. With some trepidation I agreed to go back with the stipulation that I'd be off again if they went back on their word and started treating me like a juvenile again. Thus the air was cleared and I returned to my old bedroom in number 62. My mother was so pleased as this meant she could now start planning for my 21st birthday party in the coming September. Ah, so that was it, my 21st couldn't go by without a family and friends celebration.

The invitations went out for a grand gathering at the Co-op Hall in Ladybarn Lane, Fallowfield, where food and drink were consumed in large quantities, including a toast with champagne, which was very upmarket for that time and place, that's for sure. Everybody danced to The Wailers with guest appearances by the Phantom's Trevor Jones and our occasional rhythm guitarist Tony Walmsley, with whom I would spend a great deal of time in later years. It all went very well and at the end of the evening I had arranged to take the group and some of the party to the all-nighter at the Twisted Wheel. This was an even greater success which lasted until around 6 a.m. when a few of us tipped up at our house for coffee, a bacon butty and a well-earned rest. One of the night-owls there was from our booking agency and she had the unusual name of Pym and when I asked her how it came about, she said "Oh, it's just my initials, my real name's Patricia" but she remained Pym during the course of our courtship – now there's an old-fashioned word. She didn't stay at the agency for very much longer as she moved to Stratford-Upon-Avon to help run the family hotel business there and although I visited her several times the distance separated us, putting paid to that romance.

Shortly after my party I went again to see one of my rock and roll heroes Gene Vincent at The Oasis and met him backstage for a chat and a photograph, which also included Ron and Lek. Our rock idol seemed genuinely pleased to meet his enthusiastic fans and when Lek asked him what happened to Cliff Gallup, that great guitarist in his backing band The Blue Caps, Gene just said "He didn't like the road. I think he's quit the business for good". I then said I'd got all his singles released here on the Capitol label at which he smiled and said "Yeah, it's crazy but I've had more hits here than back in the States". At that point Ron made me blush a little saying "Geoff does a very good impersonation of you and I've got a photo of him singing using a telephone as a microphone" to which Gene laughed and said "I'd sure like to see that". He then posed with us for that photo before he got ready to go on stage. What a super guy he was.

That's a treasured memory to this day. So too was the visit to Granada TV studios with Ron that November for a recording of a Little Richard Special to be aired the following January. It certainly was a hot time in the old town with many American stars coming over to play including Bill Haley and the Comets, who also appeared at the Oasis and, even though we weren't expecting too much from them, they absolutely tore the place apart playing all their hits on a most memorable evening.

Those were heady days being at the epicentre of happenings at both The Oasis and The Twisted Wheel, where I seemed to spend most of my spare time, especially as I never had to pay to get in. Visiting bands would often appear during the afternoon to set up and I'd offer a helping hand getting heavy gear down the stairs such as a Hammond organ belonging to one Clive Powell, better known later as Georgie Fame. There were regular appearances in town by Johnny Kidd and the Pirates, who featured that great guitar player Mick Green, instrumental group Nero and the Gladiators and the outrageous performer Screaming Lord Sutch, who employed both Jimmy Page and the sensational Ritchie Blackmore on guitar. Sutch's entrance from the dressing room to the stage would take him through the audience wreaking havoc and hysteria among the ladies, many of whom almost fainted with fright. On meeting and spending time with him he turned out to be a most personable guy, asking to be called Dave and happy to ferry us around town in his Chevvy Impala convertible. We felt like Kings of the Road.

With Gene Vincent, Ron & Lek

A rockin' trio Lek, me & Ron

The wailers

CHAPTER TEN

From The Wheel To My Own Wheels

Near the beginning of this book I told you about the 21st birthday present I would receive from Granny and Grampa, the princely sum of £100, which I was holding on to until a suitable car became available through Ron at Culver's Car Mart. That day came on 18th December when Ron called me on my office number DEAnsgate 8311 extension 354 (what a memory – Ron's, actually) and said he had just the car for me and I should go and have a look at it asap. I took off from work early and arrived at Culver's just before closing time and Ron pointed to "the car". I nearly fell over as he said this was within my price range and an absolute steal at £125 for, get this – a Rolls Royce. It was a 1938 Mulliner Park Ward model recently the property of Lord Webb of Chapel-en-le-Frith. This just goes to show what a great salesman Stratton is – he sold me a Rolls Royce and I couldn't even drive. No need to worry he said as he would do all the driving until I passed my test and so began an extraordinary few months of being chauffeured around by Ron with me and the boys in the band lounging about in the rear. One memorable outing took the pair of us plus Lek and Wayne Fontana to The Cavern Club in Liverpool where we met up with local legend Derry Wilkie, lead singer with The Seniors, the first group to play The Kaiserkeller in Hamburg where the Beatles would also later play. Derry was a born and bred scouser and knew his way around the city centre and all the clubs, several of which we visited that night in a club crawl, eventually ending up in the famed Blue Angel which, for reasons unknown to me, he called "The Raz". We got back to Manchester early the next morning thoroughly exhausted but entirely exhilarated by our trip to The Pool.

By way of thanking Granny and Grampa for their generosity I suggest a day out in the Rolls to take them anywhere they fancy and Granny says she'd really like to go back and have a look at Stalybridge, one of the first and most successful of the cotton mill towns. It was also where local musician Jack Judge wrote and first performed the enormously popular First World War song "It's A Long Way To Tipperary" and Jack's statue still stands outside the Old Victoria Market Hall. We had a bite to eat in the town and a walk around to rekindle some memories for Granny and all in all it was a wonderful day out for all of us.

Early on in 1964 the old Rolls was becoming a bit of a burden, what with only doing about 8 miles to the gallon, huge running costs and sitting outside Number 62 all week doing nothing, Ron and I decided on a change of vehicle. He had good contacts for a deal which saw us both buy identical Minis with consecutive number plates and me trading in the Rolls for a profit of £50 against the cost of the new car of £448. I was still on a provisional driving license when Ron dropped Clive Sayer and myself off at a dealership in Hazel Grove where we put on the "L" plates and I drove home with Clive in the passenger seat. For the next few weeks Clive and Ron both gave me driving lessons and I took a few with a driving school who declared me ready to take my test which I passed first time. Now for the open road, Mr Toad.

With the freedom gained by having my own wheels I was out and about like something demented and very often went to gigs in my own car, especially if they were local. On long distance journeys we all went together in the van and often got back home in the wee small hours and in need of a bite to eat if we hadn't managed to find a late night Indian or Chinese restaurant open along the way. To illustrate the mellowing of relations on the domestic front my mother would often be up and about and happy to make us a fry up or hot potato cakes, followed by a game of cards which usually involved me and Lek, Wal and Ron. This was a great way to finish off the night and we would sometimes play until dawn. Our favourite card game was "Shoot", which is a total game of chance and very much a gamble on the three cards you hold in your hand. Players take it in turns to beat the dealer and the pot can end up being quite large so that if you have the nerve to match what's in the pot you can go for the entire amount where you must call "Shoot" and then you either win the whole pot or you lose the equivalent amount. Dangerous times, boys, dangerous times. Nobody ever really lost a lot of money because the stakes weren't that high but it was a real buzz if you won the whole of a really big pot. Lek used to make me laugh a lot, especially in the early morning light when he left for home and did a great Max Wall impression throwing his coat tails up, sticking his bum out doing the silly walk and looking back at me with a gurning grin on his face. Great times. Lek and I spent a good deal of time together listening to music and assessing songs we might play with the group, one of which was "Shame On You Miss Johnson" by Bobby Freeman, which made Lek howl with laughter the first time he heard it and it soon became part of our act. One of Lek's favourites was Johnny Cash and although we listened to lots of his material we never did find a song we thought suitable for inclusion. On a purely social level on nights we weren't playing we'd often get together with our pals in the Parrs Wood set to play music, maybe a game of cards or a board game. On one spooky and spine-tingling evening at Billy Wright's house there were quite a few of us - Tony Walmsley, Christine Mulligan, Nobby, Veronica and Leonora Cooper – when somebody produced a Ouija board and decided to set it up for a séance so we could contact the spirit world. Lek and I thought this was a good wheeze but it all ended in tears when some of the party reacted very badly to the experience, claiming to be traumatised and very frightened by the whole thing. That session ended very abruptly and we never did it again.

Coming events were to change my life considerably as I quit The Wailers at the end of March'64. Our pcnultimate gig was a joint enterprise with Dave Lee Travis on Thursday 19th March when we rented The Servites Hall just off Bury New Road to run a dance evening, with DLT as DJ and The Runaways group supporting The Wailers, all for three shillings and sixpence, very good value. It didn't make us much money but at least we thought there was a good chance we could build upon it for the future. That would not be the case as things took a nasty turn at the next gig at a small ballroom in Rhyl in Wales on the 28th of March. I had driven there in the Mini with a pal of Lek's called Strattagaki, a lad of Greek

94

descent, who had started coming to see us play. Things seemed to be going well and we completed our first set but as we stepped on stage for the second set I announced a number but Lek said he wasn't going to play that tune. I shrugged and Wal announced we were going to do "I'm A Hog For You Baby" which Barry started to count in but Lek steadfastly refused to play and just stood there on stage with his arms folded. I was mortified by this inexplicable unprofessional behaviour and had no idea what game Lek was playing so I just said to him "Well, if you're not playing, I can't be singing" and walked off the stage into the dressing room and got changed into my civvies. I waited in the dressing room fuming at Lek's behaviour and at the end of the gig I packed my PA equipment into the back seat of the Mini and took off back to Manchester with Strattagaki, vowing never to sing with The Wailers again – and I didn't. There was a gig booked the next night and the group van pulled up outside our house and Wal came to get me to go with them. In spite of his pleading for several minutes there was no way I was going out that night and told them so in no uncertain terms. That was my exit from The Wailers and the reason for Lek's obduracy and why he had behaved so badly soon became abundantly clear to me as at the beginning of April both he and Barry signed up to play as part of Peter Noone's backing band Herman and the Hermits. They had been to an audition with the band's managers Harvey Lisberg and Charlie Silverman and although at first reluctant to join changed their minds upon seeing the date sheet for the next few weeks where they would be working almost every night and earning quite good money. I understand that this was a great incentive for an aspiring professional musician but I couldn't reconcile Lek's attitude and why he didn't just have the guts to tell me he was joining another band. After all, groups changed personnel on a regular basis and I would have accepted that without rancour and probably have wished him well.

The person who felt the split most keenly was Wal, who was in tears when it all fell apart and he wasn't invited to join the Hermits. He was a very good bass player and soon found employment with Ron's group the Spinning Tops and many years later moved south to become famous as the designer and producer of the highly-regarded "WAL" bass guitar in partnership with Rick Wakeman from the group Yes.

I must be a very forgiving person because it wasn't long after the break-up that relations between me and Lek thawed and we moved on quickly from that episode because, really, we were good mates.

Within a few days of the split I got together with my mate the guitarist Tony Walmsley to form a new, larger combo with the best musicians we knew who might be available. First up was Nick Duvall from The Country Gentlemen on bass, Neil Gibbons on sax, Alan Forbes on drums but where to find a keyboard player? As luck would have it I found him at The Bodega Club one evening when I went to see The Spinning Tops, the group Ron Stratton was managing. As I sat there watching I was aware of some guy in the shadows to the right of the stage knocking ten bells out of an upright piano. Most curious, I thought, and went over to see what he was doing, which was playing along with all the group's repertoire and doing it well. I told him he couldn't be heard and he said he knew that but he was just having a bit of fun and wasn't in the band, only a friend of theirs. I asked him if he'd like to be in a band and he said how was that possible as he had a good job at Dunn and Bradstreet in the city centre. I said I thought he had the talent and asked if he was willing to give it a go without leaving his job. He said he had no equipment and I said that could be easily fixed if he'd meet me tomorrow lunchtime at Barratt's music shop and so, without a moment's hesitation he signed up for an electric piano to play with The Six Mint Juleps. Tony Bamforth will tell you today that his life changed forever after our first meeting and that he's eternally grateful to me for bringing him into the music business, where he's since been all his life.

Tony Bamforth is one of the great raconteurs of our time with a fund of hilarious tales of his time on the road such as when he was in a dressing room with a young Michael Jackson who was very keen to please Tony and brought him cigarettes and chocolate cake. Michael was fascinated by Tony and at one point held his hand up and said "Hey, Tony, gimme five". Tony's response was "No, Michael, I don't do that shit" at which Michael fell about laughing, can you imagine. Tony B was an expert in the local dialect and would give me examples and instruction in speaking pure Glossop, which went something like this, if you can figure it out, "Ow art e mester, t'oreet?" Translated into English that greeting means "How are you, mister, are you alright?" but otherwise the outsider wouldn't have a clue what was being said. Tony was a bit of a gadabout and one night took us to a pub in Glossop to see a band with a singer calling himself James Bond and The Premiers. I took my current girlfriend, a nurse, along and had a pleasant enough evening which ended in a way that took my breath away because as we were leaving this extremely good-looking girl came up to me and said "Do you always take your Granny out on dates?" and handed me her phone number on the back of a fag packet. You probably don't need me to tell you that the nurse was history and I embarked on a fun time with Valerie from New Mills, who later moved to London to be a model.

The Juleps rehearsed hard in a room above a pub and after a short time we had a couple of sets worked out and were ready for the road. We did our first gig at Didsbury Teacher Training College and that went really well as did a few others around Manchester. Such a great group of musicians and friends, we were getting along famously until Nick, the bass player, dropped a bombshell – he was leaving. He was married with kids and had been offered a regular wage to play full-time with another group. We were all crestfallen and try though we might we just couldn't locate another bass player to fill Nick's place. Another group bites the dust.

As did the next project I got involved with and for precisely the same reason – no bloody bass player. The guitarist Vic Steele invited me to join him and his brother Eric, the loudest drummer in Manchester, to form a new group. We rehearsed a few times at Vic's house while we searched for a bass player but all to no avail and in the end we had to call it a day, a great shame. Adrian Barratt tried to help with a couple of phone calls but drew a blank and the only highlight around that time was chatting to Chuck Berry in Barratt's on May 22 the day he played at The Odeon with Kingsize Taylor And The Dominoes. Chuck was a tall guy with the most enormous hands but he seemed very gentle and friendly and happy to talk and he laughed when I told him I originally thought he played piano because of the solo on "Sweet Little Sixteen" but that I knew better now as we played lots of his songs in our act. I saw him on stage that night and he was brilliant.

After the Juleps debacle I was at a loose end when Ron came up with a suggestion for us both to have a free holiday on the Continent and I was all ears when he told me his boss, Alan Culver, wanted Ron to bring back an MG car from Geneva airport. Ron agreed and asked if he could take a friend for company and maybe have a little tour around for a week or so to which Alan also agreed. We flew from Ringway to Geneva, picked up the car and headed straight for the wine, women and song in the south of France. We didn't do well on the women front but we had a wonderful drive along the riviera corniche as we made our way via Monte Carlo towards Italy, our objective was to visit Venice. Our first stop in Italy was the coastal resort of San Remo, which is where Ron got the name for the singer in the Spinning Tops as Brian McGladdery became Remo Sands. Unfortunately, it wasn't all he got after we spent the day on the beach and Ron's skin went the colour of a lobster and he was suffering very badly from over-exposure to a heat he'd never experienced before. I had seen a red-cross type sign as we came into town and drove him there to get some help because he was in a very bad way and a soon as they saw him he was whisked away for treatment and I was told to come back later to visit as he would be in there overnight. I went back around nine o'clock that evening to check up on him and I almost fell about laughing because there he was, lying back in this bed looking for all the world like The Invisible Man. They had treated his burns, given him some painkillers and wrapped him all over in white bandages with just a slit for his mouth plus a couple of holes for his eyes. He did look a sorry sight and wasn't up for talking much so I left him to sleep and told him I'd be back next morning. Amazingly his treatment had been both timely and effective and he was discharged with a variety of creams and painkillers so that we were able to continue our journey, next destination the port city of Genoa. We arrived there around midnight and it looked like Dante's Inferno as the place was on fire with all the industrial chimneys bellowing out smoke and burning gases, all lit by strong spotlights along the wharves in the port area. We had no idea where to find a bed for the night and luckily a policeman directed us to a small hotel down a narrow alleyway in the old town. A little old lady took us in and led us to the top floor of this quite tall building, meandering though other bedrooms with people asleep on the floor. Salubrious it was not and worse was to come as we found ourselves in a twin-bedded garret on the very top floor. We got our heads down and were instantly asleep when "Bong" – we were rudely awakened as the room seemed to be shaking. "What the hell was that?" Ron shouted and I could still hear the reverberations coming from outside the window. We opened the shutters and there it was – the bell tower of a church about a leg's length away across the alley. "Oh great", or words to that effect, I said, knowing what we were faced with – hourly bongs increasing in number throughout the night. We were so tired we probably managed 55 minutes of sleep each hour and in the morning we were out of there like bats out of hell.

The drive to Venice was very picturesque and we learned from the previous night's nightmare not to leave it too late booking a hotel. We had a good look at the sights but the afternoon brought showers which meant us sheltering under an awning by the side of a canal. As we sat there smoking a fag we were suddenly aware of being bombarded by grapes – yes, grapes. Somebody was aiming them at us from the other side of the canal but we couldn't see where they were exactly so we made a run for it to the nearest café. What a strange trip this was turning out to be, eh?

As we had no planned itinerary, I looked at the map and pointed out to Ron the village of Kotschach-Mauthen across the border in Austria where I stayed in 1958. "Let's go there" he said, so off we went for one last interesting destination before beginning our journey home. Time was now running very short and we wasted none of it crossing the continent with some trepidation that we might miss our connection to get us back from France. We were booked on the flying car ferry from Le Touquet to Lydd in Hampshire at 8 o'clock in the morning and as it had taken us much longer than anticipated due to roadworks and detours we had to drive through the night to be sure of getting there on time.

Something quite marvellous happened as we drove along the coast road in the middle of the night looking for somewhere we might get a bite to eat as we hadn't had time to stop for anything substantial since breakfast. Mile after mile we went through small towns and villages with no signs of life anywhere to be seen until we entered a small hamlet with light shining through the window of a bakery. I said to Ron "Let's stop and see if they'll sell us a croissant or a baguette to keep us going", so we pulled up outside and as we entered we could hear the sound of music and laughter coming from the rear of the premises and that's when the magic happened. We made our way through the shop and opened the door into a room where there was a wedding party going on. The music stopped abruptly and all eyes turned to us as we looked at them with equal bewilderment and I managed to stutter out "Baguette, s'ils vous plait?" in mangled French. This was answered with another question "Are you English?" I said yes, we were, at which point the entire gathering erupted into spontaneous applause with bewildering jollity and bonhomie and three or four elderly men stepped forward to speak to us They said we were a good luck sign for the newlyweds, also that they would like to express their gratitude for what we did for them in the war, inviting us to join in with them and share their food and drink. The spiritual and emotional feelings engendered in us all that night have remained with me ever since. Truly the most unforgettable moment of the entire holiday.

We arrived at Le Touquet airport with a couple of hours to spare and had a bit of a kip in the car. I think the carrying capacity of the plane was about three cars and the flight over the channel only took about twenty minutes and there we were back home. We checked our finances as we were almost skint and realised we needed to be very careful not to spend too much on food at the expense of the petrol we would need to get us back to Manchester. The drive took us nearly all day and the only thing we dared to risk buying was a bag of chips, so it was a good job we'd filled up so well at the wedding feast. Ron told me the next day about Alan Culver's remarks when he looked at the mileage and realised we'd driven 3,000 miles in ten days when he said "I told you to bring the car back after you'd had a little trip not a bloody expeditionary voyage to North Africa". Ron just laughed because he knew the only thing Alan was worried about was how much that many miles had affected the car's depreciation. All was well in the end and Ron's sunburnt nose was almost back to normal.

As one door closes another one shuts, as they say, but for me that's not the way things happened. Another local group were looking to replace their lead singer and invited me to join them very shortly after giving up hope on the Mint Juleps. They were a three-piece called The Zodiacs with a bass player called Dave, a great drummer and musician in Les Winterburn and my long-time mate Trevor Lyon on guitar. They had plenty of dates in the diary and we worked up a great repertoire with good r & b tunes, a little comedy and cover versions of Beatles and Stones songs which went down really well at the type of venues we were playing, like sporting clubs and even Bernard Manning's Embassy Club. More about Bernard later. Les and Trevor were always full of fun with lots of jokes and good stories, one of which Trevor regaled me with about his dad's lecture on the "facts of life". It took place in their kitchen and it goes like this – "Well, Trevor lad, you're sixteen now, so think on". That was it, the meaning of sex in two words "think on". All was not rosy in the group, however. What the hell is it with bass players eh? This one copped out and left us adrift and unable to fulfil our bookings. I was beginning to wonder if there was any future for me in a pop group. Well, there was, but not forever I'm pleased to say.

Success had come for some of the groups in Manchester, not only in the UK but also in "the big one," America, where both the Hermits and the Hollies had visited. Lek came back raving about this great outfit he'd seen called The Mugwumps, a name that instantly brought a smile to my face. He had correctly predicted that they would be successful, although only after a name change to The Mamas and Papas. The other funny came from Graham Nash when he came back talking, in the words of George Formby – "all Yankee", with expressions like groovy, hippy and the one that really creased me up was when I asked him how had he liked America and he said "It's a gas, man". Well, then it was his turn to fall about when I queried what a gasman had to do with anything as it quickly became clear that a great deal of new terminology was entering the language, man.

An escape route to the future presented itself not long after the Zodiacs called it a day when I went for an audition at the Rex ballroom in Wilmslow with a group variously called The Gay Dogs or The Wild Dogs. They were with the Alan Arnison Agency in Stockport and had a really full date sheet at good money. I did a few numbers with them before having a chat about the possibilities for us getting together. I was quite keen as they were just the kind of band I had hoped the Mint Juleps would be with guitar, bass, drums, keyboards and sax. They asked me to join but there was a proviso and that was I would have to turn professional. I agreed to that and then they told me why they needed to replace their singer. They had been to London to audition for Larry Page, manager of The Kinks and The Troggs, and he didn't care for the singer they had and told them to come back when they had a replacement, with the offer of a recording contract if he liked the new vocalist. No pressure, then.

Chapter Eleven

I Was A Yak

That might also have made a good title for this book and you'll soon see why.

Joining this group was about to turn my life and my location upside down as we started out together with Les Heaton on lead guitar, Geoff Allen on keyboards, Pete Allen on drums, Mike Timms on bass and Roy Jones on sax, superb musicians every one and little wonder Larry Page wanted to sign them. We worked really hard tightening up the act and me bringing newer material into the mix with songs like "Baby Please Don't Go", "All Night Worker" and "I'll Go Crazy", all a bit more soul and blues than previously although we kept in some old rockers like "New Orleans", "Slow Down" and "The Girl Can't Help It". We had lots of good bookings 3 or 4 nights a week and I managed to persuade the manager of The Plaza ballroom to let us rehearse there on weekday afternoons in exchange for a reduced fee for playing there in the evenings. An excellent arrangement which worked very well. Only once did I get a complaint from the boys in the band and that was more like a cry for help than a complaint. We were doing a gig across The Pennines at a venue with tables in front of the stage which is where my girlfriend Posie was sitting. The first set went well but in the dressing room before the second set the lads asked me if Posie could move out of their eyeline as they were being distracted and unable to concentrate. I asked them why that was, what was she doing and they said just sitting there was enough because she was so pretty and with her short skirt and white stockings looking for all the world like a very sexy model. She was the epitome of a swinging sixties girl and Ron Stratton said she was the best-looking girl in town. Lucky me. Posie and I drove back home over the Snake Pass, stopping for a little light relief along the way and if you've ever had amorous inclinations in a 1960's Mini you'll be well aware you need the physical attributes of a contortionist. Apparently, we did.

We travelled a fair bit to venues like the Mojo Club in Sheffield, where I first met Peter Stringfellow, the self-styled "King Of Clubs", and to the strangely named Little Fat Black Pussy Cat Club in Bradford which I think was owned by the wrestler Big Daddy. Belle Vue in Manchester was quite a centre for grunting and grappling in those days and the local frighteners were Jack Pye, a man with a fearsome reputation, Black Butcher Johnson and Bill "Man Mountain" Benny, a larger-than-life character who owned several nightclubs including the Cabaret on Oxford Road, the Devonshire and the Levenshulme Sporting Club, formerly the Palais De Dance. I only ever went to the Cabaret club once when I was looking after one of Larry Page's proteges, a fine black singer called Beverly Mills. She was a delightful girl and I helped Larry out by getting her from gig to gig for a week or so on a tour of northern clubs. Reports of Bill's demise make for sensationally lurid reading as, according to some accounts, he died having sex with a prostitute, who had to telephone the police for help so that they could break in and rescue her from beneath the twenty stone wrestler. What a way to go. Never a dull place, Manchester, what with the gangland connections, cops and robbers and the most inappropriately named criminals The Quality Street Gang. Not that we were very much aware of any of that activity – way too dangerous territory for us good little boys.

The year 1964 ended for me at the exact same location as I had first met the group, The Creole Club at The Rex in Wilmslow. New Year's day saw us back home playing The Bodega club followed by dates at the Peppermint Lounge in Liverpool and the most bizarre performance at Prince's Ballroom in Bury. Well, the performance wasn't bizarre but the audience reaction was when one of the crowd pointed at me and said "Oh look, it's Sir". I nearly died of embarrassment realising that some of my old pupils were in the audience and had recognised me but it was all good-humoured and after the gig I had a chat with them and even signed a few autographs. How funny was that?

At the end of January we got a call from Larry Page asking us to come to London so he could hear the band again and on February 3rd we set up in Regent Sound Studio in Denmark Street, famous as the location for the recording of the Stones first album. We laid down about a dozen tracks from our stage act during that afternoon session and Larry pronounced himself well-pleased with the results. He then took us across the street to his office where we signed management contracts with him for representation and recording. We had a bite to eat in the famous Giaconda café then returned to Manchester with the expectation that both Larry and we would evaluate material suitable to record and release. However, just days after we got home we were informed that Larry had signed us to Decca Records and that our first single would be our cover version of The Coasters hit "Yakety Yak". Somewhat non-plussed at this turn of events, but at the same time delighted that we had a record coming out, we were even more surprised to be told that the group credit on the single was to be The Yaks. We accepted the bewildering speed of all these developments with equanimity and continued fulfilling the dates in the diary while waiting for Larry's promised promotion opportunities to commence. Decca Records asked us to attend their offices for a photo-shoot with their in-house photographer David Wedgbury, one of the top snappers of the sixties who many years later ran off a full set of those black and white shots for me. There was great excitement running through the group when told of our next assignment, which was to be an appearance on the TWW (Welsh and West) television pop show "Discs A Go-Go" to be recorded in their Bristol Studios on March 3rd. Also on the cast list that night were presenter Kent Walton and his young helper DJ Tony Prince, the Dave Clark Five, Anita Harris, the Walker Brothers, The Go-Jo's dance troupe and Tom Jones singing his first Number One "It's Not Unusual". The atmosphere during the show was high energy and although we were required to mime to our record it all went very well, the only downside being that we weren't in the transmission area to watch our performance. There were no domestic TV recorders in those days so we never saw our one and only exposure on the box.

"Yakety Yak" on Decca F12115 was scheduled for release on 26th March and adverts appeared in all the usual popular music magazines and I believe it received good airplay on the pirate radio ship Radio London but otherwise it was destined not to trouble the pop charts.

Dramatic changes were about to occur the day after we did our last gig in Manchester at The Oasis Club on April 7th when we got a call from Larry asking us to return to London as he had some news of an interesting project for us to consider. We agreed to travel down after another gig that same night and that's when guitarist Les Heaton got himself the nickname "Overnight" because any time there was a choice between staying in a hotel or driving through the night he would always say "overnight" with no room for discussion, for he was our leader. Very tight with money, was Les.

In Larry's office he asked us if we all had passports and got an all-round "yes" and the question "why?" He said he could fix us up with a national tour of France for the entire summer, at which we were delighted, but with a caveat, and here it comes. Larry had just agreed a contract for his newest signing to tour France but he needed a backing group. At this point everybody looked at me thinking exactly what I was thinking – "am I out?" The answer was a resounding "no" because his latest charge was Charlie Chaplin's son Michael, who was a huge media star in France and a promoter over there said he could fill theatres all around the country because of his amazingly popular celebrity status. What Larry suggested was that we open the first half of these shows as The Yaks and Michael would headline the second set. That all seemed perfectly reasonable and we prepared to begin rehearsing with Michael as the tour was due to start in June. Larry put us up at the Madison Hotel in Sussex Gardens, a place well known to hundreds of groups and artists over many years. All our expenses were paid for and we turned up regularly at an old church in Notting Hill Gate where we rehearsed and nursed Michael through his first nervous attempts at the microphone. It soon became obvious that this was not a lead singer and to help with the sound and cover any difficulties Michael had, the boys produced some wonderful vocal harmonies and I was on standby to sing along in unison while holding an acoustic guitar.

I didn't spend much time with Michael during those sessions as he was busy learning the songs but I also found him a little bit airy-fairy with his long hippie hair and, I gathered, a partiality for wacky backy in a jazz cigarette, which was something neither I nor the lads were interested in. He was very far removed from our usual sphere of influence. For the next month all went well and we really felt we had a pretty good act worked up with Michael and Larry described himself well-pleased, telling us that plans were well advanced for the coming tour.

A fellow guest at The Madison was a Norwegian journalist who had been covering The Everly Brothers tour and she asked me why we were in London. On hearing what we were doing with Michael she asked if she could come along to a rehearsal and interview him and take some photos for her magazine. I said I'd check if that was OK, which it was. Next day she came to watch proceedings and her article and full colour photos appeared in the Norwegian press. Sylvie and I got on very well together and went out for dinner a couple of times and one night she asked if she could hear our record as she just happened to have a record player in her room. That was to prove once again what a large part chance had to play at that time. Stay tuned.

During this rehearsal period our evenings were mostly free and we'd do various things together as well as apart. Coincidentally at this time Herman's Hermits were in town and I spent some time with them. I even went with Peter Noone to a photo-shoot for "Fabulous" magazine where I appeared as Pete's schoolteacher, complete with mortarboard and cape and that shot was printed in the May 22nd edition. Fame at last, except I didn't get a name check. Perhaps the most potentially reputation damaging event happened after a night out with Peter, Karl Green and Lek at the famous Ad Lib Club in central London. We'd had a great evening and a few drinks with some famous faces and as we were leaving three gorgeous "dolly birds" invited us to a party. We four got into my Mini and followed them in theirs along Park Lane and down Bayswater Road into Notting Hill. There was a guy with them who was the driver and he pulled up outside a large terraced house and we piled out of the car with a great sense of anticipation. The room we went into was decked out like some bohemian boudoir with drapes and cushions all over the place. The guy said he'd show us some of his holiday films, which were actually blue movies featuring him with these ladies and obviously filmed in the very room we were in. He then disappeared behind a curtain and I figured that was where the camera was that he was hoping to use. That was the first alarm bell and the second rang almost immediately when the ladies reached into their bags and produced some amyl nitrate poppers, which I instantly recognised as the same stuff Grampa used to crack open to ease his heart constriction. I looked at Lek, Pete looked at me and we shook our heads in unison as we stood up to leave and Pete said very forcefully "We don't do drugs and we're off, goodnight". We made a rapid exit, jumped back in the Mini and made a dash back to the hotel feeling very relieved to say the least. It did cross my mind many years later that those ladies may have been part of the infamous madame Janie Jones entourage. I guess we'll never know.

The Yaks 1965

With The Vanguards, Oslo, 1965

Gjett om det låt! Og gjett om publikum jublet! Hele salen var i et eneste kok. Sologitaristen i Vanguards, Terje Rypdal, var fra seg av fryd etter opptredenen. Maken hadde han aldri opplevet. — Ikke en prøve, og det satt som et skudd, sa han henrykt. Samtlige medlemmer av gruppen bønnfalte Jeff om å komme tilbake til Norge. Helst for godt.

Til å begynne med sa ikke Jeff stort, men etterhvert begynte han å like tanken. — Det er altfor hektisk i engelsk show-business for tiden, man er ingenting den ene dagen, stjerne den neste og så plutselig ingenting igjen. Kvalitet teller ikke så meget, det gjelder å få et «hit» og flyte på det så lenge som mulig, sa han. Her i landet lot det til at arbeidsforholdene var gode og reale, og at kvaliteten fortsatt tellet. Jo, det var nok ikke umulig at han kom tilbake.

Men først måtte han tilbake til England en stund. Han hadde gjort avtale om en turne med «Herman's Hermits». Dessuten skulle han gjøre et par plateopptak i London. Men så ....

JEFF YOUNG

gjør nordmann av seg

Norway 1965

111

With Millie Small, Oslo, 1965

CHAPTER TWELVE

Chance, Coincidence or Luck

Somebody once said to me "Your middle name should be Lucky" and I replied "My first and last names should also be Lucky" because I have been truly fortunate to have been in the right place at the right time with all the right people and for which I am exceedingly grateful. So thanks, whoever you are.

The next period of my life was to be one of intense activity and a very peripatetic itinerant existence as the Michael Chaplin association was about to come to a crippling conclusion. After all our hard work preparing Michael for the tour, he foolishly went ahead with a disastrous solo appearance on French television on June 9th. Larry Page tried to blame us for not turning up on time to go with him, insisting he had to send Michael over to Paris on his own. I think there was more to it than that but the upshot was that Michael totally bombed and the promoter cancelled the tour. This was devastating news and we drowned our sorrows over several pints in the pub knowing that we would be unemployed for some time, possibly all summer. We went back to the hotel and formed a queue to use the payphone to ring home with the news that we'd be back in Manchester the next day. Everybody, that is, except me because when Sylvie heard the news she said she was sure that if I went back home with her she could get me some work with the best group in Oslo, The Vanguards. I thought this proposition over for about half a second and the next day I was on a flight to Norway. The band wished me well as they packed up and left for home with Les Heaton kindly driving my Mini back to my parent's house. That was the last of The Yaks and the end of an era for me as a singer with an English group but there were many new adventures ahead, including an offer from Larry Page to sign a joint management agreement with him and Larry Parnes. That was never going to happen because I knew Larry "Parnes, Shillings and Pence" by reputation and his predilection for young male singers and I wasn't going there, thank you very much.

A final word on the Michael Chaplin debacle came via a letter from Larry Page dated 16th June 1965 formally cancelling our management contract where he states he's done his best to promote us but says "I am sure you yourself realize that the group boom is on the wane". What nonsense. He goes on to add insult to injury by saying he would still like to record the group but that was never likely to happen as we disbanded after that fiasco and I was off to Norway, thanks very much.

Sylvie had a flat in the centre of Oslo and we spent the first couple of days walking around so I could familiarise myself with my new surroundings. First thing in the morning I would pop down to the bakers for fresh bread having learnt how to ask for it in my broken Norwegian. I never did learn the language and all I can say now is "I don't speak Norwegian" but as soon as I say that, they think I can. Quite confusing.

Shortly after arriving Sylvie told me The Vanguards were playing at a local dancehall and we should go to see them and meet them. Their first set was excellent and they had the very best equipment, guitars and amplifiers and I was most impressed. During the break a well-known presenter called Eric Heyerdahl hosted a version of "Juke Box Jury", getting a panel up from the audience to decide whether a record would be a Hit or Miss. While that was taking place on stage Sylvie and I went backstage to meet the group who all seemed delighted to see me and after all the usual chit chat and introductions they dropped a bombshell on me by asking what songs I'd like to sing with them. To say I was taken aback would be an understatement and I said maybe we should have a rehearsal before I sang with them. Then came bombshell number two as they told me the DJ had already announced that I had arrived from England and would be singing that very night. Talk about being put on the spot. They were so enthusiastic about this and showed me a huge list of all the songs they knew and asked me to pick out three to perform. I knew most of the songs and told them the keys I sang them in and we had a very curtailed run-through in the dressing room.

As we made our way back to the stage Sylvie told me that DJ Eric had given me the biggest build-up she'd ever heard with tales of association with Manchester, The Beatles, The Hollies, Herman's Hermits and Decca Records so it should have come as no surprise to me when I walked out on stage but nothing, absolutely nothing, could have prepared me for the tumultuous reception I got that night. There were hundreds gathered around the stage and during my second number things reached fever pitch with the girls screaming as I stood too close to the edge of the stage and before I knew what the hell was going on I was dragged off the stage as a near riot broke out. To say I was manhandled is putting it mildly as my tie disappeared, my shirt got torn and further loss was avoided as I managed to scramble back on stage with as much aplomb and dignity as I could muster. I had a laugh with the crowd and told them, with good humour, to behave themselves and finished my performance with an amazing feeling of euphoria which I had never felt before. It made me realise just how The Beatles and The Stones must have felt when it first started happening to them. Sylvie meanwhile had been photographing all this with great amusement safe in the knowledge that her hunch of me making an impression in Norway had paid off.

The Vanguards finished their set and came backstage where they congratulated me profusely and asked if I would sing with them again, which I happily agreed to, especially when they handed over part of their fee to pay for my contribution. I said it wasn't necessary but they insisted and gave me about fifty quid which is more than I could have earned in a week with The Yaks back in England. As we prepared to leave via the stage-door I was told there was a crowd waiting and asking for autographs which instantly put my head in a spin – what name was I going to sign? I'd always been part of a group and now I needed a stage name as a solo singer so very quickly came up with the name "Jeff Young" which I thought would be easily understood and not difficult to pronounce. Much easier than Geoff Mullin, anyway. The Vanguards were obviously earning really good money and their group transport was a large American Plymouth Belvedere with a trailer on the rear for the equipment. The downside was the enormous distances they had to cover to get to gigs in the more remote parts of the country. We arranged to meet up for a proper rehearsal and they said they would like me to appear with them as a guest star for a set length of about twenty minutes. This didn't seem like hard work to me and I was delighted to be involved with them and the prospect of earning some decent money for a change.

Things were going really well career-wise and my star was in the ascendant with Sylvie getting me lots of publicity in various magazines and newspapers, one of which involved a photo of me with Millie "My Boy Lollipop" Small in the flat teaching Millie how to play guitar. I still treasure that shot and remember Millie as a delightful, warm and friendly girl. She also sang with The Vanguards during that tour. When we finished our practise sessions most of us enjoyed a visit to the local bowling alley for a game of tenpin and we all became pretty good at it. Despite all the close contact and readily made companions I only managed to maintain one long-enduring friendship and that was with a local lad by the name of Henning Hverven who I met early on in a club we were playing called The Hit Cavern. Henning proved to be terrific company with his great sense of fun, excellent English and a local's knowledge of Oslo and surrounding areas. Little wonder we spent so much time together with me being a stranger in a strange land.

Having more or less decided that my future lay in Norway I decided to go back to England to get my affairs in order (not those affairs) and make preparations for living full time out of the country. Almost as soon as I get home there's a phone call from Lek saying "Help, we're in deep shit, we're minus a road manager, can you please help us out?" I say I can help out for a short time and Lek says it won't be for long as they're booked for a tour of the USA starting on 19th July. That's fine by me and I take them to various gigs including one date on the 16th at Kingsway studio for the recording of "Just A Little Bit Better", which makes the charts in September. Somewhat after the event Fab magazine runs a story on August 21st that I'm the new Hermits roadie, just a little too late. Pete Noone then decides he wants me to chauffeur him around in his new Jaguar saloon. I know this also won't last long so I agree and after the recording session we leave London late at night to drive back to his parent's house in the north. Pete wants to get home fast but falls asleep on the back seat and I push on along the M1 motorway eager to stay awake and get home as quickly as possible. Then Pete wakes up and looks over my shoulder at the speedo and says "Bloody hell Geoff, you're doing 125 miles an hour – slow down", which I do, until he falls asleep again and I boot it forward again. He wakes up again and goes mental at the speed we're doing and even though I tell him I'm tired and need to get back before I fall asleep at the wheel, he's still very annoyed with me. So annoyed, in fact, that when we finally get to his home he's very grumpy and hands me my wages saying "You're fired, goodbye", leaving me standing on the doorstep like a lemon. I get home on the early morning train with some sense of relief that my helping The Hermits is over.

That's the end of me and The Hermits for a while and I call Sylvie in Oslo who is interested in what's going on in Manchester. I tell her there's an upmarket club called Mr Smith's where many top acts are due to appear, including Adam Faith the very next night. She's very interested in this and asks me if I can go to the club and interview Adam for her and send my review over to her in the post. This is intriguing and so I agree to deputise as her UK journalist representative and make myself known to the club's manager who arranges for me to interview Adam backstage. Adam is very helpful and answers all the questions Sylvie has asked for, which she translates and adds a couple of photos for the article which appears a little later in a magazine, and I still have a copy. This contact allowed me unrestricted access to Mr Smith's where I also met Tommy Cooper and Matt Monro, both of whom came on stage to start their act with a newspaper in their hands. Tommy looked at the audience and began tearing his paper into pieces, never saying a word. After about five minutes of this nonsense the audience were in hysterics as he paced the stage ripping away until, finally, he did his funny cough and laugh saying "Ha-ha-ha-Happy Birthday" as he flung the shredded paper right into the audience, who were only a few feet away, cue more hysterics – a very intimate club it was. Afterwards he asked me what I thought of the show and I told him it was terrific and that he was the only person who could get away with that opening and he said "I know, it's funny isn't it". Matt was quite the opposite, although his act contained quite a lot of humour as he started out sitting on a stool reading out amusing snippets in the paper, obviously from a prepared script. He sang like a bird and he was a lovely man with whom I would work some years later as I produced sessions with him for Radio Two. Ron and I would go down to Mr Smith's together and he'd play the tables while I spoke to the stars and then we'd have a drink, his favourite at the time being lager and lime, which I only ever tried once, just straight lager for me, thank you. I think Ron did quite a lot of business there and he was well known around the club scene as supplier of "cars-for-the-stars".

Near-death experience number five, I think it was, (have you been counting?) happened as I was making my way to Tony Walmsley's house in the Mini for a music session. The weather that day was foul with strong winds and heavy downpours and I was pretty well the only car on Burnage Lane as I passed Reynold's Chains factory, and then it happened. In the battering rain I see a car in the distance on the other side of the road begin to move forward and, as I approach, it very suddenly does a U-turn just as I'm precisely level with it. This takes me completely by surprise and there's nothing I can do except to grip the steering wheel very hard as this car scores a direct sideswipe hit sending me onto the pavement and into a concrete lamp standard. People rush out of the house where this other car was parked and the lady driver comes over quite distraught saying "I'm really sorry, I didn't see you" while the others decide to call an ambulance as I'm a bit shell-shocked. I'm taken to Withington hospital for a check-up and as there are no bones broken and I seem to be compos mentis they declare me fit to go home. My dad came to pick me up saying the police would like my account of the accident and I laughed when I saw in their report that I had "demolished a Class B upright lamp standard", which sounded as if I'd eaten it. Once again, an insurance adjuster came to call telling me that the Mini was a write-off and that my claim for new clothes and a replacement record player that was in the car would be met in full. This was in a way a blessing in disguise as I now didn't need to worry about what to do with the Mini and I certainly didn't need a record player where I was going – result.

In August I returned to Norway and started again with both Sylvie and the Vanguards who were keen to rehearse and learn a new Beatles song which was destined for the number one slot in their charts. "Yesterday" was never released here as a single but it was hugely popular in Norway and always went down very well with audiences wherever we played. Another local group were also eager to have me join them on some dates and so I often sang with The Action during the latter part of 1965 and, apparently, according to Henning, with a group called The Jailbirds as well, although I have minimal recollection of that connection.

News from home arrived sporadically and on my birthday that September I heard that The Twisted Wheel had closed down in Brazenose Street and moved to new premises so that was the end of an era, too, as I never went to the new location. Life was good in Oslo and Henning was a regular companion especially when winter arrived and he took me skiing and taught me many tips about driving in the snow and ice, which could be murderous at times. I had great respect and admiration for the skills of Norwegian drivers under those adverse conditions, they'd all make great rally drivers. I was really glad of Henning's instruction and advice for winter driving when I found I was earning enough to hire a Mercedes 190 whenever I wanted. It didn't have studded tyres but it did come with snow chains which were vital on several occasions. Temperatures could fall to minus twenty degrees, daylight was as low as six hours a day and the further north we went on gigs the darker it got so it wasn't all fun and games by any means.

I'm not entirely sure of the timeline on my activities in December but Henning and I drove from Oslo to Stockholm in a clapped-out old van in terrible weather conditions to get to a concert starring Herman's Hermits and The Hollies at the Konserthuset venue. It took us all day to cover over 300 miles but we enjoyed the concert and meeting up with both groups later on at their hotel. It was an exhausting trip and I think we both slept for some considerable time when we got back home, but it was worth it.

That December also saw the arrival of Lek in Oslo for a short holiday break and as he'd brought his guitar along he played a couple of gigs with me and joined Henning and I on a major beer drinking session at the Hit Cavern. I don't think the locals had ever seen so much consumed by so few as we stacked the table with empty bottles. Lek and Henning got on famously and Lek was delighted when we went to the ski slopes at Holmenkollen and Henning taught Lek to ski.

At the end of the year the annual popularity poll named me as the winner of the male vocalist award with Wenche Myhre winning best female singer and the top-rated group were The Cool Cats. Again, there was good coverage in the press with photos and all that.

Christmas and New Year 1965 was celebrated Norwegian style with Sylvie and her family and all was going well until, that is, Tony Walmsley arrived on January 9th. Lek had obviously told him how good things were and as Tony was at a loose end he asked if he could come over and work with the bands. That was out of the question as far as The Vanguards were concerned but The Action were happy for him to join in but it wasn't long before things started to fall apart both with work and with Sylvie. I think she got fed up with me spending so much time with Tony and one day we came back to the flat to find she had moved into the spare room and had rapidly erected double bunk beds for me and Tony. The writing was on the wall from that moment and a combination of little work during the early months of the year and our failed attempts to start a soul band meant that we were running out of money and luck. The upshot of all this came when Sylvie kicked us out of the flat and we were on the streets with only the option of a hotel to sleep in. This might have been OK except for the fact that we were only allowed to stay a maximum of three days in any one inn and so there we were in the depths of a cruel winter wandering the streets of Oslo with our suitcases and Tony's guitar. We must have been a sorry sight and I said to Tony "It's time to call it a day, mate, and fly home" whereupon Tony told me he didn't have enough money for the flight. As it happened, I did have the money for both of us and so with a combination of relief and sorrow in equal measure we left Oslo in the early spring of 1966.

CHAPTER THIRTEEN

London Calling

Back home again in Blighty and there I was with no wheels and no sounds, how am I going to cope? Never fear, a rescue is near. Lounging around the house seemed quite pleasant for a while and potting a few balls with Ron Stratton at the Slade Lane snooker hall whiled away a couple of lazy afternoons but what about earning some dough, that was the big question. Then the call that I could never have anticipated came through. It was around 8 o'clock one morning when the phone rang and a warm Lancastrian voice said "Good morning, Geoff, I'm sorry to call so early, it's Lionel Morton here from the Four Pennies, we've got a bit of a problem". I said "What's that, Lionel?" and got almost exactly the same statement I got from Lek "We're in deep shit and minus a road manager, can you help us out please?" Lionel told me they were stranded in Dundee without transport as their roadie had up and left them, dumping all the equipment in the hotel foyer. I suppressed a small giggle at this and asked what was needed and he said they had a rental agreement with Hertz and if I went to their offices in town there would be a vehicle waiting for me. He would call them immediately to arrange the van pick-up and then would I please drive up to Dundee, all expenses paid plus a good fee, and rescue them as they had a gig that night. This sounded like a splendid adventure and I was definitely up for it. See what I mean – lucky, lucky, lucky.

The Hertz office opened at 9am and I was there shortly afterwards, signed the paperwork and took off for Scotland. As soon as I arrived at the hotel Lionel asked if I could help out as roadie for a few days and I said that was fine so we packed the van and took off for the next gig on their Scottish tour, which I think was at The Bridge of Allan, a pretty town in Stirling. All went well and the lads seemed very relaxed and easy-going and I was quite enjoying myself being in the company of these popular hit-makers and touring Scotland as I hadn't visited there before. After a few days the group called me in for a conflab with Lionel, Mike Wilsh the bass player, Fritz Fryer the guitarist and Alan Buck the drummer. I kind of knew what was coming and readily said "yes" when they asked me to take the job permanently. It was to be all expenses paid and a good weekly salary, so what's not to like with travelling all over the country, having no outgoings and meeting lots of pretty females? The fulfilment of any young man's dreams at the time, I should think. So, a few days as a dep roadie turned into almost a year and what a wonderful year it was working with the only group other than The Beatles ever to play at Glamis Castle, home The Queen Mother and childhood home of Queen Elizabeth ll. Mike Wilsh well remembers making friends there with the chauffeur Gerry Austin who was an RAF fighter pilot in the second world war.

The group were still based in Lancashire and my pick-up route was Burnley for Alan, Blackburn for Fritz and Chorley for Mike with Lionel joining from London where he was living with his wife, having married the actress Julia Foster the previous August. There were times when Lionel struggled to leave London to join the band, like the time we were booked to play Glasgow University and he cried off citing a bad cold. This news didn't arrive until we were all gathered together at Fritz's house and ready to set off which caused no little consternation with the lads who were keen to do the gig as they needed the money. The proverbial bolt came out of the blue as they agreed they would do the gig and that I would stand in for Lionel Morton. Naturally, I was in shock and said I didn't know their repertoire too well and they reassured me by saying "No problem, Alan can drive the van and we'll rehearse you on the journey and work out some of the songs that you do know". All went according to plan and we managed to put on a show with no questions asked, even to the extent of me signing autographs after the show. For the life of me, I can't remember what name I signed but I do know I got Lionel's fee that night as well as my roadie fee. That was a one-off and it never happened again, thank goodness. Apart from that, I am grateful to Lionel for saving me from a beating at the end of one club gig in the North. As I was carrying the gear down a passage by the side of the club this enormous Teddy Boy stopped me and growled "You've been eyeing up my girlfriend all night and I'm gonna teach you a lesson". I protested my innocence but he was enraged and would have none of it until Lionel came along and calmly said to him "If you lay a hand on him or touch a hair on his head we will take you to court and sue you for every penny you've got". Blimey. Well said Lionel. I was more than impressed as the Ted stood there completely flummoxed by this defence, and on thinking it over for a second or two, his confused brain led him to slope off in a sulk mumbling to himself incoherently. Thanks Lionel.

We travelled extensively around the UK from Torquay in Devon to Belfast in Northern Ireland to Kirkwall in the Orkney Islands where we played to a crowd from 8-to-80-year-olds, as if the whole town was there that night, reminding me of some of the more remote locations I had played in Norway. Breakfast the next morning was wholesome and delicious and I will always remember the exquisite taste of the local white butter. Yum, some things you never forget. The boys got to that gig and back by air but I had to ferry the gear across on a boat which went, I think, from Wick to Kirkwall and the sea was not kind in either direction but I did manage to keep my breakfast down on the return trip.

Time off in Manchester was spent mostly with Ron as Lek was often away on tour and Dave Lee Travis was floating in the North Sea on board the pirate radio ship the Mi Amigo. Lots of people often say "I was there when", when in fact they weren't, but I was there on the night of May 17 1966 when Bob Dylan played Manchester's Free Trade Hall, a date which has since gone down in history. I wasn't a big Dylan fan at that point and the first half I found a bit of a yawn with him playing acoustic guitar. The second half was what caused the furore when a bloke in the audience a few rows behind me was so incensed at Dylan playing an electric guitar he shouted out at the top of his voice "Judas". That has gone down in the annals of rock music as a seminal moment and I was there.

Next came one of the most important decisions in my life when The Pennies asked me if I would go with them to London as they had decided to re-locate there in the early summer because Lionel was based there as was their manager Harold Davidson, their accountants Watermans and their record company Philips. I thought about it for less than a minute and said "yes" and what was the deal. They said they would pay my rent, up to a reasonable amount and give me a substantial pay rise. I said "yes" again. Wouldn't you? When I spoke to Tony Walmsley about this he was already living in London and we agreed it would be good fun to share a flat together and so the hunt was on for a pad in The Smoke. Within no time at all we had found our perfect pad in a beautiful white stucco-fronted house in Queen's Grove, St John's Wood just about two minutes from the tube station. We had arrived in Swinging London.

We weren't the only ones to venture south as the Pennies publicist Bill Harry and his wife asked me to help move them lock stock and barrel to London in the summer of "66. Bill was a lovely guy with a strong Liverpool accent and one time uttered a sentence which went down in Pennies folklore and was often repeated when we needed a laugh, and this was it, remember the heavy accent, when he asked me to go and collect "Thirteen purple shirts from Jermyn Street". Still makes me laugh that, and if you're wondering why thirteen, it was three shirts each for the boys with one spare, makes sense doesn't it?

Swing was the thing back then and it led to my introduction to the BBC when we were booked for a session at Broadcasting House to record inserts for a programme called "Swing Into Summer" on the Light Programme. Dear old Auntie still had some power and influence but the pop music airwaves were increasingly dominated by the pirate radio stations. Still, a gig is a gig and any exposure was welcome. This session was produced by a man called Derek Mills who, and I could never have predicted this back then, became my executive producer when I joined Radio Two some years later.

Lionel and Julia were living in Knightsbridge, Fritz was in Muswell Hill and Mike Wilsh moved into the basement flat at 87 Westbourne Terrace with two Liverpudlians, Marie Gurun and Stevie Holley, John Lennon's girlfriend. To say some interesting visitors went to Number 87 would be to put it mildly. Living above was Simon Napier-Bell who was often visited by Dusty Springfield, John Lodge of the Moody Blues also resided in that house and his future bandmate Justin Hayward went out with Marie, whom he later married. I'd pick Mike up on our way to gigs and he'd be full of stories about the constant stream of visitors and activities going on in the flat, such as the night in late September or early October when John Lennon turned up and Mike played him the new Lovin" Spoonful album, remarking on John's nose peeling from sunburn which John tells Mike he got in Spain while filming "How I Won The War" with Michael Crawford. The rest of that night Mike, John and Justin sat around chatting, jamming and smoking. If only that had been recorded, eh?

Tony was working at Sound City music shop on Shaftesbury Avenue and so most days he was out of the flat, including Saturdays, and I spent a lot of time listening to music, which is how I came to make quite a silly mistake, in retrospect. I thought it would be a good idea if there were some way to have constant music playing in the flat and to that end I borrowed Fritz's Revox tape recorder and proceeded to copy all my records onto tape. This worked brilliantly and I deemed the vinyl discs to now be surplus to requirements and sold them to a record dealer for peanuts. Some of those discs are now extremely rare and change hands for a fortune – what an idiot, who knew. I do now.

That time in London was nothing less than exhilarating almost all the time with visits to clubs being pretty much a nightly occurrence. The grooviest places in town were Scotch of St James, Blaises, Phonograph, Flamingo, Marquee and the Cromwellian, which is where Tony and I met up with bandleader Chris Barber and his wife the singer Ottilie Patterson. We chatted in the club and left at the same time as Chris who said they were going home via St John's Wood and we could share their taxi. I asked them if they'd heard of an artist called Mose Allison, which they hadn't, and I was so enthusiastic about his music that they wanted to come back to our place and have a listen, which they did. We had coffee and put on a long-player by Mose and they sat there as transfixed as I was the first time I heard him. Chris had a great pair of ears and said

"He sounds a bit like Georgie Fame" and I said "I think it's the other way round, Chris", at which we all laughed and a very enjoyable evening came to an end.

So many great things happened after our arrival that summer of "66 and I'm trying to remember all the highlights after such a distance, but this was one of the lowlights, although not entirely unproductive. I was having difficulty swallowing, especially after eating something dry, like a biscuit, and having been told at Manchester Infirmary it was nothing, just to take an aspirin for it, I wanted a second opinion and made an appointment at the ENT hospital in Gray's Inn Road. I was seen by a great young doctor who immediately said he thought he knew what it was and sent me off to have a picture taken. The x-ray confirmed his diagnosis and I was booked in for surgery to remove a blocked saliva gland just below my jaw. The doc said he was going in through my mouth so as not to leave a visible scar and I would be in for a couple of days. That was when the upside became apparent in the form of a shapely blonde nurse who took extremely great care of me. Lying flat on my back in a helpless way as she looked after me I kind of fell in love with her, and she with me. We met about a week later and she came over to the flat in her free time and revealed to me for the first time what a "Brazilian" was, and it certainly wasn't a carnival nor a monetary unit, that's for sure. So, the hospital incarceration wasn't a waste of time in any way as I was suddenly out of pain and enjoying myself as a young man should. We lost touch, as was usual with girlfriends then, because of the constant touring with the Pennies which, coincidentally, led to me knowing three girlfriends at the same time with the same name - Ann Leslie – one in Scotland, one in Manchester and one in London. That's how the cookie crumbles sometimes.

The notable sporting event of the year happened that July as England hosted and won the football world cup for the first, and so far, only time. I watched as many matches as I could and Tony and I watched the final on our tele in the flat but we decided against going into the West End that night in order to avoid the drunken excesses of the euphoric England supporters, and there were plenty of them.

Our landlady was a lovely lady called Peggy who left us very much to ourselves until one day she asked if we could be very quiet one afternoon as she had a very special guest coming for an interview. That was when we found out she was a freelance journalist and her interviewee that day was the singer and actress Millicent Martin, famous for her appearances on the television shows That Was The Week That Was and her own show Mainly Millicent. We never met Miss Martin but Peggy thanked us for our protracted period of silence, never knowing that we went out that afternoon just to be on the safe side.

Even though I had a full-time job with the Pennies there was a fair amount of down-time which I spent trying to further my own career by networking with various people in the music business, one of whom was Larry Page who invited me to rehearse in a session at Olympic Studios with his group The Riot Squad. They were a terrific outfit and I would have been thrilled to work with them but it wasn't to be as their drummer Mitch Mitchell left to find fame and fortune with Jimi Hendrix. Another singer followed me into sessions with them and his name was David Bowie, wonder what became of him? There was an oblique contact with Hendrix via Tony who met him in Sound City not long after he arrived in England on Saturday September 24th. He went in saying Chas Chandler had sent him to get whatever equipment he needed and to put it on Chas's account. He asked Tony what was the most powerful amplifier he had and as Tony showed him the latest Marshall gear, Jimi got out his white Stratocaster, plugged in and let rip a chord which Tony said almost blew the windows out. Jimi seemed satisfied with this kit and asked where he might find somewhere to jam and Tony told him to look up the Brian Auger Trinity who were playing The Cromwellian that night, which he did. Jimi came on stage wearing black shirt and trousers, Cuban heel boots and a large silver cross on a chain and launched into the most raucous and ferocious version of "I'm A Man" which blew everybody away, including Auger's regular guitarist Vic Briggs, otherwise known as "The Doctor'. Backstage later Jimi chatted to Tony and complained to him about the rotten Reslo microphone. He did sit in with the band that night and contrary to other reports of his first gig in London, I'm inclined to agree with both Tony and Brian Auger that that was what happened, The Cromwellian being Jimi's first gig in England. Is that new info for the record books?

South African music mogul Frank Fenter was another contact I made during my perambulations of the record labels and publishers in town. He was looking after Chuck Berry's publishing company Jewel Music and became head of Atlantic Records in Europe. We spent quite some discussing many of the great soul, blues and r & b artists we both admired and then he asked me what my ambitions were and would I be prepared to become part of a boy/girl vocal duo act. This was a question so totally out of the blue that it took me a minute or two to digest the idea but eventually I said that was possible and who did he have in mind to pair me up with. He told me about a great girl soul singer called Sharon Tandy, a fellow South African, who might also be interested in a double act and he gave me her phone number and said to ring her the next day, after he had told her to expect my call. This was all heady stuff with some interesting possibilities which led to more questions from Frank. He asked if I had written any songs and was I a member of the Musicians Union. I told him no on both counts and then he gave me some invaluable advice, "Always try and write your own material because song-writing is where the money is in the long term, and do join the MU or better still try to get an Equity card, which is preferable if you want to do any film or television work". That was by far the most encouraging, positive and friendly meeting I could have wished for and I left his office very much on a high.

Two things to concentrate on then, meeting Sharon and getting a union card. I first applied to the British Actors Equity Union and they sent me the application form which I duly filled in stating that I would like to use the stage name James McShane, chosen for no particular reason other than I liked the sound of it. They wrote back and said my application would be approved due to my experience as a professional singer but that I could not use that stage name because there would be some confusion with another member who was working under the name of Ian McShane. I wonder what became of him? Finally, I settled on Jason James for my professional persona and that was accepted.

Sharon took my call the next day and invited me over to her flat in Earl's Court for a coffee and a chat. She played me some songs she had recorded on the Pye label and we discussed the kinds of music we liked for most of the afternoon. Then she asked me if I'd like to go to a gig with her that evening as she was singing with a group called Fleur de Lys. "Great idea", I say, as Sharon makes us a bite to eat and feeds her cat Offley – don't ask me why, she never said. She obviously had an accent and always pronounced my name as Joffrey, which was quite amusing. I was knocked out by her performance that evening and the band were on terrific form, so much so that I was more than ready to commit to working with her, and the band, an absolute no-brainer.

We agreed to find some songs we could duet on and got together again a few days later to work through them. We thought maybe we should try and write some material but first we had to get our voices working together so we ran through numbers like Inez and Charlie Foxx's "Mockingbird" and a couple of Jerry Butler and Betty Everett songs "Ain't That Loving You Baby" and "Let It Be Me" but the one we really liked best and which we both thought would be great to record was the little-known song "Baby Baby Baby" by Bobby Byrd and Anna King, a great American soul duo. We were both equally enthusiastic about this new partnership, and each other, which cemented our relationship but brought in a whole new dynamic when she told me she was married to Frank Fenter. Sharon told me not to worry about it as they were separated and, obviously, no longer living together but it always played on my mind after that revelation. Nevertheless, we carried on our affair and polished up our vocals with the intention of writing our own songs until one day Sharon mentioned that a girlfriend of hers was writing original material with her partner and that we should go and check if they had anything suitable for us. That was how I met the girl I was to marry four years later. Her name was Caroline Stephenson, a very beautiful girl, her partner was Peter Morris, a very good pianist, and we visited them in Brendon Street, a short distance from Marble Arch. They played a few items through for us and we said we'd think about them but after due consideration Sharon and I thought we would be

129

better off trying to write our own stuff, maybe with the help of some of her band.

Sharon and I dated for some months but time and distance separated us so much that by the end of the year our relationship had all but petered out. The last time I saw her was when she invited me to see her perform on the bill with the Stax/Volt Tour of Europe when it played at the Palace Theatre, Manchester. on 23 March. That was a sensational night and backstage after the show Sharon introduced me to Otis Redding, the sweatingest man I ever saw, who just said he hoped I'd enjoyed the show and then disappeared in a rush to cool down. It was after seeing Otis perform that I began to think that maybe I wasn't putting in enough effort on stage. They say James Brown was the hardest working man in show business but I say Otis at least ran him a very close second.

The Four Pennies knew nothing of my freelance activities and my work with them carried on as normal with me collecting my weekly wages and expenses from Watermans and checking into the Harold Davidson office from time to time to check on our work schedule. That was when I first met the great singer Kiki Dee as she also turned up for a meeting and we chatted in the office of Harold's assistant Liz Gardner, a great looking and very sophisticated young woman who somehow managed to rebuff all my efforts to seduce her, even after she cooked dinner for us in her flat.

One of the more interesting engagements for the band was to perform on the Queen Mary ocean-liner. I drove down to Southampton and loaded the gear onto the ship, but regrettably I was not booked to join them on the voyage, which at least gave me quite a lot of free time back in London. When they got back from that cruise it seemed the work in the theatres and ballrooms was drying up to be replaced by work in the cabaret clubs of the north east, mainly on the famous Bailey's circuit. It was well-paid and regular and a very easy ride for me as I only had to drive to the club, set up the gear for the week ahead and helm the sound desk and lighting for the evening performances. Days were spent in the local snooker halls or cinemas as we moved around playing exotically named venues such as La Dolce Vita in Newcastle, The Marimba in Middlesbrough, La Bamba in Darlington, Latino in

South Shields and the daddy of them all the Batley Variety Club in West Yorkshire. We usually stayed the week in theatrical diggings, a form of accommodation well-known to peripatetic performers since the time of the wandering minstrel, touring troupes, vaudevillians, big bands, assorted comedians and entertainers and now it was our turn. These bed and breakfast premises comprised entirely of show-biz types and you never knew who you might meet there. One morning I came down for breakfast and sitting at the table was Frankie Howerd, one of my favourite comedians, who was appearing at a club called Tito's in Stockton. We got chatting or, to put it more accurately, I got chatted up when Frankie said he fancied a game of tennis and did I play. I said I did and he invited me to join him for a game. When I said I didn't have a racquet, shorts or shoes he said "No problem, Geoffrey, I've got a spare racquet and I'm sure I've got a pair of shorts in my room that will fit you if you'd like to come and try them on?" I knew exactly what he was after and he wasn't going to get it from me, so with as good grace as I could muster, I politely turned him down. What a naughty boy he was, that Frankie.

In the early autumn of 1966, the Pennies did one of their last recording sessions at Philips studios in Stanhope Place, laying down the tracks for a Tom Springfield composition "No Sad Songs For Me" and "Keep The Freeway Open". The usual form was to go in and see A & R man Dave Carey to discuss what to record and play him any demos or records they wanted him to hear. Dave had been a singer with the popular 1950's vocal group The Stargazers and hadn't really moved on to the 1960's with any great enthusiasm for the modern sounds. It became a standing joke every time we went into his office that he couldn't work the record player and he'd always ask the same question in his deep baritone voice "You know how to work that thing?" The group were really struggling to find or write good new material when I suggested they listen to a song from the latest Everly Brothers LP "In Our Image". They said to bring it along for Dave's evaluation and opinion, although I thought they should have made their own mind up about it, but still I took it in to Dave's office along with the boys. The song I thought absolutely perfect for them was a ballad entitled "It's All Over" written by Don Everly and although I think the group were enthused Dave Carey thought it would be better for them to record "No Sad Songs" even though it had already been recorded by The Springfields and The Walker Brothers with no discernible success. Still, what did I know, I was only the road manager but it did leave me with a lasting impression that I could spot a good song when six months later Cliff Richard had a top ten hit with it. Ha.

Near-death events numbers six and seven both happened during my time with The Four Pennies. On a late-night journey back to Manchester I was alone in the Transit van on the first section of the M1 motorway, which was unlit at the time, when the electrics failed and all the lights on the vehicle went out. For a few seconds I was driving blind then I hit the central reservation, which was a help as I managed to scrape along it while braking the van to a halt. Luckily, there was nothing coming up behind me so I was able to edge my way across to the hard shoulder where I sat in a bit of a shocked state reflecting on what had just happened. There was nothing I could do to get the lights back on so I waited for a large lorry to pass, pulled out behind and followed it to the next service station where the AA patrolman was able to repair the fault. A heart-pounding escape to say the least. Event number seven I remember very little about as I reached down for a plug on the stage floor and the next thing I knew I was on my back on the other side of the stage wondering how the hell I got there. I was told I'd had an electric shock that threw me across the stage and people were very relieved that I was alive and well. So was I.

The last major gig of note apart from the cabaret clubs was at Sheffield University in October when the Pennies were headlining and the support group was Cream. Of all possible acts to be sharing the bill with there could not have been a starker juxtaposition. I watched with interest and admiration as Cream's gear arrived and was set up on the stage, such a contrast to our amps and speakers, which were puny by comparison. I knew I would have plenty of time to erect our gear after Cream finished their set when Alan Buck came from backstage to tell me there was the mother and father of a row going on between the groups and could I go and help sort it out because Cream were refusing to go on first. In the dressing room Ginger Baker had lost his rag and shouted "These bloody students haven't come to see you lot, they've come to see us and apart from which you really don't want to be following us because the bloody audience will be deaf". Eric Clapton added his voice to this and in an effort to diffuse the situation said "Ginger may be right because we didn't know you guys were going to be on the same bill with us and we are very loud". Jack Bruce simply suggested, if we didn't think Ginger was right, that I go out into the ever-increasing crowd and ask a few punters who they'd come to see, which was quite a sensible idea. I didn't need to go and do a survey as, seemingly, this last remark had a transformative effect as the Pennies realised they were on a hiding to nothing and made the sensible decision to go on first and have an early night. In retrospect this was certainly the correct conclusion as the Pennies were accorded polite applause before Cream came on and took the place apart to a rapturous reception. They were bloody brilliant.

The early part of 1967 saw very little activity for the group until an offer came in for them to appear in a series of concerts in Istanbul because they had a hit record there with "A Place Where No One Goes". Everyone was excited about this trip to Turkey with visions of camels, sand dunes, sunshine and possibly exotic belly dancers. Preparations were made and packing included swimming trunks and sunglasses in anticipation of this rare visit to a mysterious and fascinating foreign land.

What a shock we got when we landed in Istanbul. It was snowing. We hadn't bothered to check the local weather patterns for February and as we walked through the airport in some bewilderment, we became very aware of the boob we'd made as we passed poster after poster advertising ski resorts. Some mistake. We were picked up and taken to the top-rated Istanbul Hilton and set about adjusting our expectations after our hopes of sun, sand and sex were dashed. I said I quite fancied going to the ski slopes on one of our days off and Alan Buck said he'd come and have a go even though he'd never been on skis before. There were only two official daytime engagements, both with Philips Records executives, and both very interesting. The day after we arrived we were taken to a wonderful cliff-top restaurant overlooking The Bosphorus Straits for our first taste of delicious Turkish food which we all enjoyed very much. The day after that we were booked into Philips studio to record a Turkish language version of their recent hit song. The lyrics for Lionel Morton were written down phonetically and there seemed to be general agreement that he did a fine job. The concerts were to be at the Vitesh Theatre in the city centre and we were sharing the bill with the German group Los Bravos who had a hit there with "Black Is Black". These performances were well-received and generally regarded as a big success.

Alan and I made our plans to go skiing which meant a flight from the European side to the Asian side of Turkey to a resort in the mountains which had been constructed by the American troops stationed there. We needed some local currency for the trip and the car park attendant told me he could give us a better rate than we would get at the hotel or the bank, and he did. When I asked him how this was possible, he let me into a secret regarding the eventual destination for any dollars or sterling that was exchanged on the black market. It all went through the Balkans and eventually to the USSR who paid over the odds to build up their reserves of foreign cash. Crikey, what a revelation. From landing at a small airport, we had a hair-raising taxi ride up the mountain and on getting to the top were told that we should hurry as the resort would be closing earlier than usual because reports of bad weather were coming in. Great, just what we needed. We managed a few runs and Alan got the hang of it enough to enjoy it but we were soon back in a taxi going down again. At the airport we got the news that our return flight was cancelled because of the weather and we would have to get a ferry back across to the other side. Panic set in at this news because it might well be that we wouldn't make it to the gig on time. We almost pushed that boat across the Bosphorus, willing it to go faster and we did make it but with very little time to spare. Alan and I agreed it had been a very exhilarating day, though perhaps not as much as it had been for Fritz and Lionel who had, apparently, got quite squiffy trying out the local version of cigarettes, if you get my meaning.

CHAPTER FOURTEEN
London Calling Again

The Four Pennies era ended after the Turkish trip and I decided to go back to Manchester to stay with my new girlfriend Pauline, who I met on a night out with Mike Wilsh at Le Phonographe Club just off Deansgate. She was a hair stylist and we shacked up together in a flat on Wilmslow Road we rented from Jack Jackson, which I mentioned a while back if you were paying attention. It was here that I had time to gather my thoughts, think about the future and get down to writing some songs. The first thing I laid down was "Count Me Out", which I thought would be good for Tom Jones, which led me to his publicist Chris Hutchins who invited me down to London for a meeting. Chris then told me he had struck a deal to produce some of his artists for CBS Records and said he would like to produce me if I was interested. Naturally I said I was but what about getting the song to Tom. Chris said to leave it to him and he would arrange it but that we should do a better demo of it as well. He put me in touch with a great arranger called Len Beadle and I had a session with him to run through a few songs so he could gauge my vocal range for a recording session. He also asked if I could write another song to be recorded at the same time as he would have a studio full of musicians and wanted to use up all of the studio time. Nothing wasted with Len, who had tremendous music business experience both as a musician, publisher and singer with the popular vocal group the Raindrops, which included Vince Hill, Les Vandyke and Len's wife Jackie Lee, remember "White Horses" and "Rupert"? Len also asked if I would agree to demo another song for him, which was fine by me, and the song he gave me to learn was a Mitch Murray/Peter Callander composition called "Love, You Don't Know What It Means".

Things were certainly looking up as I went back home with new song ideas whirling around in my head and within a day or two I had come up with a couple of very different themes to play to Chris and Len. The first was again a soul-type song, "Easy Kind Of Love" and the other a novelty item, "Miss Pilkington's Maid", which I thought might fit the bill for the recording session to come. All was arranged for a date at the famous and fabulous Lansdowne studios in Holland Park and when I got there I was quite nervous but at the same time energised when I saw the musicians in attendance. Among the cream of London session players were Clem Cattini on drums, Vic Flick on guitar, Arthur Greenslade on organ with The Ladybirds on backing vocals. Len had done a quite amazing job on booking these top players and I really wasn't expecting such a terrific line-up in the brass section so it was no wonder they got it down in double quick time and it seemed to go by in a flash for me as well. We got three tracks done that night, all the above except "Easy Kind Of Love" which Chris said he was holding in reserve as he had an idea about what to do with that song. It turned out that he had signed a girl singer called Mary McCarthy and he wanted the song for her, which is how it appeared on the "B" side of her CBS single "Happy Days And Lonely Nights", now a rare and valuable 45. I was at that session and was extremely impressed by Mary's performance even though I never had a chance to record it myself, which is a little bizarre.

Shortly after the recording of my three tracks Chris told me that CBS were keen to release "Count Me Out" but only as the "B" side with "Miss Pilkington's Maid" as the "A" side, and that song, dear reader, is now regarded as a 60's pop-psych classic, whatever that means. I guess Sir Tom never got to hear "Count Me Out" but I did get a cover version of it when Polydor released it by Kevin "King" Lear who was managed by Larry Page, of all people, would you believe. The third song from that session was also recorded by Paul and Barry Ryan on their album "Hey Mr Ryan" and I wonder if they ever heard my version. My first, and last, solo disc was released on 21 April 1967 under the name Jason James and Chris got to work on the publicity angle, at which he was a master craftsman. I signed as a writer with Lawrence Wright publishing and with top agency Maurice King and Barry Clayman, who also looked after the Walker Brothers. Chris introduced me to several journalists to help with record reviews, and one afternoon took me along to the London Palladium to meet another of his clients, Engelbert Humperdinck. We arrived at the star dressing room just as Enge was coming out of the rest room and into the main dressing area. We shook hands and started chatting about the business and stuff and what a great guy Chris was when out of the small room came a gorgeous-looking female who just swished by smiling, gave Mr Hump a kiss and disappeared. Whoever that lady was, Chris never said. Just a few months later Engelbert would score his second Number One record with "The Last Waltz", written by Les Reed and Barry Mason, which led to Barry self-deprecatingly telling a very funny, inside show-biz type story against himself. Apparently, Barry went into a loo where a plumber was working and whistling the tune of his big hit "The Last Waltz". Barry was very pleased with himself and said to the plumber "I wrote that song", provoking the fierce response "Oh no you didn't". Barry was shocked by this reaction and repeated "Yes, I did write it" but the plumber was having none of it and said "Oh no you didn't, Les Reed wrote that song" and Barry said "True, but I wrote the lyrics". Then came one of the best-ever put-down lines of all-time as the plumber put Barry right with the ultimate riposte "Yeah, maybe you did, mate, but I'm not whistling the effing lyrics, am I?" End of story. Barry told that story many times over the years – he loved it.

Career opportunities seemed to be very London-centric and a return to The Smoke seemed like my best bet but what about Pauline? She thought it was a good idea and said she'd come with me to see how things worked out as there were no deep connections to keep her in Manchester. We packed our bags and set off to find our new home, which we magically found on day one. A ground floor flat on the Edgeware Road near Regent's Park Canal in Little Venice, which was just perfect as the rent was acceptable, the landlady lived above and she only rented to couples, so we were in. The next thing was for both of us to find jobs as we had very little by way of savings and to see how my singing career progressed. Well, it didn't, due to nobody's fault particularly, and "Miss

Pilkington's Maid" was consigned to obscurity along with my hopes for stardom. Was I bothered? Not a bit, I had never been driven by any desperate ambition to succeed, and that's probably why I never did. Life had always been relatively comfortable and kind to me and I was forever optimistic that things would work out OK. Apart from which I wasn't prepared for the long slog and deprivation that might be required to achieve the heady heights of fame. It don't come easy. Time to go to work.

Pauline quickly found a job at one of the top hair salons in Regent Street and I started working for the S.O.S. Employment Agency at Oxford Circus, which brought in a decent living wage for the pair of us. Everything was working out fine and I was achieving good results for placing young ladies in suitable positions – don't go there. This involved a parrot-like repetition of a standard welcome address which always started like this "Hello, you've done the right thing coming to the S.O.S. Bureau", then some guff about how good we were etc, etc, followed by testing their shorthand/typing skills. Then, and only then, were we to ask what type of job they were looking for and after their reply we would look into our card index box of employers looking to hire staff which might suit them. I did quite well at this but after a couple of months I knew I didn't want to do it forever, although there was one really heart-warming episode that has always stayed with me, and it was this. One afternoon a black gentleman came in and was directed to my desk as I was the next free agent. It was unusual for men to come in looking for employment and he told me he was at the end of his tether because he couldn't find work and could I help him. I dispensed with the usual opening gambits and went straight to the point of asking him what his skills were and what kind of work experience did he have. He told me he was a qualified book-keeper with a good work record and by a somewhat unlikely coincidence, when I looked in the files there was a position for a book-keeper at Selfridges store in Oxford Street. I asked him if he would like me to call them and arrange an interview, which he did, and I did, and off he went with a spring in his step and a very warm thank you to me. That might have been the end of it except that the very next day he turned up in the office again, this time with his wife, handed me a box of chocolates and said, with a huge smile on his face, "I got the job and I can't thank you enough for your kindness to me and my family, please accept this small gift from us". Well, it near took my breath away and I can still feel a tear welling up when I think back on that day. There are some things money can't buy and that was one of them.

That summer in London was idyllic and we were beginning to make friends, me with my office buddy John Finneran and Pauline found a female pal who invited us over to Knightsbridge to visit her and her boyfriend. That started a few weeks of the most enjoyable, strange, exotic and almost unbelievable lifestyle you can imagine. The flat we went to was the penthouse and the most opulent domestic place I had ever been to because the boyfriend was an enormously wealthy man from the middle east who spared no expense having a good time. I watched awestruck as he spent dazzling amounts of money on presents for his girlfriend and her friends, including us. Every day fresh flowers and fruit would arrive from Harrods, there was a limousine parked outside on twenty-four-hour duty and every night he would take us out for a meal and a show at a nightclub. Talk about living the high life, this was it. It seemed that everywhere we went, exotic Lebanese restaurants with belly dancers, night clubs like Churchill's on Bond Street where it was the best table and champagne all night, every door was open to us. This may have had something to do with the fact that every person who opened a door or directed us to a table would receive a high denomination banknote. How the other half live, eh?

Nothing lasts forever and by the end of that summer I realised I had made a mistake in bringing Pauline to London as it began to dawn on me that I knew almost nothing about this girl who seemed somewhat reluctant to discuss her family background and life before she met me. I don't believe I ever knew her real name or even how old she was but the fact was that I couldn't see me settling down with her. We had a heart to heart about it and decided to split up with Pauline moving out of the flat to go and stay with a friend and shortly after that my office pal John Finneran moved in to share the flat with me. That worked out well as John and I shared a love of pop music and every morning we listened to the Tony Blackburn

Breakfast Show on the newly launched Radio 1, then we'd head off for a game of tennis on the courts at Regent's Park before setting off for work.

Here's where chance comes into the equation to change my life and career once again with another meeting out of the blue. One day after work at the S.O.S. Bureau I was waiting for a tube at Oxford Circus when a I heard a most mellifluous voice next to me say "Weren't you in The Yaks?", which is not a question I'd ever encountered before. I turned to face the voice, which belonged to a well-dressed gent carrying a briefcase and a brolly who held out his hand and introduced himself as Mike Hawgood. He seemed only vaguely familiar and noting my hesitancy instantly volunteered the information that he had been at Decca Records when "Yakety Yak" was released and had been part of the team who arranged the photo session and publicity material. He asked about my singing career and what I was doing just now so I told him about CBS records and my stalled attempt at stardom, at which he smiled gently and invited me to lunch the next day to listen to a proposal that might interest me.

Lunch was quite a revelation as Mike told me he was now the Advertising Manager for the music trade press paper Record Retailer, part of the American Billboard magazine group where things were so busy that he was in need of an assistant and would I be interested in seeing the music business from the other side of the fence, so to speak. It didn't take me more than a split second to show my interest as Mike outlined the job description, the salary and commission available plus quite a lot of fun being on the inside, as it were. The next thing would be an interview with the managing director Andre De Vekey at their offices in Welbeck Street, which was arranged for the following day. Andre rubber-stamped my appointment to start me off on an illuminating, entertaining and enjoyable three-year stint which began in the autumn of 1967. Goodbye to the lovely ladies of the S.O.S. Bureau and hello music press.

My work in sales mostly involved meeting the marketing executives of all the major record labels helping them plan their forthcoming releases. I never had to give anybody the hard sell, it wasn't necessary as Record Retailer began to grow in such a way as to be indispensable to the record industry. It helped, I suppose, that we printed the official Top 50 Chart which went on display in all the record outlets across the country but the compilation of that chart could occasionally be a bone of contention in some quarters when an artist, agent, manager or record label disputed their chart placing, or lack of it. Such was the case when one day I came out of my office to hear the most almighty row going on in the publisher Julian Ormond's office as a throaty female voice was haranguing him using the foulest language you ever heard – expletives not deleted. Turns out it was the singer Dorothy Squires complaining vociferously that her latest single "For Once In My Life" wasn't in the chart and she knew for certain that it had sold enough to be in the Top 40 at least. Julian explained that the data for the charts was not, and could not, be manipulated as they were compiled from the sales figures we received. This didn't pacify Ms Squires who ranted on for some time before being, almost physically, escorted from the building before she burst into flames.

The big-spending record labels then were EMI, Decca, Philips, Polydor and Pye and it was fascinating for me to visit these companies and hear about their planned releases, especially the really important ones like The Beatles, whose offices, I think I remember correctly, were in Wigmore Street just around the corner. from Welbeck Street, so very handy. There were some amazingly colourful characters everywhere in the business, none more so than some of those running independent labels, like Phil Solomon at Major Minor, David Betteridge at Island and the big boss man at Ember Records, Jeffrey Kruger, a one-time jazz pianist, film producer, artist manager, tour promoter and owner of the famous Flamingo Club in Soho. He had a finger in so many pies and I was pleased he spent so much of his advertising budget with me. I particularly liked the title of his autobiography "Angels And Arseholes My Life With The Stars". Never a truer word.

As I made my weekly way round the various advertising departments there was one I really looked forward to and that was meeting Neville Skrimshire at EMI Records in Manchester Square. The reason for this was a bit of a game we used to play regarding which records would become hits. Neville would show me a list of forthcoming releases and without me having heard them would ask me to predict which of them would be successful. With nothing to go on other than the artist's name and the song title I would perform the equivalent of blindly pinning the tail on a donkey. What surprised both of us was that I managed to correctly identify the hits about 80% of the time, which led Neville to jokingly suggest that maybe they should employ me as a consultant and save a fortune by not recording any artists or songs on my "miss" list. Lovely guy, Neville.

Fun all the way was the order of the day as I was given promotion copies of new records and invited to various films, concerts and events, for some of which I submitted reviews to the editor for his approval. Before that could happen I had to become a member of the National Union of Journalists and after my application was endorsed I covered Tim Hardin, supported by Family, at the Royal Albert Hall (Family excellent Tim Hardin not so much), The Peddlers, Lou Rawls and Ted Heath, also at the RAH, Tex Ritter at the Palladium plus various record reviews over the next three years. One of my first ever journalistic commissions for Record Retailer involved a return to Manchester and the Free Trade Hall one more time in May '68 to review The Johnny Cash Show with support acts Carl Perkins and June Carter. It was a great concert and I covered it in depth to such an extent that it was spread over almost half a page of the paper with the banner headline "Country Means Cash". Neat, eh?

On the sales side my routine was to ensure all the advertising copy and artwork arrived in my office by Friday afternoon and when all was present and correct I would wrap it up and take it to Euston station to go by Red Star parcel service on the seven o'clock train to Peterborough for collection by our printer. On Monday morning I would meet my new colleague Paul Phillips at Euston for the 9 o'clock train where we had just enough time for breakfast before we got to Peterborough. Paul was the sub-editor responsible for proof-reading the editorial content and I checked all the ads during a morning session after which we went back to the station for lunch, which more often than not was a fillet steak accompanied by a bottle of Nuits St George, Paul's favourite, although he didn't look old enough to be drinking alcohol. There was a final check in the afternoon before we left for London and the paper was put to bed for printing and publication the next day.

Not long after I started at Record Retailer my flatmate John told me he was setting up home with his girlfriend whom he intended to marry and gave me notice to quit. This could have been a problem but once again I teamed up with Tony Walmsley who was looking for a place in town as he was now the road manager for The Peddlers who had just scored a residency at The Pickwick Club in Gt Newport Street. That club became the epicentre of our nightly entertainment as it was one of the most "in" places to see and be seen and where a whole host of stars came to dine and be entertained. At any one time you might be in the presence of Frank Sinatra, Mel Torme, Michael Caine, who mentions the club in his excellent autobiography "What's It All About", Sarah Vaughan, who came in straight from her gig at Ronnie Scott's Club, and hellraisers like Oliver Reed and Richard Harris. There was great excitement the night The Peddlers performance was recorded and released by Philips as "The Peddlers Live At The Pickwick". Can you hear me clapping? It was also the night I first met David Jacobs, a smashing bloke I was to work with in later years.

Without a doubt my most memorable night there was spent in the company of another major hell-raiser, Lee Marvin, who came in looking very tanned and wearing all-white with his favoured polo-neck sweater. He sat down at the table next to me and eventually asked if he could buy a round of drinks, which was most friendly and acceptable, which led to a reciprocal offer, which led to an invitation to join him at his table. Lee asked me what I did and I said I was a friend of the band and shared a flat with Tony, their road manager, and that I had been on the road a lot myself. I said the music world was mostly a night-time occupation which meant lots of free time during the day which we filled playing snooker or going to the movies. Because of this I had seen some of his recent films and that the drunk sequence in "Cat Ballou" had me falling about laughing to which he said "Yeah, how about that, getting out-acted by a horse. That damn horse shoulda got the Oscar not me" We talked a lot about films and he said his next movie was called "The Dirty Dozen" which had been filmed in England with a pretty impressive cast and we should go and see it. I said again how much I enjoyed going to the movies and had seen him in "The Killers" with another great actor John Cassavetes but that it was Angie Dickinson I had fallen in love with and Lee said "I can understand that, she's quite sensational", which made me wonder if he had, or he hadn't, but I was afraid to ask. I made him laugh when I asked him why he hadn't got up to do the Fandango dance in "Ship Of Fools" and his response was "I can't do that kind of stuff". We carried on drinking some kind of bourbon whiskey until I had to slow down, there was no way I could hold my own with this professional drinker, and by the end of the night Lee was totally smashed and so legless I had to help him up the stairs with a shove from behind, which wasn't easy as he was bigger than me. We were both slurring and blurring as we hailed a cab for Lee and I poured him into it and told the driver to take him back to his hotel which I think was Claridge's or the Connaught. That, most decidedly, was a blurry, blurry night.

The Peddlers original manager in Manchester was Alan Lewis, who also managed The Four Pennies. He was succeeded by Joe Collins, Joan and Jackie Collins' father, with whom I would enjoy an occasional salt beef sandwich some years later. Their last manager, I believe, was the owner of The Pickwick Club, one Cyril Smith, not to be confused with the disgraced Liberal MP for Rochdale. This Cyril was a smooth and smart operator and his girlfriend was the actress Yootha Joyce who found fame in the 1970's sit-com "George and Mildred". Cyril ran a tight ship and wouldn't stand for any trouble, which sometimes reared its ugly head because of the club's popularity and success in attracting the great and the good through its doors. It was also frequented by, and of interest to, gangsters with guns from the London Underworld, although I never saw The Krays or The Richardsons in there, I'm glad to say. Why the Underworld, I used to ponder, could it be to do with Orpheus and Hades or was it something to do with the tube network?

There were many other great nights at the club, one of which was when Paddy, Klaus and Gibson played and Beryl Marsden made a guest appearance, with George Harrison in the audience. After the gig George invited us to the Phonograph club and we clambered into the group's rickety old van and headed for George's favourite table where he said "The drinks are on me, just put whatever you like on my tab" and so it was rum and coke for the rest of the night, how generous. I asked George if he remembered the party at my flat in Manchester in 1962 and he mumbled something about so much happening since then it was all a bit of a blur. I reminded him that Pete MacLaine and Wayne Fontana were there as well as two pals who would later join Herman's Hermits. George said "Who were they, then?" and I told him it was Lek, the lead guitarist and Barry the drummer, which surprised him quite a lot. I also said he didn't appear to have much trouble finding female companionship on the night as several of the girls from the Oasis were at the party. A faint glimmer of memory crossed his face and he said "It's been crazy since those early days and now we can't go anywhere without attracting loads of girls who just want a kiss and a cuddle and sometimes more". I accepted George getting the drinks in as payment for his share of the Beatles condom consignment.

The club scene during the late sixties was so vibrant with so much music and so many venues there was never a night with nowhere to go. Listing all the clubs would take up way too much room here but my favourite haunts were the two above, the Cromwellian, Ronnie Scott's, the Revolution and best of all Scotch of St James, where the great Bobcats were the house band, with regular shows by the vastly under-rated Gene Latter and The Gas. If you were around that scene then you would likely have witnessed the sensational Ike and Tina Turner Revue, without question the best of them all that I ever saw.

The first few months of the year at work found me really getting to grips with the job after my early steep learning curve and I was getting much more familiar with the record labels and their geographical locations in and around London. Flower power seemed to be on the wane but The Beatles livened things up with their Apple Boutique on Baker Street where I would meet with the terrible trio of Derek Taylor, Terry Doran and Jackie Oliver to discuss the next advertising campaign. They weren't terrible at all, very friendly in fact, and their office above the shop was impressive as every single item in it was pure white. The Apple activity was to continue unabated for the next two years and I was pleased to be part of parting them from their money. More about The Fab Four later.

Location-wise my flat was well-nigh perfect with easy access to the West End and work, a nice little Italian restaurant a few doors away and a well-stocked deli directly opposite. That was my go-to place every Saturday morning where I picked up a fresh white loaf and a large chunk of Jarlsberg cheese for breakfast, washed down with several mugs of coffee. There was a newsagents shop close by and one Saturday in late March I went in to get a paper and a cheeky little lad about ten years old behind the counter asked me if I was putting a bet on and checking the runners and riders for The Grand National. I said I wasn't really interested and he said "Oh, I am", which made me laugh but then he said "No, I'm serious, I'm putting something on a horse called Red Alligator because red is my favourite colour and I always back anything with red in the name". Blow me down, I should have listened to him because that nag came in first, and by a strange coincidence it was ridden by Brian Fletcher who also rode Red Rum to victory in 1973 and 1974. He probably made a fair profit on that horse, too, and I'll tell you more about my acquaintance with "Rummy" later on.

Early that summer I hired a Triumph Vitesse convertible and took off for a camping holiday in Spain with a new girlfriend. We took the ferry from Dover to Calais and drove through France towards Biarritz then on to Bilbao and Santander to our final destination San Vicente de la Barquera. Weather conditions were perfect, the scenery sensational, especially the Picos mountain range and all things considered it could not have been more enjoyable. When we got back we parked the car outside my flat and went to bed exhausted after the long drive. Big mistake. I didn't put the hood back up on the car and overnight it poured down. The car was soaked and it took me a couple of hours with a sponge to try to dry it out, must have been gallons in there, and it was due back that same day. I did the best I could and delivered it back to the garage and the guy asked about the trip and had the car behaved itself, the usual questions, but I couldn't wait to get out of there. I got back home with great relief and the phone rang, it was the proprietor of the garage and he asked me a classic question, he said "Did you bring the car back on the ferry or did you drive it along the sea bed?" I let out a sort of guilty laugh and asked if there was a problem and he said the car was dripping wet and would take a couple of days to dry out. I expressed surprise and denied all knowledge regarding the state of the vehicle, at which he sort of chuckled and said next time I rented a car could I please go somewhere else. My relationship with the girlfriend took a nosedive after that trip but there is a quite amazing coda that I'll tell you about later, if you're still here.

Billboard Publications had many titles under its umbrella including Hi-Fi News, Colour Photography and one for the vending machine industry, appropriately called Vend. I knew very little about this magazine and was somewhat taken aback when, in June, I was tasked with taking a sales tour of Europe to visit all the major vending machine manufacturers. First stop on my itinerary was Siemens German factory in Bingen Am Rhein, if memory serves, where I received an extremely warm welcome possibly due to my ability to speak the language. There was a tour of the facilities followed by a delicious lunch where I enjoyed my favourite dish, schnitzel with roast potatoes and a glass or two of the famous local white wine. I never knew if my visit encouraged them to place any ads in the magazine as I got no feedback whatsoever from head office in New York. Other than the time I spent at Siemens the only other memory of that trip happened in Amsterdam, where Mike Hawgood had said I absolutely must take a look at the marvellous Krasnapolsky Hotel because there were palm trees growing out of the ceiling – what? Well, he was right, it was an amazing sight but nothing compared to the night of June the 8th when I was invited to a television recording of Nina Simone in concert. There were drinks and handshakes beforehand and I was introduced to the diva as Billboard's man in London. This, I think, led her to believe I was a journalist and although she was a little cool at first, she warmed when I told her I had become a big fan of Lou Rawls after covering his concert at the Albert Hall. She pondered the fact that I was impressed by a black singer and then asked "And do you like black women singers?" At this, and don't ask me how or why, because my mouth sometimes says things before my brain engages, my response was "Well, I like the ones I've slept with". Nina's face went blank, her eyebrows raised and then she let out a roar of a laugh and said "Hey, Billboard, you're alright, maybe I'll see you in London" and with that she went off to get ready to perform. I've seen footage of that concert and sure enough, there I am standing at the top of a staircase above the stage. What a night.

By this time I had given up all thoughts of a singing career or even song-writing, but that all changed when Lek and Keith Hopwood came round for a visit and brought their guitars with them. They had decided they wanted to record some of their own material for "B" sides and album tracks even though Mickie Most insisted on selecting all the "A" sides. They asked if I would help them get a few ideas together and so we spent the whole evening and on into the wee small hours collaborating on three songs. We completed them that same night and the boys left satisfied that they had something they could present to publisher Mike Collier at Campbell Connelly Music. Mike was a great promoter and placed "Understand A Woman" with Kippington Lodge, a group he was recording and Mickie Most was happy to put "Nobody Needs To Know" on the "B" side of "Sunshine Girl". The third song, "Sultan's Daughter", Mike was unable to place with a major label but I reckon two out of three ain't bad. I was in the studio for The Hermits recording which went into the charts in July, peaking at number 8, my one and only chart success. I still get a royalty payment for that song of about £4 a year. Lek and I were at the Abbey Road studios in June for the Kippington Lodge session and as they seemed to be struggling a little with the intro I suggested a bass line to Nick Lowe. Imagine, me telling Nick Lowe what to play. Oh, the shame. Those three songs bear the writing credits Leckenby, Hopwood, Brook, which was my pen name after the heroic character Roger Brook in the Dennis Wheatley series set during the French Revolution. I also pinched his book title for the "Sultan's Daughter" song with unashamed plagiarism because I was such a fan of those novels. I have no idea now why I took on a pen name rather than use my own name unless it was a ploy to evade the attentions of the tax man.

Flushed with success from my song-writing exploits I fancied trying my hand at record production and with this in mind I recruited three of my pals who were without doubt the finest musicians I knew. An instrumental album along the lines of organists Jimmy Smith and Jimmy McGriff was what I was aiming for and to this end I booked a session for the 9th of September at Olympic Sound Studios in Barnes and assembled my top trio comprising guitarist Pete Bocking, Pete Robinson on Hammond organ and drummer Trevor Morais from The Peddlers. There was no prior rehearsal time but they gelled instantly and came up with three possibilities for recording which were "Sunshine Superman", "Eleanor Rigby" and "Windy". While they were working through their routines it became clear that the best two were Sunshine and Eleanor so they concentrated on those tunes until they reckoned they had it nailed. It sounded great to me and to Tony, who was with us that evening and I had Tony to thank for the introduction to Pete Robinson. When we were ready for a take and as the room went quiet we were aware of sound breaking through from the adjacent studio. Tony volunteered to check it out and came back saying "No wonder we can hear it through the walls, it's bloody Jimi Hendrix in rehearsal" Tony, who knew Jimi from the early days, asked if they could take a short break while we laid down our tracks and they were very happy to oblige. We came out of that session with two tracks ready to go and I hawked them around the major record labels getting pretty much the same response from them all, "No, sorry, we want bands with vocals". How disappointing it was and with great reluctance I gave up chasing for a deal. The follow on from that session will be revealed some forty years later so keep your headphones on.

At the end of September I had taken up with a young lady called Maureen who, by some quirk of circumstance, was the first of three consecutive girlfriends all called Maureen. How bizarre is that? Even weirder still, two of them married friends of mine, the aforementioned Big Wal and the other my colleague from work Lon Goddard, a gifted cartoonist, musician and journalist. At the same time I had renewed my acquaintance with Graham Nash's wife Rose, who had moved to London and was currently ensconced in Scott Walker's flat near Philips Studios at Hyde Park, I think it was in Connaught Street. Before you ask, the answer is no, it was strictly platonic between us even though I spent time at the flat and Rose sometimes cooked dinner. The subject of her friendship with Scott was never mentioned, I was too polite. Rose had begun to take a great deal of interest in things astrological and when I told her I had a copy of "Everybody's Book Of Fate And Fortune" she asked me to bring it over as it had a section on phrenology which interested her. She was delighted to read it and asked if she could borrow it for a while. It was written in the stars that I would never see that book again. Rose asked me if I'd seen the new musical "Hair" at the Shaftesbury theatre and I said no, but I was planning to go soon. She said "Leave it to me, I'll get some tickets for us", which she did and sometime in October we went to the show and got totally "confetti'd", one of the highlights for the audience as the paper burst upon us from above. That was a great show and so very much a part of the sixties.

As most people know, drugs played quite a part in the sixties counter-culture, and it lost me a friend when Fritz Fryer turned up on my doorstep one afternoon with a bunch of long-haired scruffy blokes in tow. He said they were taking a break from recording at Philips studios down the road and could they come in for a smoke. I was a bit surprised but let them in and then found out what he meant by "smoke" when they started rolling their joints ready for a weed-inhalation session. This was taking advantage as Fritz knew I didn't do drugs and I immediately told them all to go and find a "potting shed" somewhere else. Fritz took umbrage at this rejection and left in a huff, never to be seen again, not by me anyway.

On the work front things were going exceptionally well as the record company coffers piled up they spent more and more on their advertising which did wonders for my commission payments. Not only were we seeing a rise in revenue from the labels but also publishers, agents, managers, studios and many associated businesses including hi-fi equipment manufacturers. This last was of particular interest to me as it led to a meeting with John Leak, owner of Leak audio amplifiers and speakers. We got on famously as he showed me round the factory and I marvelled at these superb products which later led to him placing adverts in the magazine. More importantly, on a personal level, he asked me what I listened to my music on and when I had to admit it was very basic, he simply said "How would you like some of this kit? I can do you a very good deal". That was how I managed to bag a great sound system for the flat which stood me in good stead for many years to come.

Unfortunately, my new sound system caused some complaints from neighbours and my landlady came to tell me to keep the noise down. She also became suspicious of what was going on after a night when Wal stayed with his girlfriend Cindy and my girlfriend Maureen turned up as did Tony's girlfriend Kathy. It did get a bit raucous and she was incensed the next morning when all three ladies left at the same time. That was the limit and now she knew it wasn't occupied by a nice respectable couple she gave me notice to quit within the month. Oops. Now what to do?

I didn't see much of them after that night but strangely enough they all became Playboy Bunnies not long afterwards. My task now was to find somewhere else to live and when I mentioned my predicament to Paul Phillips he immediately volunteered to take me in until I found somewhere. That's the kind of kind guy he is and we remain great pals to this day. This arrangement worked well as we travelled to and from work together and many an evening we would bring a stack of new albums back to his house in Valley Road, Streatham and have late-night listening sessions with Aretha Franklin and the new White Album by The Beatles. This was all very well for Paul and me but his wife Wendy eventually got tired of these boy's nights and after a couple of months she told Paul either I went or she went. You'd hardly believe what Paul said to her "OK, you'd better pack your bags". Wendy didn't depart as threatened, but it spurred me on to pick up some speed in my flat search. By the most unbelievable piece of good fortune I found the most perfect pad imaginable just off Bond Street in Lancashire Court. It comprised the top two floors of number 9 with the ground floor operating as a shop. I told Tony about it and we met there to discuss the lease with the landlady, who fortunately didn't live on the premises and was happy with two men sharing.

Jason James used to be road-manager for the Four Pennies — and when that group broke up he was out of a job. But he'd already been planning a career for himself as a singer . . . he was voted Norway's number one singer some two years earlier. Now he's made his debut disc, "Miss Pilkington's Maid", on CBS . . . a number he wrote for himself. He's been signed up by Maurice King and Barry Clayman, who handle the Walker Brothers. Jason'll soon need a road manager for himself!

Jason James publicity shot 1967

CHAPTER FIFTEEN
The End Of The Sixties Is Nigh

The end of 1968 saw Tony and myself refurbishing our new abode with purple carpet and turquoise curtains from John Lewis, re-forming the lounge doorway into an octagonal shape with multi-coloured perspex sides lit from the inside to give it a very clubby feel. We had a memorable phone number, MAYfair 6969, and we changed the telephones from the old standard ones to the latest GPO TRIM phones. Many people thought they were called that because they were slim and trim but actually it was an acronym for Tone Ring Illuminator Model, and I bet you didn't know that. Saturday mornings would usually entail a much-anticipated stroll to our local supermarket, Selfridges, and their wonderfully well-stocked food hall for our weekly supplies. I'd often spend time with Mike Ashwell at his record shop in South Molten Street, just around the corner, to listen to all the latest imports before they were released in the UK. That's where I first heard Creedence Clearwater Revival, Three Dog Night and Blood, Sweat And Tears, all of which opened my ears and made them tingle. The area around the flat would be near silent from Saturday afternoon through to Monday morning as all the shops and businesses closed and a long lie-in was the order of the day on Sunday.

One day, and I'm not entirely sure of the date but it could have been March, I got a phone call from the DJ John Peel asking me for a favour. I thought "Oh no, here we go again" as he said there was a gig that night in Bristol and he and some musicians needed transport. I told him I didn't have any wheels (who needs those in London?) but he said they would pay for me to hire a vehicle which had to be big enough to accommodate Danny Thompson's double bass and several people. A fee was agreed and I picked John up first before collecting the members of Pentangle together with Roy

Harper and we set off for Bristol. I'm pretty sure the venue was the Ansom Rooms, part of the university student's union. I got to see some of the best folk musicians in the country and marvelled at the guitar skills of John Renbourn and Bert Jansch individually and collectively as Pentangle, I got them all home safe and sound after the gig and never saw any of them again, all except John Peel that is, who I saw many times at the BBC over the years that followed.

April '69 took me on my first inter-continental flight to Paradise Island, Nassau in the Bahamas to attend the first International Music Industry Conference, courtesy of my employer Billboard Inc. What an experience it was staying in an individual beach-front chalet just a short walk away from the most exotic open-air breakfast buffet bar you can imagine loaded with fresh fruit and juice and omelettes on demand – pure heaven. The price we paid for this luxury was the mandatory attendance at the lectures and meetings during the day but the evenings were free and we were able to indulge in a little night-club enjoyment at the local casino. It was a successful and blissful trip for all of us, except for poor Paul Phillips, who wasn't invited along and for whom it is still a bone of contention. Sorry, Paul, for reminding you.

Tony and I seemed to have a constant stream of visitors coming to the flat, some were girlfriends and some were mates like Alan Buck from the Pennies who was working for Burlington Music Publishers and would often turn up with a few promo copies of albums for me. He was raving about this great artist he was promoting called Nilsson and said he was sure he was going to be a major star because of his incredible voice and the unique material he was recording. History has proved Alan to be spot on in musical terms but his personal life disintegrated when his wife Jane left him and went to America in the company of a trombone player. I know it might, from one point of view, seem a little comical but Alan was devastated and never recovered from that rejection. I would call and see him at his flat near Hanger Lane on my way home along the A40 and listened to his ongoing tales of woe as he lost his job and ended up working in a shoe shop. His depression seemed to be worse every time I called in and, eventually, he ended his life in the most tragic way possible. So sad.

154

Other regulars were Pete Robinson, that gifted keyboard player who formed the progressive rock group Quatermass with an old Liverpudlian pal of ours Johnny Gustafson on bass. Pete played on The London Sessions of both Chuck Berry and Jerry Lee Lewis, as did my pal Brian Parrish. Pete also worked alongside Eric Clapton, Phil Collins, Carly Simon and David Bowie, later finding fame and fortune in America composing film scores for "Wayne's World", "Cocktail" and "World's Fastest Indian". One of Pete's fellow students at the Royal Academy, Paul Buckmaster, also came round from time to time and he became extremely well known for his orchestral collaborations with numerous stars, notably the Rolling Stones, Leonard Cohen, Miles Davis and Elton John. Those two certainly made their mark in the world of music. Not bad for a couple of mates, eh?

An old pal from Manchester looked me up unexpectedly one day and came over for a cup of coffee to tell me what he was doing in London. It was John Wright, Billy's brother, part of the Parrs Wood clique, who had joined the Household Cavalry Life Guards division and was living in the barracks near Buckingham Palace. This was interesting news to me and I asked him to tell me about his life as a soldier. He told me it was extremely testing physically and painful for the first six months from red-raw legs due to being on a horse all day long learning the ropes. I thought it really fascinating and when he invited me to visit the stables and see his mount I was delighted to accept. The stables were very impressive and the horses looked enormous to me and I said I didn't think I could handle such a beast. John asked me if I had ever ridden and I said the best I could do was a donkey on Blackpool beach. He offered to teach me to ride and although we couldn't use the army facilities, he knew of a riding school just north of London where we could go. After a few trips to Barnet I began to get the hang of it and John said I was doing well but he was called away on duty and I didn't see much of him after that. Later on I heard that he had left the army and had taken up a new life as a hill farmer in the Scottish Borders where he was on horseback much of the time. What I didn't know was that he was an accomplished musician and had made quite a name for himself in the folk world as evidenced by the albums he sent down to me during the 1990's. I recently looked at an article in the Manchester Evening News reporting his death where, among other tributes, was the information that he had been part of the mounted escort at Princess Anne's wedding and also that he had jammed with Herman's Hermits in the sixties. It's a small world, don't you know.

There was one guest who arrived at the flat late one night which surprised and delighted me in equal measure as she walked in with Tony, took one look at me and said "What are you doing here?" and I said "Well, Caroline, I live here, what are you doing here?" She told me she had just had a meal with Tony at the muso's hang-out The Kensington Garden Hotel after finishing work at Kensington Market. We chatted for a while and I remembered she had a piano so I asked her if we could come over to her place with Paul Phillips to rehearse for a gig as we were thinking of starting a band. She agreed and within a week or so we got together at her place in Brendon Street to routine a few numbers and at the end of the session she invited me to stay for a coffee, ostensibly to discuss writing some songs together. My luck had finally turned and this "dreamgirl" I had fancied since our first meeting seemed, against the odds, to be within touching distance, which rapidly became no distance at all as we became partners in a relationship that was to last almost twenty years.

Things were continuing apace at work, which was now only a short distance away as the offices had re-located to Carnaby Street, and I had been appointed Advertising Manager of the newly acquired pop title Record Mirror. This was a promotion but I was still selling space on Record Retailer at the same time, so two jobs for the price of one, what a bargain. RR had grown beyond all recognition with bumper editions sometimes running to 72 pages, which was a lot of ads and which also needed a lot more editorial entailing the recruitment of more journalists, so I guess I had provided employment for some pretty good scribblers, some of whom keep in touch and some still quite busy like Rodney Collins, Lon Goddard and the man who is proof-reading this blockbuster, Paul Phillips.

They say location is crucial and the flat was in prime position for so many things. Work was a walk down Maddox Street cross over Regent Street and there you were. Clubs within falling distance of home were The Bag O' Nails in Kingly Street, adjacent to Carnaby Street, the Speakeasy in Margaret Street, Danny La Rue's by Hanover Square and the nearest was The Revolution in Bruton Place, fabulous venues every single one. My shortest walk to a record label was to Apple Records in Savile Row at a time when their advertising spend was enormous, supporting their newly-signed artists Mary Hopkin, James Taylor, Badfinger and Billy Preston. As a regular visitor to Number 3 it never surprised me to see a famous face or a Beatle wandering about but the best ever was the day I was sitting in reception talking to Ringo about a film he was in with Peter Sellers, and the possibility of bringing in a snooker table for a game we both enjoyed, when I noticed something interesting in a waste paper basket nearby. I leant over to check it out and said to Ringo "It's one of your gold records but it looks like it's been in a fight". "Yeah", he said, "it fell off a wall over there". When I asked him why it was in the waste paper-basket he said it was destined for the rubbish bin. I said I thought that was terrible and should be saved but Ringo just said "Nah, we've got hundreds of the bloody things, you can have it if you want it". What? I could have it. Bloody hell, I was out of my chair in a flash and picked it up for a closer look. I asked Ringo if he was sure it was OK for me to take it, he said yes, and with his blessing I picked up that gem of an artefact and went back to the flat in a lightly euphoric state. This priceless iconic treasure was for "Meet The Beatles", the first of their albums to be issued by Capitol Records in the States. Thanks Ringo, the condom debt has now been repaid in full.

July 5th 1969 was a pretty interesting day as Paul Phillips picked me up from the flat to walk the short distance to Hyde Park for an open-air concert starring The Rolling Stones. We weren't prepared for the enormous crowd that had congregated and had to hustle our way through to the press enclosure right in front of the stage. We found ourselves a good central spot where we could lean back against the barriers for a bit of comfort and where we wouldn't be crushed. The weather that sweet summer day was glorious and Paul and I watched the support acts respectfully but it was the Stones we were there for. This concert has been so well-documented over the years there's little point in repeating it again here, save to say Paul and I giggled just a little when Jagger appeared in a short white dress before reciting a poem in Brian Jones honour and releasing hundreds of butterflies. We enjoyed the concert, even though the sound and performance were less than perfect because they hadn't played "live" for some time but I think we were well aware that we had witnessed a very special historical "happening".

There were many in the audience that day dressed in the most exotic, and sometimes erotic, gear and it occurred to me that I had come through three eras of youthful dressing starting with the Teddy Boy/rocker clothes in the fifties, mod style in the sixties and now pretty much a hippie going into the seventies, albeit without the sandals and kaftan, that was too much of a stretch for me.

Soon came a much more captivating and historically important event as the Apollo 11 mission on July 20 1969 successfully landed men on the moon, ushering in the beginning of a new age. Caroline and I stayed up all night to watch the drama unfold on television, drinking copious mugs of coffee and nibbling our way through sandwiches and crisps. It was riveting stuff and we could hardly take our eyes off the screen it was so enthralling. I can't remember much about the next day or even if I went to work or not, I was completely cream-crackered.

Now to a matter of some consequence for my future friendship and fortune: I don't mean that in a monetary sense, just another slice of good luck and coincidental timing. One of the perks of working in the media were the invitations to film preview screenings, which often took place in small intimate theatres in Wardour Street. If I recall correctly, I was there one evening enjoying a comedy film, I think it was "Magic Christian", when I was aware of laughter behind me that I thought I recognised and sure enough, when the lights went up I turned round to see my old mate Dave Lee Travis standing there. He looked at me and seemed surprised to see me, but not half as surprised as I was to see him. He told me he had just been given a Sunday morning show on Radio One and would be coming down to London every Saturday for the foreseeable future. Well, that was to be for the next two years, before he got a daytime show, and meant that we would see each other very regularly as he would stay with Caroline and I on the night before the show. Dave would arrive on Saturday afternoon and we would have a session listening to all the new records which often came to me well in advance of their official release date. This meant the first plays on radio for future hits by Creedence Clearwater Revival, Three Dog Night, Free, The Band and many more. Caroline and I would drive Dave to Broadcasting House on Sunday morning and join him in the studio for the show which became a sort of early "Zoo" format. I got on very well with the producer, "Whistling" Paul Williams, who was all in favour of this lively approach and he seemed impressed by my knowledge of golden oldies asking me to provide him with a list of recommendations. That was easy for me as I had already done a massive amount of research at the British Newspaper library in Cricklewood collating chart data from the early fifties right up to date with the intention of turning it into a reference book. Unfortunately, I never got round to finishing it and in 1977 The Guinness Book of Hit Singles was published rendering my research obsolete. Still, those Sunday morning studio sessions would stand me in very good stead for a future career move of some consequence.

One other film to mention at this point is "Easy Rider", which I went to see with Paul Phillips, because we still laugh about the fact that out of the whole audience, we two seemed to be the only ones to crack up at the Fraternity Of Man song "Don't Bogart That Joint" – a classic film reference in a contemporary movie. You don't hear that one on the radio these days.

The last event in 1969 of any consequence was a gig Paul Phillips organised at the Oval cricket ground where the original Wailers, Lek, Barry, Wal and me were joined by Tony Walmsley on guitar, Jack Brand on second bass, Tony Baxter on congas and Paul on piano. There were rehearsals in the afternoon but I only got a cursory run-through as they knew all the tunes but I hadn't been on stage nor held a microphone in anger for more than three years. We got through the evening in fairly good shape and Wal set up my Revox tape machine to record the gig for posterity. We only captured a very basic mono sound off a mike in front of the speaker so there was no way of improving it later but nevertheless it's a memory of the last gig the original Wailers ever played.

They say if you can remember the 60's you weren't there so I leave it up to you to decide if I was there and if I remember – waddya think? They also said it was all about "sex, drugs and rock'n'roll" and that's not true, either. Many of us got through the 60's with no drugs at all.

CHAPTER SIXTEEN

The Seventies And Stability

The early seventies saw Caroline and I become closer and closer to the point of inseparability and I began to get the feeling of finally being settled with a woman I loved. As we spent all our time with each other it became more and more obvious that we should live together permanently and to that end I relinquished my share in the Bond Street flat to Wal and moved in with Caroline at 22 Brendon Street. That was a lively time as Caroline introduced me to her social circle of friends, of which there were many – Caroline is a very gregarious lady. There was John Harrington, a somewhat eccentric young man who rented a room at the top of the house for a while, Rusty round the corner, a casino croupier and one-time landlady of Tony Walmsley, then regular visitors Patrick Starling, a sound engineer on the pirate radio ship Caroline, Brian Parrish, ace guitarist and singer, Colin Forsey, another talented musician and singer from the group Spectrum and two coin-dealer partners Alistair McKay and Michael Gouby, with whom I continue to have a solid friendship. I lost contact with Brian until we managed to find each other again almost fifty years later, but in those earlier times I would listen and marvel at his voice on the Raw Holly recording of "Raining In My Heart" which, if you've never heard it I urge you to listen on YouTube, it is brilliant. His massive talent was recognised by the Beatles producer George Martin who signed an album recording deal with him and Paul Gurvitz. Caroline and I would visit Brian and his wife Jenny in St John's Wood where Brian would sit with an acoustic guitar and play some of the songs from the album as I marvelled at his ability. Here was a great star in the making but, sadly, it never really happened for him although he still writes and performs today in his new home in Germany.

Friends of mine that we saw as a couple were Andy and Peter Marsden, who I first met in Bond Street when he was designing the inside of a shop opposite Fenwick's store. I was intrigued by what was going on in there and walked in to find out and look around. Peter had some of his paintings on show which I thought were brilliant pop-art and asked if they were for sale. I bought half a dozen of them and still have three of them now. He did similar pieces for a hotel at Heathrow airport and even though he didn't make his mark as an artist his son, Oliver Marsden, certainly did, with his work now fetching tens of thousands of pounds. Their other son, Tommy, was my godson and we remained friendly with the Marsden family for many years until Peter and Andy split up and moved away. My one regret from that period was a painting I commissioned from Peter to grace the wall of the Bond Street flat. It was a very modern piece about six feet by two feet reflecting the purple carpet theme which I left there for Wal to enjoy until some years later I asked him for it and he denied all knowledge of its whereabouts. Did he leave it in the flat when he left, did he take it with him or did he sell it? I guess I'll never know.

Tony Walmsley also went in search of pastures new finding work with American folk/rock musician Shawn Phillips who toured extensively, finally settling in Positano in Italy. At the end of his time with Shawn, Tony put permanent roots down in Italy with his wife Giovanna and now holds seminars and instruction classes in the ancient Chinese practise of Tai Chi. We're still very much in regular touch.

Early in 1970 I went to review the American cowboy star and country singer Tex Ritter in concert at the London Palladium for Record Mirror. His stage presence was amazing and he had the audience in the palm of his hand from the very start and I have to say I was impressed by just how good he was, rising above all my expectations. Not only that but backstage afterwards he proved to be the perfect southern gentleman during our interview telling me of his past, being the first artist signed to Capitol Records and his pride in his recording from the film "High Noon" winning the Oscar for best song in 1952. I was surprised and delighted when he told me he had invested in a fast-food business and anytime I visited

162

America the burgers were on him. The photo taken with him that night and my accompanying review are still in my scrap-book.

Workwise things were going along at a cracking pace with advertising continuing to increase and sales targets regularly beaten, especially at Record Retailer, which would shortly be re-named Music Week. Change was most certainly in the air with forthcoming events about to re-direct my career path once again. Wait just a minute and all will be revealed.

That summer Caroline and I booked a holiday villa near Faro in Portugal arranging to take the car, a new Ford Capri, on the ferry from Portsmouth to Santander in September. I duly booked the holiday time at work with plenty of notice but was taken aback sometime later when Julian Ormond decided to re-launch Record Mirror at precisely the time I had booked my leave. When I discussed this with him he wouldn't budge on the date and even though I assured him I would have everything in order before I left to go on holiday he insisted I was around for the re-launch. He laid it out plain and simple that I was either in the office or on holiday and if it was to be the latter my services would no longer be required. What a horrible dilemma. When I told Caroline of this nasty development she simply said that as we'd paid for the holiday we should take it and Julian could stick his job where the sun don't shine – or words to that effect.

So, I resigned and joined the ranks of the jobless but hope was on the horizon, although not till we got back from our holiday, which was wonderful except for the sailing as the ship heaved somewhat through the Bay of Biscay and so did I – never been a great sailor. The villa we rented was a Moorish-style delight, the swimming pool was warm and the weather much warmer. The food and wine were delicious and we took many drives along the coast in both directions visiting lots of superb beaches and all the while meeting the friendliest of locals. Towards the end of this trip, lying in bed one morning, I turned to Caroline and said "I suppose we should get married" – now, how romantic can you get. Fortunately, she agreed, and on our return home began making plans for the big day, which came rather sooner than I had expected, as arrangements were made for the ceremony to be held on December the 5th at

All Saints church in Marlow with a reception just over the bridge at The Compleat Angler restaurant.

Before that happened I wanted to introduce Caroline to my parents who by now had left Manchester and started a boarding house business in Blackpool. Yes, my mother was now a seaside landlady. To celebrate the engagement our first evening meal with them was accompanied by a bottle of champagne, which my mother proudly produced saying she had kept it since my 21st for just this occasion. Well, it had been standing upright in a kitchen cupboard for seven years so it was no surprise when the cork came out with not a hint of fizz – flat as a pancake and quite undrinkable. Still, the thought was there. Parental niceties having been observed and satisfied we headed back to prepare for our big day.

The reason for holding proceedings in Marlow was because Caroline's parents, Bill and Moira Stephenson, lived nearby at Winter Hill and were able to help with much of the planning and organisation. What a day it was with all our family and friends there to share it, Dave Lee Travis as best man and Ron Stratton in a white Jaguar driving the getaway car. We could have had our honeymoon in Bermuda, courtesy of Bill and Moira, but decided against it as Caroline had a fear of flying. Instead, we headed straight for Caroline's parent's farm in Blandford Forum for a couple of nights and from there to the Imperial Hotel in Torquay on the English Riviera, one of our favourite resorts. Last stop was the Tregenna Castle Hotel in St Ives and then the long trek back to reality and unemployment in London.

Time wasn't entirely wasted though, as Caroline introduced me to the Narnia novels of C.S. Lewis, A.A. Milne's Winnie The Pooh plus various others which I had never read as a child and they were certainly a better read than Rupert and Dennis The Menace, although I did read Wind In The Willows as a child. At school we read Shakespeare and Dickens, which I enjoyed, especially Great Expectations which was part of the G.C.E. syllabus, but my teenage reading comprised John Steinbeck, Mark Twain, Jack London, Sir Walter Scott, Robert Louis Stevenson, Jonathan Swift, George Orwell and Ernest Hemingway. Next came the Hobbit and Lord Of The Rings and the start of an interest in collecting illustrated books from the art nouveau period by Aubrey Beardsley, Arthur Rackham, Dulac, Detmold and my absolute favourite Kay Nielsen. These works in turn led to an appreciation of Gaudi, Klimt, Kandinsky and Hundertwasser, definitely worth checking out. Not wasted time at all, then.

I have many books on the shelf still to be read and I hope they will be as interesting as "Life Of Pi", "The Curious Incident of The Dog In The Night-Time" and the magical marvel "Jonathan Strange And Mr Norrell". Life stories usually interest me and I've enjoyed biographies of Groucho Marx, Bob Dylan, Graham Nash and Robert Mitchum but I recommend two of the very best, in my humble opinion, starting with Bruce Springsteen for his wonderful way with words and Michael Caine for his extraordinary story and the fact that his favourite restaurant in London was The Pickwick, where I never met him. The relatively recent invention of Kindle technology has led me to read some very much older literature, the most enjoyable of which I found to be "The Diary Of A Nobody", worth a read in anyone's book.

With plenty of time to talk I got to hear more details about Caroline's background and family history. Her grandfather was William Stephenson, the first British chairman of Woolworths, chairman of the Metal Box Company and owner of the London Casino, which later became Casino Cinerama before eventually returning to its original name the Prince Edward theatre. I never met this great man but I was amazed at his many successes and great fortune which afforded him the means to commission and build the "J" class yacht Velsheda, named after his daughters Velma, Sheila and Daphne. The large "J" class yachts were built to challenge for the America's Cup but, swift and impressive as they were, history records they failed in three attempts during the 1930's. Something to do with a certain Mr Vanderbilt, I understand. Bill was Commodore of the Royal Motor Yacht Club in Poole and during the 1930's his guests aboard this wonderful craft would include many of the great and good, none more so than King George V, himself a very keen sailor. There is a story the family tell of him rejecting the offer of a knighthood because his wife wasn't keen on all the social activity that such eminence would entail. Anything for a quiet life, eh? Where is Velsheda now, I wonder?

Caroline had many artistic interests, one of which was designing clothes, which she did for the Bee Gees, the Animals, singers Julie Grant and her good friend Beryl Marsden, girl drummer Honey Lantree of the Honeycombs and Sharon Tandy.

On the musical side she had been writing songs with pianist Peter Morris for their joint venture in music publishing and both she and I attended the famous Eric Gilder school of music where so many famous musicians were taught, including a young Andrew Lloyd Webber who I believe was helped considerably by Eric in his early days of composing. We also took classes in pottery and jewellery design at the Stanhope Institute for adult education so there was plenty to keep us occupied while I began to think about finding a means of generating some income.

Travis continued to stay with us on a regular basis and when I told him about my job search, he asked if I'd considered working as a producer at the BBC. That sounded like a great idea but how to go about it and the simple answer was for Dave to mention me to his boss at Radio One, Mark White. An introductory meeting was arranged and I turned up at Aeolian Hall in Bond Street, just a matter of yards away from my old flat in Lancashire Court. I wondered if I should have kept it but that was jumping to conclusions somewhat prematurely. Mark was a charming man and after he'd had a look at my resume, he made the funny remark that perhaps I was over-qualified as I'd done so many things in my various jobs. That broke the ice and we had quite a long conversation at the end of which he said he would look at where he might be able to place me, possibly doing some live music studio sessions, if that would interest me. I said I would be happy to do that and Mark said he'd be in touch shortly after he'd given it some consideration. I felt the interview had gone well and waited for a call, first one week, then two, then three and then after four weeks Mark asked me to go back to see him as he had a proposition for me. When I got to his office he explained that changes had been made and that he was no longer in charge at Radio One but he had been promoted to be Head of Radio Two. He said he hoped I wouldn't be too disappointed at this news as he could offer me some freelance work producing sessions for his new network which would be quite diverse musically ranging from singer/songwriters to small combos to large orchestras. Mark asked me if I was comfortable with those options and, with a bit of a lump in my nervous throat I said yes, I was ready to go to work. Not the hoped-for Radio One gig, then, but a whole new world of live music across an amazingly wide range of styles and personalities. I never once looked back.

Initially work arrived sporadically with a week here and there, then two or three weeks together until eventually I was given a regular three-month rolling contract which took me through the next two years listening and learning the craft of live music production. The first week was a familiarisation exercise with me visiting the various BBC studios to watch proceedings and to meet the sound engineers at the end of which I was given a schedule and my very own BBC issue stopwatch (number 1207 and still working) and thrown in at the deep end. The deepest of which happened in my very first week as I was booked for a session at The Camden studio with the great Canadian jazz trumpeter and bandleader Maynard Ferguson. This was extremely exciting for me as I was familiar with his work with the Stan Kenton Band but not so much so with the jazz/rock area he was moving into and although I could read the dots (follow a musical score) the speed and complexity required was a real roast (muso speak for the highest possible demand on your concentration and ability). Maynard came into the control room to listen to the takes and declared himself well-satisfied with the results thanking me for the session, whereas, in fact, his gratitude should have been directed at the engineer, without whom I would probably have been lost at that stage. Over the years I was always complimentary to all the sound guys for their hard work, dedication and expertise, especially as they helped me so much in those early days.

Maybe you can appreciate the trepidation I felt as a novice producer, needing all the help I could get in the studio, especially when faced with a fifty-piece orchestra and needing to stop mid-way through a take to tell them you weren't satisfied with something or other. The way to stop the take was to turn the red recording light off and over the intercom explain why to those faces glaring at you from the studio floor through the glass window into the sound cubicle. The reason could have been anything from a split trumpet note or the strings needing a tune up or maybe I might have wanted to alter the balance a little bit. Anyway, I got through those early jitters and the bands and orchestras rarely took umbrage after they began to accept I was only interested in getting the best sound for them.

Many of those sound balancers were not only technically competent but many were also good musicians and several of them were out and out characters who never failed to amuse me. The great trad jazz sound man "Mighty" Joe Young was one who always arrived in the studio and hid two bottles of Guinness behind the monitor speakers for a little "taste" in between rehearsal and recording. He never sat down at the console when working as most others did but he would respond to the music as if in a ballet, moving from control knob to control knob muttering to himself in his west-country accent "Ah, yes, little bit more of that there, a little less clarinet maybe, yes, that's lovely, what's he doing on the drums?" He always managed to get a perfect sound and every session with him was a performance. He was a one-off, for sure.

The working week for freelancers was based on ten half-day sessions, which could be morning, afternoon or evening, but nobody was ever asked to do that many as seven sessions was the accepted norm because time had to be allowed for moving from one studio to the next. No wonder, considering the locations ranged from Maida Vale, Camden, The Paris Lower Regent Street, Golders Green Hippodrome, Playhouse Northumberland Avenue, Broadcasting House and home-base Aeolian Hall. Remember, at this stage, I didn't book any of these artists, that was the preserve of the programme producer who decided which acts he wanted on his show. The exception to this rule was the allocation of the in-house orchestras into the shows most suited to showcase, let's say, the strings of the Radio Orchestra or the sound of the BBC Big Band.

It didn't take me long to realise how much I was enjoying working in this environment with the best arrangers and session musicians in the country and hearing some of the funniest stories, many not printable here. I'll give you a few so you get the idea.

Top bandleader Joe Loss was very happy to talk during breaks in a session and laughed when I told him we wore ourselves out learning the dance moves to his Madison records. Then he told me a funny from his own past when the band were playing a ballroom in Cheltenham and Joe announced that if anybody had any requests, he would try to fit them in during the evening. An Irish gentleman came up and asked if the band could play "Paddy Me Boy". Joe said he wasn't familiar with that song and asked the band if any of them knew it. They all said no and the man looked very surprised and said he thought everybody knew that song as it was so popular. Taken aback at this, Joe asked the man if he could whistle the tune or hum it, at which the guy said "I can do better than that, I'll sing it for you, it goes like this" "Paddy me boy, is that the Chattanooga Choo Choo". You can imagine the roars of laughter from the band at this revelation, they certainly knew it and they played it with great gusto..

One member of the Joe Loss band was the renowned jazz pianist and bandleader Bill McGuffie, a regular in the studios either with a small combo or with his big band. He was the most genuine of men and after nearly every session we would go for a chat and a drink, he always drank a bottle of Lowenbrau, or two. He recounted tales about his career, recordings, the film scores he had composed and remembered with a smile on his face Jayne Mansfield, with whom he appeared as the night club pianist in the London gangster movie "The Challenge", in which she sang the title song he wrote for her. He also wrote and recorded a solo piano piece for me called "A Mullin's A Mull For A' That', based on the poem of his Scottish compatriot Robert Burns. His brilliance on the piano was even more remarkable when you realise he was missing a finger from his right hand.

Benny Hill's seduction technique was revealed to me by his musical director Ronnie Aldrich who I worked with on a regular basis when he conducted the Radio Orchestra. Those sessions were quite a treat as Ronnie would augment the orchestra with four French horns, maybe a marimba or vibes and various other instruments. He told me about working with Benny and Benny's

169

success with the ladies when he invited them over to his place for dinner. After the meal Benny would suggest they play a little game, saying "Benny would like to play a game of hide and seek now" and if the lady agreed he would go off and hide while she counted to fifty. His hiding place was his bed and when he was found it was then up to the lady whether she joined him or not and, apparently, they quite often did.

Perhaps the funniest, and naughtiest, remark made at a session was when Angela Morley came in to conduct her first session after returning from America. Angela had had a sex change and a name change from Wally Stott, a famous orchestral arranger. The only other transgender person I had heard of was April Ashley back in the early sixties so this was quite something for me and the musicians, most of whom had worked with Wally. As rehearsals got under way there was a tangible air of excitement and not a little tension in the studio but all the players were showing due respect to a great musician. All, that is, except for one wag in the brass section who called out "Hey, Wally, I suppose a fuck's out of the question?" Well, if ever something was calculated to break the ice or cause a catastrophe, that was surely it as the whole place erupted in delirious laughter. Angela smiled, the laughter subsided and she proved what a great talent she was with many new and impeccable arrangements and the session ended with a huge round of applause – wonderful.

Comical one-liners were the stock in trade of many musicians like the one directed at singer Danny Street when he was told "You know Danny, if you'd been born in France you'd be called Danny La Rue" – cue more hilarious laughter.

Norrie Paramor gave me some advice in those early days when he told me never to put up my own money for a musical production, always get it paid for by a record label or publisher and if nobody would finance it then it probably wasn't worth doing. With his track record you have to take notice, I think.

I found out all kinds of background information from working with all those session musicians and all the hit records they had played on. I told the singer Rosemary Squires how I liked a record called "Frankfurter Sandwiches" by Joanne and the Streamliners when she admitted to being Joanne. I heard the guitarist Ernie

Shear tuning up by playing the intro to Cliff's hit "Move It". I said "Ernie, you've really nailed that intro" and he said "Not surprising is it, I played it on the record". On a big orchestral session I asked the bass player Eddie Tripp for a bit more attack with a guitar pick rather than using his fingers and Eddie said "Like this, you mean?" and I said that was perfect, just the sound I wanted, like Bert Kaempfert. One of the other musicians said it should sound like that because Eddie played on Bert's records, just as many others on that session had played on both Kaempfert and James Last recordings. I was loving hearing all this insider information and now you know it, too.

Quite often a date with the Radio Big Band would turn into a raucous affair, especially with the thirsty brass section and even more especially during an afternoon session. On one occasion their regular conductor Malcolm Lockyer was directing from his piano when they lit a fire with newspaper under his stool and waited for the fireworks. It was kind of funny but it could also have been quite dangerous. The Playhouse theatre was a regular venue with the stage used as a rising rostrum with the players in tiers from the reeds at the lowest level, then the trumpets above them with the trombones at the very highest level some fifteen feet from the stage floor. In the middle of a take, as I was listening and following the score I realised I couldn't hear the bass trombone. When I looked towards the stage the bass trombonist Tommy Cook was nowhere to be seen so I immediately stopped the session. Poor old Tommy had toppled backwards from his chair and was having a rest behind the rostrum. He was OK but quite unable to continue, as were some of the rest of the band, at which point I abandoned the session and sent them all home. One or two were quite rightly disciplined in the next day or two. Never a dull moment with the Big Band.

CHAPTER SEVENTEEN

My Radio Career Takes Off And
A little Treasure Arrives

By the middle of 1971 I was beginning to warm to my task and enjoying my time as a peripatetic producer overseeing such a wide variety of musical output for Radio Two. Caroline and I were getting used to married life, making improvements to our house and garden and even contemplating the arrival of tiny feet. On June 6 we went to Manchester for the wedding of Dave and Marianne Travis, a very small and private affair with me as Best Man and Caroline as Bridesmaid. There were drinks later at Dave's parent's house where a mental mynah bird seemed to rule the roost, so to speak, and never stopped talking. Maybe that's where Dave gets it from. The newly-weds soon moved to London and rented a flat in St John's Wood making them near neighbours and not weekend guests anymore. What a relief - only joking - just.

Caroline and I were beginning to wonder if central London was the right place to bring up a family, especially with the noise levels we were experiencing in Brendon Street, which was only one street away from the busy Edgware Road. At both ends of the street there were pubs which chucked out their patrons around eleven, then The Victoria Sporting Club disgorged from midnight to three and then, as we were directly opposite the rear entrance to Woolworths, we had the arrival of delivery lorries and finally the clearing of the bins around five or six in the morning. Good job we weren't light sleepers.

My health took a turn for the worse that winter as I was laid up in bed with a bout of bronchitis due to my terrible smoking habit. I was probably getting through 40 to 60 a day, with one before I got up in the morning and another in bed last thing at night. Caroline called the doctor and after he examined me, he said "Do you enjoy being in this state?" I shook my head and he pointed at the cancer sticks by the bed and said "If you don't stop smoking now, I guarantee that you'll be like this permanently before you reach the age of forty". Bloody hell – I didn't need warning twice and I knew then and there that I'd already smoked my last cigarette. Caroline joined me in giving up so we dumped our remaining packs of twenty in the dustbin and there was no nicotine no more.

A house move was on the cards, Caroline went on the hunt and came up with a charming thatched cottage in Cookham Dean not far from where her parents lived, so that was the baby-sitting problem taken care of. We moved into Woodland Thatch in Quarry Woods, reputedly the inspiration for The Wild Wood in A.A. Milne's "Winnie The Pooh" books. It was small but detached, beautifully decorated and maintained by the previous owners the Hopkins, who had an interest in a famous brand of jam, Hartley's, I think. We got friendly with their son Bill, a car enthusiast who used to race his Morgan sports car at the Castle Combe circuit. His day job was as a salesman at the Ford dealership in Slough and one day he asked me if I would help him deliver some new Fiestas to Heathrow airport, which I was happy to do. We were a bit naughty by racing these new cars and over several journeys Bill always managed to beat me, regardless of which car he was in. When I asked him how he did it he told me his secret, which was to never lift your foot off the accelerator, even when changing gears, just dab the clutch and throw the gear lever very quickly. No wonder he was getting wheelspin going into fourth gear. Bill was also very helpful in getting me a hefty staff discount on a new Cortina 2000E, a great car which I later sold to Simon Bates who said it was still running well twenty years later.

Our next-door neighbours were interesting people with the actor George Selway on one side and week-enders Ronnie and Marie Marks on the other. George was appearing in the TV series "And Mother Makes Three" with Wendy Craig who also lived locally. Ronnie was a big wheel in the audio-visual field with businesses in Tottenham Court Road, the main centre for hi-fi products in London. They were a lovely couple and Marie used to enjoy telling the story of how their son Ross arrived one day while she was on the toilet and out he popped. She swore she didn't even know she was pregnant. Ronnie introduced me to his cousin, Tony Goldstone, who asked me to help him launch a new series of TV-advertised record albums, which was right up my street. I put together a track listing, contracts were agreed and I supervised the process from start to finish which culminated in the release of "20 Star Tracks" on Ronco Records. Sales were exceptional with over half a million units shipped, resulting in my first ever Gold Disc as producer. My remuneration was to be in staged payments as various sales targets were achieved and Tony's accountant, Norman Lawrence, later to represent Pink Floyd, handed me my first cheque. All was looking very rosy and Tony asked me for more ideas for future compilation album releases, a task I set about with relish, coming up with over thirty suggestions covering various genres. Tony was delighted with these and said my rock and roll collection would be called "40 Smash Hits" and released to coincide with the David Essex film "That'll Be The Day". This all seemed to be great news until the cheques dried up as Tony withheld payment for the last tranch of "Star Tracks". When I mentioned this to Ronnie Marks he was furious and said Tony was out of order and spending too much time and money living in Mayfair near the Playboy club, driving his Rolls Royce around town in the company of various actresses and beauty queens – what a terrible lifestyle, eh? Ronnie got Tony to pay up and brought me a case of Taittinger Comtes de Champagne Rose as an apology for Tony's bad behaviour. That was the end of my association with Tony Goldstone, who never gave me a credit for my contribution to the success of Ronco Records, let alone any kind of payment. I put him down in my book as a rogue and was interested to hear some years later rumours that he had been shot dead – nothing to do with me, I might add.

On a regular basis I would pop into Aeolian Hall to pick up my schedule from one of the two Johns, Messrs Kingdon and Buckley, who were in charge of producer allocations and who would also ask for my feedback as well as offering advice and helpful hints along the way. That was as near as I got to meeting other producers or visiting the programme offices for about another year as I continued to serve my apprenticeship before I was let anywhere near a proper radio show. That came in 1972 as I joined the production team on Night Ride with Harry Walters. This was another learning curve as I was tasked with finding suitable non-needletime musical items from a vast reservoir of tapes and discs housed in a large office full of filing cabinets. These items came from a variety of sources such as the Canadian Talent Library, instrumentals from radio stations across the EBU (European Broadcasting Union), and music publishers background or library music. This was necessary to fill up the airtime as shows were restricted in the amount of commercial gramophone records (needletime) they could use due to limits agreed with the Musicians Union. This arrangement was obviously of great benefit to musicians but very restrictive as far as music radio was concerned by not being able to play as many popular records as we wanted to include. All very frustrating but just a few years later most of these restrictions were removed.

I went through all those thousands of items with a fine toothcomb, selecting what I thought were suitable for broadcast while still being responsible for most of the live music sessions on the show which went out nightly between midnight and 2am. The presenters were rotated on a weekly basis with the regulars being Ray Moore, Tony Myatt, Simon Bates, Peter Donaldson, Colin Berry, Robin Boyle, Barry Aldiss and the "enfant terrible" of late-night broadcasting Keith Skues, or Cardboard Shoes as we called him, who became forever famous as the man who broadcast nine minutes of The Speaking Clock while he went off for a pee. They don't make 'em like that anymore.

As far as I can ascertain from old copies of The Radio Times I got my first credit in the magazine on 22 October 1972 listing my session input from Kenny Ball and his Jazzmen, Pickettywitch and Paper Lace. Shortly after that first credit came sessions with Olivia Newton-John, Neville Dickie, Mickey Newbury, Roger Whittaker, The Mike Sammes Singers and Acker Bilk – all classic Radio Two acts except maybe Neville Dickie, whose banging about on an old Joanna wasn't everybody's idea of late night easy-listening. Yes, we got letters.

My first taste of an outside broadcast was on New Year's Eve when Jimmy Young came to us live from The Queen Victoria pub in Brussels and my old mucker Dave Lee Travis was at Whiskie Bill's in Cologne. All part of the regular co-operation with our European broadcasting partners. I wasn't sent abroad for those two contributions but I would be involved in many such operations over the coming years.

January 1973 saw a change on the Night Ride team as Pam Cox took over from Harry Walters as senior producer and which highlighted for me what was generally regarded as a peculiar policy in place at Radio Two. Changes in producer allocations happened on a regular three-monthly basis so that producers would wait eagerly to know what show they would be working on next. I found it somewhat de-stabilising and counter to building up good on-going working relationships. The reason given by management was that they didn't want staff getting too friendly with the turns. Ha. Getting too friendly was happening all over the place between presenters, producers, engineers and secretaries. Management wasn't blind to all that extra-curricular activity, in fact, some in management were also involved in friendly relations. It used to be said that you could only get the sack from the BBC for three things – number one was theft, number two was for not paying your license fee and number three was for having sex on the premises. Personally, I don't know anybody who got fired for this last offence so they must have been chaste, careful or just plain lucky.

Here's a run-down of artists I produced sessions with during 1973/74 which may or may not be of interest to you but as a completist I feel the need to include them. Feel free to move on to the next paragraph if you suffer from listophobia.

Cliff Richard, The Settlers, Iris Williams, Clinton Ford, Karl Denver, Dennis Lotis, Kenny Lynch, Neil Sedaka, Terry Lightfoot, New Vaudeville Band, Anita Harris, Valerie Masters, Eddie Thompson, New Seekers, Bonnie Dobson, Peter Skellern, Lorne Gibson, Edison Lighthouse, New World, Fivepenny Piece, Chas McDevitt & Shirley Douglas, Lita Roza, Frank Ifield, Don Lang, Jake Thackray, Edmundo Ross, Matt Monro, Vince Hill, Dana, Anne Shelton, Mrs Mills, Johnny Pearson and many, many more. For example, you've heard of The Two Ronnies, well, I produced the four Ronnies, namely Hilton, Carroll, Aldrich and Hazlehurst and probably some others I don't remember.

One artist I managed to book pleased me more than most as I had bought all his albums during the sixties and he didn't disappoint in the studio, reeling off a dozen or so of his best-known songs. It was John D Loudermilk unplugged as he sat on a chair, played acoustic guitar and harmonica (known by serious musicians as a "tin sandwich") using his guitar case as an improvised bass drum to keep the beat. John was delighted with the sound and the fact that I was familiar with his material, so much so that we started a friendship that was to last for years as he and his wife Susie visited us a couple of times and, although Caroline and I were never able to accept their offer to stay with them in Tennessee, I did visit them with Wally Whyton in the nineties when John regaled us with all sorts of tales from his life. More on Johnny Dee later.

One regularly booked performer was the American jazz singer Marion Montgomery who I often gave a lift back to her home in Bray where she lived with her husband the pianist and composer Laurie Holloway, who later became even more well-known as the musical director of Strictly Come Dancing. Perhaps the most unusual booking ever was when the northern comic Bernard Manning came for a session in Aeolian Hall to sing with a large orchestra. I had no idea what to expect from him vocally and when he arrived he was very personable and sat quietly in the corner of the studio while the musicians rehearsed. During the break I asked Bernard if he'd like to come to the canteen for a cup of tea but he courteously passed on the offer saying he'd prefer to wait in the studio. I brought him a cup of tea and when I arrived back in the studio he pulled out a brown paper bag from his raincoat pocket and said "I've brought my lunch with me, would you like to share a sandwich?" I thought that was very sweet but politely declined saying I had a lunch date booked after the recording. When it came time for Bernard to sing, he surprised everybody, including me, with his vocal prowess, running through his numbers like a seasoned pro. I congratulated him later and asked where he learned to sing like that and he told me of his early career as a vocalist with the Oscar Rabin band in Manchester. No wonder he knew what he was doing.

I know a really filthy Bernard Manning joke which is entirely unprintable here. Maybe after dinner one night.

Once in a while a little bit of extra special magic happens in the studio, often due to unexpected circumstances, one of which happened in March 1973 when a group called Northern Lights were due in Aeolian Studio 2 for an evening session. Their leader was Nicky North and I believe they were the house band at Streatham Locarno but the session nearly didn't happen because the sound balancer didn't turn up, leaving only myself and a young tape engineer, Bill Aitken, in the control room. The band were already setting up when I decided to do the session anyway, even though I'd never had Bill working the control desk before. I was mightily impressed, although a little anxious, with the way Bill spent extra time setting up the microphones, especially around the drum kit. As it turned out he produced the best drum sound I'd ever heard, even on record, and as close as you can imagine to the super-clean sound on the Carpenters discs. The rest of the sound was equally vibrant and commercial-sounding and the band were delighted when they heard the playback asking for copies of the tapes. You know you've got it right when the artists ask for tape copies. There was another added dimension to this particular session when Bill and I both remarked on the vocal quality of the exceptional girl singer, a young lady by the name of Tina Charles, who would go on to top the charts just a couple of years later. That was a magical night and it set my senses buzzing about this young engineer who stepped in and did such an amazing job at the controls. The very next day I went in to see Bill's boss and asked for Bill to be allocated to all my small combo sessions in future as he had done such a great job the previous evening. I was told in no uncertain manner that that wouldn't happen as Bill was merely a junior and couldn't be seen to be favoured over his more experienced colleagues. This set me back but I was determined to have my way saying Bill was an exceptional talent who had been able to provide exactly the sound I was looking for on my sessions and that I was prepared to go higher up to make this happen. It had the desired effect and Bill was perceived in a new light by his bosses, thank goodness. Bill and I became good friends, still are, and song-writing partners for a short spell. Maybe we'll release those demos one day.

Caroline said we didn't go abroad very much as I wanted to listen to the radio when my programmes went out but that wasn't the case in 1973 – I didn't stay up late to listen to Night Ride, that's for sure. In February we took off by train for the Swiss alpine village of Wengen with Caroline six months pregnant meaning that I would be skiing solo or with a group. In order to reach Wengen, which is quite remote, we travelled via Interlaken and then took the cog-wheel railway up the slopes through the most beautiful winter landscape. We stayed at the art deco style Palace Hotel where we met and made friends with two couples from Southport, the Rostrons and the Hampsons. They invited me to go skiing with them while Caroline enjoyed a hot chocolate or two relaxing on the hotel sun terrace watching the world go by with wonderful vistas of the Jungfrau and Eiger peaks in the distance. This arrangement worked perfectly well until one day the weather closed in when we were near the summit of Kleine Scheidegg, or maybe it was the Lauberhorn, and we were forced to ski down through a blizzard. It was quite frightening and John said not to worry as Sally Hampson would take the lead and get us all down safely, which she did brilliantly, being a highly accomplished skier, as was her husband Tony, who had a company producing the sweetly-named "Potter's Little Pills" – and that was long before Harry appeared on the scene.

Later that evening over a round of drinks Sally and Tony asked us if we would be watching the Grand National at the end of March. I said we sometimes put a bet on and recounted the tale of the kid who backed Red Alligator in 1968 and always put his money on red. They looked at me in astonishment and said they had a horse running that was certainly worth a punt and it also had red in its name. Sally told me it belonged to her grandfather Noel Le Mare, was trained on Southport sands and would be starting at a pretty good price on the day. We said we'd back it and what was it called? "Red Rum", she said, and when it came in first we made a bob or two, so thanks Sally. We stayed friends over the years with John and I striking up a forever friendship through our shared love of rock and roll, blues, country music and sport. In fact, it was John's enthusiasm for Tammy Wynette and Charlie Rich that made me jump all over their records when they were released by Epic, which probably helped get them in the charts, so maybe John should get a gold record as a thank you. It wasn't only our shared musical passion that kept us connected over the years as John turned out to be an ace dentist with his own practise and so we became his patients as well, and remained so until he retired many years later. Anyway, Red Rum, eh, who knew?

Caroline had a difficult pregnancy and was in Princess Margaret hospital in Windsor waiting for delivery day which happened unexpectedly on 23 May at 8.30pm. I was in London having an early evening meal with Pam Cox in a little Italian restaurant in Woodstock Street before a session in Aeolian Hall when the engineer came rushing in and said they'd had a phone call saying Caroline was about to give birth. Panic stations. Pam said "Go, I'll take the session for you, get going". I drove like mad along the M4 in torrential rain getting to Windsor just in time to be presented with my new baby daughter, Krystle Fiona Louise – what joy and a heart-bursting moment, she was lovely and Caroline was doing well, thank goodness. Just a few hours later on Night Ride presenter Barry Alldis announced Krystle's birth to the listening nation. The first of many name-checks.

Three months later the three of us went on holiday to the south of Spain driving a new Volvo but with no air-conditioning, boy was it hot. We shared accommodation there with our friends Pat and Brian Kirtley, with Brian and I attempting to play tennis in the blistering heat. We didn't stay on court too long and every day was the same but it was a good break and a much-needed holiday, especially for Caroline after the birth.

Soon after we arrived home I was invited to a meeting by pop group manager Peter Walsh, who had a proposition for me. He was managing The Troggs and Marmalade at the time and asked if I would produce their next records, which I was delighted to agree to with one proviso and that was, because of my work at the BBC, I wanted the producer credit to be Roger Brook, the pen name I had used previously. Peter agreed to this and in August we went into Sarm East studios in London for the first session with The Troggs. They were a great bunch of lads and we got on really well during the recording of Reg Presley's composition "Strange Movies" with "I'm On Fire" as the "B" side. I brought in an extra instrument to add a little heft. That was an electronic synthesizer by Hohner called a clavinet and it delivered exactly the sound I wanted for the Troggs to make the sound big and ballsy. All the reviews I've read seem to agree that we achieved that objective and it has been described in many ways such as "glam proto punk", "fathers of heavy metal" and "debauched', which it certainly was.

We were all delighted with the results and Peter was sure he could get a release on it soon and we booked another session at Sarm for me to produce Marmalade. They were another easy-going group and we laid down two tracks "Down By The River" and "Sweet Sweet Music", neither of which have ever been released and I'm still waiting for offers. Peter failed to get a release on those Marmalade songs and that's when things started to go pear-shaped. He asked me to produce another session with Hot Chocolate and I said I couldn't keep working on these recordings without some finance and a proper contract, neither of which ever materialised. To make matters worse the Troggs disc did come out on Pye records and Peter Walsh put himself down as the producer. That was the final straw, I had been well and truly stitched up by a master of manipulation, a man in whom I put unfounded trust. You live and learn, once bitten twice shy etc, etc, and the BBC was looking like a much better bet for the future.

In September 1973 Caroline and I took a break away from it all at Forest Mere Health Farm in Liphook, Hampshire. To say it was painful for me would be an understatement and although it wasn't the fault of the establishment it was the fault of the regime that caused me so much agony. It wasn't until many years later that I found out the reason for the sleepless nights and distress. There was one memorable highlight while staying there and that was meeting up with the actor Alan Lake, Diana Dors husband, who was there on his own trying to dry out after a period of heavy drinking following a riding accident in which he broke his back. He told me about the fall from the horse but not about the drinking and in the afternoon, while Caroline was having a massage treatment and facial, he said "I'm going over the wall tonight, want to come with me?" I said "What do you mean, escape?" and he said "Yes, but only to the pub down the road". He was very much "Jack The Lad", good company and very funny so I agreed to accompany him out of Stalag Mere that evening. We made our dash for freedom about nine o'clock, unobserved as far as we knew, and had a thoroughly enjoyable hour or so in total anonymity at the local hostelry. Alan talked lovingly of Diana, mentioned some of the films and TV productions he'd been in and told a few good jokes. I told him I worked at the BBC and said I liked Diana's singing on her version of "The Point Of No Return", suggesting it would be great if she could come in and do a session for Radio Two. Alan thought that was a good idea and said he'd mention it to Diana when he got home but, whether he did or didn't, I don't know because I never got to produce Diana Dors. Years later, after both Alan and Diana died in 1984, there were reports in the papers of Diana's Missing Millions and the mysterious codes she used to protect the whereabouts of the hidden hoard. It struck me that there was a good fictional story to be told about Alan giving me a series of numbers in the pub that night, swearing me to secrecy and binding me to hold them for him until he asked for their return at some future date. Wouldn't you just know it, in 2003 a TV film came out with that exact storyline saying Alan had died without ever revealing the coded numbers and their meaning. Another boat missed.

Back in Broadcasting House big decisions were being reached in response to forthcoming winter restrictions across industry to be introduced by the government to conserve fuel stocks These were to be in place from the first of January 1974 as everybody geared up for the Three-Day Week. It was a major restraint for the entire country and the BBC was not spared, with TV broadcasts ending at 10.30pm each night. Radio Two was also affected and as a consequence Mark White called me into his office to tell me the official position and how it might affect me. Was I going to be out of work again? Mark told me that all freelance contracts had to be cancelled and that would affect me in particular. I probably looked a bit downcast and said "Oh, I see", but Mark smiled and said "However, I do have one permanent producer role to fill if you'd like to consider it?" I didn't jump straight in with enthusiasm and he said "Look at it this way, it's unlikely I'll be able to offer you any work for the next few months, your other freelance activity may also be affected and where would that leave you? Also, if you take this job your immediate security is guaranteed, your salary will be more than you're earning now, you will get your own shows to produce and then, if you decide it's not for you, you can leave after six months or so". This was what we didn't call back in those days "A no-brainer" but that's precisely what it was and I thanked Mark who put my name forward for what they called a "Board", in other words a job interview. That was rubber-stamped and I became a full-time member of staff 1n December 1973. You won't be surprised to learn that I never once regretted that decision.

1974 arrived without very much change in my working life except that now I was properly on the team and becoming familiar with the day-to-day workings of various production offices, producers and presenters. I was still mainly on Night Ride but also providing support for the Jimmy Young and Pete Murray shows as well as being solely responsible for a series of short pre-recorded shows for the World Service. These I had to script, select the music and produce in the studio with various presenters at the microphone. When they received good feedback I rose to the next level of known competence. There was so much to take in, especially BBC terminology with regard to TLA's (three-letter abbreviations), of which the BBC itself is one. There was HR2 – Head of Radio Two, MDR – Managing Director Radio, LCR – London Control Room and some funny ones, like BOG – Board Of Governors, SODS – Studio Operations Duty Schedule and the best of all, seen on a memo from 1953 signed (in jest) by Old MacDonald as E.I.E.I.O. – Engineering Induction and Engineering Information Officer. Now that is an etymological mouthful. Quite a learning curve, but usually with good humour, such as these questions "Why is abbreviation such a long word?", "Why is dyslexia difficult to spell?" and "Why is phonetic not spelt like it sounds?" Questions, always questions.

There were other social conventions to get used to as well at Aeolian Hall, one of which was the daily routine of mass decampment from the office to Yates Wine Lodge in Avery Row at the rear of the building. It was customary to stay and chat for at least a couple of rounds and that was my limit as I was always conscious of having to drive home each night. I soon became aware that the drinking culture was deeply embedded across both radio and the music business, just as it had been in the print media. Some of the people I worked with suffered from the occupational hazard of alcohol dependency, very often due to the easy availability of drink and the generous expense accounts and promotion budgets of the music publishers and record labels. I'm not suggesting that I was immune to the offer of a tincture but I usually managed to keep it under control, always aware that I was at work, needed to get home of an evening and not wanting to be found by the cleaners next morning slumped over a desk or, worse still, hanging on to a toilet bowl. Oh yes, that did happen from time to time.

Mark White called me into his office one morning and waved my expenses claim at me saying "What's this, Geoff, some mistake, surely?" and I said "I'm sorry Mark, have I spent too much?" His reply was "No, it looks as though you've spent too little, why is it so low?" Then I told him that after every session in the pub the conductor always got the drinks in and sometimes wouldn't hear of me buying a round. He said I had to insist on a reciprocal drink and that we didn't want to be beholden to anybody from the music business. Obviously, I was an ingenue in this department and had much to learn. Well, I was the youngest producer there and the first of a new generation that hadn't seen military service, as most of my male colleagues had, many of them having served in the RAF, itself a form of bonding.

Caroline and I were invited by Mark White to be his guests at the Eurovision Song Contest at The Dome, Brighton in early April, which we deemed to be quite an honour and attended the event in our best bib and tucker. We had good seats in the auditorium and enthusiastically supported our entry "Long Live Love" by Olivia Newton-John but were fearful of the Italian entry "Si" by Gigliola Cinquetti and "I See A Star" by Mouth And MacNeal but the outstanding performance by Abba was the runaway winner on the night, and deservedly so. Olivia came in fourth place which wasn't bad against that kind of competition, as evidenced by the fact that her record was placed below those other entries, even in the UK charts. At the end of the presentations s we all stood up to leave the Assistant Head of Radio Two, Geoff Owen, asked me if I'd like to go backstage and meet Terry Wogan. I thought that would be fun so off we went to find Terry in the Radio Outside Broadcast vehicle waiting to interview the winners. He shook me warmly by the hand and was presumably as perplexed as I was to explain my presence there but we hit it off rather well as he asked me about my background before the BBC. I gave him a quick round-up of my career in the sixties and my time in as a singer in Oslo which seemed to interest him as we were about to have a visit from a Swedish band. Abba arrived flushed with success and gave a somewhat breathless account of their formation and performance on the night and, all in all, they gave a great interview with excellent English. I wonder if that tape has survived. When Terry introduced me to Abba he told them I had been a singer in the sixties with a group called The Vanguards in Oslo and blow me down, they had heard of the Vanguards, but not me, ha. After they left Terry turned to me, looked me straight in the eye and said "OK, so which one?" "Which one what?" I replied. "Come on, the blonde or the brunette?" "Oh, the blonde for me" to which Terry said "No, no, always go for the brunette, every time". Well, I thought, he has an eye for the ladies but surely he can't be more experienced than me in these matters, he doesn't seem cut out for it. That was my first meeting with Terry Wogan and it would be some time before we would work together, when the stars aligned in 1976.

Later that April I produced one of my last two recordings away from the BBC. The first was a duo called John and Rosalind who came in for a Radio Two session and were very taken with the way they sounded on tape. They told me they had a residency at the exclusive Factotum restaurant and would like to record a live album there and they would very much like me to produce it. I said I liked the idea but that as I was now a staff-producer I would have to get permission for such an undertaking. This was granted and I booked the Island mobile recording vehicle and brought in a four-piece group led by MD and arranger Brian Dee on organ, Laurie Steele on guitar, Russ Stableford on bass and Hal Fisher on drums, top musicians all. John Winder played acoustic guitar and wrote all the songs with Rosalind taking on most of the vocal duties. Rosalind Hanneman was also famous as the Evening Standard "Face Of The Year" in 1968, had been married to Mark Wirtz, composer of A Teenage Opera, was managed by Tim Rice, who wrote songs for her with Andrew Lloyd Webber and was now making her way with her new partner John. Another case of a star you never heard of. That evening the Factotum was packed with invited guests, one of whom was Lord Hanson, later to be my boss at Melody Radio. Small world, eh? All went off without a hitch and I later mixed the album and pressed only 100 copies of "John And Rosalind A Night At The Factotum" for all the guests in attendance that night. The sleeve was designed by the Italian cartoonist Enzo Apicella, generally regarded as one of the driving forces during the "Swinging Sixties", and the photographer at the event was Enzo Raggazzini. Caroline and I stayed friends with John and Rosalind for a while after these exhilarating times but, as with many connections in the music business, we lost touch and I do wonder where they are today.

The last commercial recording I took charge of was at the request of my old pal Pete Bocking who had moved to Margate with his wife and taken on the management of a local group called Flight 56, specialists in retro rock and roll with a terrific female singer. I booked a session at Farmyard Studios in Little Chalfont, run by another old pal, Trevor Morais, and housed in the former home of actor Dirk Bogarde. We laid down about ten tracks and everybody left that day well-satisfied with their efforts and awaited an offer from a record label. No offer ever came and I still have those recordings in my archive. Any offers? I think Pete wanted to play less as he suffered from arthritis and he wasn't too keen on touring any longer after his stint as Lonnie Donegan's guitarist.

I'm drifting a little bit sideways here because many of the sessions I was involved with were recorded on large ten-inch tape-spools which I was unable to play at home on my Sony TC355 machine. A sound engineer pal, Bob Conduct, was keen to buy it, so cash changed hands. The real reason for my diversion here is to tell you that years later Bob was speaking to some Sony bigwigs and when they heard he had an original TC355 they were keen to obtain it as the Sony Sound Museum didn't have one. They were delighted when Bob offered it to them and now my 1960's classic is in the Sony "Hall of Fame". Just thought you'd like to know that.

One regular date in the music business calendar over the years was the annual Ivor Novello Awards luncheon and in May 1974 it took place at the Grosvenor House Hotel in Park Lane. The "Ivors", as they are known, were organised by The Songwriters Guild Of Great Britain to recognise outstanding achievements in the world of popular music. The main winners that year were Elton John for "Daniel", 10cc for "Rubber Bullets" and Gilbert O'Sullivan for "Get Down". Always great to be at the "Ivors", even though some of the later awards were seen through a slightly alcoholic haze.

May that year also saw a major upswing in my career as I left Night Ride to join Frances Line as co-producer of the Tony Brandon afternoon show. The show had a large budget for live music and I was responsible for booking and producing all the big names I could entice into the studio. Over my relatively short stint on the show I managed to hold sessions with some really big-name recording stars, the first of which was Johnny Mathis, who was about to have a major career uplift and his first chart hit in over ten years with "I'm Stone In Love With You". Fellow Americans visiting the UK and happy to record for the BBC in our Maida Vale studios included Vic Damone, yet another big band crooner of Italian extraction. It really felt like a scoop getting stars of such stature and the list continued with yet another US jazz and soul singer Freda Payne, famous for her early Number One disco hit "Band Of Gold". We also had some of the best UK and European talent to draw on with appearances by Greek superstars Nana Mouskouri and Demis Roussos, soon to become known as "The Singing Frock" thanks to plays on the Terry Wogan show. UK stars in attendance were Cliff Richard, Barbara Dickson and the "Singalonga" supremo Max Bygraves among many others. Looking back I would have wanted to keep copies of those tapes but there was a system in place at Radio Two which allowed for any of these sessions to be repeated across the network so that once they had had their initial exposure on Tony's show they did a tour of most of the other shows on the station which meant I never saw them again. Like many recordings in those days they were probably held in the tape library for a while and then wiped clean for re-use.

One of the remarkable things about those sessions was the highly acceptable sound quality we managed to achieve, thanks mainly to the great skill of our sound engineers, or studio mangers as they were called. I think they were the best in the world in this kind of pressurised atmosphere, being required to deliver five perfect performances in a three-hour session, with no re-mixing. That they approximated the sound of the original commercial recordings so closely was testament to their talent and all the artists and bandleaders never failed to show their gratitude and appreciation. One story on those Tony Brandon show recordings was told to me by the ace big band balancer Robin Sedgeley, who had been with me on the Vic Damone session. He said he was working with the big band backing Tony Bennett when Tony's manager came into the control cubicle and said "Robin, I want you to stick the band up Tony's ass". Robin was quite rightly taken aback at this, never having had such an instruction before, and as he looked back for clarification he was told "You know, very tight behind Tony, no gaps, his voice should be part of the band, not noticeably separate". Robin knew exactly what was meant and said that was how he was going to do it anyway. That phrase of where to stick the band has stayed with me all this time, as you can see.

A final word on one session and the resultant repercussions was a studio date with the pianist and arranger Roger Webb. I knew Roger was Cilla Black's musical director and during a coffee break we got chatting and I told him about singing in the sixties with Lek and Barry from Herman's Hermits and he told me that he'd played piano on their hit "I'm Into Something Good", which I never knew until then. We got on well and when we discovered that we lived near each other in Cookham, Roger invited Caroline and I over to his place for a drink and a game of tennis, a suggestion that was to have huge repercussions for several people in the coming months.

We met for drinks and I played tennis with Roger and his wife Margot with Caroline sitting, sipping and spectating as she was not keen to play. Roger asked if I knew anybody locally who might join us for a foursome one day and I said we were friends with Tony Blackburn and his wife Tessa Wyatt who lived close by. That was to prove to be a fateful catalyst as introductions were made and Tony and Margot got to be friendly, which led to Roger and Tessa becoming friendly. We later heard stories that both illicit couples independently made bookings to eat in the same restaurant on the same night - talk about fireworks. That was to bring about the end of Tony's marriage to Tessa resulting in a huge amount of press coverage and Tony going into meltdown and sobbing into his microphone live on air. All extremely sad and perhaps avoidable if it hadn't been for that fateful game of tennis.

My production abilities were being gradually and gently examined and assessed by management as I produced my first solo effort on the Saturday Early Show with Bruce Wyndham. This was followed by the "Vocal Touch" series written by Ken Barnes and presented by Teddy Johnson. Nobody complained.

The highlight of the year for me personally came on December 2nd at an Anglo-American Sporting Club boxing and dinner evening at the London Hilton in honour of Muhammad Ali, the Heavyweight Champion of the World. The Welcome Address was given by Kenneth Wolstenholme then Eamonn Andrews introduced Ali who responded with gratitude for the honour in his usual eloquent manner. There were four boxing bouts that evening including one featuring the great Chris Finnegan who won his Light Heavyweight fight on points against Victor Attivor. At the end of the evening I managed to get Ali to sign my menu (still a treasured possession) and when I told him I was with the BBC he immediately asked me if I knew Harry Carpenter. I had to say that our paths had never crossed, little thinking that some years later I would help to get his teeth fixed at the Open Golf Championship at Royal Birkdale. That story still to come.

Radio Two was generally a very pleasant and relaxed environment to be working in but on the odd occasion there might be some disruption, increase in tension or an emotional

189

confrontation such as happened towards the end of 1974 when Simon Bates' producer John Meloy fell foul of his executive producer Chris Morgan. At issue was a recently released record by The Tymes called "Ms Grace" which John had programmed and played on Simon's show but which Chris regarded as highly inappropriate for exposure on Radio Two. The story goes that Chris called John to his office and told him not to play that record again, with John defending his right to choose the music for his show without interference. This is where the immovable object met the irresistible force and tempers flared with Chris receiving a black eye as witness to this meeting of minds. The upshot of this was the removal of John Meloy from the Simon Bates show and one Geoffrey Mullin being appointed the new producer. The slings and arrows of outrageous fortune where one man's loss is another man's gain – is that a mixed metaphor I see before me?

January 1975 saw major changes to the Radio Two schedule with Tony Brandon replaced by David Hamilton in a simulcast with Radio One and my new Simon Bates show was also broadcast on both networks, so technically I can claim to have been a Radio One producer, not that I need that accolade as I turned down three attempts over the coming years to drag me away from Radio Two, as you'll hear later. Simon was great to work with and we got on like a house on fire enjoying the music and laughing every day. The transition to me having my own show was seamless and I was given my own office on the third floor of Aeolian Hall and my own telephone extension so things were really looking up. The operational side of the show was so smooth that there is very little to write about other than I began to realise how important the show was to the record industry as I began to get more and more visits from pluggers, sorry – promotion executives, trying to sell me their wares. The phone was in regular use, too, and one morning it rang and a mellifluous voice said "Hello, good morning to you" and I said "Good morning Simon, how are you?" to which the voice replied "Simon, who's Simon, this is Willie Rushton, have I got the wrong number?" I could hardly contain my laughter as I told Willie that he had indeed got the wrong number. Well, anyone can make a mistake.

There was more movement on the domestic front as Caroline and I decided the Cookham cottage was a little small for our future needs and so we re-located from the sublime to the ridiculous by buying a much larger house in Bourne End. It was a wonderful turn-of-the century house with a Thames tributary stream running through the rear garden and reputedly the oldest hand-operated lock in the country. Being so close to the river was idyllic in one way but a trial in another as there was the ever-present threat of flooding, which did happen once with the water lapping up only inches from the back doorstep. We had to park the car some distance away and walk to the house across duckboards and it was amusing to see our neighbour across the stream leave his kitchen door and step into a rowing boat. Caroline's parents fared no better when a large stack of logs cut and ready for burning floated off down the Thames never to be seen again.

Krystle was walking and talking by this time and entertaining us all just by being so happy and cuddly. She was beautiful and loving and to give Caroline a little more free time we took on a Swiss au-pair girl called Irene who had good English and played the violin, so she fitted in perfectly.

Another year another Ivor Novello Awards lunch, this time in May at the Dorchester Hotel with two of the major winners about as far apart in the pop spectrum as you can imagine. The best-selling song of the year was "Tiger Feet" by Mud and the best song of the year was "Streets of London" by Ralph McTell. Without a doubt the highlight of the day was the presence of Vera Lynn, recipient of the award for Outstanding Services To British Music, which she graciously accepted and treated us to a rendition of "We'll Meet Again". I'm surprised the Dorchester managed to withstand the rapturous applause that followed this performance which almost literally brought the house down.

I didn't see Simon too often after he finished his shift as he was more than likely back home as I was waking up. My routine was to listen back to the show each morning when a "snoop" tape came back from the studio. We'd meet up for a coffee if Simon was staying in town for any reason and now and again we'd be invited to a record company reception or out for a lunch, one of which took place at The White Tower in Percy Street. Radio Two had moved from Aeolian Hall and was now operating from number 74A Charlotte Street so the restaurant was just a short stagger away, as were many more excellent eateries which welcomed our patronage with open arms and emptied many a plugger's wallet. The White Tower served the best steak souvlaki in town and as our mouths were watering sitting in the bar on the ground floor a group of four gents got up and were taken to their table on the floor above. I looked across to where they had been seated and noticed they had left an envelope on a chair and trying to be helpful I went to pick it up and take it to them. As I looked at the envelope I heard the rush of feet coming rapidly down the stairs and a man with the white face of panic snatched it from me saying "Did you look inside?" and I said "No, of course not" and with a sigh of relief he checked to see it was still sealed, said thanks and went back upstairs. That's a long-winded way of getting to the point, and when Simon asked "What the hell was all that about?" I said the envelope had OHMS stamped on it with a label saying "Top Secret", so no wonder he was wetting himself.

Charlotte Street was foodie heaven with some of my favourite restaurants all within stumbling distance of the office. They included the very old-established up-market L'Etoile, where T S Eliot used to dine, with cheap and cheerful Bertorelli's Italian at the other end of the scale. The best scampi provinciali could be had at Trattoria Pescatori and when Chez Gerard opened you just had to have chateaubriand with frites. Above all others, though, my absolute favourite was the The Little Acropolis, a Greek taverna owned and run by Nicky, where they served the best lamb kebabs and, if you asked very nicely, they would prepare amazing crepes suzette before your very eyes. I never have tasted better. Charlotte Street eateries were obviously favoured by the establishment, as witnessed by the "Top Secret" story above and the fact that The Little Acropolis was frequented by the then Prime Minister, James Callaghan. Several times I watched with interest as Nicky ushered him through the restaurant to a private dining room at the rear, never looking left or right, as if there were no other diners in the place and he was invisible. What a vote winner.

Sitting in my new office one morning at the beginning of May I was surprised and delighted when Terry Wogan walked in and asked if I had time for a chat, what a gentleman. "How are you getting on with Simon?" he asked and I said things were going very well and I was enjoying my first real solo production. Then he said something which resonated quite strongly with me, "I drive in every morning listening to Simon's show wondering why I'm enjoying his music selection so much more than the stuff I have to play on my show". I said "I take that as a compliment but what exactly do you mean?" and Terry said "Look, I'm playing anything from Max Bygraves to Shirley Bassey to Vince Hill and you're playing The Beatles, Roy Orbison and Elvis – what's going on?" I said I always tried to broaden the appeal by putting in more sixties tunes and told him he should have a word with his producer as he was the one choosing the music, which he said he would but without any discernible degree of enthusiasm or expectation. End of music discussion and on to other things as Terry said "Fancy a game of cricket?" and I said "Howzat?", which made us both laugh – a sign of things to come. He told me he was organising a charity cricket match at his local club in Taplow and was going to invite Bates and Blackburn to play, along with some celebs, and could I handle a bat and ball. I said I'd played for the First Eleven at school and once smashed a ball over the school roof which, if it had been baseball, would have been a home run. I also told him it was a cricket match that finally decided me to get my eyes tested and Terry said "Howzat?", at which we both laughed again, and that kind of repartee, good-humoured wordplay and bonhomie would underscore our friendship for many years to come. I told him that I played in a civil service game and was fielding on a distant boundary when I picked up the ball, threw it back towards the wicket and was surprised when I was called back by the captain to be told that my throw had run the batsman out. I obviously couldn't see a thing from that distance and so it really was time to get to look like Buddy Holly.

The match was arranged for June 8th and the team consisted of the two DJ's along with Terry's friend Kits Browning, Daphne Du Maurier's son, the great cricket commentator Brian "Johnners"

Johnston, Sheridan Morley, Willie Rushton and my cricketing hero Denis Compton. Others may have revered Len Hutton or "Fiery" Freddie Truman but I always thought "The Brylcreem Boy" the most dashing of them all. The Taplow boys batted first and halfway through their innings I took a fizzing catch at square leg which nearly knocked me backwards. As the batsman left the crease I saw Terry speak to Denis and nod in my direction, at which Denis chucked the ball at me and said "Now, Geoffrey, let's see what you can do". I marked my run up as in days of yore and Denis said, in a loud voice, "At last, somebody who knows how to bowl". My heart nearly burst with pride at this recognition from the maestro and I rewarded his faith by taking out the off-stump of the incumbent batsman. All in all a great day and an experience to savour. I have a great photo of Terry's winning team for posterity.

Live music was still an important ingredient in the Early Show and contributions came in from the BBC regions to be played, one per day, across the week and I was responsible for producing The London Studio Players, a small light orchestral unit led by Reg Kilbey. This was an anachronistic throwback to much earlier times which Simon and I agreed was inappropriate for that time of the morning and slowed the programme down considerably. The boss, Mark White, obviously felt differently and on the 4th of July sent me this memo – "I must congratulate you on this session. Twice when I have missed an announcement, I have thought I was listening to a record. An excellent choice of music, excellently played and balanced, well programmed so that they fit perfectly into the show". I showed the memo to Bates and suggested he didn't drop quite so many of these items in future. The juxtaposition of the of old and new styles of music was always a challenge but my placement methods seemed to keep the boss happy.

The listeners seemed to be happy too as that August we got a very high approval rating from Audience Research. This was the kind of feedback we were looking for – "Of all the ways to wake up in the mornings, Simon Bates is the best of them all", "Just right for raising one from apathy" (I like that one), "We were able to hear the delightful selection of music". They found Simon cheerful, genuine and quietly engaging with the only complaint being that the programme was too short.

It was around the time of that memo that Mark asked me into his office to tell me that he was bringing back Jack Jackson, the "Daddy of all disc jockeys", and would I please be his producer. Wow. Would I? I said I'd be delighted to work with such a legend as I'd listened to his "Record Roundabout" shows as a kid and his madcap TV shows with Glen Mason, Alfred Marks and Barbara Windsor. Mark said I should first meet Jack's agent Bunny Lewis at his office in Dolphin Square to finalise the details. Bunny was most pleasant when we met and explained that Jack had returned to England from Tenerife for health reasons as the climate in the Canary Islands was affecting his breathing. Jack was now living in Rickmansworth and would like to meet up with me at his studio there to discuss the show. Bunny told me that it was Jack who had given the BBC the famous soubriquet of "Auntie", which I hadn't known, and asked me to be gentle and not to work him too hard as he wasn't in the best of health. At my first meeting with Jack I told him I had been to these studios in the sixties when I sold advertising space in Record Retailer to his sons Malcolm and John to promote their record label Ad-Rhythm. He said "Welcome back", we laughed and that broke any ice that needed breaking as his wonderful wife Eve joined us with coffee and cake. Jack was a man of many talents, a humorous cartoonist, gifted musician and a great raconteur who regaled me with entertaining tales from his past, especially from his days as a trumpeter and dance band leader. I told him about working with Joe Loss and the "Chattanooga Choo Choo" story, which made him laugh, he told me about his residency at the Dorchester Hotel and his travels on the road with his dance band, with one tale revealing the inner workings of the song-plugging fraternity. If an influential and popular band had a broadcasting date at a ballroom anywhere in the country, there would always be a coterie of publishers standing in front of the bandstand competing with each other to get the band to play one of their songs. Such a performance could increase sales of both records and sheet music considerably and the pluggers were prepared to pay for such exposure on the radio. This insidious practise was later called "payola" and in order to get their music heard the pluggers would catch the bandleader's eye holding up one, two or more fingers to indicate the number of pounds they were prepared to pay for a play. At the end of such an evening, payments were tallied up and cash was handed over with bandleaders receiving bundles worth two to three hundred pounds, an absolute fortune back in the thirties and forties. So, the earning potential was enormous, with broadcasting fees, payments from the ballrooms and plugger's cash handouts the British big bands were really in the money. Jack told me had heard that American bandleaders like Glen Miller and Artie Shaw could earn ten times as much in a week as the top film stars of the day such as "The King Of Hollywood", Clark Gable, Joan Crawford and "The Goddess" Greta Garbo.

Our working arrangement was that I would provide Jack with plenty of background research and a stack of all the newly released records for him to choose those which he liked and which fitted into the show. Jack took about a week after I had delivered this material to put the show together and I collected the tapes to listen to back to in my office. There were five Jack Jackson shows broadcast as Bank Holiday Specials over the next two years, with one in particular getting by the censors for the inclusion of a song that would never have been heard anywhere else on Radio Two. Jack never lost his sense of humour and must have had a mischievous twinkle in his eye when he included a track from a Dr Hook album I had given him called "Roland The Roadie And Gertrude The Groupie" about life on the road in a rock band. Funny thing is, after the broadcast nobody said a word about this naughty song and the expected repercussions never materialised. Working with Jack was a joy and a privilege as he had set the template for many that followed, including my pals Adrian Juste and Kenny Everett, who cited Jack as his main inspiration, and that's not a bad accolade, either.

It's often said that it's not what you know but who you know and, for the first time in my life I became that person "who you know" as our neighbour Valerie Childs introduced us to her mother, the acclaimed piano teacher Lisa Childs. Lisa was a patron, along with the author J B Priestley, of the annual local arts and music event The Wooburn Festival, an idea originally conceived by the orchestral conductor Richard Hickox. Lisa told me it was mainly to celebrate the music popular at the turn of the century with piano recitals, chamber music and the story of Gilbert and Sullivan's comic operas. She asked if I would kindly consider becoming involved by producing an evening of more contemporary music but, she stressed, not a rock concert, rather something that might sit comfortably on Radio Two, for example. I agreed readily and then spent the next few days wondering what I had signed up for, but before the panic set in I managed to find a headline act in the shape of the singer, songwriter and musician Ed Welch, recently seen on BBC TV as the musical director for The Diane Solomon Show. Ed had also been associated with Shirley Bassey, P J Proby, Matt Monro and Spike Milligan so he knew his way around and asked me to recruit a bass player and drummer for the evening. The two I came up with were perfect for Ed's style, both top-flight musicians having played in the Dudley Moore Trio - Chris Karan on drums and Pete Morgan on double bass. I had worked with them on sessions many times over the years and I reminded Pete of seeing him at Ronnie Scott's club in The Morgan-James Duo singing their fabulous version of Damita Jo's song "Sweet Pussycat" – love that record. Finally, I roped Simon Bates in to compere the evening, which was generally regarded as a huge success, giving an added dimension to the otherwise mostly traditional festival. Much kudos in the community for me.

I saw out a very productive and enjoyable year on The Early Show working with Simon who gave me a name-check in his book "My Tune" with this brief acknowledgement "I was working for a delightful and easy-going man, who seemed permanently on the verge of collapsing with laughter, called Geoff Mullin, who functioned as my producer", end of quote. At least I functioned, and Simon always seemed to me to also be verging on laughter, we were always laughing, and it's nice that he says he was working for me, as I always assumed it was the other way round.

Dave & Marianne wedding 1971

Chapter Eighteen

The Wogan Years

Now this is where the fun really starts. Sometime towards the end of October I arrived in my office to find Terry sitting in my chair and drinking a coffee. "You're late", he said and I fell about laughing at this impertinence, who the hell did he think he was, this Wogan fella? He said he was just passing by and thought he'd pop in for a chat, at which I figured there was a little more to it than that. He told me he was still enjoying my choice of music for Simon and what would I think of the idea of producing the breakfast show. I said I'd love to but that I had absolutely no control over which show I worked on and Terry came back with the prophetic phrase "No, you haven't, but I have". After he left I pondered awhile on whether he could influence events in that way as producer allocations were always decided by the four executive producers and the head of department, currently Geoff Owen, who had taken over from Mark White. It was with great interest that I waited for the schedule due to come into force in January and sure enough, there it was in black and white, I was to be the new producer of the Breakfast Show with Terry Wogan.

There were a few green eyes at this development as the Wogan show was the one most producers hankered after and a few of the older hands thought it should be based on some kind of imagined pecking order and that I had jumped the queue. Well, I never pushed for anything nor tried to leapfrog anybody for self-aggrandisement or promotion, I just accepted what I was offered and got on with my job, so that was their problem, not mine. After that announcement I went over to see Terry in the studio at the end his show, we congratulated each other on the good news and looked forward to our new partnership. This started on Monday 5th of January 1976 between 7am and 9am with all the usual guff about

Wogan's Winners (horse-racing tips), Fight The Flab (weight-loss ideas), Pause For Thought (religious items) and a report by Henry Blofeld in Sydney on the Test match between Australia and West Indies.

For anyone who doesn't remember, Radio Two was the home of sport back then, with coverage of practically all the sports of interest to the British public ranging from the obvious to the obscure, including reports from the Isle of Man TT to the Round Britain Milk Race, from Formula One Grand Prix to Henley Royal Regatta, everything was covered.

I must divert your attention for a moment as the Henley Regatta was of particular interest to me as Caroline's father Bill always moored his boat, the Moira S, alongside the Phyllis Court Club lawn for the annual event when family and friends would gather en-masse to watch the racing, enjoy the food and drink and marvel at the stupendous firework display on the final Saturday night. It was such a tradition that the mooring next to ours was always occupied by good friend Jock McElwain, a former wing commander in the RAF, who gave me instruction in the subtle art of croquet. Krystle was only two months old at her first Henley in 1973 and admired by all as she lay in her cot, with Caroline's sister Holly and brother William keeping a watchful eye on their newly arrived niece.

My working conditions could not have been more relaxed or conducive to creative thinking, with little interference from those on high, no clock-watching or set start and end times to the day producers could come and go as they pleased. This self-regulation was open to abuse but I like to think I didn't gain the system too much, if at all, and always gave 100% to all my shows, which is probably why I always got 100% job satisfaction, and you can't get any higher than that.

Every day was beginning to seem like Christmas as each morning there would be a huge postbag which secretary Karen sorted through, replying to listeners letters and passing the more interesting on to Terry to use in the show. There were many regular contributors writing in with silly stories and amusing poems and the like giving Terry plenty of feedback and ammunition with which to entertain the nation. I thought it very astute when he figured out the ploy of getting his listeners to write all his material, putting it in a book and selling it back to them.

There were many invitations to film preview screenings and record label receptions, the first of which was that very January at The Elephant On The River restaurant to mark the Number One success of Slik's song "Forever And Ever" on Bell Records. It was also the first time Terry and I were photographed together, a moment to treasure and stick in the scrap-book.

Programming the music was an interesting exercise with two hours-worth to find every day and no repeats other than current singles. I usually gave Terry 8 items per half hour, always coming out of the news with an up-tempo number and early on trying to move the musical agenda forward a little at a time so as not to "frighten the horses", as Terry would say. It seems strange to recall now the trepidation I felt wondering what kind of telling-off I'd get the morning I programmed "All Shook Up" by Elvis to come out of the 8 o'clock news. It had never been played on the station before, to the best of my knowledge, and was certainly breaking new ground as far as I was aware. My nerves were jangling as I went into the office that morning and waited for the inevitable call from above and guess what – nobody said a thing – result. Now I could move things on apace but I'll never forget that feeling of butterflies in the tummy for maybe having pushed things too far.

As Terry was "self-op" my presence wasn't required in the studio, just an engineer behind the glass to monitor the quality and output levels, so I had a fairly normal day in the office to concentrate mainly on music selection. There was plenty of contemporary music to choose from at the beginning of the year with hits by Abba, Paul Simon, Barbara Dickson, Andy Fairweather-Low, the classic Walker Brothers "No Regrets", the sexy R & J Stone song "We Do It", the comedy duo Laurel And Hardy with "Lonesome Pine" and Terry's favourite figure of fun Demis Roussos, "The Singing Frock". These were all perfect Radio Two material which meant we were not at all as "old and fuddy-duddy" as some would like to think and in the coming years we would be as important to the success of many artists as Radio One had been in the past.

There were a few unwritten laws for programming records which meant no two female voices next to each other, no two pop groups adjacent and no two ballads one after the other. These rules were never enforced but most producers understood the reasoning.

I had observed the methodology of some of my colleagues when selecting music for their shows and it usually went like this. Working a week in advance they would arrive at work on Monday morning and think "Hmm, what shall I start with for next week?" before going to the record cabinet and browsing rows of albums deciding which artist to play first. With no way of knowing what they had programmed for earlier shows, other than memory, they were basically starting from scratch each time. I found this somewhat nonsensical and open to duplication on a massive scale as the temptation was always to go for favourites each time. That was when I decided to develop my own system of programming, in effect a manual computer, and it worked like this. I didn't see the point of randomly choosing records and thought that once I'd chosen a particular track by an artist I should pre-programme it for future use. I decided not to repeat any track during a three-month period so I went through the repertoire of each artist and decided how many of their songs were worthy of inclusion. For instance, I might choose thirteen Andy Williams tunes and place them weekly from January to March, after which they could be repeated in the same sequence ad infinitum – simple, eh? This process took some time but never required more effort than any other way of doing it and in the end I didn't need to ponder what songs to select as I'd already done the work and could be confident of going through any three-month period without duplication. I only had to consider which order to place the items across the week interspersed with the latest singles or album tracks I wished to include. This also took a heavy workload off the secretary and this is how that worked.

When I first heard I would be working on a Radio Two "Strip Show" I was more than intrigued, I can tell you. However, the reality was that those daily shows were so designated because each musical item and the information pertaining to it, such as song title, artist, duration, publisher and record label, were all typed out neatly on a strip of paper about 8 inches long and an inch wide, so nothing lascivious at all, if that's what you were thinking. Normally these strips would be placed in order on a specially constructed board with a place for each item and when complete the secretary would transfer them to clear plastic files, about four to a page, and then photocopy them as a final running order for the presenter. Wastefully, these strips were thrown away at the end of each week but I told my secretary to hold on to them as a weekly bunch and then I used them again three months later. Maybe I should have been a time and motion technician. That saved me an inordinate amount of time allowing me to spend more of my day listening to new releases, researching and searching for more varied items to include in the show. My secretary also had far less typing to do and was sworn to secrecy on my methodology as other producers wondered how I could possibly do a week's work in just one day. You mustn't ever tell anyone I told you about this, promise?

The first really significant date in the diary that year was The Eurovision Song Contest held in the Netherlands at the Hague Concertgebouw on 3rd April which meant Terry and I being there to cover the event for Radio Two. There was an added frisson of danger surrounding this particular Eurovision because of a perceived threat of terrorist activity by the Red Army Faction, also known as the Bader- Meinhof group, a west German far-left militant organisation. Security was very tight with many areas being patrolled by officers armed with sub-machine guns or assault rifles. Some delegations were considered more at risk than others and we were told that the Israeli and Irish representatives were bussed out to Scheveningen by the coast for their safety.

Terry and I went about our work without any undue hassle, visiting rehearsals, making notes and generally soaking up the atmosphere as we familiarised ourselves with the venue and our broadcast studio. As we sat side-by-side for the performance I had great difficulty suppressing my amusement at some of the things Terry said in his commentary and every now and then he would nudge me with his elbow and a smile on his face to make sure I kept quiet when he was speaking. This I managed to do but we both fell about sometimes at what we were watching on stage - fortunately Terry had an on-off switch on his microphone.

For us it was an amazing evening as Brotherhood Of Man took the trophy with a landslide victory and their winning song "Kisses For Me" has gone down in the record books as the best-selling Eurovision song of all time. You can imagine the euphoria among the British contingent immediately after the winners were announced and that high lasted well into the night as we attended the after-show party to celebrate. Terry and I were having a drink and saying "cheers" to quite a lot of people in passing and at one point we were joined by a distinguished looking gentleman who asked how the broadcast had gone and chatted for a while discussing the evening's proceedings. When he left us I said to Terry "Who was that?" and Terry said laughingly "He's on the BOG, and his name is George Howard, or Lord Howard to you and me, from Castle Howard in Yorkshire". Did you remember what BOG stands for? Board Of Governors at the BBC and friendly George would soon become Chairman Of The Board.

The atmosphere was very lively as many nationalities mixed and chatted together in the friendly way that people do when no political agenda is involved. Terry left before me and I got into a conversation with the delightful Italian conductor who asked me my name and then told me his name was Maurizio Fabrizio to which I said "Maurizio Fabrizio, what a wonderful musical name, how great". He then said "Yes, Maurizio Fabrizio, thank you" and we both had a good laugh. I told him I thought the girl singer in the Italian entry by Al Bano and Romino was very striking and he said yes, she is the daughter of the American film star Tyrone Power. You learn something every day. We parted that night on very good terms and wished each other the best for the future.

One final connection that night was a first meeting with Roberto Danova, who said he had some connection with the German entry by The Les Humphries Singers. Roberto was soon to become a familiar sight at Radio Two, promoting his songs and recordings with great enthusiasm and not a little eccentricity. He was a bit of a lad but he endeared himself to everybody with his generosity when he hosted a Christmas party for all the staff, including presenters and secretaries as well as producers. He was keen for us to play his records and sometimes seemed a little desperate but I always told him that I wouldn't play anything I didn't think good enough or that the listeners wouldn't warm to. It was a tough world out there in "pluggerland" but I never gave in to any of their blandishments and only ever played records where I was convinced of their merit. I must have been an impossible nut to crack.

There were parties everywhere at Christmas but there was one in particular we all looked forward to more than most and that was the one hosted by the singer Roger Whittaker, who was always keen to show his gratitude for Radio Two's support at a Greek restaurant in Thayer Street called The Helvetia, probably long gone by now, but remembered by many who went there, I'm sure. Roger introduced me to his agent Joe Collins, father of Joan and Jackie. We got on really well and Joe would call me up from time to time and ask me if I fancied a salt beef sandwich and a cup of coffee at his favourite restaurant in Marylebone High Street. I always accepted as he was a fascinating character with a wealth of stories to tell and I just love listening to old-timer's tales, still do, except now there are no old-timers - but I have become one.

The summer of '76 brought increased activity both professionally and domestically as we moved home (again) into a modern chalet-style house in Clifton Road in Chesham Bois, which we bought from the pianist/arranger Malcolm Mitchell, with Krystle enrolling at her first school, Heatherton House and Caroline planning to start a business selling jewellery. During an afternoon stroll around Wembley we were smitten by a fabulous-looking Ford Mustang, a metallic blue beauty which shortly afterwards featured in a BBC Schools television documentary called "Getting To Work". The premise was how the people involved in the Radio Two Breakfast Show used different modes of transport to get into work each day. Terry was shown driving from his home in Taplow along the M4 motorway into central London. The engineer, Neil, was shown taking a bus journey from home to Broadcasting House. My section showed me leaving home in this beast of a car to get to Amersham station on the Metropolitan line which was part of the London Underground network. Nobody used a bicycle – and nobody got a fee.

Terry's show was broadcast from the Montreal Olympics in July but I was left behind to supervise the playing of the records from the BH studio, lucky me. Terry took a break after his Canada trip and I persuaded management, after a bit of an arm-wrestle I must say, to let me bring in Brian Matthew as a dep. For some reason they weren't too keen but went along with me and I was vindicated almost immediately with the positive listener response we received. Brian was delighted and forever grateful for getting his chance back at the microphone, which revived his career after a long period in the doldrums. He came into the office on the second day of his stint in absolute astonishment at the effect his return to the airwaves was having and told me "I was walking up from Oxford Circus and people were passing by and sayings things like "good to hear you back, Brian", "nice show this morning, mate" and other wonderfully warm greetings. I can't quite believe it". "Well", I said, "it doesn't surprise me, when you think how many millions tune in each day". It was a real shot-in-the-arm for Brian and he went on to present many important shows in the years that followed.

The first Outside Broadcast I remember doing with Terry was from the Isle Of Wight on August Bank Holiday Monday, which the Radio Times promoted heavily with this listing for the show – "Terry talks to some holidaymakers and plays some records" – sarcastic, me? – never. I booked us into the best accommodation I could find, a charming hotel called The Peacock Vane with an excellent restaurant where we ate the night before the broadcast. Our executive producer Chris Morgan, remember him with the black eye, was with us and invited the technical crew to join us for the meal which Chris generously paid for. That was where I first came across a legendary engineer known among his colleagues as "Peter The Eater" and when I asked them why they called him that they just laughed and said "Wait and see". All was revealed at the end of each course as Peter was handed any leftovers on our plates, hoovering them up as if he hadn't eaten for a fortnight. It really was a remarkable sight and goodness knows where he put all that food considering he was as thin as Jack Spratt. I also marvelled at Chris Morgan's cavalier approach to expenses (oh to be an executive producer) and also the way the OB crew dealt with theirs as they had a choice, as did we all, and it was this. You could either go on a set daily rate or claim "actuality", which was the real cost covering all actual expenses. I always took this option as the daily rate on offer would never cover the costs of staying in the kind of hotels suited to my star performer and, naturally, I had to stay with Terry, didn't I? The OB boys had a totally different approach, as they figured out that if they stayed in accommodation priced lower than the daily rate then they could pocket the difference, which they nearly always did. Me, I would rather eat well and be comfortable, so always went for actuality, wouldn't you?

In September Caroline and I were invited to the wedding of Ron and Bente Stratton in Bente's home town of Trondheim in Norway, an offer we couldn't possibly refuse. We rather adventurously decided to drive and took the Mustang, and Krystle, with us on the boat from Newcastle to Bergen. That threw up (sorry), another example of the power of radio as when we got to the docks in Newcastle the guy processing the paperwork said "Good morning, we've been expecting you. Terry said on the radio this morning that you'd be coming up here". Blow me down, fame at last, what fun. The drive from Bergen to Trondheim was a bit scary at times going over the top of snow-covered hills on single-track roads but apparently we set some kind of a record for the time it took us to cover the distance. We stayed with Bente's sister and her husband in a traditional Norwegian house which they lit every night with copious numbers of candles and I can't tell you how meditative it made us feel sitting in the candlelight listening to Albinoni's beautiful Adagio, it couldn't have been more peaceful. The wedding and the revels that followed were an entirely different matter as a large gathering of family and friends enjoyed a typical Norwegian celebration with a festive meal and music, which capped off a very special day for them and a very special trip for us.

When I got back to work Terry asked me how the trip went and did I manage to use my Norwegian. Then I had to tell him that the only Norwegian I remembered were a couple of swear words and how to say "I don't speak Norwegian" in Norwegian, which I can deliver fluently. He was intrigued by the idea of Scandinavian profanity and asked what they were, so I told him our "F" word was also an "F" word but the funniest one was their word for farting. When I told him, in a cod accent and rolling my "r"s, that it was prumping, their description for "an explosion between the legs", he fell about laughing and said "Brilliant, I'll have to use that". I didn't think that would be a problem as nobody would know what it meant. Wrong. The next day he back-announced a record saying "Well, that was a prumping good record, wasn't it?" What we hadn't taken into account was that we were broadcasting on 1500 metres long wave which could be heard across the continent and a few days later we got letters from Norway telling us off for using a naughty word and explaining what it meant. As if we didn't know.

Elton John threw a party in October at the Aberbach Gallery in Savile Row to launch his Blue Moves album, the first to be released on his own Rocket Records label. It was a typically busy, noisy, raucous music-biz shindig and even though Elton was inundated with requests for a chat or a photo he very generously signed a limited-edition Patrick Procktor poster of the album sleeve for me, another valued treasure for the vaults.

The world's most popular singer in the years before Elvis "The King" arrived was crooner "King" Bing Crosby, the Old Groaner. He celebrated his 50th anniversary in show business with a series of dates at The London Palladium which I was lucky enough to see and get a signed copy of the tour brochure. Bing was on fine form singing all the great songs, reminiscing about his career and telling a joke against himself about the time a Hollywood car park attendant looked him in the eye and said, "didn't you used to be Bing Crosby?" The Palladium season was a triumph with standing ovations every night leading one Sunday Express reviewer to eulogise over his performance and status and posing this question "Will people be queueing to see Mick Jagger in 2015?'. Well, we know the answer to that one, don't we?

Terry was a little reluctant to do interviews on his show, possibly because we were followed by Pete Murray's chatty Open House programme, but I did manage to get Bing on there at short notice one morning and as I picked him up from BH reception and introduced myself he asked "Geoff Mullin? Are you by any chance related to a Jack Mullin?" I said I didn't know of any relative by that name and Bing volunteered the information that Jack was the man who put him on tape and this story is as fascinating as they come for anyone interested in recorded sound. Jack Mullin was stationed in Europe towards the end of the war and during a night on duty he tuned in to a German radio station and was astonished to hear a full orchestra playing at 3am in the morning. What kind of band stays up and plays in the middle of the night he asked himself and this question intrigued him for some time until he entered a radio station at the end of the war and found out the secret of those late-night broadcasts. German engineers had developed magnetic tape technology unknown outside Germany and was a closely guarded secret, leading Jack to realise just how valuable this could be. He took two of these tape machines and some reels of tape back to America where he hoped to adapt and develop them for commercial use. This is where Bing comes in, as Jack demonstrated this perfect system of sound recording telling Bing that rather than perform his radio shows live, he could record them, several at a time if need be, and spend all that free time on the golf course. Bing immediately saw the benefit of this and invested 50,000 dollars with a firm called Ampex, which became a hugely successful business and a world leader in tape technology. That's a nice history lesson and I still don't know if I'm related to Jack Mullin, but I'd like to think so.

The only other major star I can recall coming into the studio was Diana Ross, after which I pretty much gave up on the idea of live interviews and Terry certainly wasn't bothered. Wogan's wit and wisdom was enough chat for most and he'd greet me every morning with "Ah, wee Geoffrey, how's your belly for spots?" "Not too bad, Tel, thanks", I'd reply, "How's yours?" – cue silly smiles. It was becoming clear to me that the music we played on the show was gaining significance in regard to the pop charts with record labels and publishers making a great deal of effort trying to get their product played. The current singles selected for exposure on Radio Two were decided by the playlist committee, made up of all the daytime show producers, which met once a week to listen and evaluate the latest offerings from the industry. Initially this was chaired by Chris Morgan who, as I related earlier, was not at the vanguard of adventurous musical thinking, resulting in one or two heated arguments as to the suitability of certain items presented at the meeting. One such debate still makes me smile as I tried to drag the rest of the committee kicking and screaming into the modern world and the record in question was "If You Leave Me Now" by Chicago which, on reflection, I can still hardly believe the resistance, animosity even, to including it on the playlist. I was pretty vehement that we should play it, saying that it was perfect for Radio Two and was sure to be successful but they were so much in denial that I opened my big mouth and said I would make a bet that it would be a big hit. "How much?", someone chirped up and I said, hedging my bets, "Fifty pence each", which they all agreed to. That could have cost me about four quid but as history tells that disc went on to make Number One across the world becoming a multi-million seller. The only fellow producer who put his hand up, and in his pocket, was Jimmy Young's producer Harry Walters who phoned me after the meeting saying he'd had another listen and decided I was right. Lovely man, Harry, who once said at a playlist meeting there were certain records Jimmy would refuse to play and that he would break them rather than put them on air. Someone asked how he could break a vinyl 45 and I quipped back "He hits them with his wallet", which caused loud guffaws Those meetings were generally entirely good-humoured with producers mostly in agreement on what should or should not be played, except for one or two exceptions which I'll come to later. There were only two artists Terry was unhappy playing and they were Brenda Lee, because she sounded like a man, and The Stylistics because they sang like girls. Well, you can't win 'em all.

I don't know how much I personally contributed to the success of that Chicago record, probably just a smidgen, but one I would like to take some credit for is "Miss You Nights" by Cliff Richard, which almost didn't make it into the charts at all. Radio Two had been supportive of the song but after a few weeks of airplay sales had been minimal, prompting EMI to tell their promotion people to drop it as it was dead in the water. They in turn told us producers the same story and so it was dropped by some shows, except mine, because when they told me it wasn't worth playing any longer, I said "I'll decide what to play, I like this song, so does Terry, so do the listeners and I'm going to keep it on regular rotation". Two weeks later they were back saying that sales had started to pick up and pleaded with me to keep on with it, which I did, and Cliff had his first Top Twenty hit for two years. That really demonstrated the power of a play on the Breakfast Show. I bet Cliff never knew.

At the end of 1976 I looked back with some pride at the receipt of correspondence from artists acknowledging our support and thanking us for playing their records, notably a Twiggy telegram for helping her single "Here I Go Again" into the top twenty, Acker Bilk for helping "Aria" into the top five and a really grateful letter from publisher Terry Noon crediting us with getting Pussycat to Number One with "Mississippi". There was another connection with this last-mentioned disc which was released on Sonet records in the UK by Rod Buckle who, if you can cast your mind back to my childhood memories, was the one-time editor of the Beano and Dandy. Oh, you did remember, well done. Rod was so delighted with this success that not only did he present me with a gold disc he also gave me the most extraordinary gift of a unique snooker cue disguised as a walking stick as he knew I was a lover of the green baize. I'll tell you more about that sport later on as I wasn't the only one in the business who liked knocking back a pint and a few balls over a lunch hour or three.

Another of those letters came from a man I would come to know as a colleague, a friend and one of the most loved men in the business. He had been programme director on the pirate radio ship Caroline, held a similar position for Radio Luxembourg, his headed notepaper from ABC/Anchor records read "A Message from Ken Evans" and this was it – "Dear Geoff, Just a quick note to say a big thank you for the wonderful help you've given us with Don Williams. Believe me, it's been tremendously appreciated by everyone here. Look forward to seeing you soon. Best Wishes Ken". In later years I would work with both Don and Ken, who later became a producer on Radio Two and Melody Radio. After he retired, I helped him move out of his flat in St John's Wood prior to his return home to his native Australia.

1977 fizzled in without so much as a whimper but there was something special in my stocking from Santa which would sustain me throughout the coming year, the latest edition of the Egon Ronay Hotel and Restaurant Guide. This was an absolute prerequisite for my work, otherwise how was I to find suitable accommodation and places to eat when out and about with my star presenter, on actuality, naturally. Terry's profile with the public was not so high at that time as it would later become and whenever he was spotted and anybody shouted "Aren't you Terry Wogan?" he would always reply with "No, he's a much younger man", which always made me laugh. Over the years I would accompany Tel around the country whenever he was doing a BBC TV show such as "Come Dancing" or "Miss World". These were mostly evening recordings or broadcasts requiring an overnight stay and the next morning's show had to be sent remotely down the line from a local BBC facility. All we needed was a basic studio with an engineer, a telephone and a microphone to send Terry's voice down the line to London where Colin Berry would spin in the discs. It was quite exciting as we had no idea if it was working but we knew we had a skilful and experienced man in Colin at the other end if things went pear-shaped, which, to the best of my knowledge, they never did. All that was required of me was to set up these facilities with the local BBC radio stations and hold Terry's hand for a couple of days.

When we were in Cardiff I managed to set up a visit to Cardiff Arms Park, the home of Welsh rugby, where we were made very welcome and, joy of joys, we were invited to tread the hallowed turf with a stroll across the ground. Both of us being fans and former players we were delighted to have been afforded such a privilege on the very pitch where just four years previously the great Gareth Edwards scored that iconic try for the Barbarians against New Zealand in a match that has gone down in history as the greatest ever. Rehearsals that afternoon left me with nothing to do so I drove over to a cinema in Swansea to see the new Peter Sellers film "The Pink Panther Strikes Again" which had one sequence that made me fall off my seat, literally. As Clouseau checks into an alpine gasthaus he has to negotiate a large dog lying across his path so he asks the desk clerk "Does your dog bite?" to which the reply is "No, my dog does not bite". Satisfied he is in no danger, he attempts to step over the dog which takes a chunk out of his leg, prompting him to shout "I thought you said your dog does not bite", soliciting the killer comical comeback "That is not my dog". That sequence in the film was funny enough but an even more hysterical story was revealed to me some years later by Dave Lee Travis who was friendly with Graham Stark, the actor in the Hotel Alpenros reception. Graham's part required him to smoke a large Meerschaum pipe which, although he didn't normally smoke, he was reassured that it was only a harmless herbal mixture. He was happy to puff away during the filming but he couldn't understand why Sellers and director Blake Edwards kept asking for so many re-takes of that particular scene. With each new take Graham was getting more and more disorientated until finally he couldn't speak anymore nor function properly. This caused the entire crew to collapse with laughter as Graham was the only one on set who didn't know that between each take they were filling up his pipe with marijuana – he was stoned out of his mind.

For future reference Dave Lee Travis will be referred to only as DLT, Dave or Travis as his name in full takes up too much time, too much space and too much ink, so there.

Peter Sellers was a celebrity fan who listened to the show and one day sent me a note asking if we'd like to use the enclosed tape one morning to help Terry with his "Fight The Flab" crusade, which we were thrilled to do. I seem to have lost the note somewhere along the line but I still have that recording with Peter in the guise of the bumbling, dopey detective and here is the transcription – "Hello Wogan, hello Wogan, this is Chief Inspector Jaques Clouseau. There is only one way that you can defeat the demon fat and that is to stop putting it on. Why don't you realise it and give this valuable information to those poor helpless women who listen to your radio programme and are liable to suffer themselves serious medical injuries trying to carry out your well-meant but misinformed instructions. Much better that you should hire yourself a manservant to attack you wherever and whenever possible like my little yellow Cato who jumps on me at every opportunity. Use, use the fiendish power of kung fu put to melody and you may rest assured that the horrid flabby fatty lumps will vanish overnight. Otherwise, I can only recommend that you visit Doctor August Balls of Nice without further hesitation". That was a one-minute diatribe by one of our famous listeners and, I understand, we had an even more illustrious audience living in palatial properties but sadly they never sent in any tapes. I have been a bit of a hoarder of things radiophonic over many years including messages from Miss Piggy and Kermit from the Muppet Show, promo messages form Madness and the Bee Gees and the voices of the Spitting Image characters among many others. Perhaps I should put them out on social media or even a compact disc if I can negotiate the copyright laws.

Things were going along very smoothly as far as I was concerned but on the night of March 9th panic arrived in the form of a strike by BBC TV cameramen which subsequently affected much of the output including that night's broadcast of "A Song For Europe" from the New London Theatre in Drury Lane. The show went ahead in the theatre but was not shown on television and the organisers were desperate for the public to hear the songs so I was asked to mount a rescue mission by taking Terry back to BH and showcasing the songs on Radio Two. Gosh, this was exciting stuff. We rushed back to base taking over the airwaves to play all the contenders and from some good songs by The Foundations, Lyn Paul, Carl Wayne, Sweet Sensation, Mary Mason and others the winners emerged as Lynsey de Paul and Mike Moran with "Rock Bottom". They were due to represent the UK in London on April 4th but due to the ongoing TV strike the contest was postponed until 7th May which was to be a night of excitement, enjoyment and fear on my part, which we'll come to very soon. Saving the day that night (sorry) elicited a memo of deep gratitude for my efforts from on high as well as the television service but, sadly, no bonus, harrumph.

March brought another surprise when I got a Radio Times billing as the producer of the Cheltenham Gold Cup coverage. Actually, Terry was presenting the afternoon radio coverage and I was only responsible for the music that day but a credit is a credit whatever it's for.

I mentioned earlier on the vital importance to me of the Egon Ronay guide but it also lent itself to the provision of a great nickname for a colleague at Radio One, Don George, who was the producer responsible for Ed "Stewpot" Stewart and "Junior Choice" The home of Radio One was Egton House, giving rise to Don, the original legend in his own lunchtime, being dubbed Egton Ronay. Don was a lovely man who never knowingly missed a function and even if there were three or four scheduled at the same time you could be sure that he would make an appearance at each and every one. My final word on Don was the way he exited this mortal coil by collapsing with laughter watching his favourite comedy act Laurel and Hardy on TV. Not a bad way to go.

The two popular music networks were in separate buildings but we all knew who our rivals were as we saw them in BH and at most receptions, which seemed to be held on a weekly basis by one record company or another. I used to call Radio One "The Dave Network" because there were so many of them about the place, with presenters David Symonds, David Hamilton, David "Kid" Jensen, DLT (see what I did there?) and producers Dave Tate, Dave Price, Dave Atkey – did I miss anyone out? You were also in with a good chance of a job on Radio Two if both your names could possibly be your first name, for instance, Colin Martin, Ray Harvey, Ian Grant, Beverly Philips, Phil Hughes, Alan Boyd, Chris Morgan, Steve Allen, Ken Evans, Brian Stephens, Geoff Owen, Alan Owen, the two Walters Paul and Harry and, at a pinch, Tim McDonald and Charles Clarke Maxwell. This trend was also noticeable throughout the presenter line-up with Brian Matthew, Pete Murray, Alan Keith, Chris Stuart, David Jacobs, Charlie Chester, Ed Stewart, Robin Ray, Alex Lester, Cliff Adams, the fragrant Fran Godfrey and it continues today with the niftily-named Ken Bruce , not forgetting the admirable JAG, known to listeners as James Alexander Gordon, the voice of the Saturday soccer scores who had millions on tenterhooks in the hope of hearing they had won a fortune with eight score draws on their football pools coupons. Funny what weird things cross your mind, isn't it?

The boss of Radio One, Derek Chinnery, asked me to pop in and see him one day to find out if I'd be interested in joining his network and at that time, mid-seventies, the prospect quite appealed to me. I said yes to his offer and he put the wheels in motion to move me across but he was baulked when Geoff Owen called me in to ask if I was serious about this proposed move. I said I thought it wouldn't be a bad move at which he said "Well, you can't go because the grade on offer over there is MP3" to which I replied that was my current grade and Geoff said "No, it isn't, you are now MP4 and they can't afford you". So, one short conversation earned me an instant promotion and I thought right, this is how you get on in the BBC, which is only part of the story. Sometime later Derek tried again to move me over, this time offering to exchange me for two of his producers, which Geoff Owen once again refused and I'm not surprised knowing the two producers on offer – no names no pack drill – it's still a closely guarded secret, by me at least. The same thing happened many years later when Johnny Beerling wanted me to join his management team at Radio One but by that time I was off the idea as the music being played wasn't so much to my taste any longer. This attention was all very flattering and I was even urged to apply for attachments to the sports department by Patricia Ewing and also, hard to believe this, a six-month stint on Woman's Hour "to bring in a male perspective". Were they mad? You couldn't make it up, could you? Terry was always privy to these options and we discussed them in detail as he was always very supportive and gave me his best advice, besides which, I trusted him implicitly as he would warn me to beware of certain people who he said had the green eye of envy. A good judge of character was our Tel.

Before we get onto the events surrounding Eurovision, Terry and I drove up to Bradford in the Mustang for an edition of Come Dancing, staying overnight and doing the show from BBC Leeds. I bought an enormous teddy bear for Krystle and stuck it on the rear seat for the journey home, which was about as hair-raising as you could imagine, for two reasons. First, the weather was atrocious with heavy snow on the motorway and secondly because Terry was in a hurry to be back at BH by one o'clock for an important meeting. We were on the limit all the way back and by some extreme good fortune arrived back at base just before the deadline.

There are times when you can be overtaken by exciting events where previous caution and restraint get out of control, which is what happened on the night of May 7th at the Eurovision Song Contest in the Wembley Conference Centre. There was a champagne reception in the foyer where we enjoyed a couple of flutes and a chat with Pete Murray, who was commentating for BBC TV, after which we headed for our commentary position overlooking the stage. To our surprise and delight the boss had left us a half-bottle of Remy Martin cognac which Tel and I merrily sipped our way through during the broadcast. We were hoping for a win by our entry "Rock Bottom" by Lynsey de Paul and Mike Moran as five juries handed us the maximum 12 points but we were very disappointed to be pipped at the post by the French entry. There was a large post-show dinner where the wine flowed freely and we commiserated with Mike and Lynsey on their very near miss. Lynsey was delightful in defeat, chatting away to us and, once again, little did I realise that I wouldn't speak to her again for another 30 years. At the end of the three-course meal, punctuated by one or two speeches, we finally left the building around 2 o'clock in the morning. The weather was awful and Caroline and I had to make a run for it to the car park, getting well and truly soaked from a very heavy shower. The trouble happened as we were leaving the Hanger Lane roundabout taking the slip-road down to the A40. There was a stationary car without lights in the outside lane and in the downpour I didn't see it until the very last moment, causing me to swerve viciously and sending the car spinning down the slip road, finally coming to rest facing the oncoming traffic from the underpass. Luck was on my side right then as I managed to turn the car around without incident and proceed on my way until, that is, I heard and saw a police car behind me. Oh no, I thought, this is it, I'm in big trouble, as I pulled over and the cop car pulled in behind me. Without a moment's hesitation and no real idea of what I thought I was doing, I jumped out of the car as four coppers approached and, in the pouring rain, I remonstrated very loudly saying "What the hell is going on, did you see that car back there, I nearly hit it and you need to move it before someone has a nasty accident", which drew the response "Have you been drinking, sir?" It was a fair question after they had witnessed my incredible manoeuvre and with me standing there in the middle of the night dressed in my penguin suit, I ask you. I replied firmly "No, I've been working at the Eurovision Song Contest producing Terry Wogan for the

BBC", thinking a spot of name-dropping would do no harm. One of the officers was keen to breathalyse me, which I knew would not be in my best interests. The officer in charge knew he probably should have but, very fortunately and generously gave me a "Get Out Of Jail Free" card, as he said "Best be on your way, sir, and please drive with extreme caution". "Thank you, officer, I will" I said, as I climbed back into my car with the biggest sigh of relief you can imagine. They followed me for half a mile or so just to check I was in a fit state and then I was clear and very careful for the rest of the journey home. I mark that down as a major let-off and near-death experience number eight, if you've been counting. I'm not going to tempt fate by any flip comments at this stage, that's for sure. Lucky, lucky, lucky. That was the end of my drink-driving days.

Sport was very much on the agenda for me in the summer of '77 with better playing conditions than the ridiculously hot summer of '76 when you could hardly breathe for the heat. I played tennis with friends, croquet was a regular activity at Caroline's parent's place and I enjoyed a round or two with Terry at Temple Golf Club where he was a member. One racquet game I had never played was squash and when my pal Kevin Mahlia suggested I give it a try I took him on and he flattened me to such an extent that I was lying on the floor gasping for breath. I vowed never to play again but my competitive instinct cut in and I decided I needed to learn how to play this game and arranged for Kevin to take me on a few more times until eventually I had the beating of him. Not only that but I had begun to really enjoy the game and as my fitness levels improved, I applied for membership at my local squash club and began to play competitively. This keen interest led to playing games at lunchtime against my music business pals Harry Barter, who played at the Lambton club where we would often see an exhausted John Cleese lying flat on his back after a strenuous match, and ace promotion man Nick Fleming with whom I also played a regular game of snooker. Nick's dad was Paddy, a doyen of the old school of promotion men who had begun his career at the Rank Charm School for aspiring film stars, whose alumni included Petula Clark, our own Pete Murray, Shirley Eaton, every boy's fantasy when I was at school, Christopher Lee and Diana Dors, who Nick told me unwittingly broke up Paddy's marriage when his wife accused him of having an affair with her. They divorced over it and it took Paddy two years to convince her that nothing happened between him and Diana, which eventually led to a reconciliation and marrying again. That's some story, isn't it?

Another snooker-playing plugger pal was Tony "Primo" Peters, a real character who ran the London office of the Nashville publisher Acuff-Rose, one of the biggest names in country music, and with whom I would enjoy a game or two accompanied by a bacon sandwich and a pint of lager at various venues in the West End. There was a small club just off Soho Square where we were playing when one day in walks Alex "Hurricane" Higgins looking for some action. He got himself a pint and came over to watch our game and at the end he said "That's a nice-looking cue you've got there, may I have a look?" What a funny thing, I thought, but I was a huge fan and handed over my cue which he admired and then said "Fancy a game?" and I said "Not likely, Alex, I'm several planets away from you in the snooker universe". He laughed and said "OK, I'll give you forty points start and we'll play for a fiver, alright?" Well, I knew beyond any reasonable doubt that I was going to lose but the chance to play him was priceless and well worth the fiver he took off me at the end. It was one of those unforgettable chance encounters that you never forget. I did have a game against another snooker world champion but that comes later.

As a family we were settling into our new environment and making friends with neighbours, especially Krystle who became great friends with Fiona who lived right next door. I was greatly impressed by her father who handled a terrifying encounter with great aplomb and it makes a good story. Ian was driving home from work and gave a lift to a hitchhiker, who pulled a knife on him and demanded money, at which Ian remained very calm and extremely quick thinking by saying he had no cash with him but he could help the guy out with a cheque. Believe it or not he went for it and several days later was picked up by the police after trying to cash it. Nice one, Ian. Our neighbour on the other side was a company director for a large scientific company and a keen rally driver who took me for a spin through the local woods, putting his Porsche through its paces and scaring me half to death. Claud was a keen car fan and one of the first people I knew to own an Audi Quattro, which he demonstrated to me on the way into work driving through snow and ice with impeccable control. Very impressive indeed. I hankered after an Audi Quattro for years after that but I never got one.

There was a neighbour friend who prompted a long and on-going conversation between Terry and I when we discussed finances and investments. I had been invited by this neighbour to join a Lloyd's Of London Insurance Syndicate and when I mentioned it to Terry he said he had had a similar offer. We tried to evaluate the merits and pitfalls of these schemes and I said I wasn't prepared to risk everything if there was a big call on members for funds, regardless of the possibility of large financial gains. I believe Terry was thinking along similar lines and I suggested he might be best invested in Blue Chip stocks and shares as he was on a good income already and looked well set for the future. Also, how about fine wine as an investment vehicle as he could always drink it if need be, which brought forth a laugh. Many years later after getting involved in various schemes he told me he had only made money from about one in four of the businesses he had put money into. He needn't have worried as he was as astute as any expert at monetising his value as a performer and together with his clever business agent Jo Gurnett, he became the highest paid performer at the BBC.

Terry was often able to raise funds for charitable causes with personal appearances and a generally supportive role in various guises, and on a local basis I contributed to the annual fete by providing huge numbers of brand new 45rpm records as "lucky dip" prizes which got the kids very excited and raised hundreds of pounds for good causes, so thank you, British record industry.

Looking back, I do wish I had kept some contemporaneous notes about my activities over the years as now I can sometimes only rely on vague memories, which is why all I can tell you about Bank Holiday Monday in August 1977 is that Terry and I took the show along the Marine Parade in Great Yarmouth and interviewed a few holidaymakers, and that's it. Exciting, eh? Shortly after that

Terry went on holiday to France and sent me a postcard from Deauville which reads -

"Not enjoying the wonderful food, drink and weather – just counting the hours 'til I can be back with you and my listeners…… you ARE expecting me back, aren't you??.. Your *"

Made us laugh in the office as we looked forward to the return of our "star".

The last major OB of the year was scheduled for the end of September with a trip to Penzance in Cornwall. We decided to drive and I requisitioned a large, comfortable car for the journey and BBC Transport provided a Ford Granada which, to be fair, was large and comfortable. The usual routine was for us to do the morning show in BH and then head off to spend the night before the OB in the designated town, stopping en-route for a, hopefully, tasty lunch which on this occasion was to be the Horn Of Plenty at Gulworthy. I knew that Egon Ronay guide would come in useful.

During this journey it happened, a seminal moment that was to lead to many things for Terry. We were listening to Jimmy Young on the radio and about half an hour after setting out he played The Floral Dance, a new release by The Brighouse and Rastrick Brass Band, which we had also been playing. Terry amazed me by singing along both in tune and word perfect so I asked him how he knew the words and he told me his father used to sing it when he was a lad. This was it, I said "I've programmed it for the show tomorrow because we're close to Helston where it originated and you absolutely have to sing along to it just as you did then". "Oh no", said Terry, "I can't do that", but I insisted and after a little coaxing he said he would. The show next morning went extremely well, oozing with local colour and with Terry getting a rapturous reception from the crowd who all sang along with him to The Floral Dance. There was a tragi-comic event after Tel interviewed a local baker, who presented us with a specially made Giant Cornish Pasty, must have been two feet long, which we put on a shelf in the OB van. Get ready to laugh, because as we started off up a very steep hill, yes, you've guessed, the bloody pasty slid along the shelf towards the back of the van and smashed itself to smithereens against the back door. When we opened up at the back it fell out all over the road and we all thought that was a tragic waste of a good meal, especially Peter The Eater.

We thought nothing more about Terry's vocal prowess until the storm after the calm arrived. We were absolutely inundated with letters and phone calls asking where they could get Terry's record, not only from listeners but also from record shops up and down the country. I told Tel he should record it and sure enough the sharp-eared Mike Redway had the same idea and whisked Terry off into a studio to do a vocal version. The Brighouse instrumental got to Number 2 late in the year and Terry's followed in January when he appeared on Top Of The Pops singing the song while throwing flowers at the audience. His star was most certainly on the rise. The Brighouse and Rastrick Band record label, Transatlantic, presented me with a Gold Disc with inscription "For Getting There First", which we did.

As I told you, there were more than enough launch parties and receptions being held throughout the year but I did at least keep the invites to some of the more interesting of them. The first of these "Meet And Greet" functions was at The Savoy with "Starsky And Hutch" star David Soul to celebrate his million-selling Number One hit "Don't Give Up On Us". Then, in quick succession, came Neil Innes at Ronnie Scott's, David Dundas at Trader Vic's, Dolly Parton's "Cocktail Party" at The Inn On The Park, Elkie Brooks at Les Ambassadeurs – are you drunk yet? Look, here come Alan Price, Boz Scaggs and the Beach Boys, who's next? Oh yes, the Rolling Stones personal telegram invitation to "Love You Live" gig at The Marquee Club in Wardour Street and at the other end of the musical spectrum Perry Como at The Café Royal. Things rounded off with Donna Summer, Crystal Gayle and Kenny Rogers who proved to be very receptive and chatty after I told him I first heard "Ruby, Don't Take Your Love To Town" on a Roger Miller album and he said that was where he picked it up from, too.

It was becoming more and more apparent the role that Radio Two was playing in the promotion of many American country stars and that was acknowledged at the Country Music Association of Great Britain Awards Dinner at The Grosvenor House Hotel in December when Billie Jo Spears presented me with Terry's award for Disc Jockey Of The Year. Terry couldn't be there in person that night and I did wonder if Billie Jo ever knew that at the end of playing one of her records he would shout "Yee-haw, that's Billie Jo Spears, the singing harpoon" in a cod-country accent. Silly boy. When I asked Terry what he was going to do with this latest in a long line of accolades he said "I'll put it in a glass case and throw sugar at it".

Some of these exclusive personal invitations could make you feel especially privileged and I always tried to take Caroline along if it was a celebratory dinner or such. The last of the year was the British Record Industry Centenary Dinner And Ball at The Dorchester Hotel where the extra-special cabaret was provided by Cliff Richard. A marvellous night but still no thanks from Cliff.

That was a busy year, wasn't it? Especially when you add in the Ivor Novello Awards, BASCA Gold Badge Awards, Music Publishers Association luncheon and film previews for "A Star Is Born", "New York, New York", "Annie Hall" and "Close Encounters Of The Third Kind". It's little wonder I couldn't get any work done, is it?

Two pre-recorded programmes for the end of the year were a Brian Matthew Christmas Eve Special and a review of the year with Terry highlighting the most played records of 1977 on Radio Two.

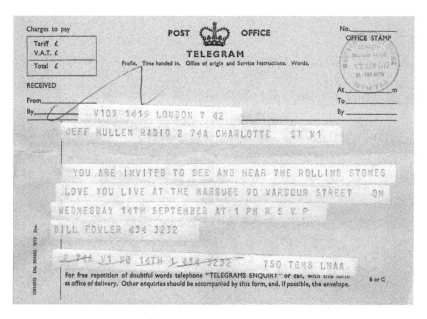

V109 1419 LONDON T 42

JEFF MULLEN RADIO 2 74A CHARLOTTE ST W1

YOU ARE INVITED TO SEE AND HEAR THE ROLLING STONES
LOVE YOU LIVE AT THE MARQUEE 90 WARDOUR STREET ON
WEDNESDAY 14TH SEPTEMBER AT 1 PM R S V P
BILL FOWLER 434 3232

W1 90 14TH 1 434 3232 TSO TGMS LNAA

Rolling Stones invite 1977

CHAPTER NINETEEN

The Wogan Years Part Two

1978 started off more or less where last year finished with receptions for Lonnie Donegan, Cliff presenting an award to The Shadows for their "Golden Greats" album, Andrew Lloyd Webber gig for "Variations" with Julian, Gary Moore and Rod Argent and "Abba: The Movie" film preview. I'm exhausted just thinking about it and, yes, it was a hard life but somebody had to do it.

There was also a change in the programme schedules in January as Terry managed to negotiate himself an extra half hour in bed together with a salary increase for working an extra half hour. If you're confused, let me explain, the show had been two hours from 7am to 9am and under the new arrangement it went on air from 7.30am to 10am. Not only that but Pete Murray and Jimmy Young swapped time slots which was the beginning of those famous handovers with all that bickering and backbiting between Terry and Jimmy. All in good humour, naturally – ha, ha.

Terry and I were in for a year of more travelling what with his commitments to "Come Dancing" and "Miss World" and the BBC's need to make its presence felt around the country with outside broadcasts. The first of those came in March with a visit to the Channel Islands where we were treated right royally by The States Of Guernsey who hosted a reception for "BBC Celebrities" (Wow) at The Bailiff's Chambers and, no, they didn't lock us up. The programme went very well and shortly afterwards we were invited to Jersey in May, which we also accepted. Was there a little jealousy or competition at play, I wonder. Two good trips, topped off for me by the acquisition of a navy-blue Guernsey and a fawn-coloured Jersey, both jumpers in case you didn't know.

Billy Joel hosted a post-concert boxing tournament at the Grosvenor House Hotel that March and he is without doubt my favourite singer/songwriter. Radio Two demonstrated yet again that it could be a major player in an artist's success with the Italian bombshell Raffaella Carra getting into the Top Ten with "Do It Do It Again". Nothing like a bit of glamour to brighten up your day and Raffaella sent a nice letter of thanks and posed for photos with me and the Radio Two crew.

At the end of the month we sent the show down the line the morning after Terry compered the "Miss Wales" competition at the Arcadia theatre in Llandudno. Another glamourous night. A couple of days later there was an invite from Elton John to a screening of his music video "EGO – A Record Breaking Film" at the Columbia theatre in Shaftesbury Avenue. It lasted a mere four minutes and attempted to show the negative side of the rock business with Elton later describing it as one of the most sincere songs he and Bernie Taupin had ever written.

Possibly the meanest, nastiest and downright cruel event of my entire career came in April when executive producer Derek Mills came into my office and told me under no circumstances was I to go into the studio the following morning. This was highly unusual and out of order as far as I was concerned so I asked why not. The fabricated response was something about the studio suites needing to be clear of all personnel because of "something important going on that nobody was to know about". I soon found out the next morning when listening to my own programme as Eamonn Andrews interrupted Terry with his Big Red Book and whisked him off while still "live" for his edition of "This Is Your Life". To add insult to injury Eamonn referred to Derek Mills as "Terry's producer". Word came back to me later that both Terry and his wife Helen asked "Where's Geoff?" with Derek telling them I was unavailable due to a prior commitment. Such a blatant lie and one I never forgave him for. Next morning I talked it over with Terry who couldn't believe what had happened and he said "What a nasty, horrible fat bastard, never trust him again". I agreed that I wouldn't and Terry warned me to keep an eye out for others he thought either untrustworthy or unfriendly, as people would disclose things to him in an effort to ingratiate themselves, making him privy to secrets that he shared with me. Maybe some people had read

Machiavelli's "The Prince" believing that was the way to get ahead but it doesn't work if you go around telling all and sundry what you're thinking. On reflection I think Derek could have been sad, lonely, frustrated and unfulfilled with a desperate need to be liked and recognised. Maybe that Elton song "Ego" would have been appropriate for this act of betrayal and self-aggrandisement. I don't think the "Me" generation is a new phenomenon.

I soon recovered from Derek's deception when I got to meet my all-time favourite female pop singer Connie Francis at a Press Conference and Reception at the Waldorf Hotel. She was delightful and quite intrigued when I told her I loved her continental songs "Al Di La", "Schoner Fremder Mann" and "Cuando Caliente El Sol" and that I used to sing one of her songs in my group back in the sixties. She said "Boys don't usually cover girl singer's songs, which one did you do?" and I told her it was the Neil Sedaka song "Fallin", which she seemed to approve of. A memorable meeting for me, indeed.

If you've never heard the story of Terry's start at the BBC, here it is. Having been successful in his native Ireland Terry thought he'd try his luck with the BBC and send them an audition tape, which landed on the desk of Mark White in 1966. Mark put the tape on and all he got was gobbledegook out of the speakers. Realising what was had happened he turned the tape around and played it properly in the right direction. He was amused by this cheeky chappie and even though he wasn't sure if it was done as a joke or just a mistake, he was impressed enough to offer this eloquent Leprechaun a job. And the rest, as they say, is a crock of circumlocutory blarney.

I knew Radio Two had the power to influence record sales but I never imagined the reaction we would get when I programmed a new novelty record on a morning in early May. Decca records had sent it in accompanied by a little blue doll with a funny white hat as a promotion gimmick. I played the disc in the office and felt a great big smile spreading across my face as something clicked in my ears that this could be extremely comical, irritating and successful all at the same time. I had never heard of this new rock group The Smurfs before, nor their leader Father Abraham, but they generated an enormous amount of interest with the listeners and record sales took them to Number 2 in the charts, where The Smurf Song stayed for 17 weeks. Decca promo man Mick McDonagh was so delighted he asked if Krystle and his daughter could be photographed together for some publicity shots. This was agreed and he gave Krystle the biggest Smurf doll you've ever seen and she was delighted. The man at Decca mainly responsible for this outrageous insult to musical taste was their Belgian manager of the international division, Marcel Stellman, the man who also inflicted Pinky And Perky on the British public. He was also responsible for the long-running TV show "Countdown", so he wasn't all bad, and I got to like him enormously. We first met after the success of his composition "A Little Love And Understanding", a top ten hit in 1975 for Gilbert Becaud, again a hit thanks mainly to plays on Radio Two. To celebrate the Smurf's phenomenal appeal, we were invited for a victory lunch in the private dining room of Decca chairman Sir Edward Lewis, where Marcel formally presented me with a Silver Disc bearing the improbable appellation "Smurfin' Geoff Mullin".

Obviously, if you had a novelty record on release, Radio Two was the place to go and over the years we had great fun and success with The Wurzels "Combine Harvester", Piero Umiliani "Mah Na Mah Na", George Zamfir "Light Of Experience" and many more. Very often the funniest thing of all was a mis-heard lyric or song title or even an artist's name by confused listeners which provided some of the most amusing moments, for instance - "Could you please play that Kenny Rogers song about the 400 children and a croc in the field". What they were asking for was "Lucille" with the words "Four hungry children and a crop in the field, you picked a fine time to leave me Lucille". Sometimes we were baffled by a request and one that got us scratching our heads for a while came during a Children In Need broadcast, when the entire network was given over to listener's requests, and this is what they asked for "Please can you play that lovely record by Freda Greaves?" We all looked at each other and said we had no idea but as she was offering a large donation to a good cause we kept her on the line and looked through all the information we had in the gramophone library but to no avail. When we asked what the song was called, she said it was very popular and went like this – "When will I see you again, when will we share precious moments". Then it clicked, and after we picked ourselves up off the floor from a bout of hysterics, we were only too pleased to play that Number One chart-topper by Freda Greaves, otherwise known as The Three Degrees.

August saw Terry off on his travels once more with a trip to Edmonton in Canada to cover the Commonwealth Games with me stuck in the bowels of BH yet again, damn. We were back on the road together later in the month with yet another outside broadcast, this time from Bridlington, which I knew quite well from holidays there with my parents. I produced the Bank Holiday Special "Jim And Terry" which Radio Times described thus – "music, mirth and merriment in the style of their regular morning encounters" – such alliteration, who writes this stuff, was it me? One last trip that month was to Bristol for an edition of "Come Dancing" at the Locarno Ballroom. We stayed at the Dragonnara Hotel, had a meal in the architecturally interesting Kiln restaurant and found time to fit in a visit to the famous Harvey's magnificent wine cellars, where we were treated to a selection of sherries. Well, it would have been rude to refuse.

Extra-curricular activity continued apace, well, it was all work-related. Bette Midler entertained us brilliantly at the opening night of her outrageous "Trash With Flash" show at the London Palladium and we got an introduction later to a reception in the Palm Court Lounge of the Waldorf Hotel thanks to WEA Records. Bette has a great singing voice, try "Mambo Italiano", and if I were having a fantasy dinner-party she would be one of the first invitees.

Next came a concert at the Empire Pool, Wembley with my old mates from Manchester, 10cc, followed by an intense round of hand-shaking in October with the launch party for Dr Hook's album "Pleasure And Pain", a meet and hear Barbara Dickson lunch, cocktails with Peter Straker at one of my favourite restaurants, Inigo Jones in Covent Garden, where I would later enjoy lunch with the lovely Amii Stewart. The last couple of free-loading opportunities came in November at a buffet lunch with Dolly Parton and a Polydor jolly for Jean Michel Jarre.

However, in among all this madcap activity there was one very special date in the diary when Terry was invited back home to Ireland for the opening night of their second television channel RTE 2 on November the 2nd. We flew into Dublin the day before the broadcast for briefing meetings with various Irish TV directors, producers and executives as this was about to be a very big deal and they wanted "one of their own, the world's most famous Irishman", to play a major part in proceedings. There was a lavish dinner that evening at a restaurant in the hills above the city centre (was it called Arbutus Lodge?) and as we walked in Terry and I both spotted the live lobster tank at the same time, looked at each other and winked, knowing full well what we would be ordering for our meal. There was much glad-handing that night and Terry and I slept soundly before doing the breakfast show from a local radio studio. With the rest of the day free I hired a car and we thought it would be a good idea to drive down to Kinsale on the coast, where we might find a decent lunch in this foodie heaven. Alas, it was not to be as we couldn't find anywhere open and so we started back to Dublin thinking to find a pub on the way. Oh boy, did we find a pub. Yes, we did, which gave us the biggest laugh of the entire trip. As we walked through an outer bar there was a smartly-dressed chap drinking alone, he looked like an accountant or solicitor, and as we walked past him he looked up, saw Terry, looked back at his drink and said "Nah, sure it can't be". He couldn't reconcile the fact that he'd heard Terry on the radio that morning and him being in a tiny pub outside Cork at lunchtime, it just didn't compute. We ordered drinks and enquired about something to eat and the landlord said "How do you fancy some queenies?" I had no idea what they were but Terry instantly said yes, that would be fine and explained to me that queenies were Dublin bay prawns. While we were waiting for our food we had a couple of games of pool, the landlord sent us over another round of drinks on the house and we repaid his hospitality by buying him a drink and we ordered another round to accompany our meal. Those prawns were more than delicious, huge chunks of white meat and never to be forgotten. The landlord then sent us another round of drinks on the house at which point I said to Terry "We should get out of here while we can still think", with which he agreed. As we left the same guy was still sitting at the outer bar but this time he didn't even look up, I think he was lost in the Irish mist. We got back to Dublin in time for Terry to take forty winks and freshen himself up, then met up with Val Doonican and his wife for a light meal in the hotel before we were all picked up to be taken to the television studios. A more than memorable trip and a great success for RTE 2 but I'll never forget that guy in the bar – classic.

After all these waist-expanding events I was rewarded for my endurance like the man who sells insurance with a note from Controller Douglas Muggeridge showing his appreciation for my durability by awarding me promotion and a pay rise, whoopee.

The year ended on a high with my old pal Paul Phillips earning himself a Top Ten chart hit as Driver 67 with his melodic novelty story-song "Car 67" about a heart-broken Wolverhampton taxi driver. It gained even more traction when the Queen Mother let it be known that it was her favourite pop song. Not a bad end to an extraordinary year by any means.

The first "unofficial" outing for Terry and I was as early as 3rd January 1979 at a luncheon hosted by Express Newspapers for the 25th London International Boat Show in Earls Court. The invitation came via my old friend and flatmate John Finneran who was now the Advertising Director of the Daily Express – didn't he do well? It must have been quite a feather in his cap to have Terry Wogan at his table, which also included big hitters, i.e. directors, from British Airways, Chrysler, Woolworths, EMI and more. An enjoyable lunch was followed by a leisurely, drooling stroll around the exhibits with no requests for autographs as the official opening was the next day, when Margaret Thatcher would do the honours. Rumour has it that John Finneran took off for Canada never to be seen again.

Telegrams were rarely sent in to us but one arrived dated 27 Feb 1979 which read "When you saw Bright Eyes you saw a hit. Art Garfunkel charted at 66 today. Many thanks for your help. Please stay with it. Best wishes Neil Ferris and the Rabbits at April Music". We stayed with it and watched it climb to Number One in April giving writer Mike Batt a million seller which stayed in the charts for 19 weeks. That song generated another deluge of letters, which brings me to this next paragraph.

The overwhelming daily mailbag of letters had become too much for poor secretary Karen Moore, who suffered from arthritis, so I requested some assistance for her but in the end, even though she was devoted to both Terry and the programme it was felt kinder to move her to a less onerous job and the delightful Pam Tarrant took her place. This proved be both prescient and apposite as the amount of correspondence doubled and then doubled again after Terry began appearing every Thursday night on BBC One with his new game show "Blankety Blank". It was very funny, sprinkled with celebrity guests and hugely successful as Terry created havoc with "Wogan's Wand" while offering the cheapest of cheap prizes, those being a model chequebook and pen, which were readily accepted by all the contestants. This show, above all others, was what set Terry on the road to superstardom and he never looked back.

There were many regular letter-writers whose contributions provided a daily diet of funny stories and varying themes which could run for several weeks or even months. There were some famous faces who put pen to paper from time to time, one of whom was Max Bygraves who, if you know his catchphrase, would always start with "I wanna tell you a story". His usual methodology was to invent some ludicrous tale which always ended with the song title of one of his recordings in the hope that he might get it played. He never did. Very often these missives would be written on British Airways airmail notepaper, giving him something to do during the flight, or on headed notepaper, such as this one from the Ouro Verde Hotel in Rio De Janeiro – "Dear Wog, it was during a nightmare you came to me. I dreamt I was in charge of the sheep on a mountain overlooking Copacabana, the ewes and the lambs were counted again and again but I couldn't account for one – I thought "hello – he's taken it on the lamb." Lo and behold – he had – will you please play as a musical memory "When I Lost Ewe" (Lingalongamax LP). Yours, till this lot ere give that bloody samba a rest. Max". He'd tell you anything to get a play, would Max.

I had worked with Max's musical director Geoff Love many times, and I was about to work with him again as I brought him in to accompany The Nolan Sisters and Patrick Moore on xylophone (not at the same time, silly) for a concert at Golders Green Hippodrome, introduced by Terry with the grand title of "Tuesday Night Is Gala Night". This took place on the 27th March, a good six months before their first lowly chart entry "Spirit Body And Soul", after which they were known simply as The Nolans and went on to great success around the world. Glad we could help. The highlight of the night for me and Terry was watching in awe as Patrick knocked ten bells out of that xylophone, bringing forth amazed applause from a delighted audience. All in all, a most successful evening.

Caroline finally overcame her fear of flying in April when she threw all caution to the winds and organised a holiday in Bangkok. No tentative trial air travel there, then. I was thinking Paris might have been a first step but no, Thailand it was. We stayed at the Oriental Hotel on the Chao Phraya river and were looking forward to seeing the sights but, unfortunately, Caroline had contracted chickenpox and was confined to the hotel for a few days. The first thing that struck me on arrival was the reaction I got from the bellboy after I tipped him for bringing in the luggage, he almost kissed my feet. I later found out that what was an average tip back home was worth about a week's wages in Bangkok. The food in the hotel was delicious but at breakfast the first day the coffee they served was an undrinkable brew the colour of molasses and thick as mud, the only downer on an otherwise splendid spread. On that first day Krystle and I enjoyed the pool and I helped her along with her buoyancy aids, checking back regularly to see how Caroline was feeling. That night I wondered what was happening to me as I couldn't sleep because of severe pains in my legs, which reminded me of the problems I had sleeping at Forest Mere. The next morning there was no improvement and Caroline and I went through a list of possible reasons including dehydration, lack of salt, lack of minerals and anything else that was different from home. After trying pain killers and all the other remedies it dawned on me what was missing from my daily routine – coffee. I ordered a cup and loaded it with sugar, held my nose and downed it in one. Twenty minutes later – no pain, which indicated to me that I was addicted to coffee and that a lack of it would bring pain, a lesson well and truly learned.

Caroline recovered sufficiently for us to get out and about to see the wonderful temples and take hair-raising rides on the onomatopoeically named tuk tuks (I love that word, no, not tuk tuk, the other one.) which were motorised rickshaws, through the unbelievably crowded streets of the city centre. We also took to the river to visit the floating markets selling fresh produce along an extensive network of maze-like canals. The thought of a trip to the beach was appealing as we had heard that Pattaya was the place to be beside the seaside and after another crazy road trip we arrived at this very average small hotel where the air-con was noisy, the night-time activity was even louder and went on till dawn. The next day we were on our way back to Bangkok much chastened but at least back in comfortable accommodation. We thoroughly enjoyed our trip and the most magical meal we had was on the riverside terrace of The Oriental where all manner of food was being freshly prepared and barbequed, with live music in the background and the warm tropical air at the perfect temperature – heavenly bliss. I think that trip cured Caroline of her fear of flying, at last.

It was quite some change of scene when I got back to find myself on another plane, this time flying to the Isle Of Man for an OB with Terry on May Bank Holiday Monday. We stayed in Douglas and did part of the programme from a horse-drawn tram along the promenade with the usual mix of chats with the locals and holidaymakers and music played in from London. We also managed to fit in a trip to Ronnie Aldrich's home near Peel where I was most taken with a lovely breed of sheep with soft brown fleeces that were more like fur. I haven't been back to the IOM since, but one day I will.

The "Come Dancing" season was in full swing and the next few months saw us visiting Cheltenham, Motherwell, Swansea and Derby, usually accompanied by Ray Moore, who did the off-camera commentary. Ray would sometimes bring along his wife Alma, a lovely lady he referred to as "Management" – which meant he was always on his best behaviour, and quite rightly so.

Probably the most fun gig of the year was in August at the Courage Brewery in Tower Bridge Road when Chas And Dave gave us a great show to promote their latest album "Don't Give A Monkey's", they were brilliant, as ever.

In September Caroline was taken by an advertisement for Timeshare Apartments which enticed us down to Torquay on the English Riviera to check them out. They were located in a beautiful Georgian terrace overlooking Meadfoot beach just outside the town centre. We were taken with it straight away and booked a spring-time week every year, which very often coincided with Krystle's half-term break from school. It was a great decision and we enjoyed many happy holidays at The Osborne Club and, in fact, still do, albeit with different partners. The Osborne had a connection with the Vaugrenier apartments in Cagnes Sur Mer, near Nice, and we took up their invitation to visit which tempted us to consider buying there. It was a wonderful secluded place in beautiful grounds with tennis courts and swimming pool, which I recommended to Terry and Helen and after they saw it they bought in immediately, as did other music biz contacts – I should have been on commission. Caroline's parents also went to have a look but decided that they would rather have a place they could visit year-round and so opted for a luxurious apartment on the Moyenne Corniche overlooking Cap Ferrat. Located on the Avenue Bella Vista, it certainly lived up to its name and Caroline, Krystle and I enjoyed our summer holidays there for several years in the 1980's. They were idyllic days and when we weren't swimming and sunbathing by the rooftop pool, we'd drive to the old hilltop villages of Eze and St Paul de Vence for a spot of lunch. The highlights each week during August were the Monaco fireworks in the Monte Carlo harbour where several nationalities would compete to present the most spectacular display. It was hard to pick a winner, each entry was equally magnificent as we sat there watching in wonderment licking our ice-creams on the harbour wall. Krystle learned a little French and was delighted when she was able to ask for bonbons in the sweet shop.

Prior to our French trips we took more traditional family holidays at the Grosvenor Hotel in Swanage at the same time every year, which many guests did, meaning that we saw the same faces every year and became quite friendly with them, as did all the children. It was something to look forward to as we got three square meals a day, indoor and outdoor pools, grass and hard tennis courts, evening entertainment and games and all with a view over the harbour. At the bar one evening an elderly gentleman engaged me in conversation and when I told him I worked at the BBC he volunteered the information that he was the composer, if that's the right word, of The Hokey Cokey, that crazy comedy song and dance. I didn't argue with him but I was always of the opinion that Jimmy Kennedy wrote that song, or at least inspired a modern version of an old folk song. Sadly, I understand the hotel was later demolished and replaced by flats.

Mentioning Jimmy Kennedy reminds me of the regular contact I had with him during the seventies as he always listened to Wogan and wrote me a letter of thanks whenever we played one of his songs. That happened fairly regularly as I often selected his hits "Harbour Lights" by The Platters, "Red Sails In The Sunset" by Fats Domino and "South Of The Border" by Frank Sinatra. He wasn't averse to writing and telling me off when he hadn't heard one of his songs for a while, either. He was a great self-promoter and when he was in London he'd take me for lunch at his favourite restaurant, Kettners in Soho, where we'd sometimes be entertained by the brilliant blind jazz pianist Eddie Thompson. Jimmy was always very generous and each Christmas he'd send me a side of smoked salmon, as did the orchestra leader Frank Chacksfield. There were many seasonal gifts arriving every December from the record industry and one year I counted 30 bottles in among the cards. As I left the office each night carrying a case of booze, I would always drop a bottle off to the commissionaire at reception. Well, that's what Christmas is all about, right?

Krystle must have been seven or eight years old when she made us roar with laughter as she came running in one day having seen an episode of Doctor Who which featured The Daleks on menacing form. She was highly excited as she held out her arm and shouted "Exterminate, exterminate, I am a garlic, I am a garlic". We laughed so hard and then told her they weren't "garlics" they were Daleks but it didn't dampen her enthusiasm any. Around about the same time we organised a birthday party for her and I used my contacts in the film world to book a private preview theatre in Wardour Street and managed to borrow a print of the children's fantasy film "Water Babies", which was just perfect for Krystle and her friends. We hired a coach to carry this troupe to London and fed them all at McDonald's in the Haymarket before the film, which all contributed to a joyous and memorable occasion for all those tiny tots. Caroline and I enjoyed it, too.

The last interesting events of the year included two comedy showcases, with Dr Hook's Christmas party and Billy Connolly's album launch for "Riotous Assembly" at Legends night club in Old Burlington Street. Fun was the order of the day and after The Singing Frock and The Singing Harpoon along came the hit song "Just When I Needed You Most" by Randy Vanwarmer, one name Terry didn't have to make up to get a laff. Oh, use your imagination.

Here's a piece of cod-philosophy which I think happens to have the ring of truth about it. As the memory fades, dates and timelines may become blurred but the reminiscences can remain in sharp focus. Here are a few things I'd like to say before the bad news arrives. A reminder that our musical mainstays during my Wogan years were The Carpenters, Abba, Neil Diamond, Barry Manilow, Billy Joel, Dolly Parton, Manhattan Transfer and Olivia Newton-John, with whom we had lunch at the White Elephant Club in Curzon Street. I mention this to amplify Terry's wicked sense of devilment and humorous teasing. We sat next to each other directly opposite Olivia and Terry leaned over and whispered in my ear "She's a real cracker, you know". I said "What do you mean?" and he replied with a twinkle in his eye "You know". In disbelief I said "You haven't?" and he looked me straight in the face, raised an eyebrow and said "Haven't I?" We both giggled and Olivia looked over and gave us a curious smile before we carried on with lunch and conversation. Being exposed to so many beautiful women during those Come Dancing and Miss World competitions we both thought we had a pretty good eye for the ladies but I never found Tel in any interesting or comprising situations, so, sorry, no dirt to dish here. We did discuss various high-profile presenters such as Selena Scott and Anna Ford and once again I went for the blonde and he went for the brunette. No change there, then.

Social gatherings and dinner parties were all part of life's rich fabric and over the years the best parties were thrown by Dave and Marianne, The Travis's, which is where, over a game of snooker, I met Ben Findon, the record producer responsible for hits by Billy Ocean, The Dooleys and The Nolans. We got chatting and discovered that we lived very close to each other, leading Ben to invite us over to his house in Fulmer for dinner and a game of snooker. That was the start of a long friendship with Ben, his wife Linda and their children Ben Junior and Charlotte, who became good friends with Krystle. They had a really magnificent property with a pool, tennis court and a full-size snooker table which Ben and I made good use of. Linda was a wonderful cook and Ben had a great cellar which he would raid for his best wines only when I was there because he said I was the only other person he knew who appreciated a fine bottle. Blimey, a fine bottle indeed. We'd start with a white Montrachet and then the amazing 1961 vintage of either a Chateau Latour or Lafite, not too bad, really. It was interesting to have the first hearing of Ben's latest recordings and I was happy to give him feedback on their prospects, one in particular, which comes later.

Ben and Linda were our guests for dinner in Chesham Bois together with Terry and Helen and their friends Kits and Hacker Browning. The evening started off with a rather too-strong offering of champagne cocktails and we did wonder how they managed to get home that night. Caroline prepared a fine meal and even though I couldn't match Ben's wines I did serve a very acceptable Chateau Ducru-Beaucaillou, which Terry thought was a wonderful wine and a great name, often referring to me afterwards as Monsieur Ducru-Beaucaillou, which I also found acceptable.

Helen was another marvellous cook and Caroline and I went over for a memorable dinner at "Wogan Towers" with several show-biz guests including Noel Edmonds and David Jason. The jokes and stories were flying thick and fast with all the blokes trying to out-do each other which made for a night of brilliant, and free, entertainment. Later Terry told me of a conversation he had with

David who said he was unhappy with the accommodation he was given when away on location. Tel was on it in a flash telling David that he was a big enough star not to accept any bullshit and either he or his agent should demand a better deal without delay. David took the advice, and the bull by the horns, and in no time at all things were resolved very much in his favour. Terry certainly knew how to negotiate, that's beyond question and not up for negotiation.

Finally, in amongst all this mayhem, came the most expensive lunch in the history of lunches, which is quite an achievement considering the obscene amount of money sloshing around the music business at the time. Simon Bates, Terry and I had never, to my recollection, been out to lunch together before but the opportunity arose when I got a phone call from a distraught record plugger. He was in great distress and begging for my help in mending a broken fence between himself and Simon. He told me he had upset Bates very badly and really couldn't afford to have a fractured relationship with such a high-profile and influential presenter, as it might even threaten his job. I asked him how he thought I could help and he asked if I could arrange a lunch where he and I and Simon could try to fix things and, if I thought it would help, bring Terry along as well. No pressure then. I spoke to Simon and Terry and they were up for a lunch but Simon said let's make it a really good one and painful to his pocket, where would I suggest. Well, I said I thought The Mirabelle was probably the best place to test out this man's intentions, and that was where we went. A limousine arrived at Broadcasting House to pick up the three of us and we arrived suitably suited and booted at this edifice to fine dining in Mayfair. We were shown into the conservatory and offered pre-luncheon drinks which brought forth murmurings of gin and tonic, maybe a dry sherry or such when I said "It's a hot, sunny day, I think I quite fancy a champagne cocktail", which settled it and the other three ordered the same. We enjoyed our first glass so much we decided on another while we browsed the menu. Then came the funny bit as the maitre 'd came over to tell us there was a gentleman at reception who claimed to be part of our party but he didn't let him in as we had only booked a table for four and besides which he was improperly dressed. We asked if this man had given a name and we were told it was a Mr Atkey, at which Simon said "Bloody hell, it's my producer Dave, he must have found out where I was from our secretary". This put our host in something of a quandary but he couldn't not let Dave join us so he asked what could be done about his attire to be told they could supply him with a jacket and tie which would be acceptable but that they couldn't offer him an alternative shirt. We soon found out why when Dave came in with a tie on and a jacket just barely concealing a lurid, brightly coloured checked lumberjack shirt. He had a huge grin on his face and we all saw the funny side of it as well. Dave wasn't going to miss this shindig for anything. Terry and Simon pored over the wine list with gay abandon and we ate the very best the kitchen had to offer, at the end of which, after a final round of vintage port, cognac and cigars, the plugger rather sheepishly asked for the reckoning. His face at first went red, then white, then red again as he handed over his credit card with an audible gulp. Limos were waiting as we staggered manfully out into the bright sunshine and Pluggerman went back to his office to hand in his expenses together with his resignation, fully expecting to be summarily dismissed. The bill was apparently astronomically humungous but to be fair to the boss he realised what had occurred with the situation beyond his employee's control and said that as he'd lunched two major stars and two important producers it was accepted but that he had better not make a habit of it. It was one for the record books and I hope you think worth the re-telling?

There was another funny moment involving Terry and Simon when we decided to play a little joke on the listeners by having them switch places during a live broadcast. One morning after the nine o'clock news Terry's show went out on the Radio One frequency and Simon went out on Radio Two. We were expecting an explosive reaction but, as it transpired, there was very little comment and the experiment fizzled out like a damp squib. Hey, maybe nobody was listening.

Now comes the worst bit, as The Bard said, "Parting is such sweet sorrow" but there was nothing sweet about what happened at the end of 1979 for either me or Terry. We were both furious and disappointed when I got a telephone call from Geoff Owen, while

I was away on holiday, if you don't mind, telling me that he wanted me to produce the new David Hamilton lunchtime show which was replacing Pete Murray's Open House. He said he was phoning me while I was away because he didn't want me to hear this news from anybody else. I said I was unhappy with this decision and surely I should stay with Terry as the listening figures were going through the roof but he said it was important to him that the best man for the job took over the lunchtime slot, what a creep. It took a while for this to sink in enough for me to accept it but Terry was so incensed that all his future contract negotiations gave him the power of veto over any change of producer. It would be another thirteen years before we worked together again as he asked for me as his producer when he came back to Radio Two after his years as a television chat-show host.

My last Terry programme at the end of those four years was on Friday January the 18th and when I arrived in the office the following Monday there was a hand-written, hand delivered letter from Terry which could not have been a better epitaph to our wonderful working relationship and friendship. This is what he wrote: -

Dear Geoff,

A brief and therefore inadequate note of thanks and appreciation for all the help, good times and good friendship that you have given me so unstintingly over the past four years. Those years have been the happiest and most successful of my professional career, and it's no coincidence that they've been spent with you as my producer and friend. May you go on to the success and promotion that you deserve, and will undoubtedly achieve. Here's to the next time – yours, Terry.

He knew how to bring a tear to your eye, didn't he? Maybe that should be the foreword for this tome as I can't think of anything better.

Krystle & Smurfs, showing early artistic promise 1978

CHAPTER TWENTY
David Hamilton – The "Diddy" Days

It didn't take more than a moment for "Diddy" David and I to strike up a good working relationship and a long-standing friendship as we both loved sport, music and the radio. Just as I had been given no particular reason for leaving Terry, there was no significant dialogue in respect of what was expected of this new lunchtime show. The format fortunately found its feet almost instantly with minimum speech and maximum music, which we both thought ideal for that time of day. The fast pace and lively music mix proved a big hit with the listeners and in very short order we had easily surpassed Pete Murray's listening figures.

Plugger pressure didn't ease off either and I was inundated with discs and invites to lunches, receptions, film previews and shows just as before. The first of these was at the end of January when we were invited to a one-off performance of a "new work" by Andrew Lloyd Webber and Don Black at The Royalty Theatre starring the marvellous Marti Webb in this one woman show. It was entitled "Tell Me On A Sunday" and the BBC filmed it for transmission on TV in February. It won great critical acclaim and gave Marti her first-ever chart entry for the stand-out song "Take That Look Off Your Face" which got to Number 3. When the album came out nearly all the producers played the song "Capped Teeth And Caesar Salad" but the record label in its wisdom decided against releasing it as a single, choosing instead the title song which only managed a meagre placing of 67.

As part of devising a new format for the show I managed to achieve a bit of a coup as we became the first BBC radio show to be given permission to do regular astral predictions. I brought in the world-famous fortune teller, sorry, astrologer, Patric Walker who gave us a daily horoscope in his unique urbane literary style. Patric was a very sociable gay and once took David and I out for drinks to a cocktail bar in Mayfair where a friend of his was playing piano mood music in the background. We were introduced and intrigued to hear about his long career as accompanist to the French chanteuse Mistinguet, at one time the highest-paid entertainer in the world. Now, for the life of me I can't recall his name, but he did expand on his experience by saying that although he was gay, he was required to relax Mistinguet in her dressing room before each performance. You might think I was making that up if it weren't so unbelievably interesting. No details, children may read this. The funny thing is, as Patric told me, he was unable to do a horoscope for himself as he didn't know exactly when he was born. How ironic is that?

On the musical side we'd mark every day by playing the hits of any artist who had been born on that date, which gave us a massive canvas to paint on. David also gave out a "Bouquet For A Bride" each Friday and we also responded to requests from listeners to play a "Musical Memory". We weren't short of ideas or feedback and the show bounced along very merrily. There was great rapport and repartee between us and David was a master of Cockney rhyming slang and he'd set me a puzzle every now and then with some outlandishly whimsical concoctions such as "How's the trouble and saucepans?" Translation, trouble and strife is wife and saucepan lids is kids hence "How's the wife and kids?" The most convoluted he came up with was "Can you sausage me a Gregory?" which means sausage and mash for cash and Gregory Peck for cheque, in other words "Can you cash me a cheque?" Ridiculous, I know, but quite good fun learning a new language.

I also selected a "Record of the Week" which was played each day and several of them became big hits such as Fern Kinney "Together We Are Beautiful", Detroit Spinners "Working My Way Back To You", Blondie "Tide Is High", Shakin' Stevens "This Ole House", his first Number One, Smokey Robinson "Being With You" and the most unlikely hit of all, which I went out on a limb with, was "And The Birds Were Singing" by Sweet People, which got to Number 4. Novelty numbers still had a part to play in the mix in those days.

Comedy also had a place in the show and we had a lot of fun with Cannon And Ball who captured the public's imagination with their catch phrase "Rock on, Tommy". They obviously listened to the show and heard their record being played prompting them to get in touch and invite us to see them in cabaret at Caesar's Palace nightclub in Luton. They were the comedy kings of their time and we had a great night with them there and a few weeks later they presented us with a silver disc as a thank you for playing their album. We liked to spread our favours far and wide, don't you know, and I'm glad to say it was reciprocated by most.

Outside broadcasts were not a regular feature of the show but we did cover a couple of Ideal Home shows with the first in March attended by Her Majesty The Queen and His Royal Highness The Duke Of Edinburgh and although we didn't get to interview them we were in close proximity. We were there again a year later and in our wander around the arena we came across former world snooker champion Ray Reardon preparing to give a demonstration. When he saw us he invited us to join him and knock a few balls about, which we did, and that was the second time I had the immense pleasure of getting well and truly thumped by one of the green baize greats.

Record company invites continued unabated with a newly popular venue being Searcys restaurant in Knightsbridge where they hosted receptions for Barbara Dickson in April and The Beach Boys in June – delicious (the food, not the Beach Boys).

Nearer to home the Chesham Chamber of Commerce had somehow managed to lobby successfully to host a "Miss Chesham" beauty contest as part of the "Miss United Kingdom" competition. I was asked to help out and got fully immersed in the whole operation, as did Caroline, who at the time was running a business in Great Missenden. I approached Tony Blackburn to ask if he would compere the evening and guess what, he jumped at the chance. We were also involved with recruiting members of the judging panel and through my contacts brought in singer Stephanie de Sykes, who wrote that year's Song For Europe, and British Songwriter of the Year Ben Findon. Caroline was also on the panel and brought in her friend Lady Campbell, better known as

The Champagne Soprano Lizbeth Webb, star of the musical "Bless The Bride", who told me, in a confidential confession that she was engaged to Peter Sellers in the early fifties. Blimey, she needn't have been so secretive about it as Peter by this time had already been seen at The Pearly Gates. This celebrity line-up was completed by local football hero Luther Blissett. The evening was a great success, Tony did a great job and I helped him on stage raising money with a raffle. One prize was a traffic cone signed by Terry Wogan, which attracted heavy bidding as they were quite the rage at the time, believe me, and all the money raised went to Stoke Mandeville Hospital.

Two major events took place in September with Frank Sinatra's appearance at the Albert Hall, one of my favourite venues where I had seen so many great acts including Creedence Clearwater Revival, Redbone, Clapton and country star Buck Owens. Sinatra was sensational and finished, inevitably, with his latest hit "New York, New York".

The second event was even more sensational but not in a good way when record label boss Chas Peate invited me to the World Middleweight championship fight between Alan Minter and Marvin Hagler at Wembley Arena. We had very good ringside seats which put us right in the firing line when the whole place erupted in a riot as the referee stopped the fight in the third round to save Minter taking any more punishment. It was a shameful night for boxing and British sport as enraged drunken fans hurled beer, bottles and anything else they could get their hands on, directly towards the ring where we were sitting. It only took us a few seconds to realise what was happening and we made a frantic dash for the exit, covered in beer, with our hands over our heads for protection. Fortunately, none of us was hurt. That night has gone down in infamy as all hell broke loose and poor old Harry Carpenter was hit on the head by a beer bottle and Hagler vowed never to fight in England ever again.

Back on the musical scene I went to a preview of Stevie Wonder's album "Hotter Than July" at Abbey Road studios, attended the Tin Pan Alley Ball at the Hilton Hotel, saw the "Cliff In London" concert at the Victoria Apollo and Barry Manilow and Queen at Wembley Arena, both considerably more civilised than my previous experience there. Caroline had been the very first to alert me to the potential of Queen after seeing them on an early Top Of The Pops appearance when she was convinced they were going to be huge. How right she was, she always had a good eye for spotting talent.

David Hamilton was a great Fulham fan and took me there to watch a game at Craven Cottage, where he was well known to the supporters as he did the commentary and announcements for many years. He also invited me to go with some of his friends to a game at White Hart Lane to see Tottenham Hotspur, and there was a great deal of fun and joshing as we gathered at his friend's house near the ground. We were all assembled and ready to go except for one late-comer, the legend that is Jess Conrad. Somebody said Jess was always last to arrive so he could make a bit of an entrance, also that I must watch the hallway as he walked in because they said he wouldn't be able to pass the mirror without pausing for an admiring glance. We all watched in anticipation for this prediction to unfold and sure enough, right on cue, he stopped by that mirror for a long, lingering, loving look, bless him.

Invitations to lunch continued unabated, mostly just on-going, keeping the wheels of industry lubricated affairs, but there were two that stick solidly in the memory. One came from Martin Grinham, the song-plugger for Valentine Music, who published what is arguably the most annoying song of all time, namely The Birdie Song which, by some cosmic quirk of fate got into the Top Ten. Maybe that's a reflection of just how good Martin was at his job, even though I don't remember playing it on David's show and, even if I did, I wouldn't admit to it now. Lunch was arranged at a hotel near Piccadilly Circus which had a help yourself carvery and we were to be joined by the then Hollies manager Jimmy Smith, a jocular man who instantly made me smile when he asked me what I wanted to drink and then, without waiting for my reply, proceeded to order three large gin and tonics. Martin and Jimmy were at the bar when I arrived and had already had a first G & T so you can probably guess where this is going. It very soon became apparent why we were eating here as Martin mounted a challenge to rival "Peter The Eater", visiting the buffet several times to sample every assorted dish on offer. Not only that but the wine was flowing freer than the Thames and the stories about the business and the characters therein were being delivered with great hilarity by a couple of real raconteurs. Nobody seemed to notice nor care about the passage of time and it was gone four o'clock before Martin asked to see the dessert trolley, which contained a large Black Forest gateau, and when the waitress asked if he'd like a slice Martin said "No, thank you, could you please just leave it on the table and we'll help ourselves". I think by this time the staff were well aware of what was going on and continued to clear away our plates with knowing smiles on their faces. Finally, we were into coffees and port and I still can't believe that two bottles of Portugal's finest were demolished, mostly by Jimmy and Martin. Then came the funniest thing I ever saw in a restaurant as this stupendous occasion entered into a final round of hilarious conflict between Martin and Jimmy as they battled over who would pay the bill. Back and forth they went at it – "I'm paying", "No, I'm paying", for several rounds, culminating in them both throwing their American Express cards on the table. Then Jimmy delivered the coup de grace by picking up Martin's card, deftly folded it in two a few times and then ripped it apart saying "I think you'll find that I'm paying, Martin". I couldn't stop laughing but Martin was crestfallen as he said "Oh no, I won't be able to go out for lunch for ages until I get a new card". We left the building just after six o'clock, very much the worse for wear and as I made my way up Regent Street my eyes were so bleary and my balance somewhat suspect I stayed very close to the walls and the shop windows. Not wanting to bump into any colleagues I avoided Oxford Circus and detoured past my old office in Carnaby Street and finally came to rest in my Charlotte Street den where I fell asleep for a couple of hours. Memorable? I'll say.

The other lunch I mentioned came via an invitation from Tommy Loftus, a delightful plugger of the old-school at RCA Records, who phoned me one morning to tell me that Mel Brooks was in town and would I like to meet him for lunch? What, lunch with Mel Brooks, are you kidding me? I was to meet them in Berkeley Square at 12.30 and the silliness started almost instantly. As I walked through the entrance door I saw the two of them sitting at the bar, Tommy saw me, nudged Mel and nodded in my direction. Mel stood up immediately and walked towards me with an outstretched hand and said "Hi Geoff, I'm Tommy Loftus, come and meet Mel Brooks". This got me at it straight away as I went to the bar, shook Tommy's hand and said "Pleased to meet you, Mr Brooks". We laughed a lot that afternoon as Mel held forth but didn't miss the chance to tell me about his new film "History Of The World" and a record he was making called "It's Good To Be King". I looked at Tommy and asked if he would be working it and was it on RCA records, at which Mel jumped in and said "No, it's on the Luggage Label", which was funny but also true. I told Mel that I really enjoyed his films "Blazing Saddles", "Young Frankenstein" and that my favourite comedy film was "The Producers". "Oh yes" said Mel, "I was hot back then", followed by "Do you know, I was the first Jew in history who ever made a buck out of Hitler?" I chortled so much I almost choked. This led on to a discussion about comedians, Jewish and otherwise, that I had enjoyed on record such as Lord Buckley, Flip Wilson, Murray Roman and Frank Gallop. Mel knew them all and said he had been listening to Frank Gallop for most of his life on radio and TV. I said one of Frank's records "The Ballad Of Irving" had been the template, some call it plagiarism, for Benny Hill's record "Ernie". Mel said "Yes, that's true, but did you know that Frank's record was itself a spoof on Lorne Green's record of "Ringo"? What goes around comes around". Such a great privilege to meet one of the funniest men on the planet and without a doubt one of the benefits of being in the business.

The opportunity to reject an offer of "Pay For Plays" never came my way in all my years in radio, and just as well as I would have shopped anybody who tried it on. However, I regarded lunches as a small token of gratitude for discs played, which came with the hope that the next offering would also merit attention. It didn't always happen that way as I judged each disc on its appeal to the listeners and couldn't be swayed by any inducement to play an unsuitable item. Most pluggers respected my judgement and decisions and they certainly didn't get too heated in debate for fear of irritating me, which, I have to say in my own defence, was not an easy thing to do.

The first London Marathon took place in March and was, naturally, a radio sport production but they asked me to provide some suitably uplifting music to fill in any gaps there might be as this was the first time they had ever attempted such a massively complicated event. All went well and they seemed to enjoy my music selection, which prompted Pat Ewing to send me a personal note of thanks for the support I gave the Sports Unit and for providing the perfect music, ending with the hope that I would be able to join "The Team" in the not-too-distant future. Praise indeed and prophetic as I would work alongside Pat and her team many times in the future. I also received a treasured piece of memorabilia from the man who headed that broadcast, Welsh rugby hero Cliff Morgan, who sent me a postcard all the way from New Zealand and this is what he wrote -

"Thank you Mr Music Man for the sounds you selected that made this "out of practise" Welsh Baptist enjoy the Marathon special despite the terror of the occasion. Sincerely, Cliff".

I talked to Cliff about his commentary on the Baa Baas v All Blacks match and he admitted to getting carried away with emotion when describing the action of the "greatest try ever scored in the greatest rugby match ever played". He was a kind and generous man who endeared himself to all who knew him and enjoyed his company.

May that year turned out to be both fascinating and infuriating as David and I heard the news that our lunchtime show was being moved to later in the day in order to accommodate the John Dunn Show in our time-slot. Now, this initiative was instigated by Controller David Hatch; who told us that as we had doubled Pete Murray's audience figures it was perfectly sensible to give this large audience over to John. What a huge insult that was as he obviously thought John was much more worthy of a large audience share than we oiks who only played pop music. David Hamilton and I had the longest telephone conversation either of us ever had, from mid-afternoon until around 8 o'clock in the evening venting our outrage and frustration at this plainly idiotic change. I set up a meeting with the two DH's and myself to try and thrash this out and change his mind but he was adamant his decision was the correct one, even though I said the audience would be exhausted by the overkill of two chat shows back-to-back and that was why the music show worked so well at lunchtime. He was having none of it and we left his office more deflated than we could have imagined by his intransigence. It was no consolation to us either when the John Dunn show failed spectacularly within six months to be replaced by Gloria Hunniford in January. David Hatch never acknowledged that he'd made a big mistake, leaving me to get on with the job of establishing a winning format for the afternoon show. Isn't incandescent a wonderful word?

That whole episode reminded me of the accuracy of classic piece of graffiti scrawled on the wall of the gent's loo in BH. It stated "Working at the BBC is like being a pubic hair on the toilet bowl of life – sooner or later you get pissed off".

There was always some wit writing funny lines or anagrams of colleague's names, especially those of our bosses, and one of the best was for the Assistant Head of Radio Two Charles Beardsall who became known to one and all as Clasher Redballs.

Barely a week after that traumatic and depressing meeting with David Hatch something rather fascinating happened at our house in Chesham Bois. The BBC location scouts had identified our property as ideal for shooting an episode of the popular TV series "Bergerac", without knowing that a member of staff lived there. We were approached for permission to film and agreed a fee of £175 for use of the house over two days. This particular episode was called "Unlucky Dip" and featured Prunella Scales living in our house and drinking heavily by the swimming pool as Jim Bergerac tried to arrest her son for stealing. We thought it all rather amusing having our house on the tele.

One morning towards the end of July I walked into my office and knew exactly who would be sitting in my chair. As I stepped through the outer door the familiar aroma of Wogan's aftershave hit me, the very distinctive whiff of Paco Rabanne. We exchanged a cheery hello and Terry told me he was taking off for an extended break for about a month and I told him we would be in the South of France during August. He asked me how I was getting on with David so I told him all was well but that I was still furious with

Hatch for switching our time-slot. He said he understood my frustration and asked what I thought of Kenny Everett. I knew something was up and simply said "Zany", which he was. "How would you like to produce him?" says Tel, and I said "Is he coming to Radio Two?" "Yes, he is, and if you fancy it, I think you would be the ideal man to work with him". I asked him how he knew all this and he said his agent Jo Gurnett was negotiating to bring Kenny to Radio Two for a Saturday morning show and he, Terry, would have some input into who would be acceptable as his producer. Wheels within wheels, eh? And that's how I ended up leaving "Diddy" David to start a three-year stint with the mega-talented comic genius. David and I parted on good terms, hoping we would work together again in the future, and at that point David said what he had said many times before, almost his "catchphrase" - "I'm just happy to be here". Weren't we all.

With Diddy David Hamilton 1980

With Cliff Richard & Simon Bates

CHAPTER TWENTY-ONE

Those Lazy, Hazy, Krazy Days
With Kenny

Where to start with this incredible character, an iconoclastic, irreverent rebel? Suppose Kenny were writing this, would he start at the end and work his way backwards? Probably, you never knew what he'd be up to from one moment to the next he was just so very mercurial. He thrived on pressure and left everything to the very last minute, revelling in the danger and excitement of how far he could push things and living on a knife-edge. I have to say it was extremely stimulating not knowing what the hell was going to happen next, even though I'd probably get the blame if it went wrong, although my mitigation would be – "Well, you know what it's like with Kenny, almost impossible to control". That was all true outside the studio but once he was in there he was the master of his environment and a consummate performer at the controls. There was never anyone that inventive, creating soundscapes and devising new techniques that went well beyond what we mere mortals call imagination. I never ceased to be amazed at his ingenuity.

Our first meeting in September 1981 was a little stilted as I visited him at his flat in Notting Hill to discuss his return to the BBC, what with our not knowing each other and Kenny unaware of what it would be like to work with me, although I'm sure Terry and Jo would have given him plenty of reassurance. We broke ground when I told him I had produced the last shows by his idol Jack Jackson, allowing some of his trepidation to disappear, after which he said "We must have a cup of coffee, darling" Then we got down to the real nitty gritty of what we could bring to this new Saturday morning show and I said I would provide him with a weekly diet of information from my research into significant dates for famous birthdays, anniversaries and forthcoming events. I also agreed to scour the BBC archives for clips of historical, comical or musical interest which he might use. He said he would provide Captain Kremen episodes and all his Memory Modules of Golden Oldies from the past but he wanted me to bring in all the newly released records. We both felt the music policy should not adhere strictly to the mainstream Radio Two playlist but be more adventurous and ground-breaking. Kenny said he was looking forward to being back on national radio, especially on the station with the Queen Anne legs. I was beginning to warm to my task by this time.

The weekly routine was then set and each Thursday evening I would visit Kenny on my way home and deliver a case full of archive clips that I had put onto tape for him, which he would work on integrating into the show by putting them onto tape cartridges in the order he wanted them. Kenny was delighted to have so much material to play with and would spend Friday compiling multiple segments to be played in between the records. He didn't always finish his work on Friday and I would often find him first thing on Saturday morning still in his pyjamas leaping about in a frantic effort to finish before we had to leave for the studio. My intention was to pick him up from home and drive to the studio, Kenny with his box of tapes and me with my box of records, but he set a precedent on that very first morning when I said I had the car outside and he said "Oh no, sweetie-pie, I'll drive", and off we went in his BMW 5 Series. He often called me "sweetie-pie" and other affectionate names over the years. He was a real "sweetie-pie" himself as I got to really like him and love him (not literally) during our time together.

That first show was on October the 3rd 1981 and it went really well, we got to the studio on time, which didn't happen very often, and for the first time in my career up to that point I sat in the studio opposite the disc jockey and passed Kenny the next record to play in sequence. This was a new and fulfilling experience for me as I felt fully part of proceedings rather than watching things unfold from behind a glass window in the control room. Because of the heightened sense of anticipation for this new show and with his pulse rate beginning to quicken Kenny went into a routine to ease the tension and help him relax. I was astounded and amused in equal parts when just seconds before he was due to announce himself on air he got off his chair, laid flat on his back and started wildly waving his arms and legs about while screaming at the top of his voice, almost to the point of exhaustion. He called it preparation and that is why, if you ever listened to one of those programmes, you would hear it begin immediately after the GTS (Greenwich Time Signal), known as the "pips", with a breathless Kenny intoning into the microphone "Good morning, darlings", instantly followed by a record so he could get his breath back. At least it got him in the mood and removed any jitters. It never lacked for the unpredictable with my boy. To extract the maximum awareness and publicity for the show another of my weekly tasks was to compose a billing for the Radio Times. This was the very first -

"Cuddly Ken returns to Auntie with an amazing display of wireless wizardry. It's wacky. It's fun. It's rubbish. Do not adjust your sets. The Producer of this show wishes to remain Geoff Mullin"

My former nemesis David Hatch was so taken by this billing he encouraged me to have as much fun with them as possible and insisted that they were never to be dropped from the magazine as he thought they were they best thing in it. Recognition at last. He also sent a very supportive note to say how much he enjoyed the show and would I pass on his congratulations to Kenny also. We were off and running. Taking David's cue regarding the billings I came up with ever more weird and wonderful editions requiring the typeface to be back to front, upside down, mirror image, strange names and bizarre situations. I'll give you a couple more later on.

As we packed up afterwards Kenny said he had loved the music, especially the disco-type stuff and hoped there would be more of the same in future. I assured him there would be as I thought we needed plenty of lively tunes which were perfect for Saturday mornings to please what would surely be a younger profile of listeners, an assumption which was later borne out by the findings from the BBC's Audience Research Unit. Then he said, on the spur of the moment, "Let's go for lunch, I'm starving". He drove us to an Indian restaurant near Regents Park where I ordered a pint of Cobra and he ordered a triple scotch. He took a large gulp, heaved a sigh and said "Ah, intravenous alcohol", which seemed to be a relief after the last two hours of intense activity. On the way home I got the first indication of the way one part of his brain worked as we drove down the high street and he pointed out various things and people along the way. His powers of observation were not only acute but also skewed at a different angle than most of us as he noticed and opined on shoppers saying things like "Oh, look at that, why do you think he's wearing that on day like this" and other such remarks, often very funny, too. He never missed a thing and often gave me a new perspective on what might otherwise have seemed mundane and ordinary.

Sometimes after a show we'd go out for a meal or drive straight back to Kenny's for lunch. Well, I say lunch but it usually consisted of one or two Pot Noodles and a glass of vodka or three. He was all for instantaneous gratification, never wanting to waste time with things on the periphery, always going for the jugular, impatient for the climax. This was never more noticeable than when he'd sit me down to watch a video he'd "edited". The first instance of this literal "cutting to the chase" was after we'd been to a preview of John Carpenter's modern take on the old sci-fi horror movie "The Thing" with Kurt Russell and he managed to get a pirate copy. After his manipulation with a razor blade there was no story, no lead-in, just the mesmerising development of the alien monster and the havoc that ensued. We went to see many films together and one that we both enjoyed very much was "Victor Victoria", a convoluted musical story about a cross-dressing female singer, Julie Andrews, who pretends to be a man doing a female impersonation act – got it? He/she was managed by a gay cabaret singer played by Robert Preston and James Garner provided the confused love interest. Henry Mancini and Leslie Bricusse came up with a terrific score and Dame Julie sang the best 1930's period song "Le Jazz Hot" with great gusto – perfect for our show. Should have been a hit.

Not only was Kenny meticulous with his work in the studio he was also fastidious around the house and I would often arrive there to find him wearing a pinafore with a feather duster in his hand flicking away the cobwebs. I did wonder if that's where his friend

Freddie Mercury got the idea for his visual performance in the "I want To Break Free" promo video. During the winter months, as you know, cars can get very dirty and one day as I was about to leave his house he came out to wave goodbye, took one look at my car and commanded "Wait there, don't go anywhere" and disappeared back inside. He came running out with a wet sponge and a dishcloth and proceeded to wash my headlights like a man on a mission saying "Geoffrey, dear heart, you can't drive around with lights like that, you might have an accident". Always concerned for my welfare was Kenny.

Not long after we started working together Kenny moved from his basement flat to a more modern apartment in Kensington and soon found out just how difficult parking was in that particular borough. To help him remember where he had parked his car, he devised a wall map covering all his nearby roads, and when he got back in he would stick a pin into the board indicating exactly where his car was. How clever is that? This was especially useful after a night on the tiles when he would otherwise have no idea where he had left his vehicle. It didn't always work, particularly if he forgot or was unable to perform this delicate task after too heavy a session. Needless to say, it was inevitable that this would happen one Friday night and on the Saturday morning we spent about half an hour wandering the streets looking for the damn thing. The corollary to this was that we were never going to get to the studio on time and as we whizzed down the Westway into town we pulled up at the traffic lights to find the car next to us was being driven by our boss. He looked at me in the passenger seat and smiled, then he looked at his watch and his face went blank as he realised we were now only three minutes away from the time we should be on air – oops. Fortunately, the newsreader on the day had the wits to realise what to do when the engineer told him we weren't yet in the studio and he simply played a jingle and segued into a record. We parked the car on a yellow line, risking a ticket, rushed into BH and pelted down the corridors as fast as we could, arriving at the transmission desk in time for Kenny to say "Good morning, darlings" in his most breathless voice ever. After that monumental cock-up I always placed two or three discs in the studio to be played if ever we were late again. And we were, several times, but nobody seemed to notice. Got away with that one, then.

Interest from both the media and the record industry intensified as awareness of the show spread and the Radio Two press, promotion and publicity units kicked into gear and worked their dark arts. We were invited to a Marianne Faithful reception for "Dangerous Acquaintances" at Chelsea Arts Club and even to the Houses of Parliament for a lunch with Johnny Mathis. Well done whoever organised that one.

Music was always my responsibility, as I handed Kenny each disc over the desk one-at-a-time, but one that captured both our imaginations was by the avant-garde performance artist and electronic music pioneer Laurie Anderson, whose hypnotic, trance-like single "O Superman" went to Number Two in the chart after we wore out our copy playing it. Kenny's favourite artists were, in no particular order, except perhaps the first two, Beatles, Queen, Elton John, Eurythmics, Cliff Richard, Electric Light Orchestra, Lulu and the one-off hit "Heartache Avenue" by The Maisonettes, their name alone sending Kenny into hysterics. I suppose it's little wonder he was so supportive, even subconsciously, of anything involving the word men, for instance "The Safety Dance" by Men Without Hats, "Down Under" by Men At Work, Miquel Brown "So Many Men So Little Time" and his absolute favourite, probably his personal anthem, was The Weather Girls singing "It's Raining Men".

Many of the discs we played had a huge appeal to the gay community as well as the public in general as they were fun and lively dance tunes guaranteed to fill any disco floor, which reminds me what Kenny used to say when I asked him after the show "What are you up to tonight?" He'd often say the same thing, "I'm going to heaven tonight darling, to revel in rapture", which I took to mean he was going to cosy up with a friend of his choice for a night of passion. And it was in a way, but it was quite a while before I found out that he was talking about "Heaven", the gay night club in the West End which he frequented on a regular basis. Well, anyone can make a mistake, can't they?

To add an extra dimension to the regular musical offerings available in the UK I would take a weekly stroll down Berwick

Street in Soho to see Jeff Weston and Howard Caplan at The Record Shack, importers of the top US disco records. They would play me the latest 12inch bangers and any that I thought would be good for the show they would loan me free of charge. They knew that with Kenny's appeal to the gay community they would pick up a fair few sales after a play on the show. This was good for both parties and our audience could be sure of hearing records they wouldn't hear anywhere else on British radio, like the pioneer of Hi-NRG and electronic dance music Patrick Cowley. Although he never had a UK hit, he had been involved with Sylvester's Top Ten disco hit "You Make Me Feel (Mighty Real)" and Kenny was highly amused when I brought in his latest offering entitled "Menergy". Bit of a theme coming through now, eh?

Of all those early Radio Times billings I concocted the one that produced the most noticeable feedback was when I spelt the title and my name backwards, which encouraged the listeners to write in to "WOHS TTEREVE YNNEK EHT" and producer "NILLUM FFOEG". For weeks afterwards I was getting letters starting "Dear Nillum Ffoeg" – were they serious? We'll never know.

The end of 1981 was especially significant for me on a personal level when quite unexpectedly I made a new friend. Krystle had a babysitter from time to time called Karin and one day she asked if she could bring a friend along with her for the evening. That was OK and we met this friend of hers called Martin Kearney, who turned out to be an excellent guitarist and all-round good egg, so no wonder we connected immediately. Martin had boundless energy and enthusiasm and helped us move house to Denham in early 1982. So bouncy was this new acquaintance that he soon became known to one and all as "Tigger", a name he has always carried with pride. I watched Martin's career develop with great interest after he left Birmingham Uni with a biochemistry degree and then his involvement in the music business via stints playing lead guitar with the band "Tall Story" and "99 Shy", neither of which, sadly, made his fame and fortune. In 1986 I introduced him to Ben Findon who took him on as a studio engineer, after which he never looked back, working at Village Studios and heading up the Wing Command production team, responsible for the thumping re-mix of the

Number One Technotronic hit "Pump Up The Jam". The bond of friendship continues uninterrupted to this day and I was at his wedding to Julie and have seen his three kids, Shaun and his twin sisters Shannon and Joanna, grow into adulthood. If you can, always encourage friendships with people younger than yourself, it keeps you young. Anyway, more about "Tigger" later.

Consecutive days in December make for interesting reading. On the 21st I managed to get tickets for a family trip to see Adam And The Ants "Prince Charming Revue" at the Dominion Theatre. Krystle was overjoyed at the prospect of attending her first rock concert and seeing her hero but it all went pear-shaped after the first few numbers when she had to leave the theatre in some distress because she couldn't cope with the ear-splitting sound levels. It was bloody loud and I wasn't at all disappointed to be taking an early bath.

Do you remember me telling you about a Beatles Gold Disc I was given by Ringo back in the late sixties? Well, on December 22nd it went into Sotheby's Belgravia Rock 'n' Roll and Advertising Art auction where it fetched the princely sum of £1700. I hadn't wanted to part with it but somehow or other I couldn't find the funds I needed to buy a new car and this seemed like the simplest solution. The car in question belonged to Caroline's mother, Moira, and it had a bit of filmic history attached to it because it was driven in the Richard Burton film "The Medusa Touch" by actress Lee Remick. If you ever see that film, look out for a silver BMW 3 Series with the registration plate RYX 141R. It was a great car and I wonder where it is today? At least parting with that Beatles treasure paid me back handsomely for the condoms and broken bed they owed me for, but it was as nothing compared to the return I received when their autographs went under the hammer. Get your bids ready and prepare to empty your pockets.

As the year end loomed this was my seasonal billing for Radio Times -

'Kenny's Office Party – get in the mood for the forthcoming festivities as the maestro rolls up the studio rug for an Exmas Extravaganza. Planned attractions will include Jugglers, Clowns, Fire-eaters, Stilt-walkers and Morris Dancers – All-time Radio favourites. The Man on the Tightrope is producer Geoff Mullin.'

Somebody was taking the mickey early in 1982 as not one but two of the little blighters arrived. One was Kenny's favourite at the time as singer, dancer and choreographer Toni Basil hit the charts with her international number one "Mickey", helped in no small part by her cheerleader outfit and dance video. The other was Krystle's favourite TV personality "Metal Mickey", whose show on London Weekend Television was enormously popular family fare. It was produced by Monkee Mickey Dolenz, appropriately, and achieved a huge audience of 12 million viewers. Mickey's synthesised catchphrase "Boogie, Boogie" caught on in a big way and Krystle was delighted to receive a personalised message from him on a cassette tape, which she treasures to this day.

There were no guest appearances on the show but we had a regular friendly visit from Paul Gambaccini as he popped in prior to presenting his review of American music and the US Top 30 on Radio One. Another Radio One personality who brought in some mail to us was Adrian Juste, as many listeners wrote in to say they listened to Kenny until the end of his show and then tuned over to "The Other Side". I can understand that perfectly. Listeners mostly communicated by letter or postcard but one day the studio phone rang and I picked up to be accosted by an irate professor who objected to a remark Kenny had just made. Kenny said he had noticed that the midnight movie didn't always go out exactly at midnight but that it didn't really matter because most viewers were probably a bit tipsy by then anyway. The prof scolded me as his producer and said "How dare you allow him to suggest such a thing?" I calmed him down by saying I'd admonish Kenny and make sure he apologised. I didn't, and to my eternal shame, I forgot. What do you mean, you don't believe me?

Kenny's all-time favourites were The Beatles, whom he worshipped, and it was a strange sort of coincidence that we had both heard the same story about them from two different sources. It concerned their first single "Love Me Do" which, it seems, could easily have been Number One but for a decision by the EMI hierarchy to prioritise the record printing presses in favour of their "big-hitters" Shirley Bassey, Cliff Richard, The Shadows and Frank Ifield, especially in the run-up to Christmas. "Love Me

Do" entered the charts in October and only made number 17 but it stayed there for 17 weeks, proving that there were enough sales to have possibly made number one. I often wonder what the total cumulative sales figures for that period would reveal?

This permissible idiocy continued apace as Kenny worked his way through a web of music and mythology, putting all the stuff I brought him onto tape. There'd be The Fascinating Fact File, Bloopers, comedy clips, historical soundbites, classical lollipops, which he called "the twiddly bits", the amazing "Story Lady" and we always had that deep basso profundo voice saying "And now, here is the weather for men". One item that got the mail flooding in was the weekly competition, which might be stuff like a Beatles track speeded up, Cliff slowed down or several short snippets of songs sewn together. There was never any shortage of prizes as the record labels gave free albums, book publishers would offer their latest titles, film companies delivered videos on VHS tape and even extremely rare memorabilia like a James Bond promo watch. Kenny was fascinated by one prize we were given, the Suzuki "Sonic Strings" Omnichord, an electronic instrument which he fiddled about with on the show and even used to assemble some of his sensational jingles.

Radio waves, brainwaves, permanent waves were all part of the merry mix of mirth and madness and we were ably supported by the irrepressible Beverley Dale, PA extraordinaire, who joined in with great enthusiasm as we lost ourselves in the ether. She had her work cut out answering all the correspondence, fielding the phone calls and turning down lunch invitations (I don't think). Her little legs never touched the ground.

Kenny and I spent quite a lot of time together away from the confines of the studio and he was the most hospitable guy with invitations to many of his other activities. There was an evening at The Comedy Store where he recorded the very risque "Kenny Everett Naughty Video Show" with Barry Cryer, John Junkin and others – very funny and very filthy. It was all done "In The Best Possible Taste", a famous catchphrase introduced by his "tart with a heart" character Cupid Stunt, queen of the double entendre. There would always be an end of run party after the last edition of his television show, which often turned into a riot with Kenny and his madcap antics taking centre stage. We once had a day out with his pals Su Pollard and Christopher Biggins but I've no idea now where we went or what we did, so it must have been a lot of fun.

Kenny's partner, Naughty Nikolai was a hunky guy, very attractive, and attracted to both sexes. With his swarthy good looks and muscular frame, he was certainly a fine figure of a man. Kenny aspired to be more athletic, fit and sporty but it proved to be an uphill struggle as he just didn't have the physique to compete. We would go for a swim and play squash together but he was just hopeless with a racquet in his hand. Nevertheless, he felt satisfied that he'd done his best after scampering round the court for half an hour chasing balls he had no chance of catching but I kept him in the game as much as possible to give him a work-out until he collapsed with exhaustion. After that we'd go out for a meal, his favourite restaurant was "Menage A Trois" in Beauchamp Place where they only served starters and desserts, a perfect menu in Kenny's eyes, and mouth.

You won't believe how generous Kenny was to me as he once sent me a birthday card and enclosed a personal signed cheque for One Million Pounds. You know, I didn't have the heart to cash it as I knew how large his mortgage was, besides which I thought it would be a nice souvenir of his magnanimity. Apart from that, I'm not sure the bank would have honoured it as it was dated June the 93rd 1980 and written in pink ink. Kenny was a good artist and he loved coloured pens, especially those with silver and gold ink, which is what he used to sign all his publicity photos.

Kenny's granny was a source of much merriment and he told stories of his time with her and how she would go all round the house each night before bed and make sure there was something plugged into all the electricity sockets in every room. When he asked her why, she said it was to make sure no electricity leaked out during the night – he swears it was true.

Continuity of Kenny's presence on the Radio Two airwaves wasn't guaranteed as he'd take time off for his TV recordings and he was a little bit fond of an exotic holiday but he did keep in touch during those absences with cards and letters, like this one written on

BA First Class notepaper when he was travelling between "London and New York, darling". It reads -

"Dearest Heartface Sweetiepie. God this is Luxury. Here we are at 98 million feet, swigging champers, watching "Thingy Without Malice" and looking forward to our first evening's boogying in a New York naughty disco – WOOPEE... Naughty postcard to follow XX Edith and Boris".

Edith was Kenny's pet name for himself and Nikolai's was Boris, him being Russian and all that.

During Kenny's absences I was diverted to various tasks like providing the music for the Jimmy Young show, producing "Sing Something Simple" with Cliff Adams or contributing to the John Dunn show, where I raided the sound archives and came up with over a year's worth of celebrity clips for the "Mystery Voice" competition. I took a bit of a flyer in convincing Barry Hearn to bring the new snooker World Champion Steve Davis into the studio for his first major radio interview. Steve won his first title in 1981 and I knew he was an articulate lad after hearing his post-match comments, so it seemed to me that bringing him in to talk to John would be something of a coup and help to widen the appeal of the show with a bit of sporting glamour. His manager Barry was very amenable, agreeable and aware that this was good publicity for his "soon-to-be" superstar of the sport but other agents weren't so obliging. When I called to ask if Tommy Steele was available, I was taken aback to hear this curt dismissal "No, Tommy's got nothing to sell at the moment". After a pause to get the full implication of this refusal, I said "Maybe not, but wouldn't it help to keep his name in front of the public?", at which the conversation ended with "I just told you, he's got nothing to sell, goodbye" and the phone went dead. Another agent I called to book a singer told me his artist was very busy and booked up for weeks ahead so there would be a six-week wait. I agreed and booked the session but the very next day I met the singer outside BH and said it was a shame we couldn't do the session sooner and got the reply "What's going on, I'm not at all busy and I want the work. I'll be having a word later". That was a bit of kidology and manipulation to try and make the artist seem more important and maybe increase their fee.

Stupid and despicable behaviour. It wasn't only agents who shot their artists in the foot, sometimes they did it themselves, and sometimes events contrived to do it for them. Shirley Bassey was a case in point at an evening reception arranged for the media aboard HMS Belfast, permanently moored on the Thames. Food and drink were served but after an hour there was no sign of The Diva. People started to get restless at this non-appearance and after another half hour had passed the food and drink ran out and many decided to call it a day and leave. There was no explanation for the delay, no apology either then or later. We never knew who or what was responsible for this star's no-show but the last thing an artist needs is a disgruntled contingent of press, television and radio influencers. It doesn't help career development, either, and it is noticeable that Dame Shirley had no hit singles between 1973 and 1987. She's back with a bang now, though, just check out "Look But Don't Touch" – super.

I wasn't idle during those breaks from my superstar. One show I really enjoyed was "Album Time" with Peter Clayton because we gelled so perfectly. I was well aware of his predilection to all things "Jazz" but he was delighted to have his eyes and ears opened to a wide variety of material that I introduced him to which made for a very eclectic playlist each week. I told Peter I had a first edition copy of his 1960 book "A Guide To Popular Music" and reminded him of what he wrote about rock and roll and rock music "It would seem to have the characteristics of a temporary craze rather than the more lasting folk element of skiffle". He admitted culpability in being well off the mark with that one and said "Yes, I got that one wrong, didn't I?" Yes, he did, but he was a lovely man and I enjoyed working with him.

The Radio Times billings continued to amuse the boss and it's not often you can use the term "Vermithrax Pejorative" without explaining that it means "Welsh Dragon", but for his first show after the break this is what I wrote -

"Kenny Happy Returns – after his sojourn among the North American primitives, the cultured goblin rises like a phoenix from the ashes of his gas, telephone and electricity bills. He's refreshed, enlivened and just as silly as ever. Travelogue: Geoff Mullin"

I don't think I would be allowed to write that in these days of political correctness.

It was as busy as ever with receptions, meet and greets and concerts for the Four Tops, Earth, Wind and Fire, Three Degrees, Foreigner, Don McLean, Blondie and Randy Edelman. One of the very best days out was arranged by Polydor Records who asked me to be at Battersea Heliport on the morning of July 18th for a special event. Very intriguing, I thought, and was delighted to be told we were being flown to Brands Hatch for the British Grand Prix – result. A small party of us were treated like VIP's with Grandstand seats, passes to the pits, wined and dined and transported back to Battersea with minimum fuss. The great Austrian driver Niki Lauda won in a McLaren-Cosworth but there were only ten finishers that day with 16 retirements, including our hero, Nigel Mansell. What a great day out that was.

My 40th birthday arrived on cue in September and I threw a little party at our new house in Denham which Kenny and Boris came to. It was a pleasant, warm late summer evening and the swimming pool looked very inviting until, that is, Kenny pushed me in at the deep end fully clothed. It was, to any onlookers, very funny but Krystle, only nine years old, was distraught and told Kenny she hated him for what he'd done. I dried off, thought nothing more of it, eventually calmed Krystle down and normal service was resumed. You just never knew with Ev what he might do next.

Shortly after that episode I got major kudos from Virgin Records for being not only the first but one of the few to recognise the appeal of a new record by Culture Club called "Do You Really Want To Hurt Me". Our colleagues at Radio One didn't rate it (we always said they had no ears) and didn't put it on their playlist, so that Radio Two got all the credit and I got what I think is a very rare personal Gold Disc. Pah, who needs The Beatles, I've got one with my name on it now. We also got a lot of credit from RCA records for supporting their new band The Eurythmics with plays of "Love Is A Stranger", another record that fitted into our format perfectly. We were having fun.

The big day of the year for Kenny came on Bonfire Night, no, not the fireworks but an invitation from CBS Records to meet and greet an act he adored, Abba, to celebrate the double compilation album "The Singles The First Ten Years". I have a lovely photo of Kenny and myself at that do as well as a set of official shots of Kenny in various poses with Abba. Ev was the "Dancing Queen" but I knew "The Name Of The Game" - me and Kenny, we loved it.

Just three days later there was another mega bash at The Hilton Hotel in Park Lane when Terry Wogan was honoured with a Tribute Luncheon by The Variety Club Of Great Britain. You can well imagine the scale of this gathering of the great and good from all walks of life as well as celebrities from the world of sport and entertainment. Before the actual lunch I was invited to a Private Reception in the Crystal Palace Suite on the second floor where all the Top Table invitees gathered for a glass of bubbly. I was quite enthralled to be able to chat to Patrick Moore again and to meet Clement Freud, Jimmy Tarbuck, Henry Cooper and those who were due to speak later. Jimmy Young took on the role of Master of Ceremonies, introducing those about to make speeches in Terry's honour. First up was Peter Alliss with his witty remarks claiming to be Terry's golfing and financial adviser and failing on both counts. David Frost noted that Terry had had three blarney stones removed, that his financial advice was "I've upped my income, up yours" and finished by saying he was the man who put corn in leprechaun. Bob Monkhouse seemed to have the measure of the man, giving the longest speech, which included some observations of his business acumen and finishing with this great line "Terry Wogan, the first man in show-business to get ninety percent of his agent's income". How true. It would be a few years before I met Bob again socially, at another of DLT's parties.

Remembering timelines can be a tricky thing but I have fond memories of Martin Kearney and his friend John Wilkins coming over to our house to watch weekly episodes of "The Young Ones", which always had us in hysterics. Later on, the three of us would get together to watch another of our favourite shows, this one starring Michael Gambon in "The Singing Detective".

End of year events included a Roxy Music concert, Julio Iglesias reception, Richard Harris and Fiona Fullerton meet and greet for the London cast of Camelot. The end of 1982 also brought Kenny's tenure on Radio Two to a temporary closure as he was needed on a more or less permanent basis producing his fantastical shows for the electronic fish tank we know as BBC One. This didn't stop us from keeping in touch but there were times when this extraordinary, fallible, frail genius of a man appeared very vulnerable, almost like a lost little boy, which led us into many episodes of deep and meaningful dialogue, more often than not about his somewhat frenetic and complex love life. Here's an example from a letter he sent after bemoaning the state of his relationship with his Russian boyfriend Nikki, otherwise known as Boris and sometimes Prince Minchkin, Kenny's camp name for him -

"Dear Geoffrey, What a jolly and useful chat the other day. However, after all that wisdom and deliberation.....I've decided in my madness, to entirely overlook Nikolai's disgraceful behaviour. At least until his next moment of mega-indiscretion. I'm just an old softy I suppose, not to mention – thick... Give Caroline all my love and see you soon. All the best, K, Edith"

So here I was at the start of 1983 without a job, well, actually picking up bits and pieces of programmes here and there to keep me occupied until Ev's return, which was never predictable. In the meantime I produced a series called "Star Choice" with Randy Edelman, Rosemary Leach, Ray Clemence, Mark Wynter and the gorgeous Fiona Fullerton, who all chatted for an hour about their favourite music. The veteran broadcaster Alan Dell was also my responsibility with his weekly shows "Sounds Easy", "Big Band Era" and "Dance Band Days", all of which I enjoyed. Alan had a bit of a reputation for being difficult to work with but we had nothing but good vibes between us, mainly because I liked the music of the thirties and forties and had a fair knowledge of it, which he liked.

There was another show I was devising after the boss, Geoff Owen, was casting about for new ideas and my propositions were for weekly specials featuring the music of the 1950's and 1960's to replace some of the more old-fashioned fare we were providing at the weekend. The first one, "The Fabulous Fifties" didn't take off right away but "Sounds Of The Sixties" was commissioned and is still running to this day. I brought in Keith Fordyce as presenter and the first show went out on Saturday February the 12th. We anticipated a short run but the show proved to be so popular we were still working together more than two years later. Keith and I became good friends and we'd call on him and his wife Anne whenever we visited Torquay, where he ran The Torbay Air Museum as a pastime and a business. I researched and wrote all the scripts for Keith and we achieved some sort of notoriety with a verbal gaffe which appeared in the magazine Private Eye in the "Colemanballs" column – "Songwriters are the unsung heroes of the music business". We all laughed at that observation, I can tell you.

Technical innovation that year brought the most significant development of recorded sound since Edison's phonograph cylinders were replaced by flat disc records, or maybe Jack Mullin nicking the German tape machines. All was revealed when an invitation arrived to attend the launch of a new product called a Compact Disc at Legends Club hosted by Decca, Phonogram and Polydor record companies. To me this was a miraculous invention and the greatest time-saving boon to radio producers and secretaries, because this is what it meant to our everyday working lives. Prior to this each disc selected had to be timed and checked for clicks and scratches which, if they were too audible had to be replaced, either with another from the office cupboard or ordered from the gramophone library. If the latter, then we waited until the following day for another copy (stop me if I'm boring you) and the whole process was repeated until an acceptable disc was found. All of that time-wasting stopped immediately with the advent of CD's as the time was displayed digitally, there was no need to check the quality and they were difficult, even for Jimmy Young, to destroy. Nirvana.

Kenny's joy was unbounded at this latest gizmo and was ecstatic when he first heard the sound quality of classical recordings plus the fact that it wasn't necessary to put a needle in a groove or turn the disc over to hear the other side. We were determined to be the first to showcase this latest cutting-edge gadget, which he called "a new-fangled doobry". However, there was a problem after we got our first demonstration disc – the BBC had no compact disc players, so I had to persuade our facilities department to buy one. They were a bit reluctant at first wondering whether the high price would be justified and even after they brought in the "one and only" CD player it was guarded like the crown jewels. I wanted one in the studio every Saturday morning but to achieve this feat I had to requisition it to be delivered and so the weekly ritual of the installation of "The BBC CD Player" was established with a lab-coated technician setting it up before the show and then returning it to safekeeping afterwards. Strange now looking back that this item seemed more precious than gold.

Anything new in that line would always capture Kenny's imagination and many a Saturday after the show we would wander along the hi-fi highway that was Tottenham Court Road to check out all the latest audio-visual merchandise available. Possibly the funniest thing he ever said to me was as a result of this interest in all things sound-related. We went to an exhibition at the Wembley Conference Centre showcasing all the latest manufacturer models coming onto the market and wandered around relatively unobserved. We were invited onto the Panasonic stand for a coffee and a chat but almost as soon as we sat down a small crowd gathered to gawp. Kenny could see people with pens and programmes at the ready and knew exactly what was coming. He signed a couple of autographs and then the panic set in as he leaned over and whispered in my ear "Geoffrey, produce me out of here". Knowing exactly what was needed I stood up and said "Kenny, we must leave now or we'll be late for the studio, come on". That did the trick and we escaped with good grace and no hard feelings. "Produce me out of here" – hilarious.

The TV show was attracting large audiences and Kenny's profile had never been higher as he introduced a diverse range of bizarre and entertaining characters such as the aforementioned Cupid Stunt, Marcel Wave, Gizzard Puke and the lovable punk Sid Snot, who even made the Top Ten with his recording of the "Snot Rap". Kenny was flying high, literally, when he sent me one of the promised "naughty" postcards from his trip to the US West Coast -

"Darlings. We're in hump city (Frisco) getting humped a lot. Bona Bona, Edith & Boris" plus a drawing of the Union

Jack and the Hammer & Sickle with the legend "Hands across the bed".

Another letter he sent said it had been "dipped in Stranded Viking" and signed off with "Edith, Queen of the waves". What a caution he was.

In July Caroline, Krystle and I were invited by our Southport friends John and Christine Rostron to accompany them to the Open Golf Championship at Royal Birkdale. Walking the course with John was a revelation as I realised he was a mine of information on the history of the club and that he was responsible for much of the negotiation that had taken place to bring the Open to Birkdale that year. He had been playing there since he was a boy, eventually becoming Club Captain and later club historian. BBC teams from both the radio and television services were there and just after we popped into the studios to say hello the TV producer pressed the panic button and all hell broke loose. The reason was that the TV sports presenter Harry Carpenter had lost the crown from his front tooth and was due in front of the camera in half an hour. I immediately stepped in to say that John was right here and could get Harry to his surgery and back in the shortest possible time. That help was gratefully accepted and John did a great job fixing Harry up so that he was able to face the cameras with a smile. The biggest smile was reserved for Tom Watson – he took the other crown by one stroke.

In September Kenny returned to Radio Two for our last season of fun, frolic and froth together and we picked up exactly where we left off. He was as daft as ever, using his favourite Omi-Palone phrases from theatrical slang to greet me in Polari-speak with "How bona to varda your dolly old eke, fantabulosa". That means he was pleased to see me and he continued calling me "Geoffreypooh", a term of affection, I can assure you.

After the show one day he said to me, in a very conspiratorial tone, "Geoffrey, I hope you're not doing anything after the show as we have to go on a special mission". I said I was free to join him on this clandestine adventure and, with no further feedback, I was intrigued as we left BH behind and headed on foot towards Oxford Street. At the rear doors of John Lewis store he pulled me inside and took me down to the basement where he searched along the rows of household goods until his eyes alighted on the object he was looking for - a bag of black plastic bin-liners. When I asked him if that was the secret mission he said "Yes, darling, I couldn't bear the thought of coming down here on my own for such a mundane purchase, let's have lunch". Thanks Kenny, I love you too.

Now, on a very personal note, sometimes in life a chance encounter might lead to long-term repercussions, never more so in my case than the night Caroline and I went to a party at her friend Rusty's house in Radlett. This was where I met the woman who would become my wife some years later and yes, little did I know etc, etc. Her name was Lesley and we chatted with her and her husband Norman for quite some time during the evening. I had brought along a few of the latest record releases and as Lesley and I danced to "Karma Chameleon" I thought "This girl is skinny as a rake, she looks in need of feeding up". At the end of the evening we exchanged phone numbers with Norman and Lesley and agreed to get together again soon. That was the beginning of a long and lasting friendship with the Davies family and their children Jamie and Kerry. We socialised at both our houses and met each other's friends, including "The Crazy Gang" from St Albans, but more of that later.

The reception area in Broadcasting House was always a bustling thoroughfare, a place to meet and greet, either by arrangement or by chance, and one of the truly great broadcasters I was lucky enough to strike up conversations with was Alistair Cooke, host of the long-running series "Letter From America", which racked up the barely believable tally of 58 years on air. We discovered we had a somewhat similar background, with him being born in Salford and going to Blackpool Grammar School, but it was a shared passion for music that really ignited our friendly chats, so much so that he generously presented me with a copy of David Ewen's book "American Popular Songs" which he signed "With all good wishes" dated October 11th 1983. Before the advent of the internet this was a valuable research tool and one which I continue to use and treasure. Mr Cooke was a gentleman of the first degree in my book.

"Rude, Kenny, rude, naughty boy" was my response to the invitation below -

"Dear Wanker, You are hereby formally required to attend this Friday October 21 at no later than 7:45 at the above address. DRINKIES... Prior to being taken by carriage to the Piccadilly Theatre in London's WEST END... to attend a performance of "Y". A sumptuous meal will be served during the cabaret which incidentally is the best show in all fucking London... Failure to appear at this event renders the member's member liable to be wrenched out of its socket and stuffed up the member's arsehole. May God have mercy on arseholes. Edith".

How could one possibly refuse, and nobody did, needless to say. The show itself was all that Kenny promised and might well be the best night of entertainment I've ever enjoyed – it was sensational. Our last social outing together was the Record Shack Christmas Ball at The Embassy Club in Bond Street, another riot from start to finish which I don't remember anything about. Finally, our last show together was on the 24th of December and was not the show he delivered the infamous Maggie Thatcher joke, that was a week earlier, and if you need reminding, this was it -

"When we were an Empire we had an Emperor and when we were a Kingdom we had a King. Now we're just a country and we've got Maggie Thatcher".

Contrary to some commentator's opinions, Kenny did not get the sack because of that joke. His Radio Two contract was not renewed because he was not available due to his long-term TV commitments. One final funny missive came from him some time after we split up, he was obviously missing me.

"Dear Geoffrey, How the devil are you? Why don't you ring me? What's wrong? Don't you love me anymore? Is it true what they say about Dixie?? Love, Edith PS…Squash?"

It was a heartfelt plea and I responded in the only way possible, I beat the crap out of him on the squash court – then we had lunch.

Three of the most memorable, funny, fulfilling and fascinating years at the Radio Two coalface.

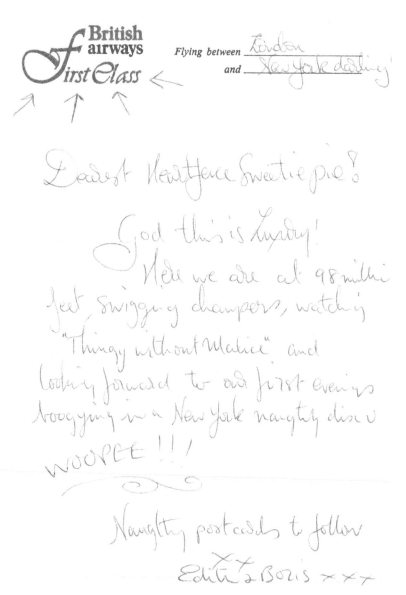

British airways
First Class ←

Flying between London
and New York darling

Dearest Heartface Sweetiepie!

God this is Luxury!
Here we are at 98 million feet, swigging champers, watching "Thingy without Malice" and looking forward to our first evenings boogying in a New York naughty disco

WOOPEE !!! /

Naughty postcards to follow

Editi & Boris x x x

Kenny Everett - note from plane

276

Kenny Everett & Boris 40th birthday card

With Kenny & Geoff Owen at Abba reception

3

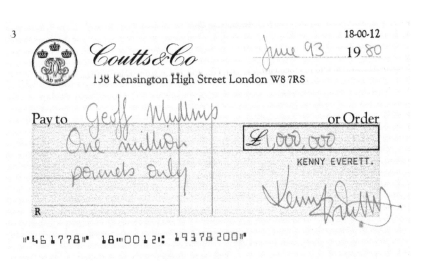

Coutts&Co
AD 1692

138 Kensington High Street London W8 7RS

18-00-12

June 93 19 80

Pay to _Geoff Mullins_   or Order

One million

pounds only

£1,000,000

KENNY EVERETT.

R

⑈461778⑈ 18⑈0012⑈ 19378200⑈

Generous Kenny

Flat E,
91, Lexham Gardens,
KENSINGTON,
London, W8.

244 9540.

Dear Wanker,
                You are hearby formally required
to attend this Friday October 21 at no later
than 7:45 at the above address,
DRINKIES!!! prior to being taken by carriage
to The Piccadilly Theatre in London's WEST
END!!! to attend a performance of "Y"
                A sumtous meal will be served
during the cabaret which incidentally is
the best show in all fucking London!!!
                Failure to appear at this event
renders the member's member liable to be
wrenched out of its socket and stuffed up
the member's arsehole.

                Mnw God have mercy on arseholes.

                Edith.

RSVP.

Kenny Everett invite to "Y"

Dear Geoffrey,

How the devil are you? Why don't you ring me? What's wrong? Don't you love me any more? Is it true what they say about Dixie??

Love, Edith
xxx

P.S... SQUASH?

Kenny Everett card - squash

CHAPTER TWENTY TWO
The Scottish Invasion Of 1984

It was a one-man invasion led by Ken (Kenneth Robertson) Bruce, a friendly, intelligent, urbane broadcaster from Glasgow with a soft Scottish burr of a voice, just perfect for Radio Two. To my credit, I think, I didn't hold against him the fact that he was a drummer. Ken was already a well-known voice to listeners in Scotland and his first incursion onto the national airwaves was presenting "Radio Two Ballroom" in the early 1980's. He was still a regular on BBC Scotland when he was given a Saturday night slot in January 1984 with me as his producer. The show ran between 11pm and 1am with a simple format consisting mostly of music, birthday and anniversary events plus a competition to engage the listeners. We did a few cheeky intros, spoken by Ken, for the audience to guess the original records, such as "Dum dum dum dummy doowah, oh yay yay yay yeah" and "Yip yip rippile de bum, diddy bum diddy". Did you get them? The first was "Only The Lonely" by Roy Orbison then "Yes Tonight Josephine" by Johnnie Ray, probably not heard much these days but quite familiar back in the early 80's. Ken would travel to London during the day, do the show, stay overnight and return to Glasgow on Sunday, a routine that lasted the entire year, by which time he had made his mark and his feet were well and truly under the studio desk. Ken and I didn't see too much of each other as my presence was not required in the studio, so most of our contact was telephonic, although I would make an appearance in the studio from time to time to make sure he was behaving himself – like as if. We got on very well and Ken remembered our first foray into late-night broadcasting together in his autobiography "Tracks Of My Years" in which he gives an accurate account of how the show was delivered to air. This is what he wrote:-

"The Saturday Late Show was produced by Geoff Mullin; he delivered a music plot, or running order, that was a little delight each week, hampered as he was by the usual lack of "needletime". The BBC's agreement with the music industry at that time was for only a limited number of commercial records to be played in any one week: the "needletime". It was never enough. Any other music needed to fill the schedules was to be by the corporation's own orchestras or session musicians, but "live" in any event, with some library music or foreign recordings bought in for good measure".

Highlights of events began in February with a Lifestyle Records "Shape Up And Dance" reception at The Fitness Centre in WC2 attended by Lulu, George Best, Patti Boulaye, Mary Stavin, Suzanne Dando and Jay Aston, which was an amazing line-up of famous fit personalities and every one a charmer. This all took place at the height of the aerobics craze and each star presented their album in the series with George and Mary doing a double-act. The albums did well, despite not really getting any airplay, and were in the charts for quite a while – did you buy one?

The Ivor Novello Awards took place in April and I was particularly honoured to be invited to join the judging panel, which voted "Blood Brothers" Best British Musical, "Going Home" by Mark Knopfler Best Film Theme and the Best Song category was won by Sting for "Every Breath You Take". Concerts were high on the agenda during spring and summer with some amazing performances by Stevie Wonder, Billy Joel, Yes and Cliff with The Shadows, the last three at Wembley Arena.

There was a "Meet and Lunch" reception for Al Stewart's new album "Russians And Americans" at the Café Royal Wine Cellars but even that was overshadowed by the shindig thrown by Andrew Lloyd Webber for "Champagne And Tea" at The Ritz with a "Starlight Express" showcase performed by Lon Satton and Ray Shell. That was my first glimpse of that marvellous roller-skating musical which went on to capture the hearts of children and adults alike over its long life. Quite a vintage year, in retrospect, I think.

My friend John Rostron had two children from his first marriage, Sarah and Tony, and in July 1981 married Christine, who had a daughter, Jocelyn, making one big happy family until another little cherub arrived on the 31st of May in the form of Katie, and I was delighted to be asked if I would be her Godfather. She's grown up now with a family of her own but she still refers to me as "The Godfather", which I rather like.

Caroline had an idea she would like another health spa retreat so we booked into Champneys in Tring to coincide with a visit there by my pal Ron Stratton, who arrived the day before us and struck up a friendship with Pink Floyd guitarist Dave Gilmour. On the first afternoon we met up with Ron and Dave who invited us to join in a game of Trivial Pursuit after dinner. As I had never heard of this game I asked if I would need my tracksuit and trainers, assuming it was some sort of track and trace race around the grounds and gardens, silly me. Ron and Dave laughed at my ignorance, then explained that it was a board game, played indoors, with general knowledge and entertainment questions. This was right up my street and that evening the four of us enjoyed a right royal battle, though I can't remember now who won – let's call it a draw. Later on we bought the game and enjoyed playing for many years afterwards, although when I was given the "History Of Music" Edition I could never get anyone to play it with me. I wonder why that was?

On my birthday that year I received a very pleasant surprise from my boss Geoff Owen who awarded me a bonus of £300 for my excellent work on Sounds Of The Sixties and my dedication to Radio Two – who's a clever clogs, then, eh. How do you spell smuuug?

My friendship with Ben Findon was still going strong and one night the phone rang around eleven o'clock with a very perplexed-sounding Ben asking if I could go round to his house as he would welcome my thoughts on a new artist he had recorded. I was used to Ben using me as a sounding-board from time to time, although not usually at that time of night, but I went over to see him anyway. He played me his latest project and said he wasn't sure what to do about it, especially as he had just started his new Spirit record label. I thought the song was quite jolly and when he told me the artist was Russ Abbott I had to metaphorically kick him on the shin, or maybe a bit higher. I said "What on earth are you dithering about?

This man is as hot as it gets right now with his hugely popular television shows and it could be a big hit at Christmas. You have to put it out". I was a bit shocked that he was so unsure about releasing it but I think I convinced him that night and the record went on to be a top ten festive hit.

Ben and I had a difference of opinion the previous year discussing Lionel Richie's latest single "All Night Long" with Ben telling me he thought it would never be a hit – wrong. A few months earlier I had been at Ben's house when his former artist Billy Ocean came to visit. I was introduced to him as Les (Charles) and we had a bit of a chinwag about the business and music generally and after he left Ben told me Billy was keen to record a new song he was working on called "European Queen". Ben said he didn't like the title and wasn't sure about working with Billy again as he hadn't had a hit for four years. Wrong again – Billy found a new producer, the title was changed to "Caribbean Queen" and was a big hit here and Number One in the States, leading to a major career revival with many more hits to come. Ah well, we all make mistakes.

The year ended with The Everly Brothers concert at the Hammersmith Odeon in November but in October I was delighted to be in the audience for a very special performance of "Chess In Concert" at the Barbican Centre. This was arranged to coincide with the album release featuring Elaine Paige, Barbara Dickson, Murray Head, Tommy Korberg and Dennis Quilley singing the songs of Bjorn Ulvaeus and Benny Anderson from Abba. That show gave Radio Two one of its most-played songs of the year and a huge Number One for the duet "I Know Him So Well" by Elaine and Barbara.

In December I was invited by the Music Publishers Association to join the judging panel for "A Song For Europe", where we would select the final 8 to go forward and compete in a BBC TV special to choose our entrant for the Eurovision Song Contest. Apparently there had been 333 original submissions, subsequently whittled down to 24, which we heard at Television Centre without any knowledge of who the writers or performers were and chose the most promising eight. Terry Wogan introduced the TV competition and, despite the inclusion of pop star Alvin Stardust, it was a ballad written and sung by Vikki (Watson) called "Love Is" that polled the most votes. Vikki took the song to Gothenburg and was placed a creditable fourth in the contest which was won by the Norwegian entry Bobbysocks with "La Det Swinge" – a prumping good winner, as Terry might have said.

More major changes to the schedules as Terry Wogan departed Radio Two for his long stint as a television chat-show host. There had been intense speculation as to who would replace him – would it be Gloria Hunniford, could it be David Hamilton or even Ken Bruce? Well, I knew the answer very early on but was very surprised on the day the announcement was made when I bumped into Simon Bates outside BH and he grinned at me and said "You must have made a pretty penny on that one?" I said "What do you mean?" and Simon said "You know, at the bookies". Then it dawned on me that although I knew it would be Ken in the frame for the Breakfast Show, what I didn't know was that there was a betting opportunity – my goodness, how naïve, I could have made a fortune. Still, we all make mistakes, or did I, would I have put a bet on? I don't know.

The most infuriating thing about Ken taking over from Terry was that I wasn't going with him as his producer, having spent a year with him building up a good working relationship. I think Ken was disappointed, too, but he didn't have the heft to influence management like Terry could. Nevertheless, onwards and upwards, what was next on the agenda?

Colin Berry was my next charge presenting the very Early Show for the whole of 1985. Once again, this was mostly music and chat with no studio attendance required of me and although we didn't see much of each other we enjoyed a very friendly working relationship. Colin was always the consummate professional, whether as a newsreader or announcer but, sadly, was always to play the bridesmaid and never the bride as far as daytime exposure on Radio Two was concerned.

January started well with a reception in "The Square Room" at the Empire Leicester Square to celebrate the 50th Anniversary of the birth of Elvis Presley which was hosted jointly by RCA Records and the Elvis Fan Club. It was a great event that lasted from 6.45pm to 3am next morning. Now that's what you call a proper celebration. At the end of the month there was a launch party for the Fascinating Aida single "Get Knotted" at the Donmar Warehouse, where I first bumped into the outrageous Dillie Keane, leader of this satirical singing comedy troupe.

Without any shadow of a doubt the musical highlight of the year for me was meeting my greatest musical hero Jerry Lee Lewis in April at the Wembley Country Music Festival which was a regular event in the Radio Two calendar. During our chat I said that in the very early days I hadn't realised I was listening to country songs that he often included on the "B" side of his rock and roll hits and Jerry Lee said "Don't get no more country than my hero Hank Williams, that's for sure, and I'll never stop playing 'em". A brief but memorable encounter and just a short while later I would re-mix the tapes of that concert for posterity.

In May I was invited to join the sports department team to provide music for the "Summer Sounds" Sunday show on Radio Two which was an immense pleasure as it combined my great love of music with sport, absolute joy. The sports director/producer was a delightful and skilful woman called Emily McMahon who was absolutely in charge in the studio, handling input from as many as twenty or more "feeds" of a multitude of sporting events from all over the country and all over the world. I was mightily impressed with her ability and speed of thought during this highly intense non-stop input of information coming at her from all directions. That's talent. We covered all the action as it happened, or very soon afterwards, with my pal Andy Peebles covering mainly cricket from grounds around the country. Andy was so well-informed, seemingly knowing every little detail, that I do wonder if he is something of a polymath. We continue to be good friends to this day. Unfortunately, the same cannot be said of the lead presenter of the series, Stuart Hall, who in recent years has become toxic in the extreme. I got on very well with Stuart during our time together and he was without a doubt "a man's man", so it came as a great shock to me to hear of his criminal activities. Sad to see such a talented man sacrifice all his achievements in such a horrendous way. He now lives alone in a small flat in Manchester with few friends and, I understand, is trying to make some kind of amends by volunteering at his local church. A terrible end to a wonderful career. On a lighter note, I heard a story about the great rugby league commentator Eddie Waring, who always got mixed up, and confused the waiting staff, when ordering his favourite meal. When he was in France he would order "chicken and frites" but when he was in England he would order "poulet and chips". This was puzzlement on an international scale, but he was a lovely a man.

1985 saw the launch of Europe's first "Video Café" at 8 Argyll Street in London, very near the famous Palladium Theatre. I went there in June to a reception hosted by Bill Wyman for the premiere of the "Willie And The Poor Boys" video. All very "state of the art" and a new avenue for exploitation.

In July I was delighted to meet Dusty Springfield at a champagne lunch party at the Hippodrome for her single "Sometimes Like Butterflies", a cover of a song written by Donna Summer. Dusty was a little intrigued when I told her I was the roadie for the Four Pennies and that we often followed her into the Philips studios in Stanhope Place for a session with Johnny Franz, who also produced her and the Walker Brothers. "Ah, yes, Johnny", she said, "so sad he's gone now, probably the fags did him in, but what a great producer he was, certainly the English equivalent of Phil Spector". I had to agree with her assessment, she was spot on. And lovely with it.

In July Caroline, Krystle and I were treated to a showcase at Wembley Arena by Torvill And Dean on their "World Tour" showcase. Then came a media only showcase gig for Sandy Dillon and Mick Ronson at Ronnie Scott's in Frith Street to promote the single "Flowers/Heavy Boys". Not only was this a good musical event, it came with an enticing invitation which told us "You will be fed and watered". As you can imagine, it was very well attended, it would have been churlish to refuse.

On the domestic side of life, we were now well-settled into our house in Denham, where one of our neighbours just a few houses down was the drummer Ginger Baker, though our paths never crossed. Another change of school was in the air for Krystle as she left St Mary's in Gerrards Cross to begin her final years of secondary education at the Rudolf Steiner School in King's Langley where she thrived in its unique environment and where her artistic talents were encouraged and developed.

With winter approaching there was a flurry of musical media activity starting with cocktails in The Crystal Room at The Mayfair Hotel for the launch of Elaine Paige's album "Love Hurts". Next came an invite from the strangely-named Frizzby Fox And Bradley to celebrate 25 years of Martha Reeves And The Vandellas with a live gig from 9pm till 3.30am. They were terrific but that's about all I can remember. No wonder things were beginning to get a little hazy as next up we were entertained by Chas And Dave at their pub in Green Lanes for a "Jamboree Bag 3" party, quickly followed by the launch party at "Bootleggers" nightclub for fifties heart-throb Frankie Vaughan's album "Love Hits And High Kicks". Everybody always said Frankie was a genuine and generous person and after meeting him that night I was full of admiration for his open personality and friendly demeanour as he was willing to talk to everyone in attendance without any sign of an ego. Lovely man. Last gig of the year for me was the Dire Straits "Live In 85" gig at Hammersmith Odeon and they were on great form, love that band.

CHAPTER TWENTY THREE
Reunited With Kenny The Bruce

Once again, the slings and arrows of outrageous fortune seemed to be hitting their mark as I was moved on to The Breakfast Show with Ken Bruce at the beginning of 1986. I was delighted at the chance to work with Ken again, especially on the major daytime show and we picked up where we left off with our friendly personal and professional relationship.

As with Terry at breakfast time, I was able to move the musical agenda along with some influence without fear of interference and over the next couple of years or so working with Ken we were able to give the audience a diet of the very best in contemporary music mixed in with the golden oldies. Among the Number One hits we championed were Diana Ross "Chain Reaction", George Michael "A Different Corner", Chris De Burgh "Lady In Red", Boy George "Everything I own", Madonna "La Isla Bonita" plus Whitney Houston and Michael Jackson chart-toppers, together with many others that didn't quite make the top spot but which certainly gave Radio Two much less of a fuddy-duddy image.

Outside broadcasts were still very much on the agenda and the first one we were scheduled to do was in February at the Scottish ski-resort of Aviemore, now there's cold, I tell you. I went up earlier for a "reccy", an old army term for reconnaissance, and met up with local tourist officials who were really helpful in suggesting where we might go and who we might speak to. In short order I had decided what the schedule would be and they got on the case to set up all our interviews and locations, and they did a perfect job for us.

Ken and I flew to Inverness and picked up a four-wheel drive Range Rover, an absolute necessity as the snow was thick on the ground, and headed south to Aviemore. In addition to the OB crew I brought along an assistant in the form of a new young producer by the name of Graham Pass, who proved a valuable asset, even though he was another bloody drummer, which certainly pleased Ken. We started the morning show with a typical Scots breakfast, porridge obligatory, then swiftly to a whisky distillery and a meeting with the local Laird and during all this Colin Berry was playing in the records from the studio in London. The programme culminated in ski novice Ken taking a lesson down the slopes clutching a microphone in his hand and with absolutely immaculate timing managed to fall flat on his derriere right at the end of the show – precision production, nothing quite like it I say.

As before, my presence was not required in the studio but Ken and I would meet after the show for a chat and a coffee and on a social level Ken and his wife visited us in Denham bringing their two young sons along with them. All was going along very smoothly until we got the news from on high that, as from April, the show was being moved to a later time slot in order to accommodate a new presenter called Derek Jameson, a former tabloid newspaper journalist. We were not amused.

There's no business like show business, they say, and the next big event was an OB in April with Ken presenting the show from the Royal Navy aircraft carrier HMS Ark Royal where he talked to the captain and crew fielding their requests and dedications. It was a great success and the plaudits came in thick and fast though strangely no more major OB's were scheduled for quite some time.

Later in April there was a press preview performance of the musical "La Cage Aux Folles" at the London Palladium with a reception afterwards in The Variety Bar where I met the stars George Hearn and Dennis Quilley, who were kind enough to pose for a photo with little old me.

As far as I can recall the summer of '86 was relatively quiet except for one rather amusing interlude, and I hope I've got the year right, but that's not the point. I was working a little later than usual in my office when I got a phone call from my friend Phil Swern, who told me he was in a nearby recording studio with Tony Blackburn, who was struggling with a song Phil wanted him to sing. I asked what he wanted me for and Phil said he'd like me to come over and have a crack at this rock and roll song he was recording.

I was surprised at this request as I hadn't sung in anger for several years, still, I said I'd give it a go just for the hell of it. Tony and Phil were all smiles when I got there and Phil played me a very good-sounding lively backing track and handed me the lyrics. I had a couple of run-throughs and then we went for a take, after which Phil said he was well-pleased and Tony said he was shocked as he didn't know I could sing like that. I said I didn't know I could still sing like that, either. The song was called "Hilary" and as far as I know it was never released – another masterpiece hiding in the vaults.

Whenever Ken took a holiday I always tried to book a well-known dep and on August Bank Holiday Monday I was pleased to welcome Bob "Blockbuster" Holness into the studio. He was a very accomplished broadcaster, having been around for many years on both radio and television, and he was a joy to work with, easy-going, friendly and keen to deliver a good performance, which he did.

As per usual there was a great deal happening in the run-up to Christmas, with a Ruby Turner gig at Limelight nightclub for her album "Women Hold Up Half The Sky", Elkie Brooks gig and meet with a champagne reception at Maxims De Paris for her album "No More The Fool" with producer Russ Ballard in attendance. I knew Elkie from way back in Manchester as her brother was Tony Bookbinder, drummer with The Dakotas. Mike Batt sent a personal letter with an invitation to afternoon tea and a performance of his new musical "The Hunting Of The Snark" in which Lewis Carroll was played by David McCallum and my old pal Kenny Everett played The Billiard Marker. The Eurythmics held a launch party for their album "Revenge", Spandau Ballet threw an after Wembley show party at The Holiday Inn Swiss Cottage, Charly Records rocked and rolled and twisted at a Hammersmith Palais party featuring the man who wrote and first recorded "The Twist", Hank Ballard And The Midnighters. I don't know about you but I'm exhausted before Santa Claus has even begun to think about putting his boots on.

Seasonal cheer was all over Radio Two that year as we got behind the silly novelty record "O My Father Had A Rabbit" which Ray Moore recorded as part of his contribution to the BBC's

"Children In Need" charity appeal. It got into the Top 30, out-performing Paul McCartney's single "Only Love Remains", which didn't. Ray was highly amused and delighted by that statistic.

My last act of any import in 1986 was to book Michael Aspel for a two-hour Boxing Day Special playing exclusively Number One Hits from the 1950's to the 1980's. Naturally, we had to have a lunch to discuss the many and varied aspects of this extremely complex show and so I booked a table at Michael's favourite restaurant, Odin's in Devonshire Street, run by the magnificent Peter Langan. The food was great, the clientele stratospheric and the walls were decorated with watercolours by Patrick Procktor among others. Over an extended lunch-hour we drank a little Gavi Di Gavi and discussed the possibility of Michael coming to Radio Two on a more permanent basis, which seemed to appeal to both of us equally, and it did happen, eventually.

As in previous years, Caroline, Krystle and I would spend Christmas with Bill, Moira, Holly and William, this year at Remenham Court, their home near Henley. It was always festive fun and I enjoyed this short break away from the hurly-burly of "The Smoke", with William or Bill entertaining us with a few tunes on the piano plus a game of chess or two. Peace on earth, for sure.

Well now, look at this, another year and still on the same programme, what on earth are management playing at? The first really interesting gig of 1987 was at the Royal Albert Hall when Paul Simon treated us to The Graceland Concert, and had I been reviewing it I would have given it Ten Stars because it was a truly wonderful performance by the whole ensemble.

The process of bringing Michael Aspel back to the Radio Two airwaves began at the end of April when he stood in for Ken Bruce – I love it when a plan comes together. The reaction to those two weeks was extremely positive, both from the audience and the bosses, so much so that serious negotiations began for Michael to have a regular weekend show starting in the autumn.

In the meantime I continued to produce Ken's daily mid-morning show and again spent summer Sundays in the studio with the sports department. I really enjoyed those exciting live broadcasts, flying by the seat of your pants, well, Emily McMahon's actually.

The series started in May and ran until October, so that was half a year of wonderful weekends for me but wasted weekends for Caroline and Krystle, the upside being I had Mondays free

August Bank Holiday Monday revived my interest in country music with a return visit to Peterborough for the Country Music Festival, where I met up with "Country Club" presenter Wally Whyton who introduced me to Hoyt Axton and his mother Mae Boren Axton. I met Hoyt many times in later years but this was my one and only meeting with Mae, who I already knew was the writer of "Heartbreak Hotel" for Elvis. What I didn't know until she told me that it was she who introduced Elvis to Colonel Tom Parker, and her connections in that world earned her the accolade of "Queen Mother Of Nashville", which I'm sure was well-deserved. Other stars I met that day were Barbara Fairchild, Nanci Griffith, Daniel O'Donnell, Jimmy C Newman, Bobby Bare, Johnny Cash and Jim Reeves' widow Mary who, when interviewed by Wally, mentioned the "lost" Jim Reeves tapes. By a strange quirk of fate, I later found those tapes at the back of an old filing cabinet and offered them to Radio Two in 2014 to mark the 50th anniversary of Jim's death and guess what, they weren't remotely interested. Maybe they can be aired in 2024? Wally was very friendly and helpful and I think we warmed to each other, which may be why I became his producer about a year later. Funny, huh?

The big day arrived in September when Michael Aspel started his regular Saturday morning shows between 10am and 12 noon. The very first guest in the studio was Jonathan Ross, later to inherit the very seat Michael was sitting in. The "Listening Panel" assembled to pronounce on the show gave it an unqualified "excellent" review and we were up and running. However, just like Kenny Everett and Summer Sport, it really messed up family weekends but, again, Mondays were my day off, which I rather liked.

We had two very good researchers on the show, Celia Toynbee and Camilla Courlander, who booked the guests and gave Michael lots of background information to use on the show. The usual modus operandi was for all this information to be collated which, together with my research and a music running order, I would deliver to Michael at his home in Claygate on Thursday afternoon.

Michael would then decide which items he felt he could incorporate into the show and write himself some sort of a working script. He was excellent with his use of words and always sounded completely relaxed on air, even though he might be reading something he had pre-prepared. Most professional, Michael. From time to time I would book a guest or two and when I wrote to Sir John Gielgud to test his interest he sent me a personal card from Wotton House, his stately home in Wotton Underwood, which is now, I understand, part of the property portfolio of former Prime Minister Tony Blair, and not too far from Chequers. Is there a plan afoot? This is what Sir John wrote -

"Dear Mr Mullin, I'm afraid I don't want to do any talk show. There is a plan to make a full-length documentary about me in the near future and that, I think, will be quite enough. Sincerely John Gielgud. Oct 21 87"

That's an upper-crust brush off, if ever there was one.

Michael was a lovely man and he invited me to his birthday party where I sat next to his friend Danny Baker who kept me entertained for most of the evening – I could hardly get a word in edgeways. Michael had what can only be described as an excellent and intriguing party trick, which he demonstrated to me one day at his home. He asked me to sit down opposite him as he sat at his grand piano and prepared to give me a private and personal performance of his amazing keyboard dexterity. I was smiling as he prepared to play, I couldn't see his hands and didn't know what to expect, when suddenly he delivered the most accurate reading of Erroll Garner's composition "Misty", complete with all the movements and grunts, as though he really was a gifted musician. I did realise before he finished that he was merely miming to the original record but, nevertheless, it was an Oscar-winning performance.

The general consensus was that Michael was a perfect choice for Radio Two on Saturday morning, with the audience enjoying his relaxed manner and choice of guests, singling out both singer Lulu and the musical comedy duo Hinge And Bracket, while awarding Michael an extremely high rating of 97% approval. Well done, Sir Michael. I wonder why he has not been knighted?

Aviemore With Ken Bruce, the Laird, the whisky distiller &
redundant piper 1986

Children In Need Appeal With Nanette Newman &
Barry Humphries 1980's

CHAPTER TWENTY FOUR
The Queen Of Mean Arrives

Michael's stints on Radio Two were as intermittent as Kenny Everett's had been because of his television commitments and in January 1988 Anne Robinson took over the Saturday morning slot.

On the 5th of January 1988 I received this hand-written letter –

"Dear Geoff and lovely team, here's a letter which only you can answer. I hope you're missing me as much as I'm missing you – in fact I hope you're missing me more. Give my best wishes to Anne Robinson. I'll see you in the Spring, and before that, of course. Regards to all, Mike (Aspel, star of R2)". Oh, he did write a good letter, the old smoothie.

Anne wasn't called the "Queen Of Mean" back then, that would come much later when she hosted "The Weakest Link" show on TV, but for now she was contracted for just three months until Michael's return in April. Fitting in right from the start she established herself as an indispensable asset to Radio Two, eventually making Saturday mornings her sole domain. When she first arrived Anne was still a sweet and gentle Liverpool lass (believe that and you'll believe anything). Not at all, she was no shrinking violet, bright, intelligent and tough enough to grab even Robert Maxwell by the proverbials when she needed to put him in his place. Her professional demeanour was at odds with her private persona and I found her to be quite charming, open, caring and very good company.

Anne was very much an investigative journalist presenter, far removed from the technically slick music DJ's, and her show came from a studio in the bowels of BH where a Technical Operator would play in the records, trailers and tapes. My job on transmission was effectively to be the DJ and guide her through every link, giving her a twenty-second warning at the end of a record, telling her to back-announce the song and artist and setting up the next item. It was very hands on for me but Anne took direction brilliantly and by the end of our time together she had become extremely confidant and competent in the complex workings of a live radio show. My work was done.

Record industry events of note started in February with a live gig and reception at Ronnie Scott's for Lyle Lovett, a great favourite of mine, and his album "Pontiac", then Godley And Creme at Rene's for the launch of their album "Goodbye Blue Sky", not an exactly uplifting title, I didn't think, and as it failed to produce either a chart placing or a hit single it was, sadly, their last studio album together.

April was a hive of activity for me as I took on production duties for two long-running shows, "Sing Something Simple" with Cliff Adams and accordionist Jack Emblow and "Your Hundred Best Tunes" with Alan Keith plus a Bank Holiday Special with Bob Holness. A little footnote to my time with Alan Keith, whose real name was Alexander Kossoff, which he changed after being accepted to study at the Royal Academy of Dramatic Art. His brother was the famous actor David Kossoff and his nephew was the guitarist in the rock band Free. He acted on the West End stage, in films and on radio before devising his long-running show way back in 1959. That October Radio Two hosted a celebratory luncheon for Alan's 80th birthday after which he dropped me a note of thanks for his present and added "I take this opportunity to tell you how much I enjoyed my time with you as my producer. So easy a time, too. Again, my thanks, Yours, Alan". Such a gentleman.

Anne's last show of the current run was on April the 9th when the boss lady, Frances Line, appeared in the studio to say thanks and goodbye. Frances seemed to be listening very intently to a record that was playing and murmuring appreciative noises, after which she said "That's a lovely record, I heard it on the station before, what's it called?" I had to hide my amusement at this because Frances had all the daytime producers in fear of her wrath if they played anything she didn't approve of. Her edict for "appropriate music" was handed down to them in a missive calling for a blend of whistling, wurlitzers, waltzes, zithers and marching music, or some such nonsense. I truly believe she wanted the musical output to appeal mainly to her parent's generation, which ran contrary to all my instincts. Fortunately, I was immune from such nonsensical dictats, being on a weekend show, and I offered "Maybe it's because it isn't on the playlist?" She seemed somewhat perplexed by this because she had no idea as to the effect she was having on producers too scared to take any kind of a chance. I told her the song was called "Perfect" by Fairground Attraction and she declared she thought it should be on the playlist. Wow, a step in the right direction away from the nadir of musical interest on the station.

The corollary of this conversation happened the following week when I was commiserating with producer Roger Bowman who came to see me after a meeting with Frances. He was very downcast and said he'd had the works thrown at him for playing "Everywhere" by Fleetwood Mac and he just couldn't see any reason why such a typically melodic song wasn't suitable for Radio Two. I agreed wholeheartedly with him and said I had played it and heard no complaints from her, and also that she liked "Perfect". He threw his hands up in the air and said "I give in, what the hell does she want?" What indeed. I think we know what she wanted and she finally achieved the pinnacle of her ambitions for the station when she commissioned the broadcast of the "European Whistling Championship"'. Oh, the joy to be outside that cycle of stupidity.

Michael returned to us in mid-April and we were straight back into the old routine with me delivering my package to him every Thursday and guests forming an orderly queue to be interviewed. Considering that on both Michael and Anne's shows we had at least two guests per week I find it hard now to remember who they all were but there were two who made an impression on me, neither of them favourable, David Frost and Jeffrey Archer. For some reason I couldn't seem to warm to either of them. Conversely, I thoroughly enjoyed the company of the cartoonist Bill Tidy, who, after many laughs, drew a cartoon in his book "The World's Worst Golf Club" and signed it "To Geoff, a man of scruples, cheers". Some you like, some you don't.

Enjoyment away from the studio, but still classed as work, were The Shadows at RAH and later a buffet reception at the Royal

Garden Hotel where they were presented with a Gold Disc. That was in May and in June the RAH also hosted a post-show reception for Randy Travis, with WEA Records delighted at the chart success of his single "Forever And Ever Amen" and, although it only made it to number 55, it was the first "country music" flavoured song to hit the charts for quite some time, thanks to plays on Radio Two.

Michael was only back with us for a brief three months but before Anne returned I had the delightful pleasure of producing a four week stint with the larger-than-life, hearty and boisterous actor Brian Blessed, who turned out to be a pussycat of a man. The show followed the same format as Michael and Anne with Brian's deep, sonorous voice just perfect for the radio. The entire crew thought he was just so lovable and I thoroughly enjoyed working with him, especially when he pressed the "talkback" key and asked me "Now then, Geoffrey, dear boy, what are we doing next, is it going to be exciting?" "It certainly is, Brian" I would say and off we'd go into the next segment of the show, often howling with laughter. My one regret is that I never got him to say "Gordon's alive." on tape. Along with Bette Midler, he would definitely be on my Fantasy Dinner Party guest list and I also wonder why he isn't Sir Brian?

Alan Keith booked a three-week break starting at the end of August and I was asked to find a suitable candidate to take over "Your Hundred Best Tunes" in his absence. Various personalities popped into my head until I remembered I had read somewhere that a great fan of the programme was none other than Earl Spencer, Princess Diana's father. Well, what a scoop that would be and so, nothing ventured nothing gained, I made enquiries as to his interest and availability, receiving the reply that the good Earl was delighted at the prospect. The Radio Two press office went into hyper-drive at this revelation and the media coverage was fantastic, publicity photos were taken in the studio, one of which I treasure, with the good Earl, myself and the wonderful and indispensable secretary Caroline Poole, sadly no longer with us.

There was a little trepidation on the part of the bosses because of the Earl's speech problems, brought on by a stroke some years earlier. That was a hurdle for both myself and his Lordship to deal with and overcome, with me asking the great man to do take after take until it was acceptable, which he did without complaint, as you will see from this letter sent from Althorp dated August 18th 1988 -

"Dear Geoffrey, I was very sorry to have our last session yesterday as I have enjoyed listening to three hours of beautiful music in technically such a perfect way. I only hope the listeners will like the programmes and not find them too heavy. I cannot thank you enough for your kindness and intelligent assessment of my choice of music. It has been a great relief to me to have your knowledge and expertise to help me through my first solo broadcast. Without your wide experience and calm acceptance of my foibles we would have got nowhere. I think the only weakness now is the quality of my speech, but that too is unquestionably better after the second time. You rightly demanded a high standard. I think we have achieved it. Now we can only wait and see how the audience reacts. But I do hope the whole idea will help the BBC and sound broadcasting. I look forward to seeing you and your wife here on Wednesday at 12.30 to meet the First Lady of Fleet Street. You should leave the M1 at Junction 16 and not go through Northampton. It will be very nice for us to see you both here. Yours Sincerely, John Spencer. P.S. Card enclosed"

The card was hand-written, but printed, with the message "I am presenting 3 music programmes on Radio Two on Aug. 28, Sept. 4 & 11 at 9 o'clock. Wherever you happen to be I hope you will be able to enjoy with me these Sunday evening programmes. John Spencer"

The card was sent to all his family, friends and contacts as he was so pleased and thrilled with the whole project. He was, as you would expect, a thorough gentleman, and he told me just how very proud he was of his daughter Diana, one day to be crowned Queen of England, an expectation sadly unfulfilled.

Caroline and I drove to Althorp on a sunny summer's day for lunch with the Earl, his wife Countess Raine and the aforementioned First Lady of Fleet Street Jean Rook, the often-outrageous Daily Express columnist, an incongruous juxtaposition of personalities, to say the least. However, lunch was a great social success, the food was delicious accompanied by some fabulous wines from the Althorp cellar. I particularly appreciated being asked by the Earl if

I liked Chateau d'Yquem and when I replied very much in the affirmative, he said "Oh good, I'll get one of the very best for you", and he did. Days like that live long in the memory and soon afterwards I received a glowing memo of thanks from Frances Line and, even better, a £600 bonus award from David Hatch for my work on the programme. An excellent reward for doing something you love, you can't beat it.

1988 was turning into a vintage year for me and one of the major highlights I always looked forward to was Paul McCartney's annual tribute to his great idol during "Buddy Holly Week". This year it was celebrated with a buffet lunch at Stefano's restaurant in High Holborn and to everybody's delight we were entertained by a set from The Crickets, who were joined later by Paul and Linda McCartney, DJ's Mike Read and Tony Prince, Chrissie Hind and Mike Berry for a raucous version of "Rave On". You can understand why my September diary was always clear for this event – it was not to be missed.

In December Simon Bates sent me a very funny Christmas card which had a cartoon on the front showing a car going into a long road-tunnel with a sign on the side saying "No Simon Bates for 600 yards". He didn't mind taking the piss out of himself and inside it he wrote "Lunch 1989?", which, of course, we did.

A call from Frances Line asking me down to her office led to one of the most rewarding and pleasurable production jobs I ever had when she said "I know you're busy with providing the music for a daily show as well as Anne Robinson at the weekend but I wonder if you could take on "Country Club" with Wally Whyton as well?" This was not so much a challenge as an opportunity to work with a musical genre I really enjoyed and with a man for whom I had the greatest admiration. My first show at the helm with Wally was on the 8th of December 1988 and we hit it off immediately as we realised our love of music stretched way beyond the boundaries of country music into jazz, swing and blues. I knew right away I was going to enjoy my time with Wal and the promise of trips to America – especially on the rather generous programme budget.

At the end of the year I produced two seasonal specials – Christmas At Althorp with the Earl Spencer, where he reminisced

303

about family traditions and music heard at his ancestral home and the other was the two-hour "Michael Aspel's Solid Gold Show". Work-wise, things couldn't have been better, I was really enjoying myself and 1989 was shaping up to be another cracker but dark storm clouds were gathering on the domestic horizon.

With Earl Spencer & Caroline Poole 1988

August 18th., 1988.

Dear Geoffrey.

I was very sorry to have our last session yesterday
as I have enjoyed listening to three hours of beautiful
music in technically such a perfect way. I only hope our
listeners will like the programmes and not find them too
heavy.

I cannot thank you enough your kindness and intelligent
assessment of my choice of music. It has been a great relief
to me to have your knowledge and expertise to help me through
my first solo broadcast.

Without your wide experience and calm acceptance of my
foibles we would have got nowhere. I think the only
weakness now is the quality of my speech, but that too
is unquestionably better after the second time.

You rightly demanded a high standard. I think we have
achieved it. Now we can only wait and see how the audience
reacts. But I do hope the whole idea will help the B.B.C.
and sound broadcasting.

We look forward to seeing you and your wife here on
Wednesday at 12.30 to meet the First Lady of Fleet Street.
You should leave the M1. at Junction 16 and NOT go through
Northampton. It will be very nice for us to see you both
here.

yours sincerely.

John Spencer.

Mr. G. Mullin,
Broadcasting House,
London. W. 1.

P. S. Card enclosed -

Earl Spencer letter of thanks

306

With Paul & Linda McCartney 1988

CHAPTER TWENTY FIVE

Nashville Here We Come

Let's get the negative stuff out of the way first. In a nutshell, after a house move to St Albans to facilitate an easier journey for Krystle on the school bus to King's Langley, my marriage to Caroline began to unravel. Things between us hadn't been great for a while and, although there were no specific reasons for it, we had simply drifted apart and so amicably agreed to a divorce. The Decree Nisi came through in May and was Absolute by October.

The family house was sold and both Caroline and I decided to stay in St Albans with Krystle staying with her mother. I put down a deposit for a new-build flat near the town centre but as it wouldn't be ready to occupy for a few months I was looking for temporary accommodation when friends Norman and Lesley offered to put me up until completion. This was all very well for me but Jamie and Kerry had to share a bedroom as I took over one of theirs. They were great kids and I hope they didn't mind too much as to all intents and purposes I became a fully paid-up member of the Davies family. So welcoming were they that I was invited to spend a family Christmas with them at Lesley's mother's house in Blewbury where I found out what a fun-loving bunch of party people they were. Lesley's mother Mary had delivered, with some assistance from husband Tony, twin sisters, Pat and Su, and two brothers, Roger and Rick, and I got to know and like them all very much over the years.

We've had many great times with the McCann family, probably more with Su and husband Brian as they were nearest to us geographically but Pat and Pete, Rick and Jacqui and Roger and Ruth all know how to give good party. I feel, as I hope all the "outsider" partners feel, that I'm lucky to be part of a happy and caring extended family.

This was my mid-life crisis, except that it was no crisis, not even a drama, as I took to my new found single status with relish, a bachelor pad and a Porsche sports car. I even indulged my passion for the fun items from my youth with a visit to a show called "Jukebox Madness" in Beenham, Berkshire where I bought an AMI Continental jukebox, a 1940's Tic Tac Toe one arm bandit and an even older arcade machine which sent ball bearings whizzing round in circles trying to land in a cup. I also wanted a pinball machine but the flat wasn't really big enough for one of those. Well, I was living on my own and needed some entertainment so what's wrong with that?

By virtue of my friendship with the Davies clan I was adopted into the Snorbans crazy gang, "The Lynton Avenue Playgroup", which consisted of the baby-sitting group Linda and Colin Cook, Pat and Graham Moody-Neale and Mel and Sandra Smout. Additionally, there were Mike Hatton, Bill and Stephanie Robinson, Willum and Merle Scott-Knox-Gore, Barry and Bronwen Knowles and Jenny and Alan Knight. A livelier bunch of ne'er-do-wells you are unlikely to meet. This great troupe became my social circle as they organised trips, birthday parties and as many ad-hoc shindigs as they could fit into the calendar year – any excuse for a knees-up. They were a hard-working bunch and at the end of each week most of us would descend on our favourite Indian curry house, The Taste Of Raj, to let off steam – which is a lot of hot air round a table of sixteen noisy loonies.

Back at the Beeb, 1989 started off with a couple of good receptions, the first for the album celebrating 30 Years of the Marquee Club in Charing Cross Road and an end of tour party for Level 42 at the Westway Studios where sushi and sake were served.

The next significant event was heart-breaking for many of us as we learnt of the struggle and eventual death of our colleague Ray Moore, loved and admired by all who knew him. A heavy smoker, he finally succumbed to throat cancer in January at the very young age of 47. His life and career were celebrated at All Souls, Langham Place on March 1st with contributions from Terry Wogan, Colin Berry and even the Syd Lawrence Band. It was as good a send-off as it gets, albeit well before its time. I produced a tribute tape featuring Ray and his novelty songs and I still have a copy to this day.

As ever, the music goes round and round: Bonnie Raitt entertained us at the Town & Country Club in Kentish Town, The Shadows celebrated 30 Years Of Hits and Bruce Welch launched his book about his time with them and Johnny Cash appeared at the Albert Hall.

The first Anne Robinson outside broadcast was on 22 April at Cannon Hill Park in Birmingham. It was part of a Healthcare Special initiative and Anne was in her element talking to the public and the health experts in attendance, one of whom I think was diet and exercise guru Rosemary Connolly, a frequent contributor to the show. Anne had several regular guests with specialist knowledge such as Matthew Parris on politics, John Tovey at the Miller Howe restaurant in Windermere for menus and recipes and Nicholas Witchell, the newsreader, for his take on current affairs. She particularly liked Nicholas because he, too, was ginger.

The "Children In Need" appeal that year came up with the bright idea of putting out a series of albums of Radio Two presenters' favourite songs and I was asked to produce one for Anne Robinson, as well as write the sleeve notes. It was called "At Your Request" and I thought what better way to kick it off than with her regular Saturday morning spiel – "Hello, Anne Robinson here. Stand by your ladders, your dusters, your ironing boards, your cookers and your gear sticks" - she always gave a fond mention to "them up a ladder". It listed various celebrity guests she enticed into the studio such as Frank Bruno, Sir Robin Day, Desmond Lynam, Pauline Collins and Anthony Newley. The music included tracks by Buddy Holly,10CC, Cliff Richard and the very first track had to be her absolute favourite "Blanket On The Ground" by Billie Jo Spears. Anne once asked me if we could play it every week but that's not how music programming works so I had to be firm on that one – you can't give the talent an inch otherwise they take a mile.

We regularly had a star guest on the show but there was one in particular I was very pleased to meet, the actor John Thaw, generally known to be a very reluctant interviewee. I took him by surprise when I said "We shared a headmaster in common". "Really", he said, "Who was that?" "Sam Hughes, he was my headmaster at Burnage Grammar", I answered. Then we got into the details of our shared Manchester heritage and discovered that we were both born in 1942, lived in the same locality and went to the same places such as the Kingsway cinema, Belle Vue and the Ladybarn youth club. After that chat John was extremely relaxed and gave Anne a brilliant interview.

By June I was six months into my stint on Country Club and decided to take the show on the road which is how we came to be at the Gedling Miners Club in Nottinghamshire to celebrate 25 Years of top British country group The Hillsiders. With the draw of Wally Whyton and Radio Two we also managed to get top acts Philomena Begley and the Brian Golbey Band to enjoy a great evening which was very well-received by the audience at home.

The big party of the year was Lesley's 40th birthday, which was well and truly celebrated at a dinner-dance with all friends and family present to marvel at this vision of the "Lady In Red". She looked absolutely stunning and, if I hadn't realised it before, I knew right then and there that I was falling madly in love with her. Little did either of us realise that precisely ten years later we would be tying the knot for the rest of our lives.

Wally always took a three-week break in August which he spent at his apartment in Benalmadena, Spain. The subject of how to fill those three weeks was up for debate – should we pre-record them with Wal or get a dep presenter such as David Allan? Wal suggested a biographical profile of three of the greats like Hank Williams, Jim Reeves, Johnny Cash or maybe Willie Nelson. Not a bad idea, I thought, but how about a series featuring all of the greats from Roy Acuff onwards and call it "The A To Z Of Country Music". I said Wal could write the script and I'd try to book a major country star to present it. Wal was delighted with this idea and asked me who would be my first choice to front this extravaganza. I said I remembered Roger Miller doing a great narration on the James Coburn film "Waterhole Number 3" and he would be my first choice, if at all possible, which it wasn't, due to Roger not being available. As luck would have it, Glen Campbell was due in the UK very soon and I managed to book him for the series. He turned out to be an excellent front-man, charming to boot, and all the recordings went off without a hitch of any kind. Glen later sent a letter expressing his gratitude for our faith in him with the hope that the audience enjoyed the programmes. By the positive amount of mail we got, that was in the affirmative, and I wrote back to tell him so. This is his letter to me -

"Dear Geoff, Thank you for the cassette copies of the epic "A-Z of Country Music". I shall always enjoy them. And thanks for the press cuttings. The series was well reviewed by the press. I can see by the enclosed letters that the listeners liked it very much. When they are happy, I am happy. Thanks much. I am sure it must have helped record sales too. Send Wally my regards and my sincere thanks for allowing me to do the show. I am sure we will meet again in the not-too-distant future, maybe for another project. I sincerely appreciate everything. Kindest regards, Glen Campbell"

Wally and Terry were both very generous friends with Terry inviting Lesley and I to visit his place in the South of France and Wally allowing us use of his place in Spain, which we visited two or three times. That was a perfect location for exploring southern Spain which we did with great enthusiasm on trips to Granada, Cordoba, Seville and Jerez, where we first sampled the delights of the luscious sweet pudding wine Pedro Ximenez – delicious. Another wonderful discovery was the romantic hideaway "La Finca De Bobadilla", an exotic five-star luxury hotel set amidst the rolling Andalucian hills to the north of Malaga.

One morning at Wally's a flash of inspiration hit me and after breakfast I said to Lesley "Why don't we go out for the day and see where we end up?" She said "Great idea, where shall we go?" and I said "Let's make it a mystery tour but bring clean knickers and a toothbrush, just In case". I had this crazy idea in my head so in anticipation I surreptitiously put our passports in my pocket and off we went, heading west towards Gibraltar. We had a look around the Rock, had a spot of lunch and then I took Les down to the harbour, where I enquired about crossing to Tangier in Morocco. We were in luck as the ferry was due to leave very soon so I got tickets and we were on our way, both of us very excited at the prospect before us. As we docked I hailed a taxi and simply said "Please take us to the best hotel in town". "Yes, sir", said the driver, and, with a big smile on his face, he took us to the fabulous "El Minzah" hotel where we booked in and made our way to a poolside bar to relax with a couple of cocktails. The next day a personal tour guide took us to all the attractions and later in the day we set off back to Gibraltar. Mission accomplished.

Just like Wally and Wogan, Anne Robinson also liked an August break and so I brought in Anna Raeburn to deputise, which she did extremely well, after all, she was another seasoned pro at the microphone and always welcome at Radio Two.

Interesting music-biz events at that time were a Bobby McFerrin meet and greet after his show at the Royal Festival Hall with the London Philharmonic Orchestra, a "Buddy Holly Week" invitation from Paul and Linda McCartney to watch the finals of the "Buddy Holly Look-A-Like" competition at the Talk of the Town and a champagne reception for Barry Manilow at the Dorchester Ballroom. My stamina and endurance was being sorely tested at this time, I can tell you, but I manned up.

Working with Wally was proving to be a joy and the highlight of the year came in October when we flew to Nashville for the Country Music Awards ceremony hosted by Kenny Rogers and Crystal Gayle. It was a long journey as there were no direct flights to Nashville so we had to change planes either in Raleigh, Virginia, Cincinnati, Ohio or Atlanta, Georgia, which became our favourite "hub". We picked up a hire car from the airport and had an early evening meal before hitting the sack at the Holiday Inn, with Wal particularly knackered from the flight. With an amazing contacts book, built up over many years, Wal spent the next day setting up interviews with the great and good in the country music fraternity and I was amazed and delighted at just how many doors opened for us. It seemed that all the major stars were in town for the awards and I don't remember Wal ever failing to get an interview he wanted as he was well-known and liked by everybody in the business. Socialising was very much on the agenda, too, as all the agents, managers, publishers and record labels were keen to showcase their talent pool from the established stars to the new acts, of which there seemed to be an endless supply, such was the allure of "Music City USA". Wal and I were not the only Brits out there on these junkets – sorry, business meetings – as we were often joined by a small contingent of journalists, publicists and broadcasters like Tony Byworth, Richard Wootton, David Allan, Alan Bailey and Head of CMA Europe, Martin Satterthwaite, all of whom were committed to the country music cause and great company to boot. There were some memorable nights at the Crazy Horse Saloon, the Rio Bravo Mexican eatery, the Texas Longhorn and many more, which caused some wag to name the town "Noshville" – clever and funny, eh?

Fortunately, a great deal of this media activity took place in the aptly-named "Music Row", a sort of pleasant village suburb where most of the big players operated. We could usually walk from one office to the next, Wally with his notes and names and me with my trusty tape recorder. Over the next few years we would meet and interview almost all the biggest stars as well as newcomers Alan Jackson, Suzy Bogguss and the biggest of them all – Garth Brooks, with whom we connected from the very beginning.

The night of the awards show was a revelation to me with its complex and spectacular stage settings, wonderful sound quality and perfect performances from a large number of singers and musicians. The word "slick" is sometimes used in a derogatory way but in this instance it fully justified its meaning as glossy and skilful. The CMA certainly know how to put on a show.

Wally was well used to everything attached to these trips to the States but for me it was a whirlwind of new sensory and social experiences and I couldn't wait to do it all over again. On our return Wal could relax a little but I had to get on with editing all the interviews and prepare them for transmission over the coming weeks. One thing that struck me was just how tiring the flights had been, especially for Wally, which prompted me to ask our office manager, Pete Mersey, if there was enough in the budget for us to travel business class in future. To my delight he said that would be fine and when I told Wally he almost kissed me and said "None of my other producers have ever managed that – you're a bloody genius" – I always like a compliment.

On my first day back in the office there was a communique from Debrett's inviting me to be included in the 1990 edition of "Distinguished People Of Today". Naturally, I hesitated for a millisecond, and said "yes", thank you very much, as it was recognition from beyond Broadcasting House. I got a name-check in there for many years afterwards.

In October I produced Don Williams in Concert at the Dominion Theatre in Tottenham Court Road and that was followed a few days later by the Radio Two "Bear Ball" for the "Children In Need" appeal, held at The Savoy in the Strand where we were extremely well entertained by the musical meanderings of Richard Stilgoe and Peter Skellern. It was a successful money-raising event and one of the joys on the actual day of the broadcasts was the time and talent so freely given by the celebrity guests who came into the studio. Over the years, among many hundreds, I had the pleasure of welcoming Nanette Newman, Barry "Dame Edna" Humphries, who came in "mufti", and Frank Bruno, who kindly donated a pair of signed boxing gloves to the appeal. It was a wonderful event to be involved with and the love and generosity was genuinely heartfelt by all involved.

Another fixture in the calendar was the annual "Radio Goes To Town" initiative to promote BBC Radio and this year we took the Anne Robinson Show to Milton Keynes, where we set up shop in a central location and Anne engaged the local populace and celebrity guests alike, although I can't recall who was on the bill. Another lack of contemporaneous notes.

The year ended with a Neil Diamond concert at Wembley Arena, a second and final "Christmas At Althorp" with Earl Spencer and an amusing letter from Michael Aspel in response to a party invitation, dated 18th December 1989 -

"Dear Geoff,

This is just to comfort you in your hour of need, because by now the party which started on 16th December will be drawing to a close and I don't expect you feel very well.

You may have noticed that I wasn't there and I am sorry about that but I enjoyed doing the Christmas programme with you and

I am going to try hard to get a series together – if you still want me darling?

Must go, I am getting emotional.

Yours

Michael"

Me too.

CHAPTER TWENTY SIX

I Become "Delicious" – Apparently.

Anne Robinson always signed off her shows with a credit to the backroom staff saying "Thanks to researcher Celia Toynbee, Camilla Courlander and the delicious Geoff Mullin", with the emphasis on "delicious". I was a bit taken aback the first time I heard her say that as it could have been open to misinterpretation. The funny thing is that for weeks afterwards I was getting letters addressed to me in the same manner, usually beginning with "Dear Delicious" – you can't buy publicity like that, can you?

The first major gig of 1990 was in January when Eric Clapton played the Albert Hall, then country star Ricky Skaggs arrived in the UK and Wally Whyton presented him with the Country Club Award for Artist Of The Decade, with which he was delighted, and pleased to have a photographic memento of the occasion with me and Wally.

On the social side of life, not only was I integrated into the local loony group but also further afield by virtue of Norman and Lesley Davies' involvement with The Radlett Players, an amateur theatrical troupe. This extremely talented team provided some of the funniest and most entertaining performances at their annual Olde Time Music Hall season every January or February. There were routines there that I had never seen before and which had the suitably-attired audience in hysterics at every sold-out show. Tables in Radlett Hall were arranged so that food and drinks could be served throughout the evening and audience participation was not only expected but actively encouraged, with Norman and others haranguing the Chairman, Ian Sutherland, with bawdy comments at every opportunity. I recorded a whole show one evening and it still makes me laugh today when I see Lesley marching the three bare-bellied bearskin-clad guardsmen around the stage and gradually losing control of them. Those shows were as good as it gets in that genre and I became aware of just what talent there was on that stage, none more so than Lesley, who I now admired as an artist as well as a friend.

In March, Mark Knopfler's group The Notting Hillbillies came into the studio for a live recording of songs from their album including "When It Comes To You", "Next Time I'm In Town" and "Tennessee Blues". Wally interviewed them and in-house promotions man Graham Lambourne took some good group shots with the band and me and Wally. It was a good session musically, quite a coup for Country Club and prompting a letter of thanks from their manager Ed Bicknell. March also saw a launch party for the European premiere of The Beatles "Help" and "Magical Mystery Tour" videos at a venue called Wall Street in Bruton Place, just off Berkely Square.

At the end of April, Anne was due to take a couple of weeks off and I managed to book Maureen Lipman as presenter. Naturally, to discuss her involvement, a date was arranged for lunch at the terribly trendy West Endy eaterie Chez Nico in Great Portland Street where we had a delightful meal and meeting. I knew Maureen would handle the show perfectly well and I hope I allayed any apprehension and fears she may have had as we parted looking forward to the shows to come. As far as I was concerned the shows went very well with Maureen the consummate professional and a natural at the microphone and it wasn't until several months later that I found out just how terribly nervous she was in the studio. Her book "Thank You For Having Me" was published in October 1990 and in it she tells of how her mind went blank, her mouth felt like cat-litter and when it came time to interview songwriter Don Black she says she was in a frothing heap. Well, you wouldn't have known it from her performance, probably down to her acting talent, and she certainly settled in nicely for the rest of that show and was much more relaxed the next week interviewing Denis Norden when she said she was as calm as a courgette (she has a good way with words, does our Mo). There was one very amusing element in that first show which she recounts with some relish and that was a letter she read out about a forthcoming wedding. She wished the couple well and we played "The Hawaiian Wedding Song". Then she writes "Five minutes later the phone rang in the control room and producer Geoff Mullin's eyes rounded beautifully. In the next record gap he came trundling into the studio to tell me that the phone call was from the bride's stepmother. She was in a fairly emotional state, in that she'd heard nothing about the wedding, wondered why she hadn't been told, and demanded to know the time and location of the ceremony". Crikey, the power of radio revelations to confuse and discombobulate the listeners. But "trundling", eh, what's that? Am I a "trundler"?

Anne's first show back was live from the BBC Big Top in St George's Square, Glasgow, as part of the "Radio Goes To Town" outside broadcasts. Our guest booked for that morning was Robbie Coltrane, who starred in the brilliant BBC TV series "Tutti Frutti" playing singer Big Jazza with The Majestics group. I loved that show, even bought the DVD. The Saturday morning regulars were pleased to note Anne's return with feedback comments to Audience Research such as "I think it is quite the best programme I have heard on Radio Two on Saturday for a long time" and this one warms the cockles of your heart "One of the greatest shows on radio". Mention of Big Jazza reminds me of an evening with the Davies clan when I said we could call Jamie Jazza, then Lesley would be Lezza, Kerry Kezza and they said what about Norman and I said he must be Nozza, which had us all in hysterics.

In May, Wally presented a one-off special, "Skiffling Again", celebrating the British music craze of the 1950's. This was something he knew a great deal about as he was one of the star performers of that era with his group The Vipers, who had Top Ten hits in 1957 with "Don't You Rock Me Daddy-O" and "The Cumberland Gap". He remembered those days with great affection and told me about starting out at the famous 2 I's coffee bar in Soho which was packed every night with desirable crumpet, otherwise known as birds or chicks. He said he had a ball during those days (being a very good-looking fella), but he settled down with the lovely Mary in a happy life-long marriage. As I later found out, Mary was a cousin of the female impersonator Danny La Rue. Small world. Wally was also an excellent talent-spotter so it was no coincidence that he drafted into the Vipers fellow performers from the 2 I's, namely Jet Harris, Tony Meehan, Bruce Welch and Hank Marvin. They would soon join Cliff Richard as the Drifters and later change their name to the Shadows to avoid confusion with the American vocal group. Another small world.

I produced "Skiffling Again" and Wally wrote a most comprehensive script covering all the bases and popular recordings from that relatively short-lived musical phenomenon. Wal and I were now getting to know each other quite well and he let me into several confidences regarding events in his early career, the first concerning his time with The Vipers. He told me that whenever they were due to appear in or around Manchester, Jimmy Savile would get in touch and offer the group the use of his house for the night, which they readily accepted as it saved a hotel charge. Apparently, Savile gave them a set of keys and stocked the house with beer and whisky for them and said they were welcome to bring back any ladies they happened to meet. They all thought this a most magnanimous gesture, which it was, until they found out why. The group happily accepted this hospitality and often paired up with a local lass for the night and got friendly in one of the bedrooms. It was while this nocturnal activity was going on that they discovered Savile was snooping on them through gaps in the bedroom doors in the manner of an arch voyeur. That was the end of their staying at Savile's place. Wally said they considered duffing him up but then thought better of it. Wal also told me a story concerning the "King Of Skiffle", Lonnie Donegan, who was looking to hire a new guitar player. Wal phoned him at the theatre, I think it was the Gaumont State in Kilburn, and Lonnie said to get over there in time for a rehearsal. Wal said he'd take the tube but when Lonnie said to get a taxi Wal replied he was down to his last ten bob and couldn't really afford to take a cab. Lonnie said not to worry he'd pay for the taxi so Wall set off with the hope of some much-needed work. As arranged, he knocked at the stage door and Donegan opened it up, took one look at Wally and said "No, you're too tall" and slammed the door in his face, leaving Wally well out of pocket and no prospect of employment – nice man Lonnie Donegan. Not all Wally's stories were negative, some were very funny, like when he told me of the night they played Brighton and after the gig they went for a drink before the pubs closed. As they were being chucked out by the landlord they saw an old boy in the corner struggling to get to his feet and offered him a helping hand. He was three sheets to the wind and pretty incoherent so they asked him where he lived and that they'd give him a lift home. As luck would have it, he told them his address in south London which was directly on their route home and so they bundled him into the group van and set off. Arriving at the old man's address around one o'clock in the morning they rang the doorbell and an upstairs window was thrown open, a young woman looked down at them and the old man and said "What the hell's he doing here, he's supposed to be on his holidays in Brighton". An apocryphal story if ever there was one.

One of the biggest events in the country music calendar took place that year in June and Wally and I flew out to Nashville to attend the annual Fan Fair at the Tennessee State Fairgrounds, where each day the audience would be treated to performances by both established artists and up and coming stars of the future who would later sit in their allocated booths to meet the fans and sign autographs. There were some heroic feats of endurance recorded during these sessions, with Garth Brooks reportedly sitting and signing for almost twenty-four hours non-stop. The music showcases were organised by the record labels, which allowed Wally set up a huge amount of interviews in the nearby press marquee, where a constant stream of artists would wander in to talk to the media. At a rough guess, there must have been about fifty stations dotted around that massive tent with journalists and broadcasters all on standby with microphones ready to grab the acts they wanted to talk to. It was very much a "given" that it was incumbent upon each artist to fulfil their media obligations and ensure the full support of their record labels. I must say they all worked extremely hard and tirelessly to present themselves as worthy of the attention they were getting.

The highlight of that trip was an afternoon visit to The House Of Cash studio in Hendersonville to interview Johnny Cash and present him with a "Heritage Award". Our journey out of Nashville was exciting, exhilarating and frightening as hell as I drove through the most atrocious thunderstorm either of us had ever known. It was like driving through a raging river and we watched open-mouthed as brilliant flashing lightning bolts travelled alongside the car about a foot above the sidewalk (sorry, pavement). We were a little bit shell-shocked and emotionally exhausted when we got to the studio, where John's sister Reba Hancock opened the door and invited us in for a welcome and refreshing afternoon tea. We were taken into the studio and before the interview began John's wife, June Carter, served the tea and we were joined by Waylon Jennings and his wife Jessi Colter. I felt somewhat overwhelmed to be in such intimate surroundings but John was so friendly and relaxed I was soon able to enjoy the proceedings as I set up the tape machine and microphones. John and his team were preparing to rehearse that evening for his radio show but he was happy to give us all the time we needed with him. Wally asked about the reasons behind his recently cancelled tour and the new tour dates going into the diary. It was a really good in-depth interview which JC said he had really enjoyed and at the end he offered "Thanks, how about a photo to mark your visit with us?" We didn't need another invitation and as I went to get my camera out John said "No need to bother with that, let's take some polaroids and then I'll sign them for you". Wow. We had our pictures taken with the great man and he signed them, a couple for Wally and two for myself, which I treasure greatly, as you can imagine. Before we said our goodbyes I plucked up enough courage to tell John that I had reviewed his Manchester concert in May 1968 and used the banner headline "Country Means Cash" which made JC, June, Waylon and Jessi laugh out loud and we left with a smile on everyone's face.

The handle "Legend" is hard-earned in Nashville but we were granted an audience with one of the true greats when guitarist/producer Chet Atkins invited us to his office on Music Row for an interview. Chester Burton Atkins was known as "Mister Guitar" and the "Country Gentleman", a name Gretsch would use in tribute on their range of electric guitars. He was warm and welcoming, offering us a cup of coffee before we even got the tape recorder out of its case, probably knowing that Wally would want to run through his entire career. To call that career extraordinary or extensive would border on understatement as Chet was credited with the creation of the "Nashville Sound", a modern move away from the old hillbilly style via his recordings in charge of production for the Everly Brothers, Elvis Presley, Dolly Parton, Perry Como and many, many more. He talked about his unique finger-picking guitar style and the influence of similarly gifted players such as Merle Travis, Les Paul, Charlie Byrd, Joe Maphis and Django Reinhardt as well as his more recent collaboration with current guitar virtuoso Mark Knopfler.

When the phone rang, Chet politely said "Excuse me, this must be important". We could only hear his end of the conversation but it gave us a good impression of what a tough, uncompromising negotiator Chet was as he said "No, my contract stipulates the provision of a Fender Twin Reverb amplifier", then a pause, then, "yes, I do have one but if you think I'm toting an amp, two guitars and a clean shirt to the airport then you're very much mistaken". Another pause and finally the coup de gras "Well, that's your problem and if I don't hear back from you by 4.30 this afternoon then I won't be getting on that plane". Chet put the phone down and said "The hell with promoters, the only thing they understand is dollar signs". We never knew if he made that gig but he did give us a great interview.

One final invitation of interest was from singer/songwriter John D Loudermilk who entertained Wally and I at his spread in rural Tennessee. We spent a hot June day there in the company of John, his wife Susan and the "Texas Tornado" Flaco Jimenez, multi-Grammy award winning singer/songwriter and virtuoso accordionist. John was very relaxed as he cooled off in the pool, which he designed in the shape of an elongated rectangle about ten feet wide and forty feet long with a maximum depth of three feet, just perfect for swimming lengths. Susan cooked up some delicious cheese-topped bread and over the course of a few beers John opened up about his early days with his great friend George Hamilton 1V, telling tales of the two of them making moonshine in the backwoods and being very aware of the local chapter of the Ku Klux Klan, which had been active in the area. John was no shrinking violet when it came to his career, telling us of the time he was short-changed on a contract and went into the office of the man in question to demand a cash settlement. It concerned a large amount of money and John explained, with a gun in his hand, that if the debt wasn't settled within 24 hours he would be back, next time with the gun loaded. That night a package of dollar bills was slid under his hotel room door. You didn't mess with John D. That became apparent when he handed me the keys to his Cadillac and suggested I take a drive around his 75-acre estate with the proviso that, if I opened in the glove compartment, I could look but mustn't touch. You'll guess there was a revolver in there. He also had some advice for walking late at night in the city centre saying "Always put one hand in your pocket and make it look as though you're carrying". "Carrying what?" I naively asked. "Why, a gun, obviously". That was an eye-opening afternoon if ever there was one.

If you think maybe that wasn't typical, listen to this. Coming back to the Holiday Inn one night I was drawn to a beautiful 1960's Corvette Stingray in the car park by reception. As I got nearer I could hear the conversation of two men standing by the vehicle and was astonished when one said "No, look, I'll give you fifty dollars for it and that's it". I thought that surely they weren't discussing the price of the car and as I passed close by them I saw the object being bartered for and yes, it was another bloody pistol. Obviously, these dealings were commonplace, as this was no surreptitious, clandestine meeting and these guys never even looked up at me as I went by. America, eh?

Wally's privileged access to the stars had been hard won over the years but newcomers welcomed him with open arms as they knew the influence he had in Europe, apart from which the initials BBC always seemed to open doors. One such new arrival was a young lad named Garth Brooks, with whom we struck up an immediate rapport, being invited to meet him at the very beginning of his extraordinary career with brunch at the Opryland Hotel. From that early introduction Garth always made himself available when we were in town, even to the extent of inviting us to his manager's office where he would sit down with an acoustic guitar and preview several of his recently-written songs. On this visit we were told that plans were afoot for a visit to London later in the year, whereupon I immediately suggested to Garth that it would be great if he came into the studio for an acoustic session just as he had done in his manager's office. He agreed to that and an interview with Wally to introduce himself to listeners in the UK. As soon as we got home I began making plans for this historic event with great relish.

July was incredibly busy as Ken Bruce and I were re-united, again, when he depped for Anne Robinson and did an excellent job while she in turn did an excellent job depping for Derek Jameson on the Breakfast Show. That summer was a whirlwind of presenter changes and the regular schedule was disrupted in nearly every time-slot with alternative hosts and celebrity guests, none more so than when Anne's husband, the journalist John Penrose, took over the reins for a three-week stint. John was very lively, a good communicator, handled being in control of a microphone very well and I enjoyed his company very much.

That July I received a Certificate of Adoption into the Davies-McCann family in St Albans, which instrument conferred upon me the full rights, duties and privileges of membership, signed by Norman, Lesley, Jamie, Kerry and myself. A friendly spoof which proved to be unnervingly prescient.

Lesley and I were invited to the European Premiere of Cirque Du Soleil in the Big Top at Jubilee Gardens on the South Bank. That was an amazing and thrilling evening of spectacular stunts which we both thoroughly enjoyed and it was special to be at the beginning of a phenomenal international success story. My next live music production was at Golders Green Hippodrome in a concert featuring the rapidly-rising U.S. country artist Alan Jackson. He brought over his full band who delivered a great set and afterwards he was happy to sign autographs and pose for photos with all the St Albans friends and family I had invited along.

The Anne Robinson Saturday shows were rolling merrily along but it was Country Club that kept me most occupied, setting up interviews and concerts with both UK and US acts. In September we set up a Cajun Party Night in Salisbury City Hall as part of Radio Goes To Town Week and invited The Crayfish Five, The Flatville Aces, R Cajun and The Zydeco Brothers to perform – you could almost smell the Creole gumbo and jambalaya – a wonderful evening was had by all. An old mate from the sixties was in the audience that night and he came backstage for a chat. It was none other than that unique and mesmerising singer from Sheffield, Dave Berry, hit recorder of "The Crying Game" and still going strong to this day.

Wally and I were off to Nashville again that October for the CMA Awards Show hosted by Reba McEntire and Randy Travis. We did our usual interviews backstage where I had the opportunity to speak with the producers and scored a major success. I asked if I could have a copy of the audio recording of the show to broadcast back home on the BBC and they said that had never been allowed before but that they'd think about it. I thought if you don't ask you don't get and sure enough a little while later I was told the tapes would be made available exclusively to me for use only on the BBC in the UK. That's all I wanted them for anyway and I guarded those tape reels like the crown jewels until we got back home. That was a notable first and after a little editing we put out the highlights from the show with an introduction from Wally, who was pleased he didn't have to select any music nor write a script nor do much speaking – it was really a night off for him. I think that's why he liked me producing so many live concerts as inserts, then his workload was much reduced – not daft, our Wally.

The lovely Sue Cook deputised for Anne in November and did a great job. I recorded Johnny Cash at the Fairfield Halls in Croydon but sadly John was having such difficulty with his voice that night that I took the difficult decision not to broadcast the concert. Another one in the vaults that's never been heard.

The final major event in our country calendar was the arrival of Garth Brooks who, true to his word, brought his acoustic guitar into the studio and delivered four of his songs "unplugged". They were "We Bury The Hatchet", "Unanswered Prayers", "What's She Doing Now" and the classic fan-favourite "Friends In Low Places". Wally and I were totally thrilled by this exclusive performance and Garth gave us a lengthy interview afterwards as well as allowing some photos for posterity. We loved Garth and his music but back then could never have conceived the stellar status he would achieve with over 170 million record sales, making him the best-selling solo albums artist in the United States. In 2021 he was honoured to perform "Amazing Grace" at the inauguration ceremony of new US President Joe Biden. In addition to all his success as a writer and singer, Garth could have made it on the comedy circuit with his great sense of humour and ability to deliver a joke and a punchline as well as anybody. At one private meeting with a few friends he gave us a wonderful rendition of "The Penguin" story, which I can't tell here because it's very naughty and very much a visual joke, so maybe after dinner one night.

1990 ended with a Michael Aspel "Sounds Of The Seventies" Xmas Special and my last-ever show with Anne Robinson. We parted the best of friends, with Annie showing her appreciation for my efforts by treating me to a splendid gastronomic lunch at Raymond Blanc's Michelin-starred restaurant Le Manoir aux Quat'Saisons in Oxfordshire. She also sent me this note on a Philippa Mills card dated December 90 –

"Dear Geoff, this comes with love and a huge amount of gratitude for all you've done for me. Without your infinite patience, skill and encouragement I would never have made it. Thank you Annie"

Now that's "Delicious"...

With Johnny Cash & Wally Whyton 1990

December 90

Dear Scott

This comes with love and a huge amount of gratitude for all you've done for me! Without your infinite patience, skill and encouragement I would never have made it! Thank you Anne x

Anne Robinson card of thanks 1990

CHAPTER TWENTY SEVEN

The "King Of The Cowboys" Tells Me A Story

I'm now back on a daily show selecting the music for "The JY Prog - there you are, you see". I had known Jimmy Young since my early days at Radio Two, at one time acting as senior producer for him and, although he usually rejected offers of lunch, I did occasionally manage to get him out into the real world. He kept himself very much to himself but would sometimes socialise with other presenters, such as the time he invited David Hamilton over for dinner at his flat. He told David about this marvellous Chinese restaurant which served wonderful food. On the night they walked in JY announced himself and got this response "Oh, so you're Mr Young – we only know you from your takeaway orders". Poor David could hardly contain himself, he was mightily amused.

Those days at Radio Two were the most staid, stolid and regressive I had ever known, with my show being sandwiched by Katie Boyle before and David Jacobs to follow. It was just like a mirror-image of the old Light Programme with a range of presenters featuring Hubert Gregg, Ronnie Hilton, Gerald Harper, Robin Ray, Richard Baker, Desmond Carrington, Charlie Chester, Victor Silvester, Steve Race, Alan Keith and Cyril Fletcher. How about that for a line-up? Guaranteed to put bums on seats, eh? Even in a moment of inspiration, Frances had to go back to 1954 and repeated the radio serial "Journey Into Space". Jet Morgan and his crew Mitch, Lemmy and Doc were welcomed back with open arms to provide a bit of light relief.

While working with Anne Robinson and Wally Whyton I had been protected from Frances Line's old-fashioned and pointless policy of appealing to her parent's generation to the exclusion of all others. I tried to counteract this blandness with a musical blend of melodic contemporary tunes mixed in with the best of the standard repertoire and lots of sixties and seventies tracks. Funny thing is, I never heard anything but praise for the music from her.

School half-term in February got the kids, Jamie, Kerry and Krystle, very excited as Lesley and I had planned a trip to Florida for them. The first week was just Les, Jamie, Kerry and me touring around the coastal resorts of Miami, Key Largo and Key West then inland across the Everglades to the gulf coast ending up in Orlando where we met up with Krystle and her friend. We did all the Disney theme parks, Universal Studios, the spectacular Typhoon Lagoon and on Saturday night we drooled over the classic car cruise in Old Town. A brilliant and memorable first holiday together with The Kinder.

Nashville came to London in many forms with shows by Glen Campbell, Kathy Mattea at the Mean Fiddler, Ricky Skaggs at the Dominion Theatre and Emmy Lou Harris at the Royal Festival Hall. In July an important reception at the American Embassy was hosted by Tennessee Governor Ned McWherter and the much-decorated US Air Force hero, General William G Moore Jnr. This was a major initiative to establish a permanent direct air service between London and Nashville and a great deal of effort was injected to help this proposition succeed. Both broadcasters and country music fans were delighted at the prospect and in 1994 American Airlines launched the first service between the two hubs. Unfortunately, this lasted only a year before the airline removed Nashville airport's international status. Nowadays British Airways will fly you there direct once again.

The weekend after meeting the General and the Governor I took Lesley and Kerry to Southport for the Open Golf Championship and, once again, we stayed with John and Christine. It turned out to be quite a memorable visit as the winner, Ian Baker-Finch, was staying just a few doors away from the Rostrons and happily agreed to bring out the trophy to have his photo taken with the locals gathered outside his house. There was much applause when he appeared cradling the famous Claret Jug and I managed to capture the whole event with my video camera, which is a great record of an eleven-year-old Kerry and The Rostron family.

Apart from JY and WW and producing all those country concerts I got together with Ed "Stewpot" Stewart for a Bank Holiday Special in August. It was off to Nashville again in October for the CMA Awards presented by Reba McEntire and attended by President George Bush. A starry night indeed but the highlight of the trip for me was meeting my childhood hero Roy Rogers, the "King Of The Cowboys", at a reception to announce "Tribute", his latest album of duets recorded with some of the greats of country music. Among those happily paying tribute were Willie Nelson, Randy Travis, Emmy Lou Harris and Clint Black, who I chatted to and asked him if he fancied being in the movies as he had the right looks, being somewhat similar to Roy, and, I thought, would fit well into a sci-fi film. At this, Clint looked at me in astonishment and said "Hey, that's something I've been wondering for a while, and you're right, a sci-fi film is a great idea". Obviously, the seed was sown as very soon after that he landed a part in the Mel Gibson movie "Maverick". Just twelve months earlier Clint had won the CMA's Male Vocalist Of The Year award and People Magazine included him in the list of Most Beautiful People In The World. He certainly had the looks for celluloid.

Anyway, back to the heading of this chapter and the subject of my boyhood hero worship. Roy was warm and friendly as I told him of my young infatuation with his movies and as we chatted a question arose in my head and I said "I liked the way you handled a gun but who else do you think was handy with a six-shooter?" "Good question" said Roy "In pure entertainment terms you don't need to look much further than Sammy Davis Junior, he's real good, but for my money you should take a look at Kirk Douglas in "Man Without A Star" 'cos that's as good as it gets". So there you have it, straight from Trigger's mouth(piece) ha ha.

There's been lots of coincidences running through this tome and here's another particularly poignant one. At the beginning of November, after many years of silence between us, I made contact again with my old pal Paul Phillips and we met for a long catch-up lunch near the Palladium. We covered many aspects of the twenty-year hiatus and were delighted to be in touch again. Paul was in good cheer as we left the restaurant and we had a chat with fellow-diner Dave Dee, the singer with Beaky, Mick and Titch. Paul's good spirits evaporated immediately upon his return to his office, where he was greeted with the news of publisher Robert Maxwell's death. Unfortunately, Maxwell had a majority stake in Paul's video magazine business and his demise rendered Paul's shares worthless overnight, a crushing blow for Paul and his writers and colleagues. That event totally overshadowed our re-union lunch and it would be several years before we rekindled our friendship.

On the 21st of November, Lesley and I went with DLT and Marianne to Manchester, where we were joined by Ron and Bente Stratton for the launch of a book called "It Happened In Manchester", about the music scene there in the 1960's. It was a gala evening at The Willows, home of the Salford rugby league team, and featured many of the groups and singers from that era. DLT was compere and introduced some of the favourite local names such as Wayne Fontana, Pete MacLaine, Johnny Peters, The Dakotas and Herman's Hermits, who persuaded me, with much encouragement from Lek and Barry, to get up on stage for a rendition of the Little Richard classic "Lucille". After more than twenty years since holding a microphone in anger it could have been a disaster but I think I just about managed to scrape by without too much embarrassment for me, the group or the audience, who filled the place to capacity. It was a fantastic night of celebration with many people seeing each other again for the first time in many years and I was particularly pleased to see some of my old group The Yaks in attendance. Apart from pure nostalgia, a condition afflicting lots of my contemporaries, there was another reason I had been invited to be there that night. I had contributed much background information and many stories from my memory banks, with over a dozen name-checks in the book.

In November I had a chat with Terry Wogan about the possibility of him presenting a seasonal special on Boxing Day and he said he would be delighted to be back on air at Radio Two. Naturally, a lunch had to be arranged, where we discussed the forthcoming show and that took all of about five minutes as we both knew exactly what to do and how. Then we enjoyed a catch-up covering the intervening years since we last shared a studio together as well as talking about a more permanent return in the future, which Terry seemed quite enthusiastic about. Watch this space.

My other contributions that year were a Christmas Day Special with Michael Aspel and Wally Whyton with "All Time Country Greats" which followed on straight after Terry's show. A good way to end the year.

1992 started off with great amusement as Wally presented me with a press release from the Nashville Chamber of Commerce which had seen fit to present me with an award for being the "1991 Shopper of the Year". It reads –

"The Confederation Of Nashville Malls met early in the New Year for their Annual Awards Show at The Opryland Hotel. Richard Ferriday, President of the Confederation, said "Some of the Malls in Nashville were in real trouble last year through the recession. Several might not have survived had it not been for the arrival, in June, of a young Englishman. This person almost single-handed put us back in the black. His sheer stamina, sometimes covering three Malls a day, was the stuff legends are made of. He carries bags within bags, suitcases within suitcases – and then like a minesweeper, he starts to sweep and swoop. A shirt here, trousers there. Perfume and scarf-leather blouson. Shoes, socks, sweaters, nothing is too much for this whirlwind – and to say our joy was unconfined when he returned in October, is putting things mildly, so we have great pleasure in naming Geoff Mullin of St Albans, England, Shopper of the Year. His Special Award will be the use of a 3 horse-power trolley, enabling him to cover the Malls 46% faster in 1992". Reuter, AP, UP & INS".

Crikey. Now I think an explanation is needed here, namely, at two dollars to the pound everything was so much less expensive than at home. Prices for housing, transport, food and clothing were always much more affordable in the US and I couldn't resist paying only half-price for Ralph Lauren and Tommy Hilfiger gear, wouldn't you? The other part of the equation was the fact that following a full day of interviews Wally and I would have dinner together, after which he would retire to his room with a glass of vodka, replay the tapes and prepare his questions for the next day. This left me at a loose end of an evening so I often met up for a drink or three with others from the UK contingent followed by a browse around Tower Records which stayed open until midnight. They always stocked a wonderful array of music reference books as well as records but my favourite haunts for finding rare records were with Mike at his Phonograph record shop or the equally amazing Aladdin's Cave known as The Great Escape where I stocked up on both classic and rare discs for my jukebox, which required the large centre holes found on US singles. As I told you earlier, I had been to the first ever Jukebox Madness Show and bought a space-age beauty, an AMI Continental, which needed feeding on a regular basis, hence the purchase of the large amounts of sustenance required. An extra suitcase was indeed needed for all this contraband as additionally I was gifted all the new albums from each record label we visited. Above and beyond the call of duty on the promotions side of the business stood the force of nature known as Reckless Johnny Wales a.k.a Bob Saporiti, a charismatic cosmic burst of energy responsible for the Warner Brothers success of Randy Travis, Dwight Yoakam, Faith Hill and Emmy Lou Harris, whose entire repertoire Bob presented me on about twenty CD albums. I had to ask for all these discs to be stickered with "Promotion Copy Only" as I couldn't possibly have paid the huge amount of customs duty they would attract. So, it was out to Nashville with one suitcase and come back with three - now I have more suitcases than records.

Another New Year change of office for me as I took up the reins scheduling the music for the new Radio Two breakfast show "Good Morning UK", presented by Australian broadcaster and controversial talk-show host Brian Hayes, with a mixture of more music, less speech. I liked Brian and we got on well although we didn't see much of each other as I didn't attend the daily three-hour transmissions between 6.30 and 9.30 – I've never been an early riser.

Sad news arrived on March 29th when I learnt of the death of Earl Spencer following a bout of pneumonia and a heart attack. Diana's father's death was noted across the media and in her Daily Mirror column Anne Robinson wrote –

"I am not in the habit of mingling with relatives of the Royal Family but I did know Earl Spencer a little. He and I shared a radio producer. His Lordship having been an inspired choice to guest-present "Your Hundred Best Tunes" on Radio Two. "I've booked Earl Spencer", I recall the producer Geoff Mullin excitedly ringing to tell me. "Oh nice", I said imagining for no good reason that the person he was referring to was some Jamaican pop star I should have heard of but hadn't. Anyway, Earl Spencer of Althorp it was. And he turned out to be rather good at the business of DJ-ing".

Wally and I were well in the groove by now and in April we went to see The Highwaymen at Wembley Arena. This was a country music supergroup consisting of Johnny Cash, Waylon Jennings, Willie Nelson and Kris Kristofferson, who was suffering with a sore throat, and at one point says to the audience very earnestly "I told Willie I was losing my voice" to which Willie said "How can you tell?" A classic comedy line which had the audience in stitches.

I produced an Easter Special with Michael Aspel and another Bank Holiday Special in May with Terry Wogan, who once again seemed keen to talk about a return to Radio Two and asking if I'd produce him – of course I would, don't be silly.

Early June and more shopping to be done in Nashville – only kidding. Wally and I were delighted when our good friend Mike Hyland from the Opryland Group invited us to a very special evening at the Ryman Auditorium, the "Mother Church of Country Music". It celebrated two important historical dates, the first being the 100th anniversary of the Ryman as well as being exactly 43 years since Hank Williams was inducted into The Grand Old Opry. The artists invited to perform that night were bluegrass legend Bill Monroe, Little Jimmy Dickens, Bill Anderson and Ricky Skaggs, all of whom we met backstage before the concert. I was aware this was a unique event and with a surge of inspiration and bravado I asked if we could plug our tape recorder into their sound system. Permission was granted to us exclusively, again, anything for the BBC and we were able to capture the entire event – a rare musical privilege which listeners were able to enjoy when we got back home.

The first trips I went on were limited to a one-week stay in Nashville until I managed to persuade management that there was so much more music and programme material available across the southern states if we could extend our stay to two weeks. Wally was overwhelmed when this was agreed and we began making plans to visit Branson, Missouri, where we met up with and were hosted by Boxcar Willie, next there was Memphis followed by New Orleans, the Crescent City, so vibrant you could almost feel the tremors and where the air itself seemed infused with the sounds of this musical melting pot. On one internal flight we were approached by two well-dressed burly blokes who very quietly asked us if we were the gentlemen from the BBC. Wally was in the window seat and I was in the aisle seat so I told them we were and asked them how they knew and why were they interested – in a very meek and mild manner, I have to add. The closest of the two said "We know the identity of every passenger on this plane because we are the security detail with the former president Jimmy Carter and he has expressed an interest in meeting you gentlemen, if you would agree?" We both said we very much agreed, at which we were told "You will kindly address him as Mr President, even though he no longer is, because that is the correct form of address for all former presidents". "Yes, sir" we chorused. Along the aisle he came with his two bodyguards, who pointed us out to him and then stood back while he spoke "I understand you are from the BBC, may I ask what brings you to our country?" I said we had a weekly national network radio programme playing country music and we were regular visitors to Nashville for Fan Fair and the CMA Awards where we able to interview the artists in person. "That's wonderful", he said "I'm from Plains, Georgia and I've been a country music fan all my life and I'm particularly fond of the music of Willie Nelson, he's a wonderful person, have you met him?" Wally said he'd interviewed Willie several times, then there was a little more small-talk before he wished us good luck and a safe journey, at which we both said "Thank you, Mr President". As he walked back to his seat Wally and I looked at each other in disbelief as the same thought crossed our minds – why on earth didn't we get the tape recorder out. Major missed opportunity.

I really can't recall all the people and places we went to but there was one where we fell about laughing so much it's inked indelibly in my memory bank. We had been invited by ex-rock'n'roller and now huge country star, Conway Twitty to visit him and attend a concert at his theatre in "Twitty City", almost as good a name as Ms Parton's "Dollywood", which we also visited at another time. Wally conducted an interview with Conway who then took us up into the empty balcony overlooking the crowded stalls area and there we sat, just the two of us, waiting for the show to begin. Great applause greeted Conway as he walked on-stage but as the noise died down and he prepared to sing a lady in the audience screamed "We love you Conway". Unfazed, he leaned in close to the microphone and said in deep husky voice "And I love you too Darlin'", at which the entire audience, mostly ladies of a certain age, screamed in rapturous adulation that was as deafening as a jumbo jet on take-off. That was when Wally and I collapsed in hysterics.

If you've ever wondered, and you probably haven't, where Harold Lloyd Jenkins got his stage name from, it was decided when he stopped at a crossroads and the signpost read left to Conway and right to Twitty. Well, that's his story, anyway. Which reminds me, nearly all the stars we spoke to had a multitude of anecdotes to tell, none more so than the funniest of them all, Roger Miller. Wally interviewed him a couple of times on our trips and he'd say things like "The place I was born was so small that the city limit signs were back-to-back" or "I was raised in Indian territory and every time we held a school dance it would rain for weeks afterwards". That's probably politically incorrect nowadays but then he did write "You Can't Roller Skate In A Buffalo Herd" and "My Uncle Used To Love Me But She Died". They don't make 'em like that anymore.

"Oh Boy. It's National Music Day" – so read the bold print on the ticket admitting listeners into Golders Green Hippodrome for "A celebration of the 50's with the cast of the West End musical "Buddy" and their special guest stars". It took place on the 28th of June, a Sunday, the cast's day off and it was a great scoop for me to book and produce the hottest London musical, with Brian Matthew as presenter. A tremendous performance acclaimed a rip-roaring success by all concerned.

More of the same music grabbed me just two months later at the launch of the compilation album "Buddy's Buddys" which featured 24 cover versions by the likes of Bobby Darin, Marty Wilde, Everly Brothers, Blondie, Hollies and Leo Sayer. The whole event was tied into Paul McCartney's celebratory "Buddy Holly Week" with a reception on the 9th of September at "Down Mexico Way" in Swallow Street, W1. I always looked forward to this, the most interesting date in the calendar, as there was no clue given to what form it would take, who might be there and who might perform. 1992 was no exception and, for me, the best ever as Paul got up on stage to sing "Rave On", "Oh Boy", "Mean Woman Blues" and "Shake Rattle And Roll", all of which he nailed perfectly as the great rock 'n' roll singer he is. Not only that, but he was joined on stage by my old mate Allan Clarke from the Hollies, Leo Sayer and Chrissie Hinde on vocals with a fabulous backing band featuring guitarists Mick Green and the truly impressive Big Jim Sullivan, the ultimate go-to session musician. To my knowledge, I had never seen Big Jim live before and it struck me then that I had now seen the greatest guitar heroes of the 1960's in a list that included Mick Green, Jimmy Page, Ritchie Blackmore, Vic Flick, Jimi Hendrix, Jeff Beck and Eric Clapton. All I can say is "Wow, lucky me". As a final memory of that day, as I was leaving the venue I had a chat with the artist David Oxtoby who had painted the superb cover art for the album. I asked him if it was possible to buy a copy and he said "No need to do that, just take one of these promo posters that are hanging about. Would you like me to sign it for you?" I said I would, and he did, signing it and adding "Rock On 1992".

The "Big Five-O" for me arrived in September and as, after my 21st birthday party, I had promised myself that if I made it to the then seemingly implausible age of fifty I would treat myself to another slap-up celebration, so I did. Family and friends were invited to a shindig at Sopwell House Hotel where we had a champagne reception, a sit-down meal, several comical toasts and dancing to my old mates Herman's Hermits, with whom I once again embarrassed myself by getting up to sing "Lucille". Lesley and I hosted the evening and stayed at the hotel that night as we were officially an item now, as were Norman and his girlfriend Cheryl. All quite harmonious, really. Coincidentally, the hotel was also hosting the Blackburn Rovers football team and, as John Rostron was friendly with their manager Kenny Dalglish, he brought him in to say hello and wish me happy birthday. A totally splendiferous evening with no serious casualties – well, there was a lot of drink consumed.

The 26th annual CMA Awards took place at the end of September and featured performances by many of the new stars including Garth Brooks, Vince Gill, Mary Chapin Carpenter, Brooks & Dunn, Suzy Bogguss and the new kid on the block Billy Ray Cyrus with his punchy hit "Achy Breaky Heart". Our friend Martin Satterthwaite, European Director of the CMA, helped us a great deal and we got interviews with all of the above but one we really wanted proved totally elusive. That was George "No Show" Jones, who walked along the corridor towards me and I asked if he could spare a few words for the BBC, without breaking step said "No, I gotta get to Houston". As Wally remarked, he was consistently rude but I comforted myself with the knowledge that I had been in the presence of a legend, albeit for only about five seconds.

As we finished our interviews, I had arranged a live link back to London for an insert into Brian Hayes breakfast show and Wally went straight for the jugular with "I thought you didn't like country music", to which Brian responded "I quite like it but a whole lot of it I would find ultimately stultifying – all those songs about dead dogs". – priceless.

I think Brian would have been intrigued by the wonderful Tanya Tucker, who was a bundle of fun, full of fizz and very sexy when we met her at a Liberty Records reception for her latest album release "Can't Run From Yourself". If you want to see Tanya in full flow check out her duet "Somethin' Else" with Little Richard on YouTube – sensational. That was a special day for me as I met a man whose music I really enjoy, the great Delbert McClinton, a rocker, a bluesman and a country star who plays a mean harp – that's American-speak for harmonica, by the way. Delbert had duetted with Tanya on her album with the song "Tell Me About It", but I had heard of Delbert back in 1962 when he played the "harp" on Bruce Chanel's million-seller "Hey Baby", and when touring the

UK had hooked up with John Lennon and given him a few tips on the old tin sandwich which resulted in it being used on The Beatles first hit "Love Me Do". Now there's a connection to savour.

Wally was rarely at a loss for words but one interview on that trip left him quite bemused and speechless. Roy Orbison's widow, Barbara, had collated an album of Roy's demos and some unfinished songs which she was promoting and, in his usual efficient way, Wally had prepared some questions for her She took one look at his list, gave him a withering look and said, very stridently, "No, Wally, I will ask the questions". Well, you've heard the expression "like a rabbit caught in the headlights" – that was Wally rendered helpless and dominated by this assault on his gentle manner. The interview proceeded well enough but I could see Wally was taken aback by Barbara's disposition and it took him a while to get over the shell-shock. Every now and then you get one, don't you?

Much more enjoyable and memorable for Wally on that trip was when Alan Jackson presented him with the "1992 Wesley Rose Foreign Media Achievement Award" at the CMA annual membership meeting. The CMA press release from Martin Satterthwaite and Bobbi Boyce noted this great achievement and finished with this quote from the biggest country star of the modern era – "He was there from day one, says Garth Brooks, who has always made time to talk to him". That was so well-deserved and Wally was delighted. I think they liked us in Nashville.

They certainly liked it when I told them that when we got back, Radio Two was broadcasting "Country Music Week" with both classic and contemporary artists in concert each day from October the 8th. We got good media coverage for it, especially in Radio Times, and kicked off with the CMA Awards show presented by Reba McEntire and Vince Gill, other highlights being London concerts by Emmy Lou Harris with her new band the Nash Ramblers, George Strait, Nanci Griffith at the Cambridge Folk Festival and Alison Kraus from the Edale Bluegrass Festival. I produced 14 shows that week and got a Radio Times credit for each one – could be some kind of a record.

I can't remember some specific dates but I guess it might have been around this time that Wally told me he had received a Royal summons from HRH Princess Margaret to join her for drinks at her place. Naturally, I asked if I was invited and Wally said no, it was a one on one. Ha – foiled again. However, when I asked how it went, he said she told him she really enjoyed his country music show and was interested to meet the voice behind the microphone. Then Wally broke protocol by telling me that after a couple of gin and tonics the most boring evening of his life ended. Probably a good one to miss – maybe.

That was one busy year, for sure, and it ended with me saying goodbye to Brian Hayes, producing Michael Aspel's Christmas Day Special followed by a three-hour Boxing Day Special with my newest star, a young whippersnapper by the name of Terry Wogan, whose Radio Times billing reads "A taster for what's in store for you in the New Year". And so, the legend continues.

THE NASHVILLE AREA
CHAMBER OF COMMERCE

161 Fourth Avenue North, Nashville, Tennessee 37219-2485

PRESS RELEASE   **January 1992**

        The Confederation of Nashville Malls met early in the New Year for their Annual Awards Show, at the Opryland Hotel.

        Richard Ferriday, President of the Confederation, said "Some of the Malls in Nashville were in real trouble last year through the recession. Several might not have survived had it not been for the arrival, in June, of a young Englishman. This person almost single-handed put us back in the black. His sheer stamina, sometimes covering three Malls a day, was the stuff legends are made of. He carries bags within bags, suitcases within suitcases –and then like a minesweeper, he starts to sweep and swoop. A shirt here, trousers there. Perfume and scarf- leather blouson. Shoes, socks, sweaters, nothing is too much for this whirlwind –and to say our joy was unconfined when he returned in October, is putting things mildly, so we have great pleasure in naming Geoff Mullins of St Albans, England, Shopper of the Year." His Special Award will be the use of a 3 horsepower trolley, enabling him to cover the Malls 46% faster in 1992. - Reuter, AP, UP & INS.

161 Fourth Avenue North, Nashville, Tennessee 37219-2485

Nashville Shopper of the Year 1992

Grafting away in the office 1990's

CHAPTER TWENTY EIGHT
The Golden Voice Returns

After a minor hiatus of just 8 years away at Television Centre, Terry was back in his spiritual home, the Radio Two Continuity Suite, and I was once again delighted to be producing the man generally regarded as the master of the microphone. This latest incarnation of the breakfast show carried the title "Wake Up To Wogan", which went out between 7.00 – 9.30am each weekday morning and was preceded by the new Early Show with Sarah Kennedy. All change for the early risers, then, and we were off and running as in days of yore, seemingly without missing a heartbeat as listener's letters started to arrive by the bucketload.

There was an important anniversary date on the horizon which needed some careful planning, to celebrate 30 Years since the Beatles first hit Number One with "From Me To You" in May 1963. As I was put in charge of producing "National Beatles Day" I got on with negotiations very sharpish having decided to ask their producer George Martin if he would be the presenter on the day and introduce their Number Ones with a potted history of each song. I waited anxiously in anticipation of agreement from the great man and was both relieved and excited when I received this fax from George's PA Shirley Burns dated 24th February 1993 – "Dear Geoff, thank you for your fax received the other day attaching the list of titles to be played on Beatles Day. Your patience has been rewarded in that George has finally said yes, he will do it. Can you let me know what day you have in mind?'

Well, that was by far the greatest hurdle overcome, and it was agreed that I would go to Air Studios in Hampstead to produce the links. George was very easy to work with and delivered the links in his friendly amiable manner, asking after each one if they were satisfactory and if I was pleased with them. Naturally, they were, and I was, as he was the ultimate authority and he gave his personal recollections on the history of each recording, after which he agreed to record some trails that I had written for use in the run-up to this important anniversary. A great man and wonderful to have such a unique and valuable contribution from the most famous record producer in the world. I came away with the tapes from that session as pleased and satisfied as I could possibly be with the knowledge that I had secured the co-operation of this unrivalled source of information of The Beatles recordings. What a scoop.

April Fool's Day quite often throws up some amusing anecdotes but for Wally Whyton and me on that day in 1993 it coincided with a sad parting of the ways as our Country Club show was shipped up to Birmingham to be produced at the Pebble Mill studios. I was very unhappy to be losing a great friend as well as my long-standing connection with the country music scene. Wally was incandescent at this major disruption to both his professional and personal life and, although he made major requests for the decision to be overturned, he had, with extreme reluctance, to accept the fait accompli he had been handed. Wally stuck it out for as long as he could but the travelling to Birmingham had a telling effect on his well-being and it is my belief that the strain on him was so great as to cause his health to deteriorate in the most dramatic and terminal way. He called it quits in September 1994 and Tony Byworth issued a press statement which quoted Wally as saying –

"The decision to relocate my producer and programme to Birmingham 18 months ago has added unfortunate dimensions. I have to rely on the vagaries of British Rail and they're having their own problems. In addition, the Pebble Mill studios have proved less than reliable and certainly not the Centre of Excellence that was being promoted then. To wait for a train that might be late, or might not arrive, and then hope to work in a studio that might not, has finally made up my mind for me".

Summing up his radio career in general he ends with "I've enjoyed every minute but I think it's time to go" All very sad and unnecessary but it wasn't quite the end of our partnership as I continued to produce Wally's programmes for the BBC World Service for the next twelve months.

I have a vague memory that was the time Controller David Hatch was considering the possibility of relocating Radio Two in its entirety to Pebble Mill, which sent shivers and shockwaves right through both the production staff and the presenters. The mere fact that it might actually happen practically brought work to a standstill as we all put our minds to the complex repercussions of such a momentous move, with Paul Walters and myself even indulging in the fantastic proposition of sharing a flat together. I put in a three-page evaluation of the pitfalls and costs of such a move whereby staff would be regularly moving between Birmingham and London for theatrical productions, film previews, artist showcases, record company launches, in-concert recordings and star interviews. Train tickets and overnight stays would be prohibitively expensive but they would pale by comparison to all the other costs of relocation. Additionally, there was no guarantee that all the presenters would join in such a mass exodus from the capital and it may be that Mr Wogan had some direct input into this debate with Mr Hatch. Did I say "may be?" Suffice to say that common sense prevailed and the whole idea was shelved, much to everybody's joint relief.

Another controversial episode that reared its ugly head in the early 1990's was "Producer Choice", a John Birt initiative that some of us viewed as ill-conceived and, in parts, unworkable. The main premise was centred around the idea that resources would be allocated to producers who would have the right to spend their budgets internally or externally of the BBC. I noticed a flaw in this "market forces" theory very early on when producers were given a budget at the same time as being told what they would be charged to request a record from the Gramophone Library. If you paid the going rate you were allowed to keep the disc for a short period before returning it. However, it didn't take us long to figure out that if we went to HMV or Tower Records we could spend the money buying discs that we could use in perpetuity. How's that for a business plan?

At an open forum meeting sometime later, Jenny Abramsky asked for any questions, comments or feedback we may have. Not being one to keep my mouth shut, I seized this opportunity to point out the ludicrous situation regarding the non-use of the Gram Library in favour of lining the pockets of record shops in the West End and elsewhere. I took pains to emphasise that this was actual cash haemorrhaging from the BBC coffers that could never be recouped and Jenny said "Is that true? Is that what is really happening?" Her face was white when I assured her that that was precisely how programme budgets were being spent. That gave her something to relay to Birt.

One of the issues with the oxymoron that is BBC management is that too much power is placed in the hands of individuals, many of whom have no commercial nous or entrepreneurial gumption, fail to grasp the reality of situations, are unable or unwilling to look ahead and are too often not held accountable for their actions. There, I've said it – but I still love dear old Auntie.

Young Terry and I were bumping along quite merrily on the breakfast show and on Easter Monday he took a break with Sarah Kennedy filling in, after which came two more of my programmes, a Jack Jackson repeat and the actress Liz Power presenting her favourite songs. Liz was currently playing Christine Hewitt in EastEnders and I found her to be quite delightful to work with and, in case you didn't know, she was married to Michael Aspel at the time. Talk about keeping it in the family – whatever next, Helen Wogan attending the microphone?

April was a busy month beyond the confines of the office with an afternoon visit to Ronnie Scott's to hear the Charlie Watts Quintet premiere the musical adaptation of the Charlie Parker book "Ode To A High Flying Bird". Then a card from EMI invited us to an "Amazing Celebration" at Jacob Street Studios for Cliff Richard's latest release "The Album", which went to Number One. That was followed by one of the very best musicals I have ever seen on the West End stage, "City Of Angels" at the Prince Of Wales theatre. It featured Roger Allam in a leading role and the clever plot revolved around a double story of a scriptwriter in the real world and the fictitious film he is working on. This was achieved by splitting the stage in two with the writer's side in colour and the film set dressed in black and white. Lesley and I thought it was a triumph that would have a long run but for some inexplicable reason it closed after just four months, despite winning an award for "Best New Musical". One explanation was that, although it had garnered many plaudits and rave reviews, the failure was blamed on the depth of the recession and the declining sophistication of West End audiences. What a terrible indictment that is.

"National Beatles Day" duly arrived on Tuesday the 4th of May and each Radio Two show featured a George Martin link and an accompanying Beatles Number One. It was well-received by the listeners, the media and was generally regarded as a good thing, I'm pleased to say.

More live concerts throughout the summer included The Everly Brothers at the Albert Hall, the Q Tips at Ronnie Scott's, a Billy Joel "River Of Dreams" Q & A at the Logan Hall, the musical "Forever Plaid", a celebration of 1950's close-harmony vocal groups and a drinks party for Cilla Black at Kensington Roof Gardens. Hectic times indeed, especially when you consider the added burden of film previews for "Falling Down" (Michael Douglas), "Dennis The Menace" (Walter Matthau), "The Fugitive" (Harrison Ford), "What's Love Got To Do With It" (Angela Bassett as Tina Turner) and "The Firm" (Tom Cruise). To think I used to get paid for all that - (?) "WORK".

I continued to produce live recordings during the autumn months featuring Don "American Pie" McLean, Nana Mouskouri, Julie Rogers, Mary Black and Suzy Bogguss, whose manager said that he'd never heard a better live sound for Suzy than the one we recorded at the Queen Elizabeth Hall that September.

Our main holiday that year was a nostalgic return for Lesley to Singapore, where she lived for a while back in the 70's. From there we went on to Hong Kong for a few days before ending our three-centre trip in the Seychelles. On the first two stops we hit all the usual tourist spots but the last was just the most relaxed place you can imagine and, in my mind, the ultimate in paradise islands. I really hope we can go back there one day.

The year came to a close with a champagne reception at The Savoy for Elaine Paige as "Piaf", a live performance by Beverly Craven at Air Studios, a Michael Aspel Christmas Day Special prior to his return to Radio Two for a regular Sunday Morning Show and, best of all, an outside broadcast with Terry in Leicester. Our guest of honour that day was brought along by Nick Fleming, who was celebrating a Number One hit with his charge, the unbelievable Mr Blobby.

Terry started the show in typical fashion "And here you find us in the very centre of the Lost City of Leicester. It's a lovely, lovely morning here, the sun is splitting the paving stones. We're at the Café Rialto tucking quick and lively into the old toast and coffee – I think I'll come and live here". He was joking about the weather because it never stopped raining all day and we got a little soaking as we left the café for the shelter of the enormous covered market, reputedly one of the biggest in Europe. Terry talked to several stallholders and sampled some local food delicacies, then we were picked up by the Lord Mayor in a horse-drawn carriage before setting off for the Mayflower Junior School where the children were waiting for us. Terry introduced our guest of honour, saying "He's pink with yellow spots and a stupid expression and Noel Edmonds is behind it". Then in he came to tremendous applause which reached a crescendo as Blobby wrestled a teacher to the ground, then chased Terry around the gym, which had them in hysterics and left poor old Terry totally speechless. When Blobby fell on the floor and rolled about the kids screamed with delight and I thought it might start a riot but they were very well-behaved and didn't join in. I bet they would have liked to. Then we were treated to a rendition of their favourite song "In The Mood" before leaving them, and us, elated and exhausted.

Next stop was to County Hall where we were entertained by a young steel band and finally a visit to the railway sidings as the vintage steam train the Sir Nigel Gresley was preparing to take off for Peterborough. Most of our movements during the programme were filmed, by a local TV station, I think, and the kid's reaction to our star guest still brings a smile to my face. What a day, a great success but little did I know that it would be my last Outside Broadcast with Terry as my life would shortly turn another sharp corner. Blobby. Blobby. Blobby.

CHAPTER TWENTY NINE
My World Turns Downside Up

At the beginning of 1994 I was invited to submit a recording of "Wake Up To Wogan" for consideration of a Sony Radio Award and I selected a programme from December which I thought might have a chance. Stay tuned for the result of that decision.

In all our years together Terry and I had never had a bad word between us but we did accept a light rivalry when Terry invited me to Twickenham for the England versus Ireland Five Nations rugby union match in February. We had a tremendous day out sitting in Terry's debenture seats enjoying a thrilling match which his team narrowly edged by one point. He was delighted with that result. I wasn't.

That was all good old-fashioned joshing between us and I was walking on air in the knowledge that I was about as lucky as can be producing a daily show with Terry, Michael Aspel's new Sunday morning show and programmes for World Service with Wally Whyton. Things could just not get any better – then they did.

In early March I took a phone call from a man called Alistair Ames, whom I did not know, and was a little surprised when he asked me out to lunch. Caution and suspicion led me to question this invitation in my usual manner as we did get crank calls, some wanting favours, others wanting to contact Wogan, journalists in need of a story and some not revealing their ultimate reasons. He told me he wanted to meet me as he thought I might be interested in what he had to say. When he finally convinced me he was on the level I agreed to meet him the next day at the Gaylord Indian restaurant in Mortimer Street. I figured if he was going to waste my time over something trivial, I might as well get a decent meal out of it. As it happens, we got on like a house on fire and spent nearly four hours over lunch with Alistair asking me lots of questions and finding common ground talking about Formula One motor racing. When I finally extracted his interest in me, he told me he was a head-hunter and had been engaged to find a suitable candidate for an important job in the music business, although he couldn't tell me what it was. This didn't satisfy me and I badgered him until he gave in and told me the position on offer was Head of Music at Melody Radio in London. When he looked at me after this revelation he said "I can tell by the look on your face that you're not impressed with this proposition. That is exactly the reaction I was hoping for because you know what's wrong with that station, don't you?" I agreed and he then said "And you know how to fix it, don't you?" Again, I said I thought I had as good an idea about reviving the station as anybody else might have. Alistair alerted me to the fact that there may be a strong field of applicants but assured me that he was well satisfied with our discussions and we parted with him saying he'd be in touch, thanking me for having lunch with him. As I walked back to the office my head was spinning with conjecture about the possibilities this might conjure up and I determined to speak to personnel the very next day – nothing ventured nothing gained.

At this point I had no idea if I would even get an interview for the job, or even if I would take it, if offered, but it intrigued me enough to take things to their logical next step and prepare the groundwork for the somewhat surreal idea of leaving the BBC. I knew there was a push for the BBC to reduce staffing levels and that generous redundancy packages were on the table. With that in mind I went to see my personnel officer, Kate Poulton, who seemed quite taken aback at the idea I would consider leaving, after all, she said, I was 52 and due to retire at 60 and surely I was happy producing Terry Wogan, Michael Aspel and Wally Whyton? I was, I told her, but I felt I was in the last-chance saloon, career-wise, and wanted to check out possibilities in the wider world. She then outlined my options for leaving, which included a payment of two year's salary, with a generous tax-free element, together with the immediate receipt of an enhanced pension, again with an attractive tax incentive. Kate and I considered all this information together, after which she said she would put the offer in writing and I would have the entire proposition on my desk the next day. Quite an attractive offer, I thought, as I stood by to watch the coming drama unfold. Guess I must always have had an element of the "disruptor" in me.

Lesley and I evaluated all this information in great depth as we considered our future together, including buying a house and moving out of the flat. We were trembling with anticipation after Alistair Ames rang to say I was on the short-list and would I agree to meet Sheila Porritt, the MD of Melody Radio. I said yes and Alistair said he would get Sheila to call me to arrange a meeting. This train was gathering pace and the fascination level was rising. The call duly came and I was invited to meet at Sheila's office in Knightsbridge. I expressed a little concern at being seen in the building as I knew my ex colleague Ken Evans was working there as were producers Zoot Money and Eddie Pumer. Sheila understood completely and arranged a clandestine meeting whereby she would open the rear garage door security gates and take me up in Lord Hanson's private lift directly into her office so no one would know I was there – James Bond eat your heart out. We had a very constructive two-hour meeting and Sheila outlined the issues at stake for Melody and seemed generally impressed with my attitude and aptitude. I left the building in a very positive frame of mind.

It had been explained to me that Melody's operating license was shortly due for renewal but the Radio Authority were concerned that the station was being run in a less than business-like manner as Lord Hanson just wrote out a check each year to keep it on air without being too much troubled by the idea of raising any revenue. He had acquired an operating license and started the station in an attempt to recreate in London the kind of "beautiful music" radio he enjoyed so much at his home in Palm Springs. However, he was forcibly reminded that this was a "commercial" enterprise and that he was setting a poor example to the industry by treating Melody as his personal fiefdom. I was told that he would phone the presenters on air and say he hadn't heard a Sinatra record for a while, and guess what, the very next disc would be by his Palm Springs neighbour, Frank.

Lord Hanson asked what he should do to be sure of continuing his franchise and was told, in no uncertain terms, that he needed to employ a sales manager, with an in-house team, and address the music policy by widening the brief with a considered expert in the field. All this was taken on board and acted upon in a most positive way, which is where I came in with regard to the music.

Then came the lightning bolt. Nobody in the business other than Alistair and Sheila knew anything about my involvement, as far as I knew, until one morning I got a call from publicist Richard Wootton, who opened up with "So what's this I hear about you leaving Radio Two?" You could have knocked me down with a feather as I said "What are you talking about?" Richard spoke in a conspiratorial way, revealing that he shared an office with Alistair Ames and had heard him on the phone talking to Sheila Porritt who told him I was her preferred candidate and the job was mine if I wanted it. Unbelievable, but true.

Now the game was truly afoot and Sheila phoned to tell me the good news and would I accept? I asked on what terms and we arranged another meeting to discuss the details. This was getting serious, I was both excited and nervous but all the tension dissipated when I assessed the salary increase, the car allowance, private health insurance, share options, a generous pension provision and a reserved parking space in Knightsbridge below my office with a leather chair and mahogany desk. In other words – a complete "no-brainer".

Sheila said the contract would be drawn up and that Lord Hanson would like to meet me. Was this a final hurdle or just a rubber-stamp job? His main office in Belgravia overlooked Buckingham Palace gardens and as we shook hands and looked each other in the eye I knew there and then that I would be working for him. I liked him from the off and after we discussed the way forward for Melody his last words were "Remember, Geoffrey, the name of the station is Melody". I assured him that I knew exactly what he meant and that he need have no worries on that score.

My new contract duly arrived and my next step was the really hard one of accepting the BBC redundancy package and telling

Radio Two that I was leaving. Throughout all these negotiations I had confided in Terry that I was considering leaving and after several coffee-morning sessions I had been given the benefit of his advice. He was genuinely supportive and understood this was a great chance for me and with uncanny prescience said "Good luck, take it, but I'm sure you'll be back here one day". Smart boy, that Wogan, especially when he sought my advice as to who I thought would be a good replacement as his producer. I had no hesitation recommending Paul Walters as the best man for the job, telling him that Paul would be very good on the music side, give him excellent production support, as well as a jolly good game of golf.

Terry and I would attend two more celebrations together before the final parting of the ways. The first was as his guest at the 47th Annual Dinner of The "Saints and Sinners" Club at The Savoy Hotel on April the 19th. Membership of this exclusive club is limited to 100 and it is left to their conscience at the dinner whether to wear the white carnation of a self-professed "Saint", while the "Sinners" wear red. I can't remember seeing too many white flowers that night. Terry was honoured to respond to the various toasts on behalf of the club, whose alumni at the time included Denis Compton, Ronnie Corbett, Lord Delfont, Michael Parkinson, Sir Denis Thatcher and H.R.H. The Prince Of Wales. Not a bad cast list, eh? A splendid evening was had by all.

The next event brought my two stars together at the Sony Radio Awards Ceremony where Terry and I were up for an award and Michael Aspel was the on-stage Presenter for the luncheon at the Grosvenor House hotel on the 27th of April. It struck me as seriously ironic when Terry accepted our Gold Award and thanked me as his producer, that in just a matter of days I would be working for the opposition.

The following day I received a hand-written note from David Hatch – "Dear Geoff, well, if you must go that's quite some style in which to do it. As Terry spelt out, the show like any other is a team effort relying crucially on a successful partnership between presenter and producer. That you achieved triumphantly. Congratulations on the well-deserved Award, good luck for life beyond the BBC and thank you for your substantial contribution to Radio 2's success over the years".

Not only that, but a few days later I got a note from the BBC Chairman, Marmaduke Hussey - "Dear Geoff, you must be absolutely delighted for winning the Gold Award in the Breakfast Show category for "Wake Up To Wogan". Very many congratulations from everyone at the BBC. All good wishes". Unfortunately, this time there was no bonus applied to my efforts.

So the dice was cast and preparations were made for me to leave Radio Two on the 29th of April and say goodbye to Wogan, Aspel, Wally and those wonderful PA's Tracey, Becky, Sara, Georgina et al. Leaving drinks were held in the Western House conference room and I was wished a fond farewell by my colleagues who gave me an original Barry Fantoni cartoon which shows two men standing by a poster of The Times with the headline "Wogan Quits Breakfast Show". One man says to the other "The end of the world must be nearer than I thought". Quite appropriate, really. They also gave me a beautifully framed picture of Broadcasting House and they now both hang on the wall as a reminder of those good old days. Most of those I'd worked with over the years also signed my leaving card, some expressed sadness, some joy (!) and some were very funny but one which was to resonate later was by Phil Hughes who wrote "Good luck – you'll need it, Selector's a pile of crap". This last was a reference to the music selection system used by most commercial radio stations, including Melody. Wogan wrote me a great leaving line "Thanks for all the LAFFS", and there were many.

Terry also wished me a personal farewell and Michael Aspel, who was on holiday at the time, sent me a funny card showing a picture of an upset baby with the printed message "I'm trying hard not to miss you so much – doggonit. It's not working". Then he wrote "Try to remember me as I was, darling. Good luck and thanks Geoff. Michael (Aspel, star)". A lovely, funny man, so he was.

Naturally, I had regrets and trepidation wrenching myself away from Radio Two, but it was to be for the best in the long run as I kept thinking of the opening lines to Roger Miller's song "Kansas City Star" – "Got a letter just this mornin' it was postmarked

Omaha, it was typed and neatly written offerin' me this better job. Better job at higher wages, expenses paid and a car but I'm on TV here locally and I can't quit, I'm a star". Always makes me laugh but unlike Roger I was prepared to move across London and take Lord Hanson's shilling.

Au revoir and auf wiedersehen, Radio Two.

With Terry Wogan 1994

With Michael Aspel 1994

CHAPTER THIRTY
Melody All The Way

My first day at Melody was Monday May 2nd 1994 and I settled into my comfy leather chair rather quickly, sitting opposite Peter Black, head of presentation, who took me under his wing, showed me around the twin studios and introduced me to the presenters throughout the day. I already knew Tony Myatt and Peter Marshall and the others I soon came to know as a friendly dedicated bunch of gents, but no ladies at the microphone, which I thought might need to be addressed. Next was Gary Johnson, head of sales, and his team, and Emma and Ronnie who were in charge of Selector, the music play-out system. Finally, the producers Ken Evans, Eddie Pumer and Zoot "Big Roll Band" Money, lovely fellers, every one.

I set to work on the music database with great relish, removing many of the duplicated songs, some of which were replicated over twenty times by different singers and orchestras. The music output was heavily skewed towards instrumental music and I reduced that quite brutally and dramatically in favour of vocals. I introduced many tracks and artists that had never been featured before on the station such as Neil Young "Harvest", Mary Black, Oleta Adams, Anita Baker, Toni Braxton and, later on, George Michael, Lighthouse Family, Aerosmith and All Saints. The feedback was really encouraging as we heard reports of many London cabbies selecting Melody on their radios, a great way to spread the word. By the end of the year the listening figures had risen from 760,000 to over a million – a huge increase, by any measure.

Not many pluggers visited us at Melody but I was still on their mailing lists for film previews, receptions and concerts and throughout the year saw Olivia Newton-John, Vince Gill, B B King and Cliff Richard plus the musicals "Oliver" and "Copacabana" with Barry Manilow.

So far so good until on June the 4th I heard the terrible news that my old pal Lek had passed away from cancer at the tender age of 51. It was a shocker, for sure, and many of the sixties musical community arranged to pay tribute with a concert in his memory. The event took place at Quaffers Club in Stockport with an extraordinary line-up of performers including his band Herman's Hermits, Troggs, Tremeloes, Merseybeats, Swinging Blue Jeans, Four Pennies, Twinkle, Dave Dee, Brian Poole, Freddie and the Dreamers, Wayne Fontana, Rubettes, Dakotas, Marmalade and Mungo Jerry with Dave Lee Travis as Master Of Ceremonies. It was a fantastic evening with an amazing cast list and Lek couldn't have wished for a better send off. May he rest in peace.

Wally Whyton would ring me at Melody on a regular basis bemoaning the state of affairs at Pebble Mill and the awful schlepp it was getting there. We were obviously missing each other and I commiserated with him but he finally called it a day at the end of September, as I mentioned earlier.

Showbiz events continued into 1995 with a reception at Planet Hollywood for the TV special "This Is Garth Brooks Too", recorded in Dallas before 65,000 fans and quite spectacular. There was a meet and greet for Lisa Stansfield at Legends club and Eric Clapton's "From The Cradle" concert at the Albert Hall.

In March I received an unexpected invitation to attend a reception in The Council Chamber at Broadcasting House for drinks prior to Terry Wogan delivering The BBC Radio Two Lecture entitled "Radio Two – The Slumbering Giant Awakes". It was great to see the old groaner again after 12 months apart and I said I was surprised to be there as I was no longer working at the Beeb. As we chatted and caught up on things Terry asked how I was enjoying Melody so I told him it was working out very well but I wondered why Frances Line had invited me to the lecture and Terry simply said "Because I asked her to". Fair enough, eh?

Less than a week later we were together again but this time on a very sad occasion as we attended the funeral service for Kenny Everett at the Church of the Immaculate Conception in Mount Street, W1. As you can imagine, it was a fuller than full house of celebrities and friends who had been part of Kenny's life, which was well and truly noted by those present that day. He was acknowledged by all as one of the greats and he left us with wonderful memories and a fabulous archive, darling.

Back in Knightsbridge everybody on the station was delighted with the attention we were drawing for our eclectic playlists and sense of adventure, especially when what we were doing was covered in an article in the Sunday Times that June. It was a case of coincidence and serendipity that our output was described as "the essential fashion accessory for the young fogies", as demonstrated by the opening of clubs like The Sound Gallery and Madame Jo-Jo's, where the exotic Count Indigo presided. There the clientele listened to a vast selection of "kitsch and cheesy" music they dubbed "the new easy listening" and the disc jockey with the best name of all was called Fred Leicester. I laughed out loud when I first heard that one.

Those clubs and their crowds of nostalgia enthusiasts were all grist to the mill giving us great publicity and when they interviewed me it was perfect timing as we could demonstrate that we were attracting lots more listeners in the important 15 to 34 age group. I had to admit I was curious about this new phenomenon as we were going in the opposite direction, slowly moving away from much of that vintage style of music by the likes of James Last, Liberace and the Mike Sammes Singers. Weird, eh?

As I said earlier, the DJ line-up at Melody was exclusively male, and in an attempt to broaden the appeal I tried to poach the fragrant Fran Godfrey away from Radio Two. She would have been a good acquisition but she refused all blandishments and stayed anchored at Radio Two. I was determined to give the station a boost and to that end I arranged a lunch with my old pal David Hamilton to check his enthusiasm and availability. I told him I wanted him to host the Breakfast Show and after the usual contract negotiations were completed, David agreed to join us. It was a good decision all round with David bringing his high-profile name and mellifluous voice to Melody, perfect for an easy-listening station's most listened to show. We were making serious inroads into the London airwaves at last.

Even though I was no longer at the perceived cutting-edge of the industry I continued to be invited to most of the prestigious happenings taking place in London. I was co-opted onto the Radio Academy steering committee for the annual Music Radio Conference held at the BAFTA offices in Piccadilly, where most of the big players gathered to discuss the state of the (radio) nation. The conference chairman was Paul Gambaccini and the whole event wrapped up with a drinks reception, naturally, and showcase gigs by Shiva and Whigfield. Not a bad day out of the office.

Other events of note were Wet Wet Wet launching their "Picture This" album in a Gothic church, the musical "Good Rockin" Tonight" at the Playhouse theatre, Emmylou Harris, Trisha Yearwood and Marty Stuart at the RAH, "Five Guys Named Mo" at the Albery theatre, Janis Ian solo performance at Ronnie Scott's, "Forever Tango" at the Strand theatre and "Riverdance" at the Hammersmith Apollo. I'm exhausted after listing that lot but there was more to come.

Lesley and I attended all those shows, what a wonderful benefit of being in the business, eh? But the two most pleasing for me personally were the rock and roll greats Little Richard, Chuck Berry and Fats Domino playing Wembley Arena. Sadly, Fats was too ill to perform that night but the other two more than made up for it. We had back-stage passes and went to a drinks reception where we chatted to Chuck for a while and afterwards Lesley remarked that she had never seen anybody with hands bigger than Chuck's. She still remembers it whenever his name comes up in conversation.

I was a huge fan of Neil Sedaka and had seen him in cabaret at The Talk of the Town but never met him. That all changed after he played the Shaftesbury theatre and we were invited to shake his hand after the gig. He was charm itself and happily responded when I said "I Go Ape" was one of the first records I ever bought and that I absolutely loved the "B" side "Moon Of Gold" and wondered if he ever included it in his act. He then volunteered the information that he didn't because "I'm not sure how many people would remember it as "I Go Ape" never charted in the States, but I'm so glad you like Howie's and my attempts at a real rock and roll record, thank you". Then he was whisked away by his PR minder and

I never got to tell him about playing his music on the Wogan show in the 70's. Still, it was a thrill for me nevertheless.

Certainly, the most important national event in August 1995 was VJ Day, the 50th Anniversary of the end of the Second World War with a Service of Remembrance at Buckingham Palace which the entire Royal Family attended. Lesley and I had reserved seats opposite Buckingham Palace for the afternoon celebrations and the RAF fly-past, but this was not by dint of her being an army brat nor my standing in the radio world. No, this was because, of all the radio stations in London, Melody Radio had been selected to provide the music for the enormous crowds gathered along the Thames in the evening for another fly-past and fireworks display. I put a music running order together with all the greats of the wartime era including Anne Shelton, Joe Loss, Glenn Miller, Andrews Sisters and Vera Lynn. It was relayed all along the Thames in London and the crowd sang along with great gusto. That wasn't the end of our involvement as Melody broadcast the evening's proceedings live from a high-vantage point overlooking the river with David Hamilton providing a running commentary during a live two hour outside broadcast. We got tremendous feedback and kudos for that event which really put us on the map.

The final, and extremely special, highlight of 1995 happened on Sunday December 3rd when Lesley and I went to a birthday party. Doesn't sound too riveting, does it? But this party was at the invitation of the Ambassador of the United States of America and his wife Mrs Crowe, requesting the pleasure of our company at a reception to celebrate Dave Brubeck's 75th birthday at Winfield House in Regent's Park. How extraordinary to meet and speak with the jazz legend and then be entertained in such an exclusive setting with performances of "Take Five", "Rondo A La Turk" and "It's A Raggy Waltz", among others. A perfect way to end the year.

As a postscript, on the musical front, I was wondering if our support for Mike Flowers recording of the Oasis song "Wonderwall" would be the Christmas Number One but it was not to be as it stalled at Number 2, beaten to the top spot by Michael Jackson's "Earth Song". Is there no justice?

A week later we were back at the same venue, this time taking our friends Linda and Colin Cook as our guests, (well, guests of Epic/CBS actually, as I remember the tickets were an outrageous amount of over £100 each) to witness the powerhouse performer from Canada, Celine Dion. She was magnificent that night and arrived at the after-show party in CTS Studios much as I imagine the Queen of Sheba would have made her entrance at such a function – totally imperious – a true diva.

During the year, Melody Radio was cruising along nicely with David Hamilton firmly ensconced in the Breakfast Show, which finished at ten o'clock, after which we'd have breakfast together in a great Italian deli just a few steps from the studios. I think it was called Caffe Concerto, and it served great coffee, cheese and ham croissants and scrambled eggs with smoked salmon – delicious. Our rapport was as good as ever and I was delighted when David took me to watch a match at Craven Cottage between Fulham and Brighton. Over the course of many conversations David filled me in on some of the many funny background stories from his long career, two concerning his association with Ken Dodd, with whom he worked for many years. In fact, I believe it was Doddy who named David "Diddy" after the Diddy Men who worked down the famous Jam Butty Mines in Knotty Ash. One day he turned up at Ken's house to take him to an engagement and, as usual, he was asked to wait in the vestibule. Ken came to greet him and said "David, you've never been inside the house before, come on in and I'll give you the guided tour". At this, David was shown around with Ken pointing out every piece of furniture and proudly stating its provenance "That's from a well-known store in Manchester, that's from Leeds" and so it went on with Ken having received practically all these goodies in lieu of cash each time he made a personal appearance or opened a store. David was most amused at this revelation of Ken's attempts to evade the taxman but, as we know, they caught up with him eventually. The other story that baffled David somewhat was when he and Ken were appearing at separate shows on the same night in the same town. Ken said to David "Come round to the theatre and I'll take you out for dinner and a drink". "Wow", thought David, "This is a first" and couldn't wait for his unexpected treat. They met as arranged and Ken led the way to a small fish and chip café near the theatre where Ken produced the menu and said "Have whatever you like" and then proceeded to pull two bottles of beer out of his raincoat pocket saying "I told you I'd buy you a drink". Well, David's flabber had never been more gasted.

The other story concerns the high-profile TV quiz show host Hughie Green, most famous for "Double Your Money" and the long-running talent discovery show "Opportunity Knocks". When David was the television continuity announcer for ITV he apparently infuriated Hughie with this classic put-down "And now, following Opportunity Knocks, the evening's entertainment will begin with Coronation Street". Hughie's ire and indignation at this insult was entirely palpable and not altogether mis-placed. David was a very cheeky chappie in those days, and he hasn't changed.

The forward march of Melody was enhanced by a change of radio frequency, which gave us a wider footprint around London and therefore access to many more potential listeners. This coincided with a major advertising campaign and a change of name when I suggested we call the station the much more contemporary-sounding "Melody FM". This was welcomed by everybody, including Lord Hanson, but especially by the sales team.

On June 15th we heard of the death of jazz diva Ella Fitzgerald, which prompted me to prepare a two-hour tribute to her presented by David Jacobs. It was a labour of love for me and well received, prompting Lord Hanson to write this little letter -

"Dear Geoff, please accept my thanks and congratulations on your contribution to the Ella Fitzgerald Programme. It was an excellent review of her professional life. A great deal of work by all concerned must have gone into the script, music selection and overall presentation. As ever, H".

Well, that was very nice, except that the good Lord had no idea that I had done all the research, script-writing, music selection and production. There was no team effort, just me and the charming David Jacobs. Still, a pat on the back is always welcome. We entered the programme into the "Specialist Music" category for the 1997 Sony Awards but didn't get a gong.

On the domestic front I was taking Krystle out for a meal nearly every week, usually to our favourite Italian The Cosa Nostra in central St Albans and even though she was now 23 with a life of her own I felt it was important to have a regular date.

Lesley and I decided it was time to move out of the flat and look for a house as we fully intended to stay together for the long term. We must have looked at about 40 different properties before we settled on 11 Lancaster Road, which suited us very well, was within walking distance of the railway station and had lots of scope for improvement. We moved in, appropriately, on July the 4th – Independence Day.

CHAPTER THIRTY ONE
The Homecoming

The saddest of sad news started 1997 off with the death from lung cancer on January 22nd of my great pal Wally Whyton. He was such a wonderful person and a really good companion during our years together. I still miss him.

On a professional level the Wheel Of Fortune began to turn in my favour yet again as I was invited to apply for the newly created post of Head Of Music Policy at Radio Two, thus enabling me to return to the BBC, as predicted by the prescient Mr Wogan. This opportunity came completely out of the blue and initially I was in two minds about leaving Melody as things were going so well at the station both in terms of advertising revenue and big increases in the listening figures. Still, I was persuaded to send in my application form and await a date for an interview. Working on my presentation to the board I was helped enormously by friends Pat and Graham, both well-versed in such matters, with Graham preparing some excellent overhead slides from info I supplied regarding the state of the market and the various players. They listened to my first stab at delivering my thoughts and immediately told me to cut it in half and rehearse till I was word perfect, which I did.

The interview went extremely well. I was relaxed and confident as I hit them right between the eyes telling them that I was passionate about music, passionate about Radio Two and in order to address their current malaise they needed to look at the presenter line-up with a view to the future and make drastic improvements to the music database. For instance, why were they still playing such old-fashioned items as "Woodman Spare That Tree" by Phil Harris and "I'm A Gnu" by Flanders and Swann yet ignoring the current hit single "Older" by George Michael which would be perfect for the Radio Two playlist. This brought some slightly shocked facial expressions and one member of the panel said "Is that true?" in disbelief. I assured them that it certainly was true and when asked what would be my solution to this state of affairs I came up with a three-word phrase that was much quoted later on when I said "With this database you have to Remove to Improve".

I was satisfied with my performance that day and so too were the powers that be as I was offered the position and asked to "Come Home where you belong". Then the hard part started with negotiations regarding various conditions including salary, car parking, private health insurance and pension rights, all of which had been available and generous at Melody. Eventually, after some hard bargaining they made an offer I could accept and on the 12th of February a press release was issued noting that I had been appointed Head of Music Policy at Radio Two and Jeff Smith had taken the same position at Radio One. Director of Radio, Matthew Bannister said "I am delighted to have two of the most experienced music experts in the country re-joining BBC Radio. They both combine a passion for music with a knowledge of BBC Radio and the commercial sector".

That went well, then, and I felt I left Melody in good shape with a contemporary music playlist featuring Paul Young, Shola Ama, Gabrielle, Wet Wet Wet, Bryan Adams, Tony Braxton and The Lighthouse Family. Now to get down to sorting out Radio Two!

When my former colleagues heard the news of my return I'm sure there was a little touch of envy somewhere in the air but they welcomed me back quite warmly as the devil they knew being the best option. One wag, on hearing that I was going back into the pension scheme called me "Geoffrey Two Pensions", and that stuck for a while. I was fortunate to have two great colleagues working alongside me with former producer Paul Newman managing the day to day running of the music database and the highly motivated and lively personal assistant Melissa Lyon, who could always be relied upon to be bang up to date with all the latest pop music trends. Her knowledge, enthusiasm and efficiency were merits that I very much treasured. She has since gone on to ably assist many of the top management team at BBC Television. An absolute treasure.

While my time at Melody had been rather on the comfortable side the pace of life increased exponentially at Radio Two both in the office and at outside events with invitations to meet up with Cliff Richard at a reception on Valentine's Day after a successful performance of "Heathcliff" at the Hammersmith Apollo. Then a media gig for the singer Jewel at the Café de Paris, a trip to Ardwick Green Apollo in Manchester to see the Everly Brothers, Disney's Beauty and the Beast at the Dominion, Tottenham Court Road, Michael Jackson Ghost premiere with Blood on the Dancefloor at the Odeon Leicester Square. In May it was the annual Radio Goes To Town, this time in Manchester with gigs by Stevie Winwood, Jaques Loussier Trio and Deniece Williams Gospel Train concert. It was good to be back in my old home city for a few days, especially as I could show Lesley around and stay in comfort at the Midland Hotel – luxury.

Special Event of the year happened on Friday 13th of June as BBC Chairman Sir Christopher Bland invited a small group of Terry Wogan's family and friends into the Council Chamber at Broadcasting House to celebrate his Honorary OBE, presented by The Rt Hon Chris Smith, Secretary of State for National Heritage. This took place at 9.15am and was followed by "A Breakfast" attended by, among others, John Birt, Ken Bruce, Bill cotton and Sir Colin Cowdrey. It was a great privilege to be at such a rare occasion and to witness Terry being duly honoured.

After three months of "removing to improve" the music database, both the producers and I were happy that there would be no more moans and groans when the music playout system delivered the running orders for the week ahead.

As Chair of the weekly playlist committee, it was very satisfying to push the contemporary music agenda along and although there were grumbles from Radio One that we were encroaching on their territory we stood firm. I was adamant regarding crossover tracks and told them "We're not concerned who the artist is or what genre they fit into, if it's a ballad, melodic, and won't frighten the horses, we're going to play it. Why don't you stick to rock, grunge, garage, punk, rap and brit-pop and leave the good stuff to us". Radio One had never had a monopoly on the charts and we held our ground because you can't intellectualise about popular music so we played Boyzone, Robbie Williams, Spice Girls, Gary Barlow, Shawn Colvin, 911, Cathy Dennis, Prefab Sprout, Beautiful South, All Saints etcetera and eventually their protestations died down. They knew they weren't going to win that one.

An interesting take on the progress of Radio Two appeared in The Times in July as we were enjoying great success with the Sarah Brightman and Andrea Bocelli song "Time To Say Goodbye", a number two hit due almost entirely to exposure on Radio Two. The article quoted the Huey Lewis line "It's hip to be square", noting that "Time To Say Goodbye" was still in the Top 30 more than two months after its release and that Radio Two now had a market-leading 12.6 percentage share of listeners with Radio One trailing on 11.6. I was quoted in the article and when asked "How long will the divine Sarah's single, recently awarded gold disc status, linger on the playlist?", I replied "It's already stayed active much longer than most things we play, simply because listeners continue to react strongly in favour of it, as witnessed by its very slow decline in the charts. At some point, though, a value judgement will be made. There will come a point when we decide it is past its sell-by date, and let it join the database of classic tracks". We loved our listeners and their great sense of taste and that article surely helped to confirm our position at the top of the radio tree.

That summer saw an influx of invitations to various events including a very rare opportunity to visit the BT Tower in London, lunch with Simon Cowell at Sheekey's fabulous fish restaurant and a fund-raising gala hosted by Dave Dee where I was seated next to Alice Cooper, who was in town for a concert at the Astoria as part of his "School's Out For Summer 1997" tour. He was charming and most engaging in conversation – a thoroughly nice chap. Then there was diva Dionne Warwick live at the Royal Festival Hall, not bad going so far.

August 31st brought the awful news of the death of Diana, Princess of Wales, in a car crash in Paris, which I first became aware of via a frantic phone call asking me to get back to base to organise a much more suitable and sombre musical output as the normal schedules were scrapped. Unfortunately, Lesley and I were on holiday in Bruges, Belgium, with no chance of returning to London in time to be of any help. However, the production staff rallied round and did a sterling job of selecting suitable music for such a sad occasion. It was a magnificent effort.

Just two weeks later Lesley and I were invited to attend "An Audience With Elton John" at London Weekend Television studios with the full package of pre-show drinks and supper after the show. It was a marvellous, funny and hugely entertaining event with Elton asking the star-studded audience if they had any questions. The most poignant of the evening came from George Martin, who had produced the tribute version of "Candle In The Wind/Goodbye England's Rose" which Elton performed at Diana's funeral on September 6th. George asked if Elton would ever sing that song again and was firmly assured that he would never sing that version of the song as it was a one-off performance and never to be repeated. That's love and integrity for you.

This was turning out to be an extraordinary year in so many ways and one of the later highlights was a trip to Nashville with Lesley for the CMA Awards show in late September. It was no surprise when Garth Brooks picked up the "Entertainer of the Year" award and it was refreshing to see newcomer Deana Carter receive the "Single of the Year" award for "Strawberry Wine" which also won in the "Song of the Year" category. The song was co-written by Matraca Berg and included on Deana's hilariously titled debut album "Did I Shave My Legs For This?", which also contained a song written by the great Kim Carnes. The reason I've gone into so much detail here is because Lesley and I were invited to a very special private performance by these artists at Green's Grocery, a bijou music venue in Historic Leiper's Fork, not far from the Old Natchez Trace in Franklin, Tennessee. It was a privilege to be there on that most memorable night and see these artists up-close and personal in such an intimate acoustic setting.

By complete contrast another invitation took us to the original Grand Ole Opry venue at the newly-renovated Ryman Auditorium in downtown Nashville to see the amazing, blazing John Fogerty who shook the old place to its wooden rafters playing all the old Creedence Clearwater Revival hits. It was part of John's "Blue

Swamp Tour" and one of the best concerts I've ever seen, perhaps an even more powerful performance than the one I saw in London way back in the sixties. As electric bayou music goes - it was sensational.

Two other things to say about this visit were a small luncheon at Morton's restaurant hosted by Joe Gallante, President of RCA Records, where he introduced us to country superstar Lorrie Morgan. This was followed by the undoubted honour of being presented with a personal CMA Award for my "Exceptional Contribution To The Development Of Country Music Worldwide". It doesn't get any better than that in Nashville.

We finished off 1997 musically with a terrific Status Quo concert at Wembley Arena featuring all their hits including the great John Fogerty song "Rockin" All Over The World". Extremely lively.

1998 came in at a pace, well Hale And Pace, actually (sorry about that). The comedy duo were appearing on the BBC TV series "Jobs For The Boys", which set them the challenge of writing an entry for the "Song For Europe" competition, and they offered for consideration their effort "More Than Enough For One Life" – a snappy title if ever there was one. I was on the judging panel with my colleague Paul Walters, songwriter Gary Osborne and four others who met at Television Centre to listen to the final shortlist, from an initial list of 800 entries. We selected what we considered the best 8 songs to go forward to "The Great British Song Contest" where the viewers and listeners would have the final say on the winning song. It was a close-run thing but singer Imaani emerged the winner with her song "Where Are You". As for Hale And Pace, they didn't make the cut.

Memorable music nights that year included an invitation to the Brit Awards in February at the London Arena with pre-show dinner and drinks, which is always a good start to an evening. Ben Elton was the host, introducing performances by The Spice Girls, Fleetwood Mac, Tom Jones, Robbie Williams, Texas, All Saints, winners of both Best Single and Best video awards, and The Verve who were voted top in the Best Group, Best Album and Best Producer categories. Such a fantastic array of stars to entertain us but possibly the one thing that night that most will never forget was when the drummer from Chumbawamba ran out and chucked a bucket of water all over Deputy Prime Minister John Prescott. Showbiz and politics – should they ever mix?

From one highlight night to a very lowlight night when top plugger Jackie Gill invited Lesley and I to the Queen's Theatre in Shaftesbury Avenue to a preview in March of a campy new whodunnit musical "Saucy Jack And The Space Vixens". We might have known from that title not to raise our expectations too high and we weren't disappointed because it was dire. So bad was it, in fact, that for the very first time in my life I left the theatre during the half-time interval. The next day Jackie called in to see what I thought of the show and I said "Well, I can only tell you what I thought of the first half". Jackie nodded in agreement as I mentioned the appalling sound quality and the below par performances for a West End show. Little wonder it only ran for 85 performances.

Two weeks after the sadly lacking "Saucy Jack" show Jackie Gill invited us to a far better offering at the Vaudeville Theatre to see the South African musical "Kat And The Kings" which deservedly won the Laurence Olivier Award for Best New Musical and, in an unusual move, the Best Actor In A Musical award was presented to the entire cast.

Exciting things were happening in the charts for Radio Two that March as Shania Twain had her first hit "You're Still The One" which entered the top ten thanks in a large part to enormous support from the station. That song came from the 40 million-selling album "Come On Over" which also contained her huge hits "That Don't Impress Me Much" and "Man I Feel Like A Woman". I bet you didn't know her real name was Eileen Regina Edwards, did you?

Two events in April are worth remembering for their uplifting effect. The first was an invitation from impresario Bill Kenwright to attend the 10th anniversary performance of the musical Blood Brothers with the wonderful Barbara Dickson returning to her starring role. Those of us privileged to be there left the Phoenix Theatre for an after-show reception at the Waldorf hotel where we ate and drank and chatted to Bill and Barbara and the cast. A wonderful evening, indeed.

Next up an invitation from Andrew Lloyd Webber who splashed out big-time to celebrate his 50th birthday with a concert in the Royal Albert Hall. No expense was spared in mounting this once-only spectacular and the stars turned out in force, among whom were Michael Ball, Kiri Te Kanawa, Sarah Brightman, Boyzone, Antonio Banderas, Elaine Paige, Glenn Close, Donny Osmond and Bonnie Tyler. That's a sumptuous array of talent which was matched by the VIP hospitality we enjoyed in Box 15 being served champagne and a hot and cold buffet. Happy birthday Andrew.

As promised, here is the coda to a story that reverberated down the years from 1968. I was sitting in my office one morning when the phone rang and a man asked if I was Geoff Mullin. Being wary of such questioning I asked why he wanted to know and he told me he was a private investigator who had been hired to find a man by that name who had driven to Spain in 1968 with a young lady in an open-top sports car. When I questioned him some more, he said this lady would like to get in touch and only if I agreed would he pass my details on to her. Thinking nothing of it, I said "By all means, she can contact me here at the BBC". Two days later I got a call from said lady who told me of her life and I gave her an outline of my career and we agreed to meet next time she was in London. I wasn't expecting that event to be just three weeks later, when she rang and said "Hi Geoff, I'm in town and wondered if you were free for dinner this evening?" I thought that was pretty rapid and a bit last minute but said I'd be at her hotel at 7.00pm. In the meantime, I booked a table at a nice Italian restaurant just around the corner from the hotel and looked forward to meeting up with her again after such a long time. At the front desk I was told I was expected and directed to the penthouse suite, if you don't mind, where she had laid on champagne and after a glass and a brief chat, I suggested we carry on our conversation at the restaurant. "Oh, I thought we could stay in and order room service", she said, but I insisted on going out as I had booked for dinner. That was when the funny vibes started as I could tell she was not happy with this arrangement, but we went out anyway. Over dinner she explained that she wanted to write about our trip to Spain and, to help her remember everything, she wanted to do the journey all over again - with me. That's when the funny vibes multiplied exponentially. She was crestfallen when I told her that was a non-starter as I was all loved-up with Lesley and couldn't possibly contemplate such a venture. The air was a bit frosty, to say the least, as we finished our meal and I walked her back to the hotel. That's when the air became positively frozen as I graciously declined her offer of a nightcap in the penthouse, saying it was rather late and I had to be getting home. They say hell hath no fury like a woman scorned and, although I had agreed to meet her on the most innocent of terms, she was clearly angry at her plans being thwarted, accusing me of causing her a wasted journey. Well, that was enough for me and I told her, in no uncertain terms, that I had given her no reason whatsoever to expect anything more than a friendly lunch or dinner. At this she stomped off into the hotel, never to be heard from again. I couldn't wait to get back in my car and head for home with the accelerator planted firmly to the floor. Let that be a lesson to me.

Back at Radio Two in Western House, (now named Wogan House in Terry's honour), things were moving along nicely, especially the consensus of opinion among the producers about the musical direction we were taking. This was never more noticeable than at a playlist meeting in April when we first heard the Mavericks single "Dance The Night Away", which brought a big smile to every face in the room as we knew we'd be playing it to death until it charted. And it did, getting to Number 4, with the station taking much credit for that success. As the single began its slow decline after 18 weeks on the chart the plugger from MCA Records came in to see me and asked for my opinion on a follow-up single from their album Trampoline. The obvious candidate was "Someone Should Tell Her", a song in similar up-tempo vein, which I said I would support and my hunch was that all the producers would feel the same, and they did. You can imagine our dismay when the next single turned out to be "I've Got This Feeling", a somewhat sombre song which only managed Number 27, sounding the death-knell for the group in terms of UK chart success. A year later MCA tried to resurrect their chart career by finally releasing my original suggestion but it was too little too late and "Someone Should Tell Her" stalled at Number 45. I was very disappointed as I loved the group, singer Raul Malo is a personal favourite and one of the great voices of our time in my opinion.

The Eurovision Song Contest took place at the National Indoor Arena in Birmingham following Katrina And The Waves winner "Love Shine A Light" the year previously. Terry Wogan and Ulrika Jonsson hosted the event which was won by the Israeli entry "Diva" sung by the transsexual artiste Dana International. The UK entry "Where Are You" by Imaani came a very creditable second. There were the usual after-show celebrations and next day we tramped back down to The Smoke, otherwise known as London.

July saw Lesley and I travelling north again to stay with John and Christine Rostron who had invited us to The Open Golf Championship at Royal Birkdale where we were lucky enough to be in the clubhouse as the Masters champion Mark O'Meara won his second major of the year, holing his final putt to take victory after a play-off with Brian Watts. It had been a wet and windy weekend in Southport but that didn't stop us enjoying a most sociable visit with our very good friends.

Holiday entitlement at the Beeb was quite generous at 5 weeks per annum and Lesley and I took off for Florida in September with our good pals Linda and Colin Cook. We flew into Tampa and stayed in Longboat Key at a condo owned by a friend of the Cooks but little did we know how interesting our sunshine stay was going to be. After a few days on the beach we headed for the delights of Orlando where Lesley had managed to get free theme park tickets through a friend at work. We had fun staying at Wilderness Lodge where we made the mistake of asking for tomato ketchup with our breakfast. This request immediately prompted our waitress to shout at the top of her voice "Ketchup over here, ketchup, ketchup right now" and within seconds we were inundated with bottles brought over by the table who had previously asked for it, helped by the waiting staff, until our table could take no more. The regulars in there knew what was coming and fell about laughing, as did we. At one point I left the restaurant and came back to find Lesley, Linda and Colin demonstrating the fine art of the dance routine to the Hokey Cokey, which the yanks call the Hokey Pokey and do quite a different version to us. Gradually all the others in the line stopped to watch the Brit version performed by the 3 olde tyme music hall experts. They then had to teach the waiting staff the Brit version as they decided it was much more fun.

Back in Longboat Key I realised we were only days away from the CMA Awards gala night in Nashville and thought it would be wonderful if we could go and take the Cooks along, too. A couple of phone calls later we were added to the guest list and then scrambled to get flights booked. We arrived in Nashville and headed straight to the mall to get me a jacket, trousers and shoes as I had only brought beach-type gear with me. Fully kitted out we checked into the Opryland Hotel and got ready for the biggest night in the country music calendar. Vince Gill was the host and the winners that night were Garth Brooks, George Strait, Trisha Yearwood and the Dixie Chicks with Tammy Wynette and Elvis Presley finally being inducted into the Country Music Hall Of Fame. It was a great night and the Cooks were overwhelmed by the experience, especially the post-show hospitality of unlimited food and drink.

Sobriety was the order of the day when we arrived back at our condo in Florida as warnings were everywhere about the incoming Hurricane George. We were told we could only stay overnight and must vacate the area early next morning. We managed to get dinner at a nearby restaurant and as we were the last to leave we helped the staff putting up the chairs on the tables and securing the place to face the storm force winds. The next morning we left for Tampa airport but were unable to get a flight as BA had cancelled all their scheduled flights. Luckily they were able to arrange to get us home with Virgin if we were prepared to drive to Orlando, which is what we did. That was some beach holiday.

CHAPTER THIRTY TWO

Spliced Again

Three of the top promotion men in the business were very helpful to me in early 1999 by way of delving in to their company archives and putting some of my old recordings onto compact disc from the original master tapes. Gary Farrow at CBS did me a copy of "Miss Pilkington's Maid" and later Dave Shack got me the "B" side "Count Me Out" and even unearthed my version of "Love, You Don't Know What It Means", which I didn't even know existed. What a result that was. Over at Decca Records the great Bill Holland raided the vaults to get me master copies of the Yaks "Yakety Yak" and "Back In "57". I feel a compilation album coming on. Well, why not?

Dave Shack was also involved in a major project for RCA Records with a set of compilation albums marking out Elvis Presley as the "Artist Of The Century" to coincide with the millennium. I was very pleased and very proud when Dave asked me if I would kindly give him some personal quotes to be included on the sleeve notes. Wow, what an honour to have my name associated with Elvis. These were my quotes, "Elvis was the hero to every red-blooded male of his generation and broke down enormous musical and social barriers" and "He made me want to start a rock and roll band and I did". Thanks Dave. The follow-on from that was a letter in July from Todd Slaughter of the Elvis Presley Fan Club who wrote "I really liked the nice one-liners you are quoted as saying in the sleeve notes of the new Elvis Presley Artist of the Century release". Thanks Todd.

Yet another top plugger came into my office in early 1999 asking for my advice on a record he had been asked to plug but wasn't sure if he should take it on. It was the afore-mentioned Nick Fleming, who handed me the single to listen to and stood waiting for my response. Well, I was floored by this track and, with a very quizzical look on my face, said to Nick "What are you thinking about, what's the problem?" and he said "Well, I wasn't quite sure, do you think it will be a hit?" My reply was succinct "Number One, you only have to listen to the intro to hear the magic", to which Nick said "Oh, right, if that's what you think I'll take it on", which he did, and at the end of February Britney Spears entered the chart with "Baby One More Time", her first chart-topper. That was one of the easiest hits to predict and a turn of the century pop classic.

When Radio Two got behind this great pop song it caused a bit of a stir in the media as it brought up once again the question of the demarcation lines between Radios One and Two. Both stations felt entitled to play it and I said so in an interview when the cameras rolled into my office to pose the question "Where is popular music being played with regard to Radio One versus Radio Two?" I told them there was no "versus" as each channel played the records they thought their listeners would like to hear, that there was no media frenzy and it was all just a storm in a teacup.

The poet Tennyson wrote "In the spring a young man's fancy lightly turns to thoughts of love", and so it was with me, spring chicken that I am, or was. The reason being Lesley's forthcoming 50th birthday on July the 8th and my being in a quandary as to what to buy her and how to celebrate it. One day, without any previous thoughts on the matter, I muttered a stuttered mumble of incoherent ramblings about getting hitched and having a party. What a birthday present eh? – me. This was readily agreed and we booked the delightful venue of St Michael's Manor in St Albans where the ceremony took place and also seated our 50 guests for a slap-up luncheon. We very nearly missed our great date as, due to a lack of hot water, I had to wait to have a shower which put us behind schedule and we turned up half an hour late just seconds before the registrar was preparing to leave for her next appointment. Saved by the skin of our teeth. As we stood together waiting to get spliced a loud cry was heard behind us from sister Pat's baby, Shannon, to which I responded "It won't be long now darling till we have one of those". This brought forth much laughter and certainly eased the tension after such a long wait. We were fortunate to enjoy a wonderfully warm summer's day just perfect for our wedding photographs on the lawns and by the lake in the beautiful grounds of the Manor.

It was a truly wonderful afternoon but we weren't done there as we invited everybody back to our house to continue the celebrations with an evening meal provided by a local Indian restaurant. It was such a balmy evening we ate outside on the rear patio and garden and as we relaxed after our second large meal of the day Lesley's brother Roger was prompted to stand up and demand our attention, something he's very good at, a polished public performer. He said that as I had had three best men at the wedding, namely Ron Stratton, John Rostron and Dave Lee Travis, he thought it only fair that he should say something more in honour of Lesley. Well, it was the speech of the day and it had us all in stitches as he regaled us with his memories of Lesley in her younger years and, as I recall, it wasn't completely complimentary. It would have been good to have a copy of that speech but sadly Roger's reminiscences were completely impromptu although he did have a copy of the words of the song he sang to the tune of "Sisters" which was equally funny. So ended a wonderful day for the newly-weds and all their family and friends.

Our honeymoon took us to the magical Burgh Island hotel, a magnificent art-deco building on this unique private island just across from Bigbury on Sea in Devon. Leaving our car on the mainland we boarded the high-riding sea tractor which ferried us across the sand just as it had done for decades. When you arrive at the hotel you enter a time capsule where everything reflects the style of the 1930's when so many high society house parties took place here. We were lucky enough to experience something of the feeling of that era when we donned dinner jacket and evening dress for a dinner dance accompanied by a small band playing the music of the period. Its iconic status is well-deserved as it has been seen in many films and television shows and is also famous as the venue where Agatha Christie wrote "And Then There Were None" and the Hercule Poirot mystery "Evil Under The Sun". It's a wonderful place and we will return when we are able.

Lesley was not the only one in our group of local friends to celebrate a 50th birthday in 1999. There were four others, Jenny Knight, Jo Bates, Merle Scott-Knox-Gore and Barry Knowles, who came up with a great plan for us all to go to Hungary and stay at Lake Balaton where we would get the best possible view of the total eclipse of the sun on the 11th of August. We all thought this a brilliant idea and together with spouses and other mates our party numbered sixteen (I think) so we booked two houses and two minibuses which Barry, Willum and I volunteered to drive. The fun started when we arrived at Budapest airport and went to pick up the vehicles, only for Willum to realise he didn't have his driving license with him, it was miles away at the terminal where the rest of the party were waiting for us. Willum said he really wanted to be a named driver and was told he could register in the Budapest office later, and so on the day before the eclipse we drove back to Budapest to have a look around and get Willum his accreditation. I asked Willum why he was so keen, because if he couldn't drive he could have a drink, a no-brainer in my book, but he said he was very keen and would like to drive back that evening. We enjoyed a hearty meal and plenty of the local brew with poor old Willum going tee-total. We set off home in the dark with me riding shotgun as navigator in the front passenger seat and Willum doing well as the driver until we approached a set of traffic lights which turned red but Willum wasn't slowing down. At first I said "Red Light, Willum". No response. Then I said it again but louder. Still no slowing down and in the end I screamed at him to stop but he just sailed on through. I was shocked and asked him why he didn't stop and he nonchalantly replied "Well, all those other cars went through". That's some logic, that is. And here's the funny part, maybe, when I said to Willum "You'd better pull over mate there's police car behind you with its lights flashing". He didn't believe me, carried on and then said "Oh shit, you're right, I'll pull over". Good idea, I thought, as we came to a stop and Willum got out of the car to talk to the police. A minute later he came back and asked me to help him with the police as one of the officers was swinging a pair of handcuffs and Willum was in panic mode. I asked the officers if they spoke English as we had no Hungarian at all but they just pointed at Willum and indicated that they were going to put him in the police car. Then I asked them if they spoke German and they said yes, they had some German and explained that Willum was going back to jail in Budapest for the night and would face a magistrate in the morning as he had so blatantly broken the law with his dangerous driving. I relayed this to Willum and he went white. That's when the parlay and international negotiations began as I explained that we couldn't come back the next day to collect Willum as we would be watching the eclipse. That cut no ice and I began pleading for mercy on Willum's behalf, saying what an idiot he was and how he was truly sorry and wasn't there some way they could let him off. Well, there was, and after about twenty minutes or so of hard bargaining, they agreed to let us go on our way, Willum included. Phew. Everybody agreed that watching the eclipse was a magical, almost out of body experience and we determined to do it again at the next possible accessible event. That's when Les and I became what is known in astronomical circles as umbraphiles or "shadow chasers", which I like better.

This exciting year climaxed with a media furore over the single "Millenium Prayer" by Cliff Richard, whose incensed fans accused Radio Two of banning the song. They are a formidable force, those die-hard Cliff supporters, who protested every way they could with letters, phone calls and any other means they might employ to get the media on their case. They got plenty of attention alright as opinion was sought and printed in the press, some good some not so good. Even television thought this a good enough story to get in on the act and so, in early November, I was invited to appear on the GMTV Breakfast Show to be harangued outside Broadcasting House by a group of ardent Cliff fans. Being the nice guy I am, and not wanting to meet a rotten tomato, I mollified their mock anger (they're nice people, after all) by reminding them that Radio Two had always championed Cliff and would continue to do so. I told them that the record had not gone on the Radio Two playlist because early November is too soon to be playing Christmas records and the suggestion that it was banned simply wasn't true, it was all blown up by the media. That calmed them down and in the end they thanked me for coming to talk to them and so a fist fight between me and Cliff was avoided. Lucky Cliff. Funny old game this music biz.

Prince, also "The Artist Formerly Known As Prince" (crikey), had a minor hit in 1983 with these very predictive lyrics "2000, zero zero, party over, oops, out of time so tonight I'm gonna party like it's 1999". Well, we couldn't resist joining in with that chorus and so Lesley and I invited all our local friends to celebrate with us to bring in the new millennium and, as New Year's Eve parties go, it was a belter. Goodbye to the twentieth century, that, too, was a cracker.

Do you remember me telling you how I was cruelly side-lined for Terry Wogan's "This Is Your Life"? Well, this time it was different and I managed to get in on the act and received a very nice letter from researcher Sue Venables "Thank you so much for helping to make our This Is Your Life tribute to Dave Lee Travis such a great success. Without your help with the initial research the show would have proved to be very difficult. What you said on the show was just perfect. I hope Lesley enjoyed it too". She certainly did and it was great to catch up with Michael Aspel again and the original members of Herman's Hermits as I hadn't seen them for a very long time. That show went out on BBC1 at 8.30pm on Monday 14th February 2000 – Valentine's Day, indeed.

That summer Radio Two was riding higher than ever before and a music trade magazine did a two-page feature interviewing me on all things regarding the station, with a photograph, naturally. It highlighted the fact that we were now officially Britain's most popular radio station with over ten million listeners. I explained the success was down to an evolutionary process over the last three years with policies to attract more younger listeners while not alienating the older ones. The music was brighter and less old-fashioned and our presenter line-up now included former Radio One stalwarts Johnnie Walker and Steve Wright who brought a fresh new sound to the network. Our progress was often down to being ahead of the curve and programming songs before other stations, the classic case in point was the huge Aerosmith hit "I Don't Want To Miss A Thing", which most other stations initially ignored, including Radio One, but it was well-championed by Radio Two and sold over a million copies. Another totally topical track we got behind was "Smooth" by Santana which had been a top ten hit back in April. Strange thing is, there were questions about its suitability for Radio Two from up above (no, not that high) and I defended it by simply saying "That's exactly the kind of record we should be playing and the reason you brought me back to Radio Two". I fielded the same query about the Blondie single "Maria", but it was fine when it got to Number One. We weren't doing things too badly, then.

Michael Terence Wogan, to give him his full name, had once again put pen to paper and in August I received a card which read "BBC Worldwide would like to invite you to celebrate the launch of Terry Wogan's autobiography "Is It Me" on 5th September at The Park & Garden Room of the Four Seasons hotel on Park Lane". The great and the good populated the place, as you can imagine, what with free champagne and all that stuff but I did manage to have a word with Terry and as we were talking a PR person came along and asked if I would like a copy of the book. I was just about to say yes, please when Terry told her not to bother as he had a copy ready for me. Well-prepared as ever, he retrieved a book from a nearby table and handed it to me. I looked inside and the inscription read "Geoff, so many years – so many laughs Terry". Those words say it all, really.

At the heart of the music industry there are many key organisations, one of which is BASCA, The British Academy of Composers & Songwriters, who hold a special event every year in honour of the great and good in the business. Known as The Gold Badge Awards, it is a highly prestigious occasion which this year was held in October at the Savoy Hotel. I was involved on two fronts, firstly, Tony "Primo" Peters, who I mentioned earlier, was due to receive an award and asked me to write a tribute piece to him for inclusion in the brochure. I mentioned his relentless good humour and his catalogue of awful jokes such as "A man orders a pizza and is asked if he wants it cut into 4 pieces or 6. The man replies "Oh, just 4 please, I couldn't possibly eat 6". I also told of his competitive spirit, although it was amazing on the snooker table, whenever he had an easy black to win the game, I only had to mention the Radio Two playlist for him to manage a miraculous miss.

Another recipient that year was Alan Keith, who I had produced back in the 80's and for whom I now hosted a luncheon party of ten at the event. It was perfect timing as Alan celebrated his 92nd birthday that week and there were references to the amazing fact that he made his first radio broadcast in 1933. Alan was very moved by all the attention and next day sent me this note "I wish to thank you for a wonderful afternoon and for the honour you have bestowed on me". It's always nice to get a letter of appreciation and another arrived from David Jacobs who I had invited onto our table "That was a splendid lunch party you hosted today, thank you for including me". What gents.

I had known and enjoyed David Jacobs company for many years and, like many urbane and sophisticated gentlemen, he had a wicked sense of humour and told the filthiest jokes. I had the good fortune to sit between him and George Melly at a memorable dinner in the Reform Club and I can't remember when I laughed so much as they traded stories all through the evening. George remembered me producing him at a concert in Rickmansworth and I said I remembered some of his naughty double-entendres and innuendo and he said "Yes, it hurts, doesn't it?" Nuff said.

Jokes and laughter have always been part and parcel of life in the media and never more so than at some of the regular get-togethers at the DLT's homes. Fellow DJ's such as Mike Read, Paul Burnett, Adrian Juste and Tony Prince would often be there as would comedian Bob Monkhouse, with whom I enjoyed long chats, particularly about some of the old-time comics like Ken Platt, Sonny Roy "The Funny Boy" and one of my childhood favourites Albert Modley, now largely forgotten but very popular in their day. There were others like Sue Cook, Jan Leeming, Anita Harris and Lynsey De Paul, who told the most brilliant jokes and for such a petite and demure lady some of them are unprintable here. Prankster Jeremy Beadle would entertain us with a quiz session and was happy to take questions from us in return, some of which I managed to catch him out on with musical questions. One of the last lunches before Covid hit saw ace piano player and singer Elio Pace doing his stuff with Martin Kearney on guitar, Dave Mann on bass and Travis and I alternating on drums. Dave was good, I was rubbish. Mention of Paul Burnett reminds me of the story of him leaving Broadcasting House to be confronted by an irate woman, who threw a pot of paint all over him and yelled "Take that David Hamilton!" The business of show, eh?

During my second stint at Radio Two there had been some contentious issues and I can tell you without hesitation that being part of the management team was nowhere near as much fun as being at the coalface as a producer.

There was a conflict of interest when the radio research team came in to tell me they had secured funding for a major project to song-test tracks in our music database. I was horrified and told them we had tried it at Melody Radio and it was a waste of time, effort and money. They were adamant it had to go ahead and had already contracted a German firm to carry out the study. So much for being in charge of my own department. The research was conducted at vast expense and what it told us was that we should cut out a very large number of popular songs, many by major artists such as Roxy Music and Blondie, as they had not tested well. It was hogwash, once again, and our producers were much more qualified to decide when a song had reached its sell-by date than groups of disparate listening panels up and down the country. I nodded imperceptibly in the way of the results and six months later we were back at square one after a quarter of a million pounds had left the building and the BBC.

Our tailor-made play-out system also came in for scrutiny when the powers that be were told at an industry event that Radio Two was not using the industry standard system Selector. Once again, I railed against this as I knew its limitations when we used it at Melody where Emma and Ronnie had to work hard each day to customise the output, otherwise it would have been a shambles. All to no avail, as very soon machines were installed and a consultant programmer engaged to run the system. It wasn't up to the task and was still being tested when I left.

A knock on the door and a man in a lab coat walked in and asked if he could measure my window sills. I asked why and he said the whole of the management floor was to have hydroponic plants on each window sill and he would come in every week to clean and feed them. I told him not to bother as I wouldn't be having any plants installed in my office. I stormed down the corridor to confront those who thought this a good idea and asked them what sort of message was it sending out when that very same day three of the most experienced and loyal secretaries had been made redundant. No plants grew there for a while.

One final recollection comes from one of the regular "Away Days" when the management team would hole up in some country house hotel for a couple of days brainstorming sessions. We'd arrive for drinks, dinner and sometimes a convivial game of snooker, as on this occasion when one of the guest attendees was Trevor Dann, Head of BBC Music Entertainment. Having worked with the top presenters in the business I always took a keen interest in our on-air talent and had pushed very hard for both Johnnie Walker and Steve Wright to be given daily shows on the network. Up for debate and discussion was our current presenter line-up and one suggestion that came up quite forcibly was the replacement of Ken Bruce. Well, who did they have in mind for this important switch, I wondered, could it be Noel Edmunds or maybe Chris Tarrant? All was revealed when the name of Alex Lester was put forward. Well, I nearly flipped and opposed this idea vehemently because although Alex is a perfectly good DJ there seemed to me no point whatsoever in replacing Ken who was very popular and delivered good audience figures. Anyway, I really liked Ken. Fortunately, I was supported in my opinion by Trevor Dann and the whole idea was dropped. Ken's subsequent success and longevity is a matter of record, although I'm not sure if Ken ever knew anything about this near miss.

So, how's that for a bunch of gripes?

The last major musical event I remember was a rather splendid evening as guests of WEA Records for the launch of the new Enya album "A Day Without Rain". Dinner was in The Admiralty restaurant at Somerset House, after which we watched a specially organised fireworks display on the opposite bank of the Thames. They knew how to throw a party at WEA. As a footnote, Enya's album and the single "Only Time" were later used extensively in the

American media coverage following the 9/11 attacks on the Twin Towers in New York.

In December we flew over to Vienna to see my old friends Fritz and Christa and Bobby and Georg. There was a wonderful atmosphere everywhere and we walked around the Christmas markets drinking various mixes of the hot alcoholic Punsch. It wasch a wunnerful chrip.

As Lesley and I had never needed an excuse for a party it was no surprise when we decided to host another millennium shindig, just in case we'd jumped the gun the year before, you understand. With relatives and friends, we managed to sit 28 down for a New Year's Eve feast, followed late into the night with some strenuous boogieing. That's the last I remember of the year 2000.

Wedding of the Year 1999

A bull riding retirement

CHAPTER THIRTY THREE

Freedom

The mandatory retirement age at the BBC back then was 60 but my leaving date was brought forward somewhat by more top management meddling when Gregg Dyke slashed several key radio posts in his great restructuring initiative. Out went Gwen Hughes, Head of Radio Three Music Policy, Mike Lewis, Deputy Head of Radio Five Live, a couple at Radio One and others that I don't recall. That's what you call a major staffing overhaul. I would have liked to have seen my time out there but yet another redundancy package eased my exit and softened the blow to my bruised ego, after all I'd done for the bastards. I left the station in good health and it's since gone on from strength to strength. It was a great ride from the Manchester clubs to Broadcasting House. Thanks.

When I left the building I was allowed to take all my records, hi-fi equipment and tape recorders plus my trusty companion over the years – BBC stopwatch Number 1207, a rare classic, like me. Another thing that happens if you have achieved a certain level of notoriety is a "Leaving Do" in the Governors Dining Room at Broadcasting House. Mine was on Thursday 3rd of May 2001 and my guests that day included several colleagues, presenters and pluggers who had been alongside me for most of my journey, about 24 in all. Lesley was presented with a huge bunch of flowers and I was given an antique BBC microphone mounted on a stand with the inscription "Presented to Geoff Mullin with the affection of all his colleagues in BBC Radio". Also, they had managed to find and frame the Top Twenty chart listing page from the New Musical Express edition of Friday 26th March 1965 which carried a Decca Records advert for "Yakety Yak" by The Yaks. All in all, an excellent send-off, and the very last time I set foot in Broadcasting House.

Not many things bring an emotional tear to my eye, and leaving the BBC was not one of them. That has only happened twice in a theatrical setting, the first being at a performance of the ballet Swan Lake and again when that good man from Decca Records, Bill Holland, invited Lesley and myself to see the wonderful Luciano Pavarotti in Hyde Park that July. He was sensational and I was very moved by his passionate rendition of some of the greatest pieces from the operatic canon.

I took to retirement like a duck to water and embarked on the major tasks of sorting out my books, records and tapes, both video and audio, which I transferred to DVD and compact disc. Lesley was still working at this time so I was able to muck about to my heart's content – bliss.

On my birthday in 2001 we were enjoying lunch at the Cosa Nostra when Simon, the owner, came rushing in from the kitchen with a look of absolute shock and terror on his face blurting out "They've blown up a skyscraper in New York". We were all dumbstruck and asked him for details but all he could say was it was happening now, live on the television. We paid the bill very smartly and rushed back home to watch this dreadful event unfold over the next few hours. That was a birthday I'll never forget.

Back in 1999 John Rostron had called me to tell me that The Crickets were playing in Liverpool and what did I think the chances were that he might persuade them to come and play in Southport on their day off in aid of the osteoporosis charity. I told him to go for it, which he did, and they did, and ever since John has had a very friendly relationship with them, especially drummer Jerry Allison. Which brings me to October 2001 when once again they came to perform at The Floral Hall in Southport and this time Lesley and I went to stay with John and Christine to attend the concert. The best part of that visit was not only seeing The Crickets live but enjoying their company over dinner at the Rostron's home and hearing stories of their time with Buddy Holly and many others. How great to be in the company of these influential legends of rock and roll, and although I had met guitarist Sonny Curtis when producing Country Club with Wally Whyton, it was great to hear the southern drawl of Jerry Allison, bass player Joe B Mauldin and ace pianist Glen D Hardin, who played with Elvis Presley in his TCB band. What a great night that was.

I can't let a mention of Buddy Holly's band go by without acknowledging my friend John Beecher from Roller Coaster Records, an acclaimed Crickets expert, who has helped me enormously with advice and contacts to improve my personal music recordings. As John would probably say, "They needed it". He's so laconic and a very funny man (I think). Even funnier is the fact that, although we live only fifty miles apart, we've never actually met. Something that must be remedied.

Another bit of interesting information about John and Christine's home, especially for a Manchester boy like me, was that it had previously been owned by a man called Monty Bloom, a great patron and friend of the artist L S Lowry, who often visited Monty, and at one time there were reputed to be a hundred Lowry paintings in his house. One for the Fascinating Fact File.

Our major holiday that year was another visit to Miami, which I wouldn't mention except for one incident that demonstrated the American attitude to commerce and business. We did the usual touristy things and, remember this was not long after 9/11, it was relatively quiet and we were made very welcome, none more so than when getting into the lift at our hotel. We were joined by a tall, distinguished gentleman who asked us where we were from and what we were doing in Miami. When we said we were on holiday he said "Well thank you so much for spending your vacation dollars here with us in the U.S.". The bottom line is very important over there.

While we were away we heard of the tragic death of George Harrison and later it set me to thinking about two things, my Beatles autographs and my big 6-O birthday coming up. Our builder friend John Wilkins had just completed converting our garage into a games room where I intended to put a pool table, one-armed bandit, penny-in-the-slot fairground machine, pinball table and a jukebox. After measuring up I realised either the pinball machine or the jukebox had to go, and as this was to be a party room, music was essential, so the pinball machine bit the dust. I had my eye on a new Rock-Ola box which played a hundred compact discs, giving me ten times more tunes than the vinyl box, but at £6,000 it was very pricey. This got me wondering what my Beatles autographs were worth and I made an appointment to see Stephen Maycock at Sotheby's for an expert opinion. He was intrigued by the fact that it was on Oasis club paper and had the signatures of The Big Three on the reverse. He looked at it for a while and then put his nose to it for a good sniff, finally declaring it had great provenance and we should put it up for auction with a reserve price of £3,000. Sotheby's "Rock/Fashion" auction took place on the 14th of June 2002 at Olympia, London and Lesley and I sat nervously waiting for Lot 300 to come up. We were shocked when the final bid came in at £6,000, and rather than going for a meal as we had planned, we headed straight back home all a bit shaky and astounded at our good fortune. That completed the games room set-up and we had so much more enjoyment from all the music than a set of autographs quietly sleeping in a scrap book. Thanks again Rose, the Oasis, The Big Three and The Fab Four.

Foreign travel now became an important part of our lives as it was time to start hitting "The Bucket List" which we did with great enthusiasm and when we weren't actually on holiday we were busy planning one. The local mob were also organising regular trips abroad and this year we were in Delft, with previous visits to Honfleur and Oudenaard having set the tone for cultural programmes revolving around gourmet food and wine. What's not to like?

There were annual trips organised by Sandra Smout where we took over an entire Youth Hostel for a weekend which were always great fun, if sometimes a little uncomfortable, particularly if you hadn't had enough to drink or were banished to the "snorers and farters" bedroom. One of these visits was to Essex and there was much comment around the dinner table about the local accent, glottal stops and vowel sounds, which prompted me to pipe up with "They call that irritable vowel syndrome". Got a good laugh. It happened again when, I think, Alan Knight was telling us about a really expensive newly-built house where the plumbing had failed and the toilet had leaked under the raised floor of the building and out into the garden. I couldn't resist a comment on this and said

"That's what they call the effluent of the affluent". I guess you had to be there.

Lesley did some terrific planning for my 60th birthday which we celebrated at Number 11 with the usual group of suspects who enjoyed a tasty meal and copious amounts of champagne. The pool table and the jukebox got hammered, as did most of the guests, and that counts as a great success round these parts. Another one bites the dust.

Lesley also researched and booked all our holidays and in 2003 came up with two great adventures, one of which might well have been near-death experience number nine (been counting? – keep up). The first was a fabulous five-week trip around Australia and then South Africa where, on an evening safari, we got caught up in a skirmish between rampaging elephants and a pride of lions. The noise-level was unbelievable and my heart was pounding as a bull elephant approached our open-top Land Rover with an evil glint in his eye. That was enough for our driver who smashed into reverse gear and got us out of there in the nick of time. Very exciting, yes, but also ridiculously frightening, our blood pressure must have been off the scale.

There was a sad end to the year with the death from prostate cancer of Bob Monkhouse and sometime later his widow Jacquie asked me if I could help her find a home for Bob's record collection. I went to their house in Egginton to have a look and realised there was quite some value there which I managed to get her a good price for. She donated the funds from the sale to her favourite charity. While I was there Jacquie showed me the garage which she wanted to clear out, including a whole stack of large metal film canisters, which she said were destined for the dump. I was horrified at this and pleaded with her not to throw away Bob's unique collection until I could get a film expert to look at it. She agreed and I contacted a friend from the British Film Institute to take a look. He declared it a treasure trove of rare worth and arranged for it to be stored in a climate-controlled environment where it would be catalogued and preserved for future generations of film enthusiasts. I was pleased it was saved from an ignominious end in a skip.

The travel bug was alive and kicking as we joined the local group for a trip Les Andelys to visit Monet's marvellous garden and from there Lesley and I drove along Germany's fabled Romantische Strasse, a wonderful adventure which included a visit to the beautiful medieval town of Rothenburg Ob Der Tauber and the spectacular fairy tale castle of Neuschwanstein. A year later, in 2005, we went to a family wedding with Mel and Sandra in Italy, in October the local group went to Madrid to see an annular eclipse of the sun and we went over to Ballycastle in Northern Ireland to see my daughter Krystle and my new-born grandson Finlay. A year later we saw our third eclipse along with Lesley's brother Roger in Antalya, Turkey and finished our travels in late November with a week on each of the main islands of Hawaii. Mele kalikimaka to you.

Over the years we travelled around America more than anywhere else, wearing out many hire cars with trips along Route 66, the Blue Ridge Parkway, Yosemite and Yellowstone National Parks. We let the train take the strain when Auntie Maureen joined us on a visit to Canada with a spectacular ride on the Rocky Mountaineer. We had a marvellous 7-week drive around New Zealand and following that, thanks to Barry and Bron we saw our fourth eclipse in Cairns, Australia where quite a few of the St Albans crew also turned up at the other end of the world. We saw the Northern Lights in Lapland, where Les fell off the dog-sled she was (not) controlling and into the snow but astonishingly came out quite unharmed.

Possibly the most memorable trip of all was to The Old West where we visited Cheyenne, Laramie, Deadwood, the Badlands, the Black Hills, the Little Big Horn, Mount Rushmore, the astonishing Crazy Horse Monument and the Devils Tower, which was the focal point of interest in the film "Close Encounters of the Third Kind". It was great to hear authentic tales of Wild Bill Hickok, Calamity Jane, Buffalo Bill, Butch Cassidy and The Sundance Kid and The Hole in the Wall Gang.

Fate tried hard to intervene on that trip by dealing us a hand to take us in a decidedly different direction when we were both offered employment in the town of Duchesne. The drive into town along a beautiful valley was going smoothly until the dashboard flagged up a slow puncture. Panic – we had no spare, Duchesne was about twenty miles away with nothing in between. We crawled along watching the tyre pressure drop in equal measure to the miles we were covering and just made it before the tyre ran completely flat. At the tyre depot we asked for help and the guy said "Sure, swing around the back and old George'll fix you up". So we swung around the back and there he was, old George, the epitome of a mountain man, with denim dungarees, long hair and a beard as big as a xmas tree. We pointed to the problem tyre, he nodded and grunted, took the tyre off, removed a nail and spat on the hole to watch the bubbles come out. He nodded, grunted again and proceeded to attack the tyre with an instrument of torture that looked like an enormous corkscrew. Satisfied that he'd completely destroyed the offending rubber he took out a large plug, covered it in glue and hammered it into the tyre. He pumped it up, checked it out, put it back on the car, nodded, grunted and walked away without a word.

Well, that was the most amazing piece of industrial dexterity I've ever seen and when we went to settle the bill the boss man said "That'll be five dollars, please". I couldn't believe that price and insisted on paying more because of the trouble we'd been saved but the most he would accept was ten dollars, so I said I'd give old George a fiver for his efforts. Then we got into a conversation, which is when he asked Lesley if she was computer literate, which she was, and he asked me if I could drive, which I could, obviously. Then he said he had plenty of well-paid work for us if we'd like to come and live in America. That's not an offer you get every day but we politely declined saying we had family responsibilities back in England. When I gave old George his fiver he changed his modus operandi, giving us a grunt first, then a nod. All in all, a fascinating day, don't you think?

Lesley wrote notes on all our adventures and I'm sure there's a travelogue ripe for publishing.

With grandson Finlay

That was some BBC leaving do 2001

CHAPTER THIRTY FOUR
Big Change Is Gonna Come

So sang Peter Green and he was spot on. Now we come to "The Curious Incident Of The Noise In The Night-Time". Have you ever been shaking and tingling with a combination of fear and anticipation of something weird about to happen? I certainly had the collywobbles one night when I was woken about 2am by the sound of a dull thud. I listened out for a few minutes then went back to sleep. There it was again, and my curiosity got the better of me so I put on my dressing-gown to investigate. Lesley woke up and I told her what I'd heard and suggested she stay in bed while I went downstairs to investigate. I didn't turn any lights on and peered through the curtains into the front garden where I saw the dim shape of someone bending over. I thought they were stealing a bush or some plants so I called the police who told me not to turn on any lights and by no means confront this person in the garden. They said there was a patrol car nearby which would approach silently with no lights on and I was not to open the door until they arrived and knocked. I was all a-quiver by this time as I heard yet another dull thud and then the sound of running feet. I'm getting the same feelings again just writing this, for goodness sake. Eventually, a copper knocked on the door and told me what had been going on. By this time Lesley was up and about and judged this young cop Adrian to be very hunky and just right for Kerry. Always matchmaking, is Lesley. He said the guy was stripping the lead from next door's garage roof and dropping it onto our garden, hence the thuds. He told us how he chased the guy for a while but lost him in the large gardens behind us and then asked me for a hand to put all the lead into our garage to store overnight rather than wake up our elderly neighbours. Adrian said he had taken control of the guy's bike and that there would have been an accomplice nearby with a van to transport the lead, which is why we had to get it into a safe place otherwise they would come back for it. What a nerve-jangling saga that was, but I'm alright now.

And so to the big change, no, not the car, the house. We had been thinking of moving away from St Albans for a quieter life and the opportunity came in early 2010 when estate agent Nick Hill told us there were people very interested in properties in Lancaster Road. We sold very quickly to the lovely Acharya family and the hunt was on for somewhere new to live, causing us to criss-cross the south west until we finally settled on marvellous Marlborough in wonderful Wiltshire (that's supposed to be funny). Exceptionally, we decided to sell off most of our furniture and chattels, which was an adventure in itself. Neighbours Vince and Camilla bought the old vinyl jukebox, the guy who bought the pool table dismantled it, rebuilt it on a flat-bed truck and took it to southern Spain. I can just imagine the looks and comments he must have got on the way down there with this blue baize table trundling along the road. Next to go was the lounge and dining room furniture which went to a film and TV props company who sometime later hired it out to the BBC for an edition of the popular "New Tricks" series. We were most amused to see it in some professor's house.

After the dust settled, we decided a break was in order and I thought it might be nice to visit Norway again. As luck would have it my former P.A. Melissa Lyon, little star that she is, said she could get us tickets for the Eurovision Song Contest if we were In Oslo in May. Offer accepted and we planned our trip around the fiords to fit in with the contest date. That's serendipity, for sure.

Our sporting activities in Marlborough, besides the regular drinking competitions, included the bowls club, the croquet club and the golf club, where we met and became great friends with Jim and Julie Raff. They in turn introduced us to their friends Steve and Margaret Hobson, Roger and Denise Grant and Ros and Alan Brooks, lovely people one and all. Yes, even you, Roger (ha ha). Fortune favoured us again as one of Lesley's oldest friends from her days in Germany, Margaret Fletcher, was living nearby with her husband Martin and not too distant were Michael and Valerie Gouby and Rob and Judy Crompton, so three more jolly couples for the team. Other regulars on the party invite list include those young whippersnappers Mark and Sus Howard, Mike and Sophie Booth and neighbours Alan and Claire Taylor-Wheeler and Sarah and Ian Coulson, who are about to get hitched as I write.

My old pal, plugger and squash nemesis Harry Barter celebrated his 70th birthday in July 2011 and threw a brilliant afternoon lunch party in his garden where lots of his music-biz pals got up and sang a song or two. Travis and I were dragged up, completely unprepared, and did some kind of acceptable version of the Ray Charles classic "What'd I Say", backed by The Swinging Blue Jeans.

Music must have been in the air that year as I spoke to Trevor Churchill, an old contact at Ace Records and suggested to him that my 1968 recording of "Sunshine Superman" by Bocking, Robinson and Morais might be suitable for inclusion on one of their "Mod Jazz" series of CD's. Trevor put the wheels in motion and in January 2012 that dusty old track came out on "Mod Jazz Forever" with the promo script reading "As you leave the room to the previously unreleased British jazz cut "Sunshine Superman" by Bocking, Robinson, Morais you will be feeling as sharp as ever. Another mod jazz miracle". I'll buy that for a recommendation, wouldn't you?

Since my rugby and cricket playing days I hadn't been a regular spectator anywhere but Lesley and I were fortunate enough to see a couple of major football matches at Wembley Stadium and tennis during the Wimbledon Fortnight. Lesley had never been to a rugby match so I was delighted to get a pair of tickets for the 2015 World Cup match that October between Italy and Romania at Sandy Park in Exeter. We had good seats, it was a great game, Lesley found it very exciting, and Italy won.

Another sad start to the year in 2016 when my old mucker Sir Terry Wogan passed away from cancer. He was always so generous to me and at one time helped me with a speech I had to make. I still have his hand-written notes, this one for a friend's birthday "We've been chums for years. There's nothing in the world I wouldn't do for him, and there's nothing in the world he wouldn't do for me. And that's how we've spent the last 25 years – doing nothing for each other". He was a great man, certainly a national treasure, and I wish he were still with us.

On a more joyful note, 2016 was drummer Barry Whitwam's 70th birthday and Lesley and I were invited to his party in July. Sadly, Lesley didn't make it because she wasn't well but she insisted that I go. She's so lovely. Over drinks in the bar I met up with Norwegian journalist Olaf Owre, number one Herman's Hermits fan and chronicler of all their activities and anyone connected with the group. I was astounded at his knowledge of my small part in their story as he reeled off a list of practically everything I've recorded or written. He knows more about me than me – which is rather scary. I was on a table with Ron and Bente Stratton, Dave and Jean Chalmers and my cousin Judith, who was an old schoolfriend of Barry's wife Pat. We were entertained by The Ivy League, who were terrific musically and also hysterically funny and the birthday dinner was a resounding success.

It's a great joy, I think, to make contact again with good old pals from the past and thanks to Facebook I've been able to talk again to Andy Peebles, Brian Parish, Pete Howarth and Trevor Lyon from The Zodiacs, who told me he'd been playing note perfect versions of the Shadows numbers for many years. He said the group was called The Shedows and when I laughed and said how come that name, he said because they used to practise in the garden shed. You couldn't make it up, could you.

I took a solo trip to Manchester and stayed with Ron and Bente, who hosted an intimate dinner party with Leonie Leckenby and ex-Hermit Keith Hopwood. All the old stories and memories came flooding back and a jolly good evening was enjoyed by all. Anyway, or "any road up" as the say in Manchester, who wouldn't enjoy an evening with Bente's delicious cooking and Ron's fine wines.

By some strange serendipity, the very next day there was another re-union comprising Dave Chalmers, Pete MacLaine, Tony Bamforth and John Wilson. John had been very successful in the world of insurance and later invited me to join him and his wife Michelle for lunch on his hospitality table at the Etihad stadium and watch the Manchester derby between City and United. It was a fabulous day and a privileged way to be at a football match with great food, great seats and above all great company. That same day I was introduced to Noel Gallagher and Johnny Marr, with whom

I had quite a long conversation about the Manchester music scene back in the sixties and he said he hoped there would soon be a museum covering all the music associated with the city and perhaps I could be involved in the project. That was a wonderful gesture by John, which he later generously extended to Lesley and I for yet another Manchester derby. We hope to join him again one day, all things being equal.

As Lesley was celebrating her 70th birthday in July 2019 I had thoughts about damaging a microphone again and recording a couple of songs for her as, for some bizarre reason, she enjoyed listening to me singing along to Elvis songs. I suppose mildly amused might be a better term. I mentioned this to my pal Rob Crompton when we visited him and his wife Judy for dinner. Rob showed me his music recording set up and asked me what songs I had in mind. I said "Love Letters" and "Don't" and left it at that. Two days later Rob called and "I've got them" and I said "Got what?" "The backing tracks for your songs, when can you come over and put the vocals on?". I was completely taken aback by this unexpected development and on some dubious pretext or other to allay Lesley's suspicions, I went over to Rob's to sing a song or two. The backing tracks he had downloaded were absolutely note perfect, including the vocal chorus, so now it was up to me. After a couple of hours of Rob doing his engineering thing trying to make me sound half-decent, we declared ourselves satisfied with the end product. Rob put the two songs onto a CD which I put in Lesley's birthday card. A little tear came into her eye when she heard it, especially as I had customised both songs to include her name, and she thought it was a lovely thing to do. On the day of her party the guests asked if they could hear it and she agreed – cue applause.

Serendipity is a wonderful word and a wonderful thing. The most recent manifestation of this curious phenomenon happened only days ago after I sent the Gene Vincent photo to John Beecher. He loved it and told me he was working on a tribute album to Gene and would I consider laying down a track for inclusion. Would I? I'd be delighted and honoured to record what might be the very last outing for my vocal chords.

Ace musician the brilliant Martin Kearney recorded the backing tracks and backing vocals, and at the end of August 2022 I laid down the vocal for Jezebel and the track which was chosen - *She She Little Sheila*. The Rollercoaster CD tribute to Gene Vincent should be released by Christmas, amazing – the wrinkly rocker lives on!

Our last holiday before the awful Covid pandemic hit was a road trip around Atlantic Canada taking in Nova Scotia, New Brunswick and Prince Edward Island. I look forward to the time when we can start travelling again, when this dreadful war in Ukraine is over and all the hopes of my youth for a peaceful world might come true.

Well, there you have it, the story of my journey through life, and most of it is true. I can only hope you've enjoyed it as much as I have. I wish you a fond goodbye and, as Terry wrote on my final, final BBC leaving card "You've left your mark on me". Likewise, Terry undoubtedly left his mark on me and I hope I might at least have left just a faint impression on you. I'll sign off with Roy Rogers famous farewell – "Happy Trails".

Happy Christmas with Kerry, Lesley & Jamie

LIST OF PHOTOGRAPHS

Lightning Source UK Ltd.
Milton Keynes UK
UKHW020513091222
413588UK00011B/156